OT 27:
Operator Theory: Advances and Applications
Vol. 27

Editor:
I. Gohberg
Tel Aviv University
Ramat-Aviv, Israel

Editorial Office

School of Mathematical Sciences
Tel Aviv University
Ramat-Aviv, Israel

Birkhäuser Verlag
Basel · Boston

$$v_{n+1}^{(m)} = \hat{v}_{n+1}^{(m)} = v_n^{(m)}(1 - \alpha_{n+1}^{(m)}\hat{\alpha}_{n+1}^{(m)}) \tag{3.2c) p.30}$$

$$z^m A_n^{(m)}(z) = Z^{(m)}(z)Q_n^{(m)}(z) - R_n^{(m)}(z) = \hat{Z}^{(m)}(z)Q_n^{(m)}(z) + P_n^{(m)}(z) \tag{4.3a) p.38}$$

$$z^m \hat{A}_n^{(m)}(z) = Z^{(m)}(z)\hat{Q}_n^{(m)}(z) - \hat{R}_n^{(m)}(z) = \hat{Z}^{(m)}(z)\hat{Q}_n^{(m)}(z) + \hat{P}_n^{(m)}(z) \tag{4.3b) p.38}$$

$$B(p)_n^{(m)}(z) = Z^{(p)}(z)Q_n^{(m)}(z) - R_n^{(m)}(z) = \hat{Z}^{(p)}(z)Q_n^{(m)}(z) + P_n^{(m)}(z) \tag{4.7a) p.40}$$

$$\hat{B}(p)_n^{(m)}(z) = \hat{Z}^{(p)}(z)\hat{Q}_n^{(m)}(z) - \hat{R}_n^{(m)}(z) = \hat{Z}^{(p)}(z)\hat{Q}_n^{(m)}(z) + \hat{P}_n^{(m)}(z) \tag{4.7b) p.40}$$

$$\Theta_{n+1}^{(m)} = \begin{vmatrix} V_n^{(m)}(z) & \hat{V}_n^{(m)}(z) \\ zU_n^{(m)}(z) & z\hat{U}_n^{(m)}(z) \end{vmatrix} = \frac{1}{f_m} \begin{vmatrix} 1 & \tfrac{1}{2}f_m \\ -1 & \tfrac{1}{2}f_m \end{vmatrix} \begin{vmatrix} A_{n+1}^{(m)}(z) & \hat{A}_{n+1}^{(m)}(z) \\ Q_{n+1}^{(m)}(z) & \hat{Q}_{n+1}^{(m)}(z) \end{vmatrix} \tag{4.13) p.44}$$

$$[S_n^{(m)}(z) \ \ \hat{S}_n^{(m)}(z)] = [S_{n-1}^{(m)}(z) \ \ \hat{S}_{n-1}^{(m)}(z)]\theta_n^{(m)} \ , \ \ \theta_n^{(m)} = \begin{vmatrix} 1 & -\hat{\alpha}_n^{(m)} \\ -z\alpha_n^{(m)} & z \end{vmatrix} \tag{3.6) p.33}$$

$$S_n = P_n, R_n, Q_n, B(p)_n, A_n, U_{n-1}, V_{n-1} \ , \ \ \Theta_n^{(m)} = \theta_1^{(m)}\theta_2^{(m)} \cdots \theta_n^{(m)}$$

$$t_n^{(m)} = \frac{w - \alpha_n^{(m)}}{1 - \hat{\alpha}_n^{(m)}w} \qquad \qquad , \ \hat{t}_n^{(m)} = \frac{w - \hat{\alpha}_n^{(m)}}{1 - \alpha_n^{(m)}w} \tag{6.4) p.56/57}$$

$$\frac{S_n^{(m)}(z)}{\hat{S}_n^{(m)}(z)} = t_n^{(m)} \begin{vmatrix} S_{n-1}^{(m)}(z) \\ z\hat{S}_{n-1}^{(m)}(z) \end{vmatrix} \qquad , \qquad \frac{\hat{S}_n^{(m)}(z)}{S_n^{(m)}(z)} = \hat{t}_n^{(m)} \begin{vmatrix} z\hat{S}_{n-1}^{(m)}(z) \\ S_{n-1}^{(m)}(z) \end{vmatrix} \tag{6.5) p.56/57}$$

series (Chap. 6)

$$\Pi_n^{(m)}(z) = L_-(Q_n^{(m)}(z)/\hat{Q}_n^{(m)}(z)) \ , \ \hat{\Pi}_n^{(m)}(z) = L_+(\hat{Q}_n^{(m)}(z)/Q_n^{(m)}(z)) \tag{6.6) p.57}$$

$$\Gamma_n^{(m)}(z) = R_n^{(m)}(z)/(z\hat{R}_n^{(m)}(z)) \quad , \quad \hat{\Gamma}_n^{(m)}(z) = z\hat{P}_n^{(m)}(z)/P_n^{(m)}(z) \tag{6.6) p.57}$$

$$\Sigma_n^{(m)}(z) = L_+(U_n^{(m)}(z)/V_n^{(m)}(z)) \ , \ \hat{\Sigma}_n^{(m)}(z) = L_-(\hat{V}_n^{(m)}(z)/\hat{U}_n^{(m)}(z)) \tag{p.60}$$

$$\Omega_n^{(m)}(z) = A_n^{(m)}(z)/Q_n^{(m)}(z)) \quad , \quad \hat{\Omega}_n^{(m)}(z) = \hat{A}_n^{(m)}(z)/\hat{Q}_n^{(m)}(z) \tag{p.61}$$

parameters/rhombus rules (Chap.7)

$$a_{n+1}^{(m)} = (1 - \alpha_n^{(m)}\hat{\alpha}_n^{(m)})\hat{\alpha}_{n-1}^{(m)}/\hat{\alpha}_n^{(m)} \qquad , \hat{a}_{n+1}^{(m)} = (1 - \alpha_n^{(m)}\hat{\alpha}_n^{(m)})\alpha_{n-1}^{(m)}/\alpha_n^{(m)}$$

$$b_n^{(m)} = -\alpha_n^{(m)}\hat{\alpha}_{n-1}^{(m)} \qquad , \hat{b}_n^{(m)} = -\hat{\alpha}_n^{(m)}\alpha_{n-1}^{(m)}$$

$$F_n^{(m)} = -a_n^{(m)} \qquad , \hat{F}_n^{(m)} = -\hat{a}_n^{(m)}$$

$$G_n^{(m)} = a_{n+1}^{(m)} - b_n^{(m)} = \hat{\alpha}_{n-1}^{(m)}/\hat{\alpha}_n^{(m)} \qquad , \hat{G}_n^{(m)} = \hat{a}_{n+1}^{(m)} - \hat{b}_n^{(m)} = \alpha_{n-1}^{(m)}/\alpha_n^{(m)}$$

$$\rho_n^{(m)} = a_n^{(m)}b_n^{(m)} = a_n^{(m+1)}b_{n-1}^{(m)} \qquad , \hat{\rho}_n^{(m)} = \hat{a}_n^{(m)}\hat{b}_n^{(m)} = \hat{a}_n^{(m-1)}\hat{b}_{n-1}^{(m)}$$

$$\sigma_n^{(m)} = a_n^{(m)} + b_n^{(m)} = a_{n+1}^{(m)} + b_n^{(m-1)} \qquad , \hat{\sigma}_n^{(m)} = \hat{a}_n^{(m)} + \hat{b}_n^{(m)} = \hat{a}_{n+1}^{(m)} + \hat{b}_n^{(m+1)}$$

On this card we give some formulas that will be used frequently during our exposition. For quick reference they are gathered on this card so that they can be taken along as one is progressing in the text.

Moebius transforms

$$t_n(w) = \frac{a_n + c_n\, w}{b_n + d_n\, w} \quad , \quad t_0 \circ t_1 \circ \cdots \circ t_n(w) = t_n(w) = \frac{A_n + C_n\, w}{B_n + D_n\, w} \qquad \text{p.12}$$

$$\begin{bmatrix} C_n & A_n \\ D_n & B_n \end{bmatrix} = \begin{bmatrix} c_0 & a_0 \\ d_0 & b_0 \end{bmatrix} \cdots \begin{bmatrix} c_n & a_n \\ d_n & b_n \end{bmatrix} = \begin{bmatrix} C_{n-1} & A_{n-1} \\ D_{n-1} & B_{n-1} \end{bmatrix} \begin{bmatrix} c_n & a_n \\ d_n & b_n \end{bmatrix} \qquad \text{(2.5-6) p.12}$$

$$C_n B_n - D_n A_n = \prod_{k=0}^{n} (c_k b_k - a_k d_k) \qquad \text{(2.7) p.13}$$

continued fractions

$$(A_n/B_n) = \frac{a_0}{b_0} + \sum_{k=1}^{n} \frac{a_k\rfloor}{\lfloor b_k} \quad , \quad S_n = S_{n-2}a_n + S_{n-1}b_n \quad , \quad S = A \text{ or } B \qquad \text{(2.16) p.19}$$

$$F = \frac{a_0}{b_0} + \sum_{k=1}^{n} \frac{a_k\rfloor}{\lfloor b_k} - \frac{R_n\rfloor}{\lfloor R_{n-1}} \quad , \quad R_n = FB_n - A_n \qquad \text{(2.17) p.19}$$

$$A_{n-1}B_n - B_{n-1}A_n = (-1)^n b_0^2 a_1 a_2 \cdots a_n \qquad \text{(2.18) p.20}$$

formal Laurent series

$$F(z) = \sum_{k=-\infty}^{\infty} f_k z^k \quad , \quad \Pi_{m:n}F(z) = \sum_{k=m}^{n} f_k z^k \quad , \quad F_*(z) = \sum_{k=-\infty}^{\infty} \bar{f}_k z^{-k} \qquad \text{p.22-23}$$

$$Z^{(m)}(z) = \tfrac{1}{2} f_m + \sum_{1}^{\infty} f_{m+k} z^{m+k} \quad , \quad \hat{Z}^{(m)} = -(\tfrac{1}{2} f_m + \sum_{1}^{\infty} f_{m-k} z^{m-k}) \qquad \text{(4.2) p.38}$$

$$T_n^{(m)} = [f_{m+i-j}]_{i,j=0}^{n} \quad , \quad T_n^{(m)} = \det T_n^{(m)} \qquad \text{p.29}$$

$$T_n^{(m)} Q_n^{(m)} = [v_n^{(m)}\ 0\ \cdots\ 0]^T \quad , \quad T_n^{(m)}\hat{Q}_n^{(m)} = [0\ \cdots\ 0\ \hat{v}_n^{(m)}]^T \qquad \text{(3.1a) p.30}$$

$$q_{0,n}^{(m)} = 1 \quad , \quad Q_0^{(m)} = 1 \quad , \quad \hat{q}_{n,n}^{(m)} = 1 \quad , \quad \hat{Q}_0^{(m)} = 1 \qquad \text{(3.1b,c) p.30}$$

$$P_n^{(m)}(z) = \Pi_{-\infty:m}(F(z)Q_n^{(m)}(z)) = v_n^{(m)} z^m + O_-(z^{m-1}) \qquad \text{(3.5a) p.32}$$

$$\hat{P}_n^{(m)}(z) = \Pi_{-\infty:m-1}(F(z)\hat{Q}_n^{(m)}(z)) = \hat{u}_n^{(m)} z^{m-1} + O_-(z^{m-2}) \qquad \text{(3.5b) p.32}$$

$$R_n^{(m)}(z) = \Pi_{m+1:\infty}(F(z)Q_n^{(m)}(z)) = u_n^{(m)} z^{m+n+1} + O_+(z^{m+n+2}) \qquad \text{(3.5c) p.32}$$

$$\hat{R}_n^{(m)}(z) = \Pi_{m:\infty}(F(z)\hat{Q}_n^{(m)}(z)) = \hat{v}_n^{(m)} z^{m+n} + O_+(z^{m+n+1}) \qquad \text{(3.5d) p.33}$$

$$R_n^{(m)}(z) = F(z)Q_n^{(m)}(z) - P_n^{(m)}(z) \quad , \quad \hat{R}_n^{(m)}(z) = F(z)\hat{Q}_n^{(m)}(z) - \hat{P}_n^{(m)}(z) \qquad \text{(4.1) p.37}$$

$$\alpha_{n+1}^{(m)} = u_n^{(m)}/v_n^{(m)} \quad , \quad \hat{\alpha}_{n+1}^{(m)} = \hat{u}_n^{(m)}/\hat{v}_n^{(m)} \quad , \quad \hat{\alpha}_n^{(m)} = 1/\alpha_n^{(m-1)} \qquad \text{p.30/67}$$

Adhemar Bultheel

Laurent Series and their Padé Approximations

1987

Birkhäuser Verlag
Basel · Boston

Author's Address:
Adhemar Bultheel
K. U. Leuven
Dept. Computer Science
Celestijnenlaan 200A
3030 Leuven-Heverlee
Belgium

Library of Congress Cataloging in Publication Data

Bultheel, Adhemar:
   Laurent series and the Padé approximations.
   (Operator theory, advances and applications ; vol. 27)
   Bibliography: p.
   Includes index.
   1. Laurent series.   2. Padé approximant.   I. Title.
II. Series: Operator theory, advances and applications ; v. 27.
QA331.B795   1987   515   87–24297
ISBN 0-8176-1940-2 (U.S.)

CIP-Kurztitelaufnahme der Deutschen Bibliothek

Bultheel, Adhemar:
Laurent series and their Padé approximations /
Adhemar Bultheel. – Basel ; Boston : Birkhäuser,
1987.
   (Operator theory ; Vol. 27)
   ISBN 3-7643-1940-2 (Basel)
   ISBN 0-8176-1940-2 (Boston)
NE: GT

© 1987 Birkhäuser Verlag Basel
Printed in Germany
ISBN 3-7643-1940-2
ISBN 0-8176-1940-2

CONTENTS

Preface ix

2. Introduction 1
   2.1 Classical Padé approximation 1
   2.2 Toeplitz and Hankel systems 2
   2.3 Continued fractions 3
   2.4 Orthogonal polynomials 4
   2.5 Rhombus algorithms and convergence 5
   2.6 Block structure 5
   2.7 Laurent-Padé approximants 6
   2.8 The projection method 7
   2.9 Applications 7
   2.10 Outline 10

3. Moebius transforms, continued fractions and Padé
   approximants 11
   3.1 Moebius transforms 11
   3.2 Flow graphs 14
   3.3 Continued fractions (CF) 18
   3.4 Formal series 22
   3.5 Padé approximants 24

4. Two algorithms 29
   4.1 Algorithm 1 29
   4.2 Algorithm 2 32

5. All kinds of Padé Approximants 37
   5.1 Padé approximants 37
   5.2 Laurent-Padé approximants 39
   5.3 Two-point Padé approximants 43

6. Continued fractions 47
   6.1 General observations 47
   6.2 Some special cases 49

7. Moebius transforms 55
   7.1 General observations 55
   7.2 Some special cases 57

8. Rhombus algorithms 65

8.1 The ab parameters (sawtooth path) 65
8.2 The FG parameters (row path) 72
8.3 A staircase path 73
8.4 $\rho\sigma$ paramaters (diagonal path) 75
8.5 Some dual results 77
8.6 Relation with classical algorithms 81

9. Biorthogonal polynomials, quadrature and reproducing
   kernels 83
   9.1 Biorthogonal polynomials 83
   9.2 Interpolatory quadrature methods 90
   9.3 Reproducing kernels 94
   9.4 Other orthogonality relations 98

10. Determinant expressions and matrix interpretations 103
    10.1 Determinant expressions 103
    10.2 Matrix interpretations 112
         10.2.1 Toeplitz matrices 112
         10.2.2 Hankel matrices 122
         10.2.3 Tridiagonal matrices 127

11. Symmetry Properties 132
    11.1 Symmetry for $F(z)$ and $\hat{F}(z) = F(1/z)$ 132
    11.2 Symmetry for $F(z)$ and $G(z) = 1/F(z)$ 136

12. Block structures 141
    12.1 Pade forms, Laurent-Pade forms and two-point Pade
         forms 141
    12.2 The T-table 143
    12.3 The Pade, Laurent-Pade, and two-point Pade tables 149

13. Meromorphic functions and asymptotic behaviour 155
    13.1 The function $F(z)$ 155
    13.2 Asymptotics for finite Toeplitz determinants 156
    13.3 Asymptotics for infinite Toeplitz determinants 159
    13.4 Consequences for the T-table 163

14. Montessus de Ballore theorem for Laurent-Padé
    approximants 167
    14.1 Semi infinite Laurent series 167
    14.2 Bi-infinite Laurent series 170

15. Determination of poles 173
    15.1 Rutishauser polynomials of type 1 and type 2 173
    15.2 Rutishauser polynomials of type 3 179
    15.3 Rutishauser polynomials and Laurent series 181

15.4 Convergence of parameters 183

16. Determination of zeros 187
     16.1 Dual Rutishauser polynomials and semi-infinite
           series 187
     16.2 From semi-infinite to bi-infinite series 189
     16.3 Convergence of parameters 193

17. Convergence in a row of the Laurent-Padé table 195
     17.1 Toeplitz operators and the projection method 197
     17.2 Convergence of the denominator 199
     17.3 Convergence of the numerator 203

18. The positive definite case and applications 207
     18.1 Function classes 207
     18.2 Connection with the previous results 212
     18.3 Stochastic processes and systems 219
     18.4 Lossless inverse scattering and transmission lines 224
     18.5 Laurent-Padé approximation and ARMA-filtering 230
     18.6 Concluding remarks 231

19. Examples 233
     19.1 Example 1 233
     19.2 Example 2 248
     19.3 Example 3 253

References 257

List of symbols 263

Subject index 271

PREFACE

The Padé approximation problem is, roughly speaking, the local approximation of analytic or meromorphic functions by rational ones. It is known to be important to solve a large scale of problems in numerical analysis, linear system theory, stochastics and other fields.

There exists a vast literature on the classical Padé problem. However, these papers mostly treat the problem for functions analytic at 0 or, in a purely algebraic sense, they treat the approximation of formal power series. For certain problems however, the Padé approximation problem for formal Laurent series, rather than for formal power series seems to be a more natural basis.

In this monograph, the problem of Laurent-Padé approximation is central. In this problem a ratio of two Laurent polynomials in sought which approximates the two directions of the Laurent series simultaneously.
As a side result the two–point Padé approximation problem can be solved. In that case, two series are approximated, one is a power series in z and the other is a power series in z^{-1}. So we can approximate two, not necessarily different functions one at zero and the other at infinity.
To connect this problem to the previous one, we just have to glue the two series together to get a formal Laurent series. When the classical definition of Padé approximation is applied to a Laurent series instead of a power series, we get a numerator which is a polynomial plus infinitely many negative powers of z which are generated by the terms with negative powers in the Laurent series. Thus if the Laurent series has no negative powes of z, i.e. when it becomes a power series, the classical Padé approximant appears as a special case.

The first part of this volume (up to chapter 11) is purely algebraic. Three types of recursive algorithms are presented to find the solutions of the three types of Padé problems mentioned above. The first one is in principle the Trench–Zohar algorithm for Toeplitz matrix inversion. The second one is a nonsymmetric version of the Schur algorithm for deciding whether a function is a Schur function. Both these algorithms are based on a "Toeplitz approach", which means that Toeplitz matrices are a basic working tool, whereas the algorithms commonly used in the classical Padé literature (Euclid, Routh, Kronecker a.o) are more "Hankel minded". A third type of algorithm is of rhombus type and this is essentially the Rutishauser qd algorithm from numerical analysis.

From the engineering literature, the flow graph representation of electrical networks is used to represent the algorithms. This will be most useful in getting a visualization of the computational flow.

The recurrences of the algorithms can often be interpreted as recurrences associated with continued fractions and formal orthogonal polynomials. These interpretations are also treated to some extend, including reproducing kernels and Christoffel-Darboux-type formulas.

When the algorithms are used in a linear algebra context, formulas will be found for Toeplitz and Hankel matrix inversion and triangular factorization.

Finally, the block structure of the classical Padé table will be extended to describe the blocks of Laurent-Padé and two–point Padé tables.

The second part of the volume is analytic in nature. The Padé approximation problem is considered for meromorphic in $\mathbb{C} \setminus \{0\}$ functions. Classical and more recent results on the asymptotic behaviour of Hankel and Toeplitz determinants and the projection method are used for proving convergence in columns and rows of Padé tables. In classical Padé theory the convergence of columns is well established and the convergence of the rows can be obtained from a simple duality principle. For the Laurent-Padé problem, convergence of the columns is essentially the same as in the classical case. For the row convergence however, some new methods had to be used, and it is one of the most important results of this monograph. From these convergence results it is derived how the poles and zeros of a meromorphic function given by a Laurent series can be computed. The computation of poles is related to column convergence and the computation of zeros is related to row convergence.

Chapter 17 contains some interpretation of the Padé approximation problem in other theories like Carathéodory and Schur function classes, Szegö polynomials orthogonal on the unit circle, prediction theory and inverse scattering. My interest in the last topics was the inital motivation for writing this monograph. Therefore it is my sincere hope that this text will not only be appreciated by specialists in Padé approximation, continued fractions, orthogonal polynomials and Toeplitz matrices but also by people with a more applied mathematical background e.g. from stochastic processes, time series analysis, signal processing, linear systems theory or inverse scattering.

I realize that it will take some time for the reader who is not familiar with the subject to get accustomed to the large number of different types of polynomials, series and parameters. To help him, a quick reference of the most important formulas is included on a separate card which can be taken along as a bookmarker.

It remains to express my appreciation to the Computer Science department of the K.U.Leuven where I had the opportunity to prepare this text. The typesetting is done with the equipment and software provided by the department. Paul Levrie read an earlier draft of the manuscript. He pointed out a number of errors and made valuable suggestions for improvement of the text. Lieve Swinnen prepared a first draft for the typesetter.

I also wish to thank Prof. I. Gohberg, editor of this series who encouraged me to rewrite an internal report, which was the fetal version of this monograph, in a readable form.

The staff of Birkhäuser Verlag, Basel is thanked for expert advise in editing and production.

Adhemar Bultheel

Leuven, Belgium
May 1987.

Chapter 1

Introduction.

1.1 Classical Padé approximation

Padé approximants for a formal power series are well known [BGM]. The basic idea is to approximate a formal power series $F(z) = \sum_0^\infty f_k z^k$ by a rational function of the form $A_m(z)/B_n(z)$ where $A_m(z)$ and $B_n(z)$ are polynomials of given degrees m and n respectively such that the formal expansion of the approximant in increasing powers of z is $\sum_0^\infty \phi_k z^k$ and $f_k = \phi_k$ for $k = 0,1,2,...,N$ with $N \geqslant m + n$.

There are many applications of this type of approximations. They range from the solution of all types of operator equations, over convergence acceleration, linear system theory, network theory, stochastic processes etc. E.g. the partial realization problem in linear system theory is in many aspects the same as the Padé approximation problem [GRL]. An extensive bibliography on the use of Padé approximation in model reduction is given in [BU8]. Many books appeared on the subject of Padé approximation as well as many conference proceedings. Claude Brezinski has compiled a list of hundreds of references on Padé approximation and related topics. One of the basic references on Padé approximation is a paper by W.B. Gragg [GR2] giving a survey of a number of basic properties of Padé approximation. The techniques used in the study of Padé approximation are related to many other fields of mathematics. One of the basic tools are simple recursive algorithms to compute the Padé approximants. Perhaps the most striking example is the Euclidean algorithm and related algorithms like the Routh [HEN] or Viskovatoff [BU6] algorithms. These algorithms can be used to construct successive Padé approximants of type (m,n), $(m+1,n)$, $(m+1,n+1)$, $(m+2,n+1)$, $(m+2,n+2)$, $\cdots$. These recursive algorithms use the knowledge of two successive approximants in this sequence to construct the next element in the sequence in a simple manner. If you look at the Padé table, which is the matrix with as (m,n) entry the (m,n) type Padé approximant, then the previous sequence describes a staircase sequence in this table. Such a staircase sequence is only one of the possibilities for sequences that can be constructed by recursive algorithms. In fact it is possible to compute from two adjacent elements in the Padé table any of the surrounding elements. A survey of such relations is given in [BU5]. In the Routh algorithm as in many other related algorithms, the fundamental problem is to find the denominator of the approximant. To see this, suppose that the constant term of the denominator is nonzero. Then the Padé approximation problem can be formulated as a linear problem. Indeed, the defining relations of the Padé approximant can be rewritten as

$$\sum_{k=0}^{n} f_{i-k}b_k = r_i \ , \quad i = 0,1,... \tag{1.1}$$

where f_k with $k < 0$ is supposed to be zero. b_k for $k = 0,1,...,n$ are the denominator coefficients of the Padé approximant of type (m,n). $r_k = a_k$ for $k = 0,1,...,m$, where the a_k are the numerator coefficients. $r_k = 0$ for $k = m+1,m+2,...,m+n$. These equations for $i = 0,1,...,m+n$ fix the numerator coefficients a_k , $k = 0,1,...,m$ and the denominator coefficients b_k , $k = 0,1,...,n$ up to a normalization. The remaining coefficients r_k for $k \geqslant m+n+1$ are defined by (1.1) in terms of the f_k and the b_k. We can chose b_0 to be one for normalization, so that the denominator coefficients are the solution of the system

$$\sum_{k=1}^{n} f_{i-k}b_k = -f_i, \quad i = m+1,...,m+n. \tag{1.2}$$

and the numerator coefficients are found by a simple evaluation of the first $n+1$ relations in (1.1):

$$a_i = \sum_{k=0}^{n} f_{i-k}b_k, \quad i = 0,1,...,m. \tag{1.3}$$

1.2 Toeplitz and Hankel systems

As you can see from this, the fundamental problem is to solve a system of linear equations of Toeplitz type or, if you reverse the order, of Hankel type. A Toeplitz matrix has the following form :

$$\begin{vmatrix} t_0 & t_{-1} & t_{-2} & \cdots & t_{-n} \\ t_1 & t_0 & t_{-1} & \cdots & t_{-n+1} \\ t_2 & t_1 & t_0 & \cdots & t_{-n+2} \\ \vdots & \vdots & \vdots & & \vdots \\ t_n & t_{n-1} & t_{n-2} & \cdots & t_0 \end{vmatrix}$$

and a Hankel matrix has the form

$$
\begin{bmatrix}
h_0 & h_1 & h_2 & \cdots & h_n \\
h_1 & h_2 & h_3 & \cdots & h_{n+1} \\
h_2 & h_3 & h_4 & \cdots & h_{n+2} \\
\vdots & \vdots & \vdots & & \vdots \\
h_n & h_{n+1} & h_{n+2} & \cdots & h_{2n}
\end{bmatrix}.
$$

Normally a linear system of dimension $n \times n$ can be solved in $O(n^3)$ operations by classical system solvers. Because a Toeplitz system is highly structured, it can be solved in $O(n^2)$ operations. These fast Toeplitz solvers are recursive procedures that perform so to speak the same operations as those appearing in procedures like the Euclidean algorithm. This means that a number of results on Padé approximation can be cast into a linear algebra formulation to give fast methods to factorize a Toeplitz or a Hankel matrix into its lower-upper triangular factors [GR3,BU7]. Other algorithms than the Euclidean or Routh algorithm do exist. E.g. Trench [TRE1,TRE2] and Zohar [ZOH1,ZOH2] and later many others developed fast algorithms for the solution of Toeplitz and Hankel type systems. A survey of these Toeplitz algorithms is given in a thesis by D.Sweet [SWE]. See also [MUS] and [BU9]. There are matrices that are not Toeplitz or Hankel but still have a certain structure that makes them not completely arbitrary. A measure for the complexity of such systems was introduced by Kailath and his coworkers [KAI]. They define the displacement rank of the matrix. The displacement rank measures by how much the matrix differs from a Toeplitz or Hankel matrix. Hence it is related to the complexity of the algorithm needed to solve a system with such a matrix. Algorithms similar to the algorithms for plain Toeplitz matrices were designed to solve systems with a matrix that is of low displacement rank. The operation count is then of the order of $O(\alpha n^2)$ where α is a number between 0 and n which is essentially the displacement rank. By applying a divide and conquer principle (or doubling strategy) and fast fourier techniques, it is possible to reduce the operation count even further from $O(n^2)$ to $O(n(\log_2 n)^2)$ [BGY]. A lot of information on these fast algorithms with applications to linear dynamical systems, signal processing and VLSI implementation are found in [LAN]. Another excellent survey is given in [HER]. Although it is possible to generalize at least some of the results given in this volume to matrices with low displacement rank, we shall not pursue this any further for the time being. Also the "superfast" algorithms will not be treated.

1.3 Continued fractions

The three term recurrence relations like those used in the Routh algorithm are immediately connected with continued fractions. Indeed, if we consider the recursion $Q_{n+1} = b_{n+1}Q_n + a_{n+1}Q_{n-1}$ with $Q_{-1} = 0$ and $Q_0 = b_0$, then these Q_n are the denominators for the successive convergents of a continued fraction

$$\frac{a_0}{b_0} + \frac{a_1}{\lvert b_1} + \frac{a_2}{\lvert b_2} + \frac{a_3}{\lvert b_3} + \cdots \qquad (1.4)$$

The difference relation for Q_n is nothing but the forward evaluation scheme for the successive convergents. The corresponding recursion for the numerators is exactly the same: $P_{n+1} = b_{n+1}P_n + a_{n+1}P_{n-1}$ but with initial conditions $P_{-1} = b_0$ and $P_0 = a_0$. Algorithms like the Routh algorithm are simply algorithms to obtain a continued fraction expansion of the given power series by successive long divisions. I.e. they compute the terms a_k and b_k [BU6]. Hence the Padé approximants on the staircase sequence mentioned before become the successive convergents of the continued fraction constructed by this algorithm.

1.4 Orthogonal polynomials

Three term recurrence relations are also related to orthogonal polynomials. In a formal setting, the orthogonality can be expressed with respect to a linear functional λ depending on some positive integer m and related to the power series $F(z)$. It is defined for all polynomials by $\lambda^{(m+1)}(z^k) = f_{k+m+1}$, $k = 0,1,2,...$ for some $m \geqslant 0$. If the denominators of the Padé approximants on the diagonal $(m+n,n)$, $k = 0,1,...$ of the Padé table are $Q_n^{(m+n)}(z)$, then it can be shown that the polynomials $z^n Q_n^{(m+n)}(1/z)$ are orthogonal with respect to $\lambda^{(m+1)}$ [BRE] and it will be illustrated in this volume that several other orthogonality properties can be found.

The orthogonal polynomials are in their turn related to interpolatory quadrature formulas where $F(z)$ now plays the role of a weight function. This connection will also be treated.

The Routh-Hurwitz stability criterion is another instance where the Routh algorithm pops up. I.e. it can be used to check if all the roots of a polynomial are e.g. in the left half plane or not. The theory of Padé approximation will therefore also be related to these stability problems. So will the algorithm of Trench have a close connection with the Schur-Cohn stability test which checks if all the roots of a polynomial lie inside the unit disc.

1.5 Rhombus algorithms and convergence

The division algorithms like the Routh and Euclid algorithm are not the only possibility to compute the Padé approximants. The qd (quotient–difference) algorithm of Rutishauser [RUT] and its variants construct by simple rhombus rules a table of coefficients that contains the numbers a_k and b_k for a continued fraction expansion like (1.4). This qd algorithm can again be used at least in principle, to compute the roots of a polynomial. For the development of these results, we need an analytic theory as opposed to the formal algorithmic approach that was used to obtain the previous results. We now need the convergence of the formal power series. It should be the McLaurin expansion of a meromorphic function analytic at the origin. One of the major convergence results in Padé approximation is the theorem of Montessus de Ballore. It states that under certain conditions the Padé approximants of type (m,n) for a fixed n and for m tending to infinity converge to the given function $F(z)$. Convergence is on compact subsets of a disc centered at the origin containing exactly the n smallest poles of $F(z)$ in its interior. This convergence is uniform, except of course at the poles. With this convergence result, we can show the existence of a convergent sequence of polynomials whose zeros are in the limit some of the poles of the given function. These polynomials are essentially factors of the denominators of the (m,n) Padé approximants for $m \rightarrow \infty$. In the ideal case, that is if the poles of $F(z)$ are separated in modulus, they can be found one by one. The coefficients of these polynomials are expressed in terms of elements of the qd table. Hence, zeros of a polynomial are found as the poles of the function which is one over this polynomial. For this function the qd table is constructed and column limits are computed, giving in the limit factors of the given polynomial. A classical proof of the Montessus de Ballore theorem depends heavily on asymptotic expressions for finite Hankel determinants whose entries are coefficients of the given power series [BGM]. Most important is that these asymptotic expressions involve the poles of $F(z)$ so that the results on the pole positions are obtained. Similar results may be obtained for the zeros of $F(z)$. This involves the convergence in rows of the Padé table. I.e. convergence of the sequence of (m,n) approximants where now n tends to infinity and m remains constant. This type of convergence is easily derived from the Montessus de Ballore theorem through a symmetry that exists between the Padé table for $F(z)$ and the Padé table for $1/F(z)$. These tables are each others mirror image in their main diagonal.

1.6 Block structure

The study of all these problems in the simplest case where all the elements in the Padé table exist is not too difficult. However, as can be seen from the system (1.2), problems can be expected when this system is singular. To find the structure of the Padé table we have to look at the Toeplitz determinants $T_n^{(m)} = \det(f_{m+i-j})_{i,j=0}^n$ and see when they become zero. It turns out that zero determinants in the T-table, i.e. the table with entries $T_n^{(m)}$, will always appear in square blocks. These blocks will define square blocks (called singular blocks) in the Padé table. Upon and above the antidiagonal of such a singular block all the Padé approximants can be reduced to the same irreducible form which is the left top element in the singular block. Below this antidiagonal in the singular block, no Padé approximants exist as defined in the first paragraph of this introduction. There we only have Padé forms that solve the linearized problem (1.2-3) without the restriction that the constant term of the denominator has to be nonzero.

1.7 Laurent-Padé approximants

All these results are found in classical references on Padé approximation and in the paper [GR2] we have mentioned before. The extension of the idea of Padé approximation for a formal power series to some Padé–like approximants for a formal Laurent series has led to the notion of Laurent-Padé approximants. To define this type of approximations we proceed as follows: given a formal Laurent series $F(z) = \sum_{-\infty}^\infty f_k z^k$, we can split it up into the two series $Z(z) = \tfrac{1}{2}f_0 + \sum_1^\infty f_k z^k$ and $\hat{Z}(z) = \tfrac{1}{2}f_0 + \sum_1^\infty f_{-k} z^{-k}$. Then find two rational approximants $R(z) = A_m(z)/B_n(z)$ and $\hat{R}(z) = \hat{A}_n(z)/\hat{B}_n(z)$ such that the expansions $R(z) = \tfrac{1}{2}\phi_0 + \sum_1^\infty \phi_k z^k$ and $\hat{R}(z) = \tfrac{1}{2}\phi_0 + \sum_1^\infty \phi_{-k} z^{-k}$ match the coefficients of $Z(z)$ and $\hat{Z}(z)$ in a Padé sense. I.e. such that $f_k = \phi_k$ for $k = 0, \pm 1, \pm 2, ..., \pm N$ with $N \geqslant m+n$ and in addition such that the sum $R(z) + \hat{R}(z)$ is a rational expression with as a numerator a Laurent polynomial of degree m and as denominator a Laurent polynomial of degree n.
The notion of Laurent-Padé approximation was introduced in other papers of Gragg [GR1], [GRJ]. The essence of this volume is to give generalizations of the results given in [GR2] concerning Padé approximation to include the Laurent-Padé case. Of course there is a close connection with classical Padé approximation, so that results similar to the classical ones can be expected. Again the coefficients of the two denominators $B_n(z)$ and $\hat{B}_n(z)$ are found as the solutions of two Toeplitz systems similar to (1.2). The only difference is that now f_k need not be zero for $k < 0$. Essentially the same techniques are used and the same algorithms will do the job for Laurent-Padé approximation. Many of the tables that can be constructed in connection with classical Padé approximation like the T-table, the qd-table, the table of orthogonal polynomials etc. can be extended to the Laurent case. The main difference is that the rows of these tables for the classical case were numbered from 0 to ∞ because f_k was zero for negative k while for the

Laurent case this row numbering extends almost trivially to $-\infty$. The block structure of the Laurent-Padé table will also be more complicated because it will be defined by a superposition of the block structures for its two parts $A_m(z)/B_n(z)$ and $\hat{A}_m(z)/\hat{B}_n(z)$. Convergence theory when the numerator degree $m \to \infty$ and determination of the poles will give no special problem, but convergence for the denominator degree $n \to \infty$ will be a more serious problem because the simple symmetry argument that is used in the classical Padé case will not be applicable anymore. It turns out that to study this type of convergence we need asymptotic expressions for the Toeplitz determinants $T_n^{(m)} = \det(f_{m+i-j})_{i,j=0}^{n}$ but now for $n \to \infty$. There is an extensive literature on the asymptotics of infinite Toeplitz determinants where the f_k are the Fourier coefficients of a function satisfying some extra conditions [GRE], [GOF], [BOT1], [BOT2]. None of these directly give us the result we need. Our Toeplitz determinants are based on the coefficients in the Laurent expansion of a meromorphic function and what we need are asymptotics that involve the zeros of this function. However, it will be possible to combine the results of [BOT1] and the asymptotics for finite Toeplitz (or Hankel) determinants of the classical Padé theory to get the results we need. In this context we shall also need Wiener-Hopf type factorizations for the symbol $F(z)$ of the Toeplitz operator. Here we closely follow the method of [GOF]. All this will lead to convergence results for rows of the Laurent-Padé table that are in their final appearance straightforward generalizations of the classical results. E.g. the zeros of $F(z)$ can be obtained by considering row limits in the qd-table for its Laurent series.

1.8 The projection method

Linear systems with a Toeplitz or Hankel matrix have many other applications that go beyond the Padé approximation problem. E.g. convolution type equations can be discretized to give such a system that is in general infinite dimensional. The Wiener-Hopf equation

$$\sum_{k=0}^{\infty} f_{i-k} b_k = r_i , \quad i = 0,1,... \tag{1.5}$$

can be solved by the projection method. That is by successively solving the subsystems

$$\sum_{k=0}^{n} f_{i-k} b_k^{(n)} = r_i , \quad i = 0,1,...,n \tag{1.6}$$

for $n = 0,1,2,...$ and eventually there is convergence of the subsolutions $(b_k^{(n)})_0^n$ to the solution of the infinite equation. Such convolution equations have been studied by I. Gohberg and I.A. Feldman [GOF]. This connection makes it quite clear why some results of [GOF] were needed in the study of the convergence of a row of the Laurent-Padé table. The convergence results we obtained can also be interpreted as convergence results for the projection method to solve the equation (1.5). Our type of convergence is uniformly on compacts, whereas the convergence treated in [GOF] is convergence in l_p norm.

1.9 Applications

Toeplitz operators and Toeplitz forms have many other applications. E.g. in problems of random walk, prediction theory, stationary Gaussian processes, network theory, digital filtering and the study of linear dynamical systems [GRE]. In these type of applications, the Toeplitz forms are based on the Fourier coefficients of a positive definite function on the unit circle of the complex plane. Consequently, the Toeplitz matrices are positive definite matrices. Many of the previously defined formal concepts get in such a situation their classical meaning. The symbol of the Toeplitz operator $F(z)$ is now a genuine weight function in the definition of an inner product which is the weighted l_2 inner product for functions defined on the unit circle. The polynomials orthogonal with respect to this inner product are known as Szegő polynomials [SZE]. Besides the three term recurrence relation for these polynomials, there is also a nice coupled recurrence for these polynomials $Q_n(z)$ and their reciprocals $z^n \overline{Q_n(1/\overline{z})}$. The parameters involved in this recurrence are called Szegő parameters. The sequence of Szegő parameters completely characterizes the sequence of orthogonal polynomials and hence the weight function $F(z)$. It was pointed out by Akhiezer [AKH] that these Szegő parameters are exactly the same as the sequence of parameters generated in an algorithm due to Schur [SCH] which he used in the study of functions in the Schur class. These are functions analytic and bounded by one in modulus in the open unit disc. The Schur functions are somehow equivalent with Carathéodory functions which are analytic and have a nonnegative real part in the open unit disc. Therefore the Schur functions, Carathéodory functions and positive definite functions can be studied parallelly. They are extensively used in the study of the classical moment problems [AKH].

Szegő's polynomials and therefore also the Schur-Szegő parameters appear in several engineering applications. It is e.g. shown in [DED] that the Szegő recurrence relation can be recovered from a Darlington synthesis procedure known in circuit theory. In fact this method solves an inverse scattering problem [RED] for transmission lines. Applications in linear estimation theory for stochastic processes and digital filtering are also well known [GRE], [OPS], [MAR]. E.g. the construction of an autoregressive predictor involves the computation of Szegő polynomials orthogonal with respect to the density function of the given stochastic process [GRE]. In this respect the well known Levinson algorithm is worth mentioning [LEV]. The construction of a digital filter is essentially the same problem [OPS], [MAR]. The Levinson algorithm computes the predictor polynomial from the covariance information and this is done by computing the Schur-Szegő parameters and evaluating the polynomials through the coupled recursion of Szegő. In this context, the Schur-Szegő parameters are called partial correlation coefficients, a term suggested by the stochastic approach, or reflection coefficients, a term stemming from scattering theory. The algorithm of Schur and the Levinson algorithm can be seen as duals in the sense that the Levinson algorithm gives the triangular factors of the inverse of the covariance matrix, which is a selfadjoint positive definite Toeplitz matrix, whereas the Schur algorithm computes the elements of the triangular factors of the covariance matrix itself.

All the problems in this sphere are related to the Laurent-Padé approximation problem in the special case of a positive $F(z)$ and of a numerator degree equal to zero. The other types of Laurent-Padé approximants applied to these problems may lead to unstable results (the poles of the approximant are not where they should be) or it may be impossible to factor the numerator into its stable/unstable factors. The $(0,n)$ Laurent-Padé approximants give predictors that are of so called autoregressive (AR) type only [OPS]. More general predictors, i.e. predictors with a numerator that is not a constant, are said to be of ARMA (Autoregressive-Moving Average) type. They can be obtained by an interpolation version of the Schur algorithm which was constructed by G. Pick and R.Nevanlinna [PIC], [NEV]. Whereas the Schur algorithm constructs a rational approximant of a Schur function by successive interpolations at the origin, the Pick-Nevanlinna algorithm will construct rational interpolants for the same function that interpolate in a sequence of points that can be chosen arbitrarily inside the unit disc. In the special case that all these points coincide at the origin, we obtain the Padé-like Schur algorithm again.

For a nonselfadjoint Toeplitz matrix, the original Schur and Levinson algorithms have to be slightly adapted. Due to the asymmetry of the problem, we have for each step in the recurrence relation of the algorithms two Schur-Szegő parameters that become complex conjugate in the selfadjoint case. Although it is conventional to use Routh or Euclid like algorithms as the starting point in Padé approximation, we shall put the generalized Levinson and Schur algorithms central in our development. These generalized algorithms are in fact the algorithms proposed by Trench and Zohar to solve a Toeplitz system [TRE1], [ZOH1].

1.10 Outline

The outline of the contents of this volume is as follows. Up to chapter 11, the approach is a formal algebraic one. Central in the development are the algorithms given in chapter 3. These are the generalizations of the Levinson and Schur algorithms for nonselfadjoint Toeplitz matrices. As we noted before, this is less conventional since in the classical approach recursive relations for a staircase or a diagonal in the Padé table are considered. The algorithms in chapter 3 give relations between two adjacent rows in the Padé table. The rhombus rules, which are natural extensions of the classical qd relations are derived from the recursions treated in chapter 3. They can be found in chapter 7. The different types of Padé approximants, continued fractions and more general Moebius transformations that are related to these recursions are treated in chapters 4–6. The denominators of the approximants are orthogonal polynomials with respect to some linear functionals. These are given in chapter 8. Expressions in terms of Hankel and Toeplitz determinants are given in chapter 9 together with the interpretation of the algorithms as factorization algorithms. If the formal Laurent series is symmetric then the upper halves of the bi-infinite tables associated with it are essentially replicants of the lower halves as explained in chapter 10. Chapter 11 is the last chapter on formal series. It extends the classical block structure of Padé tables to Laurent-Padé tables.

Chapters 12–16 treat convergence theorems if the Laurent series represents a meromorphic function. Poles and zeros of such a function can be recovered from limits of rows and columns in the bi-infinite tables associated with its Laurent series.

In chapter 17, we give a special case of the previous theory, relating it to the theory of Schur, Levinson, Szegő polynomials, moment problems and digital filtering. These theories are essentially concerned with the Fourier series of a positive function on the unit circle of the complex plane and study the central row in the Laurent-Padé table for it. It were these ideas that triggered our interest in extending these results to the complete Laurent-Padé table of a formal Laurent series.

Finally chapter 18 gives some worked examples to show how the algorithms and formulas work in practice.

Chapter 2

Moebius transforms, continued fractions and Padé approximants

In this chapter we shall introduce some basic tools and definitions. Some of the definitions will be slight modifications of the classical definitions. These modifications are needed since we shall treat formal Laurent series rather than formal power series which causes some problems for the definition of the quotient and product of such series. Moebius transforms are simple linear fractional transforms. They are important because continued fractions, to be treated in the third subsection, can be defined as a sequence of Moebius transforms of a special type. Another tool we shall introduce in the second subsection are flow graphs. These are extensively used in the engineering literature to give a graphical representation of an algorithm or an analog network realizing this algorithm. Some of the flow graphs we shall give will probably look very familiar to readers who know the ladder or lattice realizations of prediction filters. It may help them to understand the theory and it will be advantageous for others to have a clear and concise representation of a certain algorithm. To introduce our formal concepts of different types of Padé approximants, which is done in the last subsection, we need some definitions and notations to work with formal series. These are given in subsection 4.

2.1 Moebius transforms

We shall now give the definition of a Moebius transformation and some elementary properties that are so trivial that we give them without proof.

A linear fractional transform or *Moebius transform* is defined for the extended complex plane (or some other field extended with an element ∞) by

$$z = t(w) = \frac{a+cw}{b+dw} \quad , \quad ad-bc \neq 0. \tag{2.1}$$

If $w = p/q$ and $z = x/y$, we can write it as a linear transformation :

$$\begin{vmatrix} x \\ y \end{vmatrix} = \begin{vmatrix} c & a \\ d & b \end{vmatrix} \begin{vmatrix} p \\ q \end{vmatrix}. \tag{2.2}$$

We call the transformation defined by (2.2) a *Moebius transform for pairs*. The transformation (2.2) will also be represented by a notation like (2.1).

$$(x/y) = t(p/q) = (aq + cp/bq + dp)$$

where $(\cdot/\cdot)$ has to be understood as a notation for a couple of elements. It is obvious that the difference between a Moebius transform and a Moebius transform for pairs is only spurious if we identify w with the couple $(w/1)$ and $(a/0)$ with ∞. We shall mix both concepts and use the notation that will be the most suitable one in the context. If you find a notation like a/b you should read it as a quotient or as a pair of elements as will be appropriate. We give some elementary properties of Moebius transforms.

PROPERTY 2.1. *The inverse transformation of t as defined in (2.1) is given by*

$$t^{-1}(z) = \frac{a-bz}{-c+dz}. \tag{2.3}$$

□

We shall often need the composition of a sequence of Moebius transforms.

The next property says that the composition of a number of Moebius transforms is again a Moebius transform and the parameters of the global transform are easily found by multiplying out 2 by 2 matrices like the one in (2.2).

PROPERTY 2.2. *Let $\{t_n\}$, $n \geqslant 0$ be a sequence of Moebius transforms based on the parameters $\{a_n, b_n, c_n, d_n\}$:*

$$t_n(w) = \frac{a_n + c_n\, w}{b_n + d_n\, w} \quad , \quad a_n d_n - b_n c_n \neq 0 \ , \ n \geqslant 0.$$

Define recursively the successive compositions of these Moebius transforms by $t_0(w) = t_0(w)$ and $t_n(w) = t_{n-1}(t_n(w))$, $n \geqslant 1$. Then these are again Moebius transforms. Indeed:

$$t_n(w) = \frac{A_n + C_n\, w}{B_n + D_n\, w} \tag{2.4}$$

with A_n, B_n, C_n and D_n defined by

$$\begin{vmatrix} C_n & A_n \\ D_n & B_n \end{vmatrix} = \begin{vmatrix} c_0 & a_0 \\ d_0 & b_0 \end{vmatrix} \cdots \begin{vmatrix} c_n & a_n \\ d_n & b_n \end{vmatrix}. \tag{2.5}$$

□

Note that in the recursive definition

$$\begin{vmatrix} C_n & A_n \\ D_n & B_n \end{vmatrix} = \begin{vmatrix} C_{n-1} & A_{n-1} \\ D_{n-1} & B_{n-1} \end{vmatrix} \begin{vmatrix} c_n & a_n \\ d_n & b_n \end{vmatrix} \tag{2.6}$$

we could start with the initial conditions

$$\begin{vmatrix} C_{-1} & A_{-1} \\ D_{-1} & B_{-1} \end{vmatrix} = \begin{vmatrix} 1 & 0 \\ 0 & 1 \end{vmatrix}.$$

If we express that the determinant of the left hand side of (2.5) equals the product of the determinants of the matrices in the right hand side we obtain a useful relation that is known as the *determinant formula* :

$$C_n B_n - D_n A_n = \prod_{k=0}^{n} (c_k b_k - a_k d_k).$$ (2.7)

With the Moebius transform of (2.1) we associate a *dual transform* viz.

$$\hat{t}(w) = \frac{d + cw}{b + aw} .$$ (2.8)

This dual transform corresponds to the transposition of the 2 by 2 matrix in (2.2).

PROPERTY 2.3. *Let the Moebius transforms t and its dual $\hat{t}$ be defined by (2.1) and (2.8) and set $i(z) = 1/z$. Then*

a) $t^{-1} = (-i) \circ \hat{t} \circ (-i).$ (2.9a)

b) *If moreover $b = c$ in (2.1), then*

$$t = i \circ \hat{t} \circ i.$$ (2.9b)

□

As you can see, this dual transform is somehow related to the inverse of the original Moebius transform. This becomes especially useful when we consider the composition of a sequence of Moebius transforms as you will see in the next property.

PROPERTY 2.4. *Let t_n and $t_n = t_0 \circ t_1 \circ \cdots \circ t_n$ be as in property 2.2 and denote their duals with a hat. Then*

$$\hat{t}_n = (-i) \circ t_n^{-1} \circ (-i) = \hat{t}_n \circ \hat{t}_{n-1} \circ \cdots \circ \hat{t}_0,$$ (2.10)

with as before $i(z)=1/z$. If A_n, B_n, C_n, and D_n are associated with $\{t_n\}$ as in property 2.2, and if

$$[S_n \ R_n] = [S_{-1} \ R_{-1}] \begin{vmatrix} C_n & A_n \\ D_n & B_n \end{vmatrix} = [S_{n-1} \ R_{n-1}] \begin{vmatrix} c_n & a_n \\ d_n & b_n \end{vmatrix},$$ (2.11)

then

$$S_n / R_n = \hat{t}_n(S_{n-1}/R_{n-1}) = \hat{t}_n(S_{-1}/R_{-1})$$ (2.12)

and

$$R_{-1}/S_{-1} = i \circ \hat{t}_n^{-1}(S_n/R_n) = -t_n(-R_n/S_n).$$ (2.13)

□

2.2 Flow graphs

A *flow graph* will be very useful for a graphical representation of transformations and algorithms. It can be defined as a network of directed *branches* connecting *nodes*. A node is indicated by a circle and a branch by an arrow between nodes. To each node is associated a *node value* and to each branch a *transmittance*. Let (jk) be the branch from node j to node k with transmittance f_{jk} and let w_j be the node value of node j. The *output* of branch (jk) (at node k) is then $f_{jk} w_j$. The node value at node k is the sum of all outputs of branches entering node k. If no transmittance is indicated we suppose it to be 1. External input to the network is via *source nodes* and outputs can be extracted at *sink nodes*. There are no branches entering a source node and a sink node has only entering branches. If the number of source and sink nodes of a flow graph is the same, we can couple them in pairs. Such a pair is called a *port*. If there are m such ports, the network is called an *m-port*.

As an example consider the flow graph in fig 2.1.

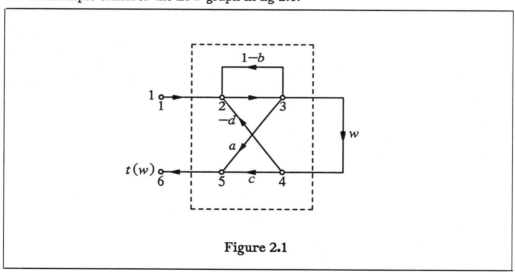

Figure 2.1

Node 1 is a source node with value $w_1 = 1$ (external input) and node 6 is a sink node with value $w_6 = t(w)$ (output). Let w_k in general be the node value for node k. Then we clearly see that

$$w_6 = w_5 = aw_3 + cw_4$$

$$w_4 = w\, w_3$$

$$w_2 = w_3 = w_1 + (1-b)\, w_3 - dw_4.$$

These equations can be solved to give the transfer from w_1 to w_6 as :

$$w_6 = \frac{a + cw}{b + dw} \, w_1.$$

Thus fig. 2.1 is nothing but a flow graph representation of a Moebius transform. A simplified representation of fig. 2.1 is a 2-port with a *load* w. This is done in fig. 2.2a.

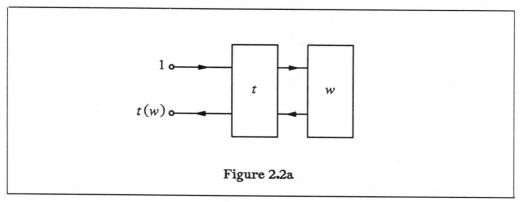

Figure 2.2a

The composite transformations (2.4) and (2.10) can be represented as a cascade of such 2-ports with a load w. See fig. 2.2b and 2.2c.

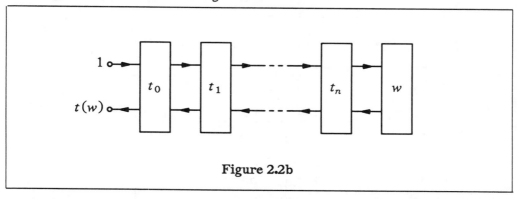

Figure 2.2b

If the Moebius transform is defined as acting on a pair (see (2.2)), then it is represented by a two-port as in fig. 2.3. This gives for the sequence of transforms in (2.5) the cascade of fig. 2.4. For the input $(p,q) = (1,0)$ you obtain $(x_n,y_n) = (C_n,D_n)$ as output and for $(p,q) = (0,1)$ you obtain $(x_n,y_n) = (A_n,B_n)$.

Let us come back to the lattice section of fig. 2.3a. The recursion for (R_n,S_n) given in (2.11) can be respresented as in fig. 2.5 or equivalently by the ladder forms of figs. 2.6. These lattice and ladder forms are very popular in filter realization. A cascade of these transforms is easily implemented. The output of one section gives the input for the next section and each section is identical in structure. They differ only by the values of the transmittances.

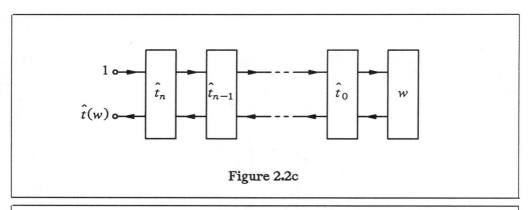

Figure 2.2c

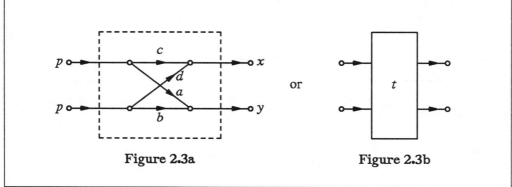

Figure 2.3a   Figure 2.3b

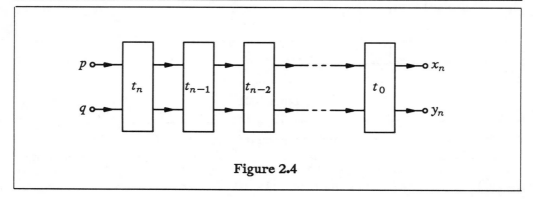

Figure 2.4

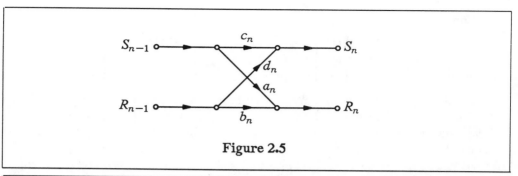

Figure 2.5

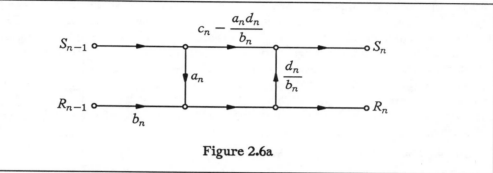

Figure 2.6a

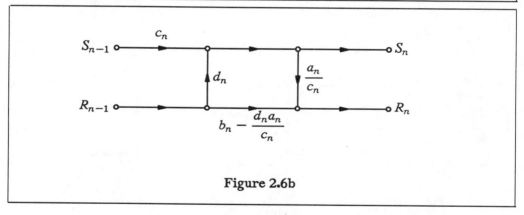

Figure 2.6b

2.3 Continued fractions (CF)

In this section we give some definitions and elementary properties of continued fractions. These and many other results can be found in [JOT].

A recursive definition for a continued fraction could be as follows: a *continued fraction* is a term plus a ratio of a numerator over a denominator. A numerator is a term and a denominator can be a term or a continued fraction. A term is an element from a field. This illustrates the origin of the name continued fraction. As we said, our approach is purely formal so that a CF need not converge in any sense. Moreover this definition would lead to situations where we have to take the ratio of elements for which the quotient is not defined as we shall see in the next subsection on formal series. It will therefore be useful to concider the numerator/denominator configuration as a pair of elements, rather than as a quotient. The Moebius transforms introduced in the first subsection had the possibility that they could be discribed as transformations involving a quotient or as transformations for pairs of elements. That is why we redefine a continued fraction as a special case of a sequence of Moebius transforms $\{t_n\}$. Special because we must have in the notation of property 2.2

$$b_0 = c_0 \neq 0, d_0 = 0 \text{ and } a_n \neq 0, c_n = 0, d_n = 1, n \geq 1.$$

Thus

$$t_0(w) = \frac{a_0}{b_0} + w \text{ and } t_n(w) = \frac{a_n}{b_n + w}, n \geq 1.$$

As we have said before, this is trivially transformed into transformations for pairs whenever necessary. To represent $t_0 \circ t_1 \circ t_2 \circ \cdots$ we use the classical notation

$$\frac{a_0}{b_0} + \frac{a_1}{\lceil b_1} + \frac{a_2}{\lceil b_2} + \cdots \quad \text{or} \quad \frac{a_0}{b_0} + \sum_{k \geq 1} \frac{a_k}{\lceil b_k}. \tag{2.14}$$

If as before $t_n = t_0 \circ t_1 \circ \cdots \circ t_n$, we define the *n-th convergent* of the CF as $t_n(0)$.

Each Moebius transform in the sequence depends only on two parameters a_n and b_n. The composition of these Moebius transforms is again a Moebius transform as we have seen in property 2.2. The composite Moebius transform will also depend on only two parameters A_n and B_n. As you can see, we have in (2.5) $C_n = A_{n-1}$ and $D_n = B_{n-1}$. Indeed (2.5) becomes in the special case of a CF

$$\begin{vmatrix} A_{n-1} & A_n \\ B_{n-1} & B_n \end{vmatrix} = \begin{vmatrix} b_0 & a_0 \\ 0 & b_0 \end{vmatrix} \begin{vmatrix} 0 & a_1 \\ 1 & b_1 \end{vmatrix} \cdots \begin{vmatrix} 0 & a_n \\ 1 & b_n \end{vmatrix}, \tag{2.15}$$

as can be easily verified. Now it becomes clear that a CF is inherently related to a *three-term recurrence relation*. It directly follows from (2.15) or equivalently from

$$\begin{vmatrix} A_{n-1} & A_n \\ B_{n-1} & B_n \end{vmatrix} = \begin{vmatrix} A_{n-2} & A_{n-1} \\ B_{n-2} & B_{n-1} \end{vmatrix} \begin{vmatrix} 0 & a_n \\ 1 & b_n \end{vmatrix}$$

that

$$A_n = A_{n-2}a_n + A_{n-1}b_n$$

and

$$B_n = B_{n-2}a_n + B_{n-1}b_n,$$

and the same recurrence relation exists for any combination of A_n and B_n.

(2.15) also implies that in (2.11) S_n becomes R_{n-1} in case of a CF. By setting $S_{-1} = 1$ and consequently $R_{-1} = b_0$, we have $S_n = R_{n-1}$ from $n = 0$ on. As a consequence of these observations, equation (2.4) and property 2.4 we get the next property.

PROPERTY 2.5. *Let (A_n, B_n) be defined as in (2.15). Then the convergents of the CF (2.14) are given by*

$$t_n(0) = \frac{a_0}{b_0} + \sum_{k=1}^{n} \frac{a_k}{\lceil b_k} = (A_n/B_n) \tag{2.16}$$

and if R_n is defined by $R_n = FB_n - A_n$, then

$$F = \frac{a_0}{b_0} + \sum_{k=1}^{n} \frac{a_k}{\lceil b_k} - \frac{R_n}{\lceil R_{n-1}}. \tag{2.17}$$

PROOF. (2.16) is (2.4) with $w = 0$ and (2.17) follows from (2.13) if you take $[S_{-1} \ R_{-1}] = [-1 \ F]$.

$\square$

At this point we can be somewhat more precise about why we will sometimes need to define the Moebius transforms as a transformation of pairs especially when they are of CF type. We shall meet situations where A_n/B_n and R_n/R_{n-1} will be the ratio of formal Laurent series for which the quotient is not defined. In those cases, the convergents A_n/B_n of the CF have to be understood as a pair of formal Laurent series rather than as a quotient. These pairs forming the convergents are then defined by a relation like (2.15). I.e. with initial conditions $A_{-1} = b_0$ and $B_{-1} = 0$ we get

$$\begin{vmatrix} A_0 \\ B_0 \end{vmatrix} = \begin{vmatrix} b_0 & a_0 \\ 0 & b_0 \end{vmatrix} \begin{vmatrix} 0 \\ 1 \end{vmatrix} = \begin{vmatrix} a_0 \\ b_0 \end{vmatrix}, \quad \begin{vmatrix} A_1 \\ B_1 \end{vmatrix} = \begin{vmatrix} A_{-1} & A_0 \\ B_{-1} & B_0 \end{vmatrix} \begin{vmatrix} a_1 \\ b_1 \end{vmatrix} \quad \text{etc.}$$

This is the same as interpreting the Moebius transforms as acting on pairs, or if you wish, applying the three-term recurrence relation. In this way we introduce an ambiguity since only the ratios A_n/B_n are uniquely defined and not the numerator and denominator separately. Therefore we introduce the notion of equivalent pairs. We call two nonzero pairs (A_n/B_n) and (A'_n/B'_n) *equivalent* if $A_n B'_n = A'_n B_n$. A notation like $F = (A_n/B_n)$ means that $F B_n = A_n$. Two CFs are called *equivalent* if they have an equivalent sequence of convergents. More precisely if (A_n/B_n) and (A'_n/B'_n) are the convergents of two CFs, then these CFs are equivalent if

$$A_n B'_n - A'_n B_n = 0, \quad n = 0,1,2,\dots .$$

Now we continue with properties for CFs. The determinant formula (2.7) becomes for a CF :

PROPERTY 2.6. *Let* (A_n/B_n) *,* $n = 0,1,\dots$ *be the convergents of the CF (2.14). Then*

$$A_{n-1} B_n - B_{n-1} A_n = (-1)^n b_0^2 \, a_1 a_2 \cdots a_n; n = 0,1,2,\dots \tag{2.18}$$

$\square$

PROPERTY 2.7. *CF (2.14) is equivalent with*

$$\frac{a_0 k_0}{b_0 k_0} + \frac{k_1 a_1}{\lceil k_1 b_1} + \sum_{i \geqslant 2} \frac{k_{i-1} k_i a_i}{\lceil k_i b_i} \quad , \quad k_i \neq 0. \tag{2.19}$$

PROOF. By applying the three term recurrence relation, you can easily check that the convergents of CF (2.19) are $(k_0 \cdots k_n A_n/k_0 \cdots k_n B_n)$, $n = 0,1,2,\dots$, where (A_n/B_n), $n = 0,1,2,\dots$ are the convergents of (2.14). Hence the convergents of (2.14) and (2.19) are equivalent.

$\square$

The *even part* (or the *even contraction*) of a CF with convergents (A_n/B_n) is a CF with convergents (A_{2n}/B_{2n}). The *odd part* is similarly defined as a CF with convergents (A_{2n+1}/B_{2n+1}). We have the following property:

PROPERTY 2.8. *The even part of (2.14) is*

$$\frac{a_0}{b_0} + \frac{a_1 b_2}{\lceil a_2 + b_1 b_2} + \sum_{k \geqslant 2} \frac{-a_{2k-2} b_{2k-2}^{-1} a_{2k-1} b_{2k}}{\lceil a_{2k} + (b_{2k-1} + b_{2k-2}^{-1} a_{2k-1}) b_{2k}} \tag{2.20}$$

and the odd part is

$$\frac{a_0}{b_0} + \frac{a_1}{b_1} + \sum_{k \geqslant 1} \frac{-a_{2k-1} b_{2k-1}^{-1} a_{2k} b_{2k+1}}{\lceil a_{2k+1} + (b_{2k} + b_{2k-1}^{-1} a_{2k}) b_{2k+1}}. \tag{2.21}$$

PROOF. To prove (2.20) note that if the convergents of (2.14) are (A_n/B_n), then the three term recurrence relation gives:

$$S_{2n} = a_{2n}S_{2n-2} + b_{2n}S_{2n-1},$$
$$S_{2n+1} = a_{2n+1}S_{2n-1} + b_{2n+1}S_{2n},$$
$$S_{2n+2} = a_{2n+2}S_{2n} + b_{2n+2}S_{2n+1},$$

where S could be A or B. By eliminating the S with an odd index between these three relations, you obtain the general three term recurrence relation of (2.20). The initial conditions are involved in the first term. They can be verified easily. The proof of (2.21) is similar.

□

Thus a contraction of a CF is another CF, i.e. a sequence of Moebius transforms of CF type. The rather complicated expressions in (2.20) and (2.21) are due to the fact that here a sequence of CF-type Moebius transforms is represented. It is much simpler if a contraction of (2.15) is defined as a sequence of general Moebius transforms, i.e. not necessarily of CF-type, which is obtained by multiplying out two successive factors in (2.15). This will be is done now.

Let (A_n/B_n) be the n-th convergent of (2.14). Define $R_n = a A_n + b B_n$ for arbitrary a and b. Two successive lattice sections like in fig. 2.5 become now as in fig. 2.7 .

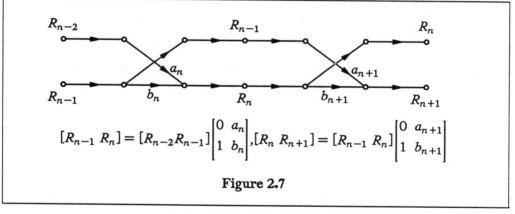

Figure 2.7

This can be "contracted" to the ladder section of fig. 2.8.

A CF was defined as a special sequence of Moebius transforms. We can also associate with a sequence of general Moebius transforms a CF as follows:

PROPERTY 2.9. *Consider a sequence of Moebius transforms $\{t_n\}$. Let the parameters for t_n be $\{a_n, b_n, c_n, d_n\}$ and let $\{A_n, B_n, C_n, D_n\}$ be associated with the composite Moebius transforms $\{t_n\}$ as defined by (2.5). Then there exists a CF with successive convergents (C_0/D_0), (A_0/B_0), (C_1/D_1), $(A_1/B_1),...$, (C_n/D_n), $(A_n/B_n)...$ It has the form*

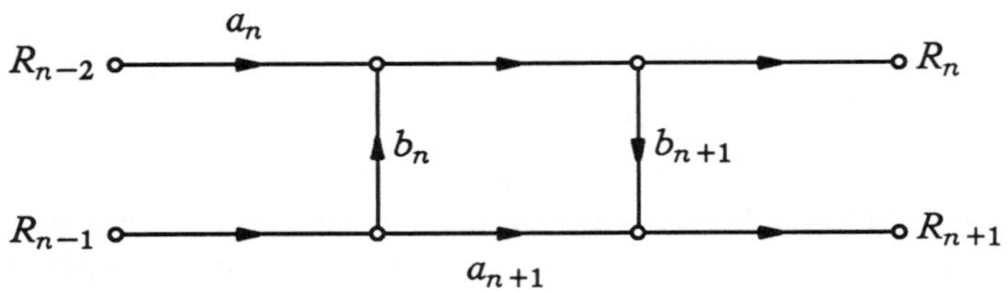

$$[R_n \; R_{n+1}] = [R_{n-2} \; R_{n-1}] \begin{vmatrix} a_n & a_n b_{n+1} \\ b_n & a_{n+1} + b_n b_{n+1} \end{vmatrix}$$

Figure 2.8

$$\frac{c_0}{d_0} + \cfrac{(a_0 d_0 - b_0 c_0)d_0^{-2}}{b_0 d_0^{-1}} + \cfrac{c_1}{d_1} + \cfrac{(b_1 c_1 - a_1 d_1)c_1^{-1}}{a_1 c_1^{-1}} + \cdots$$

$$+ \cfrac{c_n}{d_n} + \cfrac{(b_n c_n - a_n d_n)c_n^{-1}}{a_n c_n^{-1}} + \cdots \qquad (2.22)$$

PROOF. The first two convergents are directly verified. With some algebra, the other convergents can be shown to satisfy the recursive definition of (2.6).

□

It is equally simple to obtain CFs with convergents (A_0/B_0), (C_0/D_0), (A_1/B_1), (C_1/D_1), ... or by a contraction we obtain a CF with convergents (A_0/B_0), (A_1/B_1), ... or (C_0/D_0), (C_1/D_1), ...

2.4 Formal series

A theory on formal Laurent series can be found in [HEN]. However in Henrici's book Laurent series only have a finite number of negatively indexed coefficients. We need operations for bi-infinite series. Therefore we have to be careful in defining products and quotients of such series. These and some other definitions will be introduced in this subsection.

With a bi-infinite sequence of complex numbers $\{f_k\}_{-\infty}^{\infty}$ we associate a *formal Laurent series (fls)*

$$F(z) = \sum_{-\infty}^{\infty} f_k z^k.$$

We shall allow ourselves to take subsections of a fls by defining a projection operator working on fls. The *projection operator* $\Pi_{m:n}$ is defined by

$$\Pi_{m:n} F(z) = \sum_{k=m}^{n} f_k z^k.$$ (2.23)

With such a subsection we associate a Laurent polynomial. A *Laurent polynomial* is an expression like in the right hand side of (2.23) with m and n finite. Its *degree* is $\max\{|n| : f_n \neq 0\}$.

If in a fls the nonzero coefficients extend only to one side, which can be $+\infty$ or $-\infty$, it is useful to have a notation to indicate which part of the fls is zero. To this end we introduce the notion of *order*. Notations O_+ and O_- are defined via

$$F(z) = O_+(z^m) \quad \text{iff} \quad \Pi_{-\infty:m-1} F(z) = 0$$ (2.24a)

and

$$F(z) = O_-(z^n) \quad \text{iff} \quad \Pi_{n+1:\infty} F(z) = 0.$$ (2.24b)

Sup $\{m : F(z) = O_+(z^m)\}$ is called the $+$ *order* of $F(z)$ and we denote it as ord$_+(F)$. Inf $\{n : F(z) = O_-(z^n)\}$ is called the $-$ *order* of $F(z)$ and we denote it as ord$_-(F)$.

If a fls $F(z) = O_+(z^0)$, we call it a *formal power series (fps)*.

Now we come to the problem of defining operations on power series. Addition and substraction give no difficulty since we can define the sum of two fls as the fls with kth coefficient the sum of the kth coefficients of the given fls. Multiplication of two fls can be defined in the usual way as a Cauchy product and poses no problem if both have finite $+$ order, both have finite $-$ order or if at least one of both is a Laurent polynomial. The multiplication of two general fls will be difficult to define. Fortunately we shall never have to compute such a general product and leave this definition open. For a division we have to be more careful. We start by defining what we mean by the inverse of a fls with a finite $+$ order or a finite $-$ order.

PROPERTY 2.10. *If $F(z)$ is a fls and* ord$_\pm(F(z)) = m$, *then there exists a unique fls $G(z)$ with* ord$_\pm(G(z)) = -m$, *such that $F(z)G(z) = 1$.*

PROOF. This is trivial to verify. The fls $G(z)$ can be simply obtained by long division.

$\square$

If a fls has infinitely many nonzero coefficients and has finite $+$ or finite $-$ order, then its *inverse* $F(z)^{-1}$ is uniquely defined as the fls $G(z)$ in the above property. If $F(z)$ is a Laurent polynomial, it can have an inverse of finite $+$ or finite $-$ order. To distinguish between expansions of $F(z)^{-1}$ with infinitely increasing or decreasing powers of z we use the notation $L_+(F(z)^{-1})$ and $L_-(F(z)^{-1})$ respectively. The *quotient* of two fls is defined as $F(z)/G(z) = F(z) G(z)^{-1}$ if both have finite $+$ order or finite $-$ order. If both are Laurent polynomials we specify what we mean by the prefix L_+ or L_- :

$$L_+(F(z)/G(z)) = F(z) \, L_+(G(z)^{-1})$$

and

$$L_-(F(z)/G(z)) = F(z) \, L_-(G(z)^{-1}).$$

A fls need not converge. It is however convenient to introduce the notation $F(0)$ or $F(\infty)$ in the following sense

$$F(0) = \Pi_{0:0} \, F(z) \quad \text{if} \quad F(z) = O_+(z^0)$$

$$F(\infty) = \Pi_{0:0} \, F(z) \quad \text{if} \quad F(z) = O_-(z^0)$$

As we said in the introduction, the simplest development of the theory is associated with normal Padé tables. To avoid all the difficulties that occur in Padé tables with singular blocks, we shall suppose initially that our fls will generate a normal Padé table. Such a fls will be called normal. Thus we have the definition: A fls $F(z) = \sum_{-\infty}^{\infty} f_k z^k$ is called *normal* if all the Toeplitz matrices $T_n^{(m)} = (f_{m+i-j})_{i,j=0}^{n}$ for $m = 0, \pm 1, \pm 2, \dots$ and $n = 0, 1, \dots$ are nonsingular. A fps $\sum_0^{\infty} f_k z^k$ is normal if this is satisfied for $m, n = 0, 1, 2, \dots$.
In chapters 3–10 we shall suppose that the fls is normal. Only in chapters 11–16 we investigate what can be said about non–normal series.

2.5 Padé approximants

We shall introduce Padé approximants in a formal setting and give some generalizations of this concept. The generalizations we shall need are two–point Padé approximants and Laurent–Padé approximants. We start with ordinary Padé approximation. Classically a Padé approximant is defined for a formal power series. Let $F(z)$ be a fps and $A_m(z)$ and $B_n(z)$ polynomials of degree at most m and n respectively. $A_m(z)/B_n(z)$ is called a *Padé approximant (PA) of type (m/n)* for $F(z)$ if

$$F(z) - L_+(A_m(z)/B_n(z)) = O_+(z^{m+n+1}) \ , \quad B_n(0) \neq 0. \tag{2.25}$$

As we already noted in the introduction, we can linearize the problem if the contant term of $B_n(z)$ is nonzero. This is done in the next property.

PROPERTY 2.11. *Condition (2.25) is equivalent with*

$$F(z) \, B_n(z) - A_m(z) = O_+(z^{m+n+1}) \ , \quad B_n(0) \neq 0. \tag{2.26}$$

PROOF. Just multiply both sides of (2.25) with $B_n(z)$. Because $B_n(0) \neq 0$, the order of the right hand side doesn't change. Conversely, by multiplying both sides of (2.26) with $L_+(1/B_n(z))$ the order is again maintained.

$\square$

If $F(z)$ is a fls, rather than a fps and $B_n(z)$ is a polynomial, we can not expect that there exists a polynomial $A_m(z)$ so that (2.26) is satisfied. If $A_m(z)$ is generalized to be a fls $A_m(z) = O_-(z^m)$ (m can be $0, \pm1, \pm2, ...$), then (2.26) is solvable for $B_n(z)$ and $A_m(z)$. Note that we could not use (2.25) since $L_+(A_m(z)/B_n(z))$ is not defined. Therefore $(A_m(z)/B_n(z))$ should again be understood as a notation for a pair of elements rather than as a quotient.

The following property can be found in any classical reference on Padé approximation. The extension to our generalization of Padé approximants for a fls is trivial.

PROPERTY 2.12. *If $F(z)$ is a normal series, then all PAs $(A_m(z)/B_n(z))$ of type (m/n) exist and the $-$ orders of $A_m(z)$ and $B_n(z)$ are exactly m and n respectively. The $+$ order of the residual $R(z) = F(z)B_n(z) - A_m(z)$ is exactly $m+n+1$. The pair $(A_m(z)/B_n(z))$ is uniquely defined up to a multiplicative constant for numerator and denominator.*

PROOF. Suppose $A_m(z) = \sum_{-\infty}^{m} a_k z^k$ and $B_n(z) = \sum_0^n b_k z^k$. Define the vectors $A_m = [\cdots\ a_{m-2}\ a_{m-1}\ a_m]^T$ and $B_n = [b_0\ b_1\ \cdots\ b_n]^T$. The Toeplitz matrices $(f_{m+i-j})_{i,j=0}^n$ are denoted by $T_n^{(m)}$. We suppose that if $F(z)$ is a fps, we set as before $f_{-k} = 0$, $k = 1,2,....$ Normality of $F(z)$ means that all the appropriate $T_n^{(m)}$ are nonsingular. It follows from (2.26) that we have to look at the solution of

$$\sum_{k=0}^n f_{i-k} b_k = a_i, \quad i = ...,m-2,m-1,m \tag{2.27}$$

and

$$\sum_{k=0}^n f_{i-k} b_k = 0, \quad i = m+1,m+2,...,m+n. \tag{2.28}$$

The coefficients r_i for $i = m+n+1, m+n+2,...$ of the residual $R(z)$ are given by

$$\sum_{k=0}^n f_{i-k} b_k = r_i, \quad i = m+n+1,m+n+2,... . \tag{2.29}$$

A_m is completely defined by the first equations in terms of B_n and B_n has to be a solution of the second set of equations. This second set of equations always has a nontrivial solution with $b_0 \neq 0$. A solution with $b_0 = 0$ is impossible since then $T_{n-1}^{(m)}$ would be singular. Because b_0 is not zero we can normalize the ratio $A_m(z)/B_n(z)$ by taking $b_0 = 1$. Moreover, property 2.11 says that a solution of the previous equations, i.e. of (2.26) will give a Padé approximant. Because we have set $b_0 = 1$, the second set of equations can be rewritten as

$$\sum_{i=1}^{n} f_{k-i} b_i = -f_k , \quad k = m+1, m+2, ..., m+n.$$

Since the matrix of this system is nonsingular, its solution is a unique. This solution in turn defines A_m uniquely by the first equations. Hence the Padé approximant is uniquely defined up to a multiplicative constant in numerator and denominator. The coefficient b_n cannot be zero because this would imply that $T_{n-1}^{(m+1)}$ is singular. Finally, because

$$T_n^{(m)} B_n = [a_m \; 0 \; 0 \; \cdots \; 0]^T,$$

a_m can only be zero if $T_n^{(m)}$ is singular. Similarly if

$$T_n^{(m+1)} B_n = [0 \; \cdots \; 0 \, r_0]^T$$

then r_0 cannot be zero. Now, r_0 is the coefficient of z^{m+n+1} in the residual $R(z)$. This completes the proof.

□

The *Padé table* for $F(z)$ is a table with as (m,n)-th entry the (m/n) PA for $F(z)$. Thus if $F(z)$ is normal, all the elements in its Padé table exist and since the Padé approximants are essentially unique, all the entries in the Padé table are different from each other.

For a non-normal series, there may not exist a solution to (2.26) with ord$_+ B_n(z) = 0$, ord$_- B_n(z) = n$, ord$_+ A_m(z) = 0$ and ord$_- A_m(z) = m$. Equation (2.26) always has a solution if we relax these conditions to $B_n(z) = O_+(z^0), B_n(z) = O_-(z^n)$ and $A_m(z) = O_-(z^m)$. However the solution need not be unique any more. The pair $(A_m(z)/B_n(z))$ is then called a (m/n) *Padé form* (PF).

There are other ways to define PAs for a fls $F(z)$. A possible alternative is the *Laurent-Padé approximant* (LPA) of a fls.

Let $F(z) = \sum_{-\infty}^{\infty} f_k z^k$ be a fls and define $Z^{(0)}(z) := \frac{1}{2} f_0 + \sum_1^{\infty} f_k z^k$ and $\hat{Z}^{(0)}(z) := -(\frac{1}{2} f_0 + \sum_1^{\infty} f_{-k} z^{-k})$. Let m and n be nonnegative integers. Let $R(z)$ and $\hat{R}(z)$ both be ratios of two Laurent polynomials such that

(1) The denominator of $R(z)$ is a polynomial in z and the denominator of $\hat{R}(z)$ is a polynomial in z^{-1}. Both polynomials have degree at most n.
(2) $Z^{(0)}(z) - L_+(R(z)) = O_+(z^{m+n+1})$.
(3) $\hat{Z}^{(0)}(z) - L_-(\hat{R}(z)) = O_-(z^{-(m+n+1)})$.
(4) $R(z) + \hat{R}(z)$ is equivalent with $A_m(z)/B_n(z)$ where $A_m(z)$ is a Laurent polynomial of degree at most m and $B_n(z)$ is a Laurent polynomial of degree at most n.

We shall then call the pair $(R(z), \hat{R}(z))$ an (m/n) *LPA for* $F(z)$. This is clearly an extension of the classical notion of PA. Indeed $L_+(R(z)) + L_-(\hat{R}(z))$ is a fls which matches the coefficients of z^k in $F(z)$ for all $|k| \leqslant m+n$, while $R(z) + \hat{R}(z)$ can be brought into the form of a ratio of two Laurent polynomials with numerator degree m and denominator degree n.

We preferred to define a LPA as a pair of ratios, rather than as its sum because in our formal setting we can always find $A_m(z)/B_n(z)$ from the pair $(R(z), \hat{R}(z))$, but the way back is not uniquely defined. This way back is only defined in a situation where $F(z)$ is a Laurent series of a function analytic in $r < |z| < R$ and if $R(z)$ is analytic in $|z| < R$ and $\hat{R}(z)$ analytic in $|z| > r$. Only in that case will the Laurent series of $A_m(z)/B_n(z)$ in the region $r < |z| < R$ match the coefficients of z^k in the Laurent series of $F(z)$ for $|k| \leqslant m+n$.

Like for the Padé case it is possible to show [GR1,GRJ] that for a normal series $F(z)$ all the LPAs exist and are essentially unique. If $R(z) = P(z)/Q(z)$ and $\hat{R}(z) = \hat{P}(z)/\hat{Q}(z)$, then one can show that for a normal series $F(z)$ $\mathrm{ord}_+ Q(z) = \mathrm{ord}_+ \hat{Q}(1/z) = 0$, $\mathrm{ord}_- Q(z) = \mathrm{ord}_- \hat{Q}(1/z) = n$ and if $R(z) + \hat{R}(z)$ $= A_m(z)/B_n(z)$ with $B_n(z) = Q_n(z)\hat{Q}_n(z)$ then $\mathrm{ord}_+ A_m(z) = -m$ and $\mathrm{ord}_- A_m(z) = m$. The proof of this property is similar to the proof of property 2.12. It depends on a constructive method to find the LPAs. The algorithms to construct the approximants will be given in the next chapter. Because they can be computed, the existence of the LPAs follows directly. The statements about the precise order of numerator and denominator follow then easily like in property 2.12. They can also be derived from the determinant expressions given in chapter 9. About this matter, see also chapter 11 on the block structure.

For a non-normal series we shall have to relax the definition of a LPA to what we call a *Laurent-Padé form (LPF)*. It is defined as follows. $(R(z), \hat{R}(z))$ is a LPF if $R(z) = P(z)/Q(z)$ and $\hat{R}(z) = \hat{P}(z)/\hat{Q}(z)$ satisfy conditions (1) and (4) as in the previous definition of the LPA and (2) and (3) are replaced by

(2) $\quad Z^{(0)}(z) Q(z) - P(z) = O_+(z^{m+n+1})$
(3) $\quad \hat{Z}^{(0)}(z) \hat{Q}(z) - \hat{P}(z) = O_-(z^{-(m+n+1)})$.

Again a LPF may not be unique but it always exists.

We now introduce the concept of a *two-point PA*. More general definitions than the one given here are possible but for our purposes the following is sufficient. Let

$$L(z) = \sum_{k=0}^{\infty} c_k z^k \quad \text{and} \quad \hat{L}(z) = \sum_{k=0}^{\infty} \hat{c}_k z^{-k}$$

be two fls. Suppose $A_n(z)$ is a polynomial of degree m and $B_n(z)$ a polynomial of strict degree n with $B_n(0) \neq 0$ such that for some m, $0 \leqslant m < 2n+1$:

$$L(z) - L_+(A_n(z)/B_n(z)) = O_+(z^{m+1}),$$

$$\hat{L}(z) - L_-(A_n(z)/B_n(z)) = O_-(z^{m-2n}).$$

Then $A_n(z)/B_n(z)$ is called a *two-point Padé approximant* for the pair $(L(z), \hat{L}(z))$ of type (m,n), $(0 \leqslant m < 2n+1)$.

Again we could relax this definition to obtain *two-point Padé forms* (*two-point PF*). Let $A_n(z)$ and $B_n(z)$ be polynomials of degree at most n, such that

$$L(z) B_n(z) - A_n(z) = O_+(z^{m+1})$$

and

$$\hat{L}(z) B_n(z) - A_n(z) = O_-(z^{m-n}).$$

Then we call the pair $A_n(z)/B_n(z)$ a *two-point PF* for the pair $(L(z), \hat{L}(z))$ of type (m,n).

Chapter 3

Two algorithms

In this chapter we give two possible algorithms related to the recursive computation of elements in a Padé table for a fls. The successive approximants have the same numerator degree but the denominator degree increases as we proceed. This means that we move from left to right on a horizontal line in the Padé table. The algorithms are well known methods for the solution of Toeplitz systems [TRE1],[ZOH1] and are related to the methods of Levinson and Schur known in digital filtering theory. Much information on these algorithms and many related ones can be found in a thesis by D.R.Sweet [SWE].

Algorithm 1 is in fact the algorithm as described by Trench and Zohar. It will become clear here and in the next chapter that this algorithm computes the denominators of the PAs that can be found in two adjacent rows of the Padé table. The parameters $\alpha_n^{(m)}$ and $\hat{\alpha}_n^{(m)}$ that appear in the recursion for these polynomials are direct generalizations of the Schur-Szegö parameters. This will be explained in chapter 17. Algorithm 1 can be seen as a generalization of the Levinson algorithm. Another interpretation of the first algorithm is that it computes the triangular factors of the inverse of a Toeplitz matrix. This will be explained in chapter 9.

The second algorithm, that is directly obtained from the relations in algorithm 1, gives a continued fraction expansion of the fls $F(z)$. This is explained in more detail in chapter 5. The successive convergents of this CF are the same PAs as those obtained by the first algorithm. The recursion is not on the denominators $Q_n^{(m)}(z)$ as before, but on the corresponding numerators $P_n^{(m)}(z)$ and the residuals $R_n^{(m)}(z) = F(z)Q_n^{(m)}(z) - P_n^{(m)}$. Again the same parameters $\alpha_n^{(m)}$ and $\hat{\alpha}_n^{(m)}$ that appeared in algorithm 1 will be computed but in a different way. The latter algorithm is a nonhomogenious generalization of the Schur algorithm. In terms of linear algebra, we could say that this algorithm computes the triangular factorization of the Toeplitz matrix itself, and not of its inverse.

Algorithms of rhombus types to solve the same problem will be given in a later chapter.

3.1 Algorithm 1

Suppose $F(z)$ is a normal fls so that all the Toeplitz matrices $\mathbf{T}_n^{(m)} = (f_{m+i-j})_{i,j=0}^n$ are nonsingular. Consequently the following equations have a solution.

$$\mathbf{T}_n^{(m)} Q_n^{(m)} = [v_n^{(m)}\ 0\ \cdots\ 0]^T \text{ and } \mathbf{T}_n^{(m)} \hat{Q}_n^{(m)} = [0\ \cdots\ 0\ \hat{v}_n^{(m)}]^T \tag{3.1a}$$

with

$$Q_n^{(m)} = [q_{0,n}^{(m)}\ \cdots\ q_{n,n}^{(m)}]^T\ ,\ q_{0,n}^{(m)} = 1 \tag{3.1b}$$

$$\hat{Q}_n^{(m)} = [\hat{q}_{0,n}^{(m)}\ \cdots\ \hat{q}_{n,n}^{(m)}]^T\ ,\ \hat{q}_{n,n}^{(m)} = 1. \tag{3.1c}$$

The problem of solving these equations is clearly related to Padé approximation. The first Toeplitz system represents equations (2.28) with the last equation of (2.27) prepended. Hence $Q_n^{(m)}(z) = [1\ z\ \cdots\ z^n]Q_n^{(m)}$ is the denominator of the (m/n) PA of $F(z)$ with a comonic normalization (i.e. the denominator has a constant term equal to 1). $v_n^{(m)}$ is the corresponding coefficient of the highest degree term in the numerator. The second Toeplitz system in (3.1a) is the set of equations (2.28) with the first equation of (2.29) appended, but for m replaced by $m-1$. Therefore $\hat{Q}_n^{(m)}(z) := [1\ z\ \cdots\ z^n]\hat{Q}_n^{(m)}$ is the denominator of the $(m-1/n)$ PA of $F(z)$. Now, the normalization for the denominator is a monic one. I.e. with highest degree coefficient equal to 1. $\hat{v}_n^{(m)}$ is the leading coefficient in the residual.

Property 2.12 showed that $q_{n,n}^{(m)}$, $\hat{q}_{0,n}^{(m)}$, $v_n^{(m)}$ and $\hat{v}_n^{(m)}$ are nonzero and so are

$$u_n^{(m)} = [f_{m+n+1}\ \cdots\ f_{m+1}]Q_n^{(m)}$$

and $\tag{3.2a}$

$$\hat{u}_n^{(m)} = [f_{m-1}\ \cdots\ f_{m-n-1}]\hat{Q}_n^{(m)}.$$

As can be seen from (2.27-29), $u_n^{(m)}$ is the leading coefficient in the residual for the (m/n) PA and $\hat{u}_n^{(m)}$ is the highest degree coefficient in the numerator of the $(m-1/n)$ PA with the normalizations mentioned.

It is easily verified that the solutions of (3.1) satisfy the recursions (see [TRE1,ZOH1]):

$$Q_{n+1}^{(m)} = \begin{vmatrix} Q_n^{(m)} \\ 0 \end{vmatrix} - \begin{vmatrix} 0 \\ \hat{Q}_n^{(m)} \end{vmatrix} \alpha_{n+1}^{(m)},$$

$$\tag{3.2b}$$

$$\hat{Q}_{n+1}^{(m)} = \begin{vmatrix} 0 \\ \hat{Q}_n^{(m)} \end{vmatrix} - \begin{vmatrix} Q_n^{(m)} \\ 0 \end{vmatrix} \hat{\alpha}_{n+1}^{(m)},$$

with $\alpha_{n+1}^{(m)} = u_n^{(m)}/v_n^{(m)}$ and $\hat{\alpha}_{n+1}^{(m)} = \hat{u}_n^{(m)}/\hat{v}_n^{(m)}$,$n \geqslant 0$, while

$$v_{n+1}^{(m)} = \hat{v}_{n+1}^{(m)} = v_n^{(m)}(1 - \alpha_{n+1}^{(m)}\ \hat{\alpha}_{n+1}^{(m)}). \tag{3.2c}$$

The initial conditions are

$$Q_0^{(m)} = \hat{Q}_0^{(m)} = 1 \quad \text{and} \quad v_0^{(m)} = \hat{v}_0^{(m)} = f_m. \tag{3.2d}$$

The values of $u_0^{(m)}$ and $\hat{u}_0^{(m)}$ are found from (3.2a). These recursions are easily verified by noting that if $Q_n^{(m)}$ and $\hat{Q}_n^{(m)}$ satisfy (3.1), then

$$\mathbf{T}_{n+1}^{(m)} \begin{vmatrix} Q_n^{(m)} & 0 \\ 0 & \hat{Q}_n^{(m)} \end{vmatrix} = \begin{vmatrix} v_n^{(m)} & 0 & \cdots & 0 & u_n^{(m)} \\ \hat{u}_n^{(m)} & 0 & \cdots & 0 & \hat{v}_n^{(m)} \end{vmatrix}^T,$$

so that $Q_{n+1}^{(m)}$ and $\hat{Q}_{n+1}^{(m)}$ of (3.2b) satisfy the defining equations (3.1) with n replaced by $n+1$.

With the interpretation given in the previous comments, we could say that (3.2) describes a recursive algorithm to compute the denominators of two adjacent rows in the Padé table.

Using a polynomial notation, (3.2b) can be rewritten as

$$[\, Q_{n+1}^{(m)}(z) \;\; \hat{Q}_{n+1}^{(m)}(z)\,] = [Q_n^{(m)}(z) \;\; \hat{Q}_n^{(m)}(z)] \begin{vmatrix} 1 & -\hat{\alpha}_{n+1}^{(m)} \\ -z\alpha_{n+1}^{(m)} & z \end{vmatrix}. \tag{3.3}$$

This gives us the algorithm displayed in fig. 3.1 below.

$$Q_0^{(m)}(z) = \hat{Q}_0^{(m)}(z) = 1$$

$$v_0^{(m)}(z) = \hat{v}_0^{(m)} = f_m$$

for $n=0,1,2,...$

$$u_n^{(m)} = \Pi_{0:0}(z^{-m-n-1}F(z)Q_n^{(m)}(z));$$

$$\hat{u}_n^{(m)} = \Pi_{0:0}(z^{-m+1}F(z)\hat{Q}_n^{(m)}(z));$$

$$\alpha_{n+1}^{(m)} = u_n^{(m)}/v_n^{(m)} \quad ; \quad \hat{\alpha}_{n+1}^{(m)} = \hat{u}_n^{(m)}/\hat{v}_n^{(m)}$$

$$[Q_{n+1}^{(m)}(z) \;\; \hat{Q}_{n+1}^{(m)}(z)] = [Q_n^{(m)}(z) \;\; \hat{Q}_n^{(m)}(z)] \begin{vmatrix} 1 & -\hat{\alpha}_{n+1}^{(m)} \\ -z\alpha_{n+1}^{(m)} & z \end{vmatrix}$$

$$v_{n+1}^{(m)} = \hat{v}_{n+1}^{(m)} = v_n^{(m)}(1-\alpha_{n+1}^{(m)}\hat{\alpha}_{n+1}^{(m)})$$

Fig. 3.1: Algorithm 1

A worked example using this algorithm can be found in chapter 18. Note that $\{\alpha_k^{(m)}, \hat{\alpha}_k^{(m)}\}_1^n$ completely define $\{Q_k^{(m)}(z), \hat{Q}_k^{(m)}(z)\}_0^n$ with the normalisation imposed. To evaluate the polynomials $Q_n^{(m)}(z)$ and $\hat{Q}_n^{(m)}(z)$ we could use the Horner scheme with the polynomial coefficients as input, but it is equally simple to generate the polynomial values from the recursion (3.3) using the coefficients $\alpha_k^{(m)}$ and $\hat{\alpha}_k^{(m)}$ as input. The coefficients $\alpha_k^{(m)}$, $\hat{\alpha}_k^{(m)}$ are thus as important as, and are in a lot of situations a substitute for the polynomial coefficients. $\alpha_k^{(m)}$ and $\hat{\alpha}_k^{(m)}$ are the direct generalizations of the Schur-Szegő parameters as we mentioned in the introduction. How the original Schur-Szegő parameters can come out as a special case will be explained in chapter 17. These coefficients will play a central role in the further development of the theory. From now on we shall refer to them as the *SS (Schur-Szegő) parameters of $F(z)$*.

The next algorithm is a method to compute them without computing the polynomials $Q_n^{(m)}(z)$ and $\hat{Q}_n^{(m)}(z)$.

3.2 Algorithm 2

This algorithm will find the numbers $\alpha_k^{(m)}$ and $\hat{\alpha}_k^{(m)}$ by recursive computation of formal series that go along with $Q_n^{(m)}(z)$ and $\hat{Q}_n^{(m)}(z)$. These series are defined by

$$P_n^{(m)}(z) = \Pi_{-\infty:m}(F(z)Q_n^{(m)}(z)) \; ; \; \hat{P}_n^{(m)}(z) = \Pi_{-\infty:m-1}(F(z)\hat{Q}_n^{(m)}(z))$$

and   (3.4)

$$R_n^{(m)}(z) = \Pi_{m+1:\infty}(F(z)Q_n^{(m)}(z)) \; ; \; \hat{R}_n^{(m)}(z) = \Pi_{m:\infty}(F(z)\hat{Q}_n^{(m)}(z)).$$

With the previously commented interpretation of (3.2) as a part of the Padé equations (2.27-29), it is easily seen that $P_n^{(m)}(z)$ is the numerator of the (m/n) PA and $R_n^{(m)}(z)$ the corresponding residual. Similarly, $\hat{P}_n^{(m)}(z)$ and $\hat{R}_n^{(m)}(z)$ are the $(m-1/n)$ numerator and residual.

Observe that the first nonzero terms in these series are the coefficients $v_n^{(m)}$, $\hat{u}_n^{(m)}$, $u_n^{(m)}$ and $\hat{v}_n^{(m)}$ that appeared in algorithm 1. (See (3.1) and (3.2a)):

$$P_n^{(m)}(z) = v_n^{(m)} z^m + O_-(z^{m-1}),$$ (3.5a)

$$\hat{P}_n^{(m)}(z) = \hat{u}_n^{(m)} z^{m-1} + O_-(z^{m-2}),$$ (3.5b)

$$R_n^{(m)}(z) = u_n^{(m)} z^{m+n+1} + O_+(z^{m+n+2}),$$ (3.5c)

$$\hat{R}_n^{(m)}(z) = \hat{v}_n^{(m)} z^{m+n} + O_+(z^{m+n+1}). \tag{3.5d}$$

Thus, with these coefficients, we can again construct $\alpha_{n+1}^{(m)}$ and $\hat{\alpha}_{n+1}^{(m)}$. It is a simple matter to fill in the recursion (3.2b) for $Q_n^{(m)}(z)$ and $\hat{Q}_n^{(m)}(z)$ into the definitions of $P_n^{(m)}(z)$, $\hat{P}_n^{(m)}(z)$, $R_n^{(m)}(z)$ and $\hat{R}_n^{(m)}(z)$ to find that these series satisfy the same recursion as the polynomials $Q_n^{(m)}(z)$ and $\hat{Q}_n^{(m)}(z)$. Hence

$$[S_{n+1}^{(m)}(z)\ \hat{S}_{n+1}^{(m)}(z)] = [S_n^{(m)}(z)\ \hat{S}_n^{(m)}(z)] \begin{vmatrix} 1 & -\hat{\alpha}_{n+1}^{(m)} \\ -z\alpha_{n+1}^{(m)} & z \end{vmatrix} \tag{3.6}$$

where S is Q, P or R.
The initial conditions are

$$Q_0^{(m)} = \hat{Q}_0^{(m)} = 1, \tag{3.7a}$$

$$P_0^{(m)}(z) = \Pi_{-\infty:m} F(z) \quad , \quad \hat{P}_0^{(m)}(z) = \Pi_{-\infty:m-1} F(z), \tag{3.7b}$$

$$R_0^{(m)}(z) = \Pi_{m+1:\infty} F(z) \quad , \quad \hat{R}_0^{(m)}(z) = \Pi_{m:\infty} F(z). \tag{3.7c}$$

Algorithm 2 can thus be described as follows : for $n = 0,1,2,...$ we take the leading coefficients of the series (3.4) as in (3.5). With these we can contruct $\alpha_{n+1}^{(m)} = u_n^{(m)}/v_n^{(m)}$ and $\hat{\alpha}_{n+1}^{(m)} = \hat{u}_n^{(m)}/\hat{v}_n^{(m)}$. Then recursion (3.6) is used to construct $S_{n+1}^{(m)}(z)$ and $\hat{S}_{n+1}^{(m)}(z)$ for $S = P$ and $S = R$. Next we take the leading coefficients again etc. This is described in fig 3.2. A worked example using this algorithm can be found in chapter 18. This second algorithm is related to algorithms computing CF expansions of $F(z)$. This will become clear in chapter 5. As a special case, we can obtain the Schur algorithm from it, as will be shown in chapter 17. In comparison with the previous algorithm, we could say that algorithm 2 does a recursion on numerators and residuals of the PAs on two adjacent rows of the Padé table, whereas algorithm 1 performs the recursion on the denominators of the same PAs.

Throughout the rest of this volume, we shall use the notations $Q_n^{(m)}(z)$, $P_n^{(m)}(z)$, $R_n^{(m)}(z)$ and the corresponding notations with a hat for the quantities related to $F(z)$ as they are defined in this section, even if it is not explicitly mentioned. We shall refer to them the *Q-polynomials* or *polynomials of the first kind*, the *P-series* and *R-series* associated with $F(z)$.

The recurrence relation (3.6) and its parameters $\alpha_n^{(m)}$ and $\hat{\alpha}_n^{(m)}$ will be essential in our further development. We now give a property of the parameters $\alpha_n^{(m)}$ and $\hat{\alpha}_n^{(m)}$ that will be useful for further reference.

$$P_0^{(m)}(z) = \Pi_{-\infty:m}(F(z)) \quad ; \quad \hat{P}_0^{(m)}(z) = \Pi_{-\infty:m-1}(F(z))$$

$$R_0^{(m)}(z) = \Pi_{m+1:\infty}(F(z)) \quad ; \quad \hat{R}_0^{(m)}(z) = \Pi_{m:\infty}(F(z))$$

for $n = 0,1,2,...$

$$u_n^{(m)} = \Pi_{0:0}(z^{-m-n-1} R_n^{(m)}(z)) \; ; \; \hat{u}_n^{(m)} = \Pi_{0:0}(z^{-m+1} \hat{P}_n^{(m)}(z))$$

$$v_n^{(m)} = \Pi_{0:0}(z^{-m} P_n^{(m)}(z)) = \hat{v}_n^{(m)} = \Pi_{0:0}(z^{-m-n} \hat{R}_n^{(m)}(z))$$

$$\alpha_{n+1}^{(m)} = u_n^{(m)}/v_n^{(m)} \qquad ; \quad \hat{\alpha}_{n+1}^{(m)} = \hat{u}_n^{(m)}/\hat{v}_n^{(m)}$$

$$\begin{vmatrix} P_{n+1}^{(m)}(z) & \hat{P}_{n+1}^{(m)}(z) \\ R_{n+1}^{(m)}(z) & \hat{R}_{n+1}^{(m)}(z) \end{vmatrix} = \begin{vmatrix} P_n^{(m)}(z) & \hat{P}_n^{(m)}(z) \\ R_n^{(m)}(z) & \hat{R}_n^{(m)}(z) \end{vmatrix} \begin{vmatrix} 1 & -\hat{\alpha}_{n+1}^{(m)} \\ -z\alpha_{n+1}^{(m)} & z \end{vmatrix}$$

Fig. 3.2: Algorithm 2

THEOREM 3.1. *Let* $\alpha_n^{(m)}$ *and* $\hat{\alpha}_n^{(m)}$ *be the SS parameters of the normal s* $F(z)$. *Then* $\alpha_n^{(m)}\hat{\alpha}_n^{(m)} \neq 0$ *and* $\neq 1$ *for all* $n = 1,2,3,...$ *and* $m = 0, \pm 1, \pm 2,... $.

PROOF. By definition, $\alpha_n^{(m)} = u_n^{(m)}/v_n^{(m)}$ and $\hat{\alpha}_n^{(m)} = \hat{u}_n^{(m)}/\hat{v}_n^{(m)}$. Since $u_n^{(m)}$ and $\hat{u}_n^{(m)}$ are nonzero, as we already said, also $\alpha_n^{(m)}$ and $\hat{\alpha}_n^{(m)}$ are not zero. Moreover, by (3.2c), $v_n^{(m)} = v_{n-1}^{(m)}(1 - \alpha_n^{(m)}\hat{\alpha}_n^{(m)})$, which is not zero, so that $\alpha_n^{(m)}\hat{\alpha}_n^{(m)} \neq 1$.
□

This theorem implies an order property for polynomial solutions of (3.6).

COROLLARY 3.2. *Let* $S_0^{(m)}$ *and* $\hat{S}_0^{(m)}$ *be nonzero constants. Let* $S_n^{(m)}(z)$ *and* $\hat{S}_n^{(m)}(z)$ *for* $n = 1,2,...$ *be defined by (3.6) taking* $S_0^{(m)}$ *and* $\hat{S}_0^{(m)}$ *as initial conditions. Then* $S_n^{(m)}(z)$ *and* $\hat{S}_n^{(m)}(z)$ *are polynomials of exact degree n with nonvanishing constant terms.*

PROOF. $S_n^{(m)}(z)$ and $\hat{S}_n^{(m)}(z)$ have to be polynomials of degree at most n. The constant term of $S_n^{(m)}(z)$ is :

$$S_n^{(m)}(0) = S_{n-1}^{(m)}(0) = \cdots = S_0^{(m)} \neq 0$$

and the constant term of $\hat{S}_n^{(m)}(z)$ is

$$\hat{S}_n^{(m)}(0) = -\hat{\alpha}_n^{(m)} S_{n-1}^{(m)}(0) = -\hat{\alpha}_n^{(m)} S_0^{(m)} \neq 0.$$

We can similarly show that the coefficient of z^n in $\hat{S}_n^{(m)}(z)$ is $\hat{S}_0^{(m)}$ and the coefficient of z^n in $S_n^{(m)}(z)$ is $-\alpha_n^{(m)} \hat{S}_0^{(m)}$.

$\square$

Chapter 4

All kinds of Padé Approximants

In this chapter we shall give different Padé interpretations for the quantities introduced in chapter 3 and related quantities that are introduced in this chapter.

It was already explained in previous chapter how $P_n^{(m)}(z)$, $Q_n^{(m)}(z)$ and $R_n^{(m)}(z)$ of (3.1) and (3.4) as well as the corresponding series with a hat are related to Padé approximation for $F(z)$, so that we can be very brief about that. However, it is also possible to construct with algorithm 1 and algorithm 2 Laurent-Padé and two-point Padé approximants. How this is done is explained in this chapter.

4.1 Padé approximants

We start with Padé approximants. The proof of the following theorem is given in previous chapter. We give it here for further reference in a concise form.

THEOREM 4.1. *For $n \in \mathbb{N}$ and $m \in \mathbb{Z}$, let $P_n^{(m)}(z)$, $Q_n^{(m)}(z)$, $R_n^{(m)}(z)$ and the corresponding series with a hat be related to the normal fls $F(z)$ as in algorithms 1 and 2 or, what is the same, by defining equations (3.1) and (3.4). Then $(P_n^{(m)}(z)/Q_n^{(m)}(z))$ is an (m/n) PA of $F(z)$ and $(\hat{P}_n^{(m)}(z)/\hat{Q}_n^{(m)}(z))$ is an $(m-1/n)$ PA of the same series. The series $R_n^{(m)}(z)$ and $\hat{R}_n^{(m)}(z)$ are the corresponding residuals. These are defined by (3.4) and hence satisfy the relations*

$$R_n^{(m)}(z) = F(z)Q_n^{(m)}(z) - P_n^{(m)}(z) \tag{4.1a}$$

and

$$\hat{R}_n^{(m)}(z) = F(z)\hat{Q}_n^{(m)}(z) - \hat{P}_n^{(m)}(z). \tag{4.1b}$$

$\square$

Observe that we here use the generalized definition of PA for a fls. Indeed $P_n^{(m)}(z)$ and $\hat{P}_n^{(m)}(z)$ have infinitely many negative powers of z. Only if $\Pi_{-\infty:-1}F(z) = 0$ and if $m \geqslant 0$, we have a PA is the classical sense.

4.2 Laurent-Padé approximants

To come to a Laurent-Padé approximant we need another pair of polynomial solutions for recursion (3.6). These polynomials $A_n^{(m)}(z)$ and $\hat{A}_n^{(m)}(z)$ are sometimes called *polynomials of the second kind*. We shall first define some polynomials $A_n^{(m)}(z)$ and $\hat{A}_n^{(m)}(z)$ and then show that they are solutions of (3.6).

Define for some integer m the series $Z^{(m)}(z)$ and $\hat{Z}^{(m)}(z)$ as

$$Z^{(m)}(z) := f_m' \, z^m + f_{m+1} \, z^{m+1} + f_{m+2} \, z^{m+2} + \cdots \tag{4.2a}$$

$$\hat{Z}^{(m)}(z) := -f_m' \, z^m - f_{m-1} \, z^{m-1} - f_{m-2} \, z^{m-2} - \cdots \tag{4.2b}$$

with $f_m' := \tfrac{1}{2} f_m$. Clearly $F(z) = Z^{(m)}(z) - \hat{Z}^{(m)}(z)$. Use this in the relation $F(z)Q_n^{(m)}(z) - P_n^{(m)}(z) = R_n^{(m)}(z)$ to find

$$Z^{(m)}(z)Q_n^{(m)}(z) - R_n^{(m)}(z) = \hat{Z}^{(m)}(z)Q_n^{(m)}(z) + P_n^{(m)}(z). \tag{4.3a}$$

The left-hand side is $O_+(z^m)$ and the right-hand side is $O_-(z^{m+n})$. Thus (4.3a) represents something of the form $z^m A_n^{(m)}(z)$ where $A_n^{(m)}(z)$ is a polynomial of degree n.

Similarly we can define polynomials $\hat{A}_n^{(m)}(z)$ of degree n by

$$z^m \hat{A}_n^{(m)}(z) = Z^{(m)}(z)\hat{Q}_n^{(m)}(z) - \hat{R}_n^{(m)}(z) = \hat{Z}^{(m)}(z)\hat{Q}_n^{(m)}(z) + \hat{P}_n^{(m)}(z). \tag{4.3b}$$

Observe that these definitions for $A_n^{(m)}(z)$ and $\hat{A}_n^{(m)}(z)$ can also be given in a form independent of $P_n^{(m)}(z)$ and $R_n^{(m)}(z)$:

$$A_n^{(m)}(z) := z^{-m} \, \Pi_{m:m+n}(Z^{(m)}(z)Q_n^{(m)}(z)) \tag{4.3c}$$

and

$$\hat{A}_n^{(m)}(z) := z^{-m} \, \Pi_{m:m+n}(\hat{Z}^{(m)}(z)\hat{Q}_n^{(m)}(z)). \tag{4.3d}$$

Since it follows from (3.6) that

$$\begin{vmatrix} P_{n+1}^{(m)}(z) & \hat{P}_{n+1}^{(m)}(z) \\ Q_{n+1}^{(m)}(z) & \hat{Q}_{n+1}^{(m)}(z) \end{vmatrix} = \begin{vmatrix} P_n^{(m)}(z) & \hat{P}_n^{(m)}(z) \\ Q_n^{(m)}(z) & \hat{Q}_n^{(m)}(z) \end{vmatrix} \begin{vmatrix} 1 & -\hat{\alpha}_{n+1}^{(m)} \\ -z\alpha_{n+1}^{(m)} & z \end{vmatrix}, \tag{4.4}$$

we obtain by multiplying (4.4) from the left with $[1 \; \hat{Z}^{(m)}(z)]$ once again recursion (3.6) where S can now also be replaced by A. The initial conditions are $A_0^{(m)} = -\hat{A}_0^{(m)} = f_m'$.
The determinant formula (2.7) gives that

$$A_n^{(m)}(z)\hat{Q}_n^{(m)}(z) - \hat{A}_n^{(m)}Q_n^{(m)}(z) = z^n f_m \prod_{k=1}^{n}(1-\alpha_k^{(m)}\hat{\alpha}_k^{(m)}) = z^n v_n^{(m)}.$$

Indeed, we have to replace in (2.7) a_k by $-\alpha_k^{(m)}$, b_k by z, c_k by 1 and d_k by $-z\alpha_k^{(m)}$. Thus after a division by $Q_n^{(m)}(z)\hat{Q}_n^{(m)}(z)$, we get:

$$\frac{A_n^{(m)}(z)}{Q_n^{(m)}(z)} - \frac{z^{-n}\hat{A}_n^{(m)}(z)}{z^{-n}\hat{Q}_n^{(m)}(z)} = \frac{v_n^{(m)}}{(Q_n^{(m)}(z))(z^{-n}\hat{Q}_n^{(m)}(z))}. \qquad (4.5)$$

Observe that relations (4.3) allow us to conclude that we have the following order relations:

$$\begin{vmatrix} -1 & z^{-m}Z^{(m)}(z) \\ -1 & z^{-m}\hat{Z}^{(m)}(z) \end{vmatrix} \begin{vmatrix} A_n^{(m)}(z) & \hat{A}_n^{(m)}(z) \\ Q_n^{(m)}(z) & \hat{Q}_n^{(m)}(z) \end{vmatrix} = z^{-m} \begin{vmatrix} R_n^{(m)}(z) & \hat{R}_n^{(m)}(z) \\ -P_n^{(m)}(z) & -\hat{P}_n^{(m)}(z) \end{vmatrix}$$

$$= \begin{vmatrix} O_+(z^{n+1}) & O_+(z^n) \\ O_-(z^0) & O_-(z^{-1}) \end{vmatrix}. \qquad (4.6)$$

From this we can directly derive theorem 4.2 below.

THEOREM 4.2. *For $n \in \mathbb{N}$ and $m \in \mathbb{Z}$, define the polynomials $Q_n^{(m)}(z)$ and $\hat{Q}_n^{(m)}(z)$ by (3.1) and $A_n^{(m)}(z)$ and $\hat{A}_n^{(m)}(z)$ by (4.3). Then $(\dfrac{A_n^{(m)}(z)}{Q_n^{(m)}(z)}$,*

$$-\frac{z^{-n}\hat{A}_n^{(m)}(z)}{z^{-n}\hat{Q}_n^{(m)}(z)}) \text{ is a } (0/n) \text{ LPA of } z^{-m}F(z).$$

PROOF. It follows from theorem 4.1 and theorem 2.12 that $\mathrm{ord}_+ Q_n^{(m)}(z) = 0$ and $\mathrm{ord}_- \hat{Q}_n^{(m)} = n$. Hence, the (1,1) relation in (4.6) can be written as

$$z^{-m}Z^{(m)}(z) - L_+(\frac{A_n^{(m)}(z)}{Q_n^{(m)}(z)}) = O_+(z^{n+1}).$$

Similarly, we find from the (2,2) relation of (4.6) that

$$-z^{-m}\hat{Z}^{(m)}(z) - L_-(-\frac{z^{-n}\hat{A}_n^{(m)}(z)}{z^{-n}\hat{Q}_n^{(m)}(z)}) = O_-(z^{-n-1}).$$

Now, (4.5) showed that $A_n^{(m)}(z)/Q_n^{(m)}(z) - z^{-n}\hat{A}_n^{(m)}(z)/z^{-n}\hat{Q}_n^{(m)}(z)$ is a constant over a Laurent polynomial of degree n. Hence $(A_n^{(m)}(z)/Q_n^{(m)}(z)$, $-z^{-n}\hat{A}_n^{(m)}(z)/z^{-n}\hat{Q}_n^{(m)}(z))$ is an LPA for $z^{-m}Z(z) - z^{-m}\hat{Z}(z) = z^{-m}F(z)$ and it is of type $(0/n)$.

$\square$

The previous theorem showed how to find a $(0/n)$ type LPA for $z^{-m}F(z)$. It is a natural question to ask for a generalization to (m/n) type LPAs for $F(z)$ or shifted versions of it : $z^{-p}F(z)$ where p is an arbitrary integer. To this end, we have to generalize the polynomials $A_n^{(m)}(z)$ and $\hat{A}_n^{(m)}(z)$ to Laurent polynomials which will be denoted as $B(p)_n^{(m)}(z)$ and $\hat{B}(p)_n^{(m)}(z)$. These are introduced first. Take expression (4.1a), i.e. $F(z)Q_n^{(m)}(z) - P_n^{(m)}(z) = R_n^{(m)}(z)$, and replace $F(z)$ by $Z^{(p)}(z) - \hat{Z}^{(p)}(z)$ with $Z^{(p)}(z)$ and $\hat{Z}^{(p)}(z)$ as defined before in (4.2). Rearrange the terms to obtain

$$Z^{(p)}(z)Q_n^{(m)}(z) - R_n^{(m)}(z) = \hat{Z}^{(p)}Q_n^{(m)}(z) + P_n^{(m)}(z) =: B(p)_n^{(m)}(z). \qquad (4.7a)$$

Checking the orders of the left hand side and right hand side of the first equality sign, we find that $B(p)_n^{(m)}(z)$ is a Laurent polynomial with powers of z ranging from $\min(p,n+m+1)$ to $\max(m,p+n)$. Similarly, starting from (4.1b), i.e. $\hat{R}_n^{(m)}(z)\hat{Q}_n^{(m)}(z) - \hat{P}_n^{(m)}(z) = \hat{R}_n^{(m)}(z)$, you can define $\hat{B}(p)_n^{(m)}(z)$ by

$$\hat{B}(p)_n^{(m)}(z) := Z^{(p)}(z)\hat{Q}_n^{(m)}(z) - \hat{R}_n^{(m)}(z) = \hat{Z}^{(p)}(z)\hat{Q}_n^{(m)}(z) + \hat{P}_n^{(m)}(z) \qquad (4.7b)$$

and find that it is a Laurent polynomial with powers of z ranging from $\min(p,n+m)$ up to $\max(m-1,p+n)$. Multiplying (4.4) from the left with $[1\ \hat{Z}^{(p)}(z)]$ and using definitions (4.7), we see that in (3.6) we can also replace S by $B(p)$. The initial conditions are easily checked. They are:

$$B(p)_0^{(m)}(z) = f'_p z^p + f_{p+1} z^{p+1} + \cdots + f_m z^m \qquad \text{if } p \leqslant m \qquad (4.8a)$$

$$= -f_{m+1} z^{m+1} - \cdots - f_{p-1} z^{p-1} - f'_p z^p \quad \text{if } p > m \qquad (4.8b)$$

and

$$\hat{B}(p)_0^{(m)}(z) = f'_p z^p + f_{p+1} z^{p+1} + \cdots + f_{m-1} z^{m-1} \text{ if } p < m \qquad (4.8c)$$

$$= -f_m z^m - \cdots - f_{p-1} z^{p-1} - f'_p z^p \quad \text{if } p \geqslant m. \qquad (4.8d)$$

Note that $z^{-m}B(m)_n^{(m)}(z) = A_n^{(m)}(z)$ and $z^{-m}\hat{B}(m)_n^{(m)}(z) = \hat{A}_n^{(m)}(z)$ or in the special case that $m = 0$ $B(0)_n^{(0)}(z) = A_n^{(0)}(z)$ and $\hat{B}(0)_n^{(0)}(z) = \hat{A}_n^{(0)}(z)$.

The Laurent polynomials $B(p)_n^{(m)}(z)$ and $\hat{B}(p)_n^{(m)}(z)$ appear in the numerator expressions of an (m/n) type LPA for $z^{-p}F(z)$. This is given in the following theorem.

THEOREM 4.3. *Let m,n and p be nonnegative integers and define for a normal fls $F(z)$ the polynomials $Q_n^{(k)}(z)$ and $\hat{Q}_n^{(k)}(z)$ as in (3.1) and the Laurent polynomials $B(p)_n^{(k)}(z)$ and $\hat{B}(p)_n^{(k)}(z)$ as in (4.7). Set further by definition*

$$K(p)_n^{(m)}(z) := \left(\frac{z^{-p} B(p)_n^{(p+m)}(z)}{Q_n^{(p+m)}(z)} \;,\; -\frac{z^{-(n+p)} \hat{B}(p)_n^{(p-m)}(z)}{z^{-n} \hat{Q}_n^{(p-m)}(z)} \right) \qquad (4.9a)$$

and

$$\hat{K}(p)_n^{(m)}(z) := \left(\frac{z^{-p} \hat{B}(p)_n^{(p+m)}(z)}{\hat{Q}_n^{(p+m)}(z)} \;,\; -\frac{z^{-(p+n)} B(p)_n^{(p-m)}(z)}{z^{-n} Q_n^{(p-m)}(z)} \right). \qquad (4.9b)$$

Then $K(p)_n^{(m)}(z)$ is a (m/n) LPA for $z^{-p} F(z)$ if $m \geqslant 0$ and $\hat{K}(p)_n^{(m)}(z)$ is a $(m-1/n)$ LPA for $z^{-p} F(z)$ if $m > 0$.

PROOF. We only give the proof for $K(p)_n^{(m)}(z)$ with $m \geqslant 0$. The rest is similar. We begin by checking the order of approximation. Since $Q_n^{(p+m)}(z)$ is comonic and $\hat{Q}_n^{(p-m)}(z)$ is monic of degree n and since $z^{-p} F(z) = z^{-p} Z^{(p)}(z) - z^{-p} \hat{Z}^{(p)}(z)$, it follows from (4.7) that

$$z^{-p} Z^{(p)}(z) Q_n^{(p+m)}(z) - z^{-p} B(p)_n^{(p+m)}(z) = z^{-p} R_n^{(p+m)}(z) = O_+(z^{m+n+1})$$

and

$$z^{-p} \hat{Z}^{(p)}(z) [z^{-n} \hat{Q}_n^{(p-m)}(z)] - z^{-(p+n)} \hat{B}(p)_n^{(p-m)} = -z^{-(p+n)} \hat{P}_n^{(p-m)}(z)$$

$$= O_-(z^{-(m+n+1)}).$$

Hence these orders are as they should be for an LPF. The order properties of $Q_n^{(p+m)}(z)$ and $\hat{Q}_n^{(p-m)}(z)$, i.e. they both have $+$ order 0 and $-$ order n, are sufficient to make (4.9a) an LPA if we can prove that the sum of the two ratios in (4.9a) is the ratio of two Laurent polynomials of degree m and degree n respectively. This degree condition is clearly satisfied for the denominator. Thus we only have to prove that the numerator, which is

$$L(p)_n^{(m)}(z) :=$$

$$z^{-(n+p)} [B(p)_n^{(p+m)}(z) \hat{Q}_n^{(p-m)}(z) - \hat{B}(p)_n^{(p-m)}(z) Q_n^{(p+m)}(z)] \qquad (4.10a)$$

is a Laurent polynomial of degree m. Now we obtain with some simple algebra the following train of equalities (Use successively (4.7a), (4.1a), (4.6), (4.1b) and (4.6) again.)

$$z^{n+p} L(p)_n^{(m)}(z) = [Z^{(p)}(z) Q_n^{(p+m)}(z) - R_n^{(p+m)}(z)] \hat{Q}_n^{(p-m)}(z)$$

$$- [\hat{Z}^{(p)}(z) \hat{Q}_n^{(p-m)}(z) + \hat{P}_n^{(p-m)}(z)] Q_n^{(p+m)}(z)$$

$$= F(z) Q_n^{(p+m)}(z) \hat{Q}_n^{(p-m)}(z) - R_n^{(p+m)}(z) \hat{Q}_n^{(p-m)}(z)$$

$$- \hat{P}_n^{(p-m)}(z) Q_n^{(p+m)}(z)$$

$$= [P_n^{(p+m)}(z) + R_n^{(p+m)}(z)]\hat{Q}_n^{(p-m)}(z) - R_n^{(p+m)}(z)\hat{Q}_n^{(p-m)}(z)$$

$$- \hat{P}_n^{(p-m)}(z)Q_n^{(p+m)}(z)$$

$$= P_n^{(p+m)}(z)\hat{Q}_n^{(p-m)}(z) - \hat{P}_n^{(p-m)}(z)Q_n^{(p+m)}(z) = O_-(z^{p+m+n})$$

$$= [\hat{P}_n^{(p-m)}(z) + \hat{R}_n^{(p-m)}(z)]Q_n^{(p+m)}(z) - R_n^{(p+m)}(z)\hat{Q}_n^{(p-m)}(z)$$

$$- \hat{P}_n^{(p-m)}(z)Q_n^{(p+m)}(z)$$

$$= \hat{R}_n^{(p-m)}(z)Q_n^{(p+m)}(z) - R_n^{(p+m)}(z)\hat{Q}_n^{(p-m)}(z) = O_+(z^{p+n-m}).$$

Since the left hand side is both $O_-(z^{m+p+n})$ and $O_+(z^{-m+p+n})$, it follows after dividing out z^{n+p} that $L(p)_n^{(m)}(z)$ is a Laurent polynomial of degree m. This completes the proof of theorem 4.3.

□

In previous theorem, m took only nonnegative values because (m/n) LPAs are only defined for nonnegative m and n. Formally, there is nothing against allowing negative values for m in (4.9). These are again LPAs as you can see from the following trivial identity:

$$\hat{K}(p)_n^{(-m)}(z) = -K(p)_n^{(m)}(z)\begin{vmatrix} 0 & 1 \\ 1 & 0 \end{vmatrix} \tag{4.11}$$

for any integer m.

From the previous proof it follows that if $L(p)_n^{(m)}(z)$ is as defined in (4.10a) and $\hat{L}(p)_n^{(m)}(z)$ is similarly defined for $\hat{K}(p)_n^{(m)}(z)$, i.e.

$$\hat{L}(p)_n^{(m)}(z) :=$$

$$z^{-(n+p)}[\hat{B}(p)_n^{(p+m)}(z)Q_n^{(p-m)}(z) - B(p)_n^{(p-m)}(z)\hat{Q}_n^{(p+m)}(z)], \tag{4.10b}$$

then it is possible to replace $B(p)$ in (4.10) by one of the symbols P or $-R$. This result is formulated as a corollary.

COROLLARY 4.4. *Let* $L(p)_n^{(m)}(z)$ *and* $\hat{L}(p)_n^{(m)}(z)$ *be defined by (4.10a) and (4.10b). Then*

$$z^{n+p}L(p)_n^{(m)}(z) = S_n^{(p+m)}(z)\hat{Q}_n^{(p-m)}(z) - \hat{S}_n^{(p-m)}(z)Q_n^{(p+m)}(z) \tag{4.10c}$$

and

$$z^{n+p}\hat{L}(p)_n^{(m)}(z) = \hat{S}_n^{(p+m)}(z)Q_n^{(p-m)}(z) - S_n^{(p-m)}(z)\hat{Q}_n^{(p+m)}(z) \tag{4.10d}$$

where S can be P, −R or B(p).

PROOF. (4.10c) was obtained during the proof of theorem 4.3. (4.10d) can be deduced similarly.

□

If you allow negative values for m, then the symmetry relation given in (4.11) for $K(p)_n^{(m)}(z)$ and $\hat{K}(p)_n^{(m)}(z)$ can also be derived for the numerators $L(p)_n^{(m)}(z)$ and $\hat{L}(p)_n^{(m)}(z)$. The definitions (4.10) give us directly the following result:

COROLLARY 4.5. *Let* $L(p)_n^{(m)}(z)$ *and* $\hat{L}(p)_n^{(m)}(z)$ *be as defined in (4.10). Then*

$$L(p)_n^{(-m)}(z) = -\hat{L}(p)_n^{(m)}(z).$$

□

This concludes our derivation of LPAs. We have seen how the parameters $\alpha_n^{(m)}$ and $\hat{\alpha}_n^{(m)}$, computed by algorithm 1 and algorithm 2 are sufficient to define the recursion (3.6). This recurrence relation can be used to generate from the appropriate initial conditions all the quantities needed to obtain LPAs. Thus, if we add to the algorithms 1 and 2 recursion (3.6) for $S = A$ or $S = B(p)$, we find that these algorithms can then be used to generate LPAs.

We shall look at two–point PAs in the next subsection.

4.3 Two–point Padé approximants

It will turn out, as we shall see in this subsection, that we can use algorithms 1 and 2 again to generate two–point PAs, at least for the special class of two–point PAs that we defined in chapter 2. A first set of two–point PAs may be obtained with the polynomials $A_n^{(m)}(z)$ and $\hat{A}_n^{(m)}(z)$ (defined in (4.3)) as numerators. Indeed, observe that (4.6) implies the following relations:

$$z^{-m}Z^{(m)}(z) - L_+ \left(\frac{A_n^{(m)}(z)}{Q_n^{(m)}(z)} \right) = \frac{R_n^{(m)}(z)}{z^m Q_n^{(m)}(z)} = O_+(z^{n+1}), \tag{4.12a}$$

$$z^{-m}\hat{Z}^{(m)}(z) - L_- \left(\frac{\hat{A}_n^{(m)}(z)}{\hat{Q}_n^{(m)}(z)} \right) = -\frac{\hat{P}_n^{(m)}(z)}{z^m \hat{Q}_n^{(m)}(z)} = O_-(z^{-n-1}), \tag{4.12b}$$

$$z^{-m}Z^{(m)}(z) - L_+ \left(\frac{\hat{A}_n^{(m)}(z)}{\hat{Q}_n^{(m)}(z)} \right) = \frac{\hat{R}_n^{(m)}(z)}{z^m \hat{Q}_n^{(m)}(z)} = O_+(z^{n}), \tag{4.12c}$$

$$z^{-m}\hat{Z}^{(m)}(z) - L_- \left(\frac{A_n^{(m)}(z)}{Q_n^{(m)}(z)} \right) = -\frac{P_n^{(m)}(z)}{z^m Q_n^{(m)}(z)} = O_-(z^{-n}). \tag{4.12d}$$

Note that this is only true if $Q_n^{(m)}(z)$ and $\hat{Q}_n^{(m)}(z)$ are of strict degree n and if their constant term doesn't vanish. This is so if $F(z)$ is normal as we showed in property 2.12.

Relations (4.12) are exactly the order properties we need to show that we get two–point PAs. Hence they prove the following theorem:

THEOREM 4.6. *Let $m \in \mathbb{Z}$ and $n \in \mathbb{N}$. Let $F(z)$ be a normal fls and let the polynomials of degree n $A_n^{(m)}(z)$, $\hat{A}_n^{(m)}(z)$, $Q_n^{(m)}(z)$ and $\hat{Q}_n^{(m)}(z)$ be related to $F(z)$ by (4.3) and (3.1) and define $Z^{(m)}(z)$ and $\hat{Z}^{(m)}(z)$ by (4.2). Then $A_n^{(m)}(z)/Q_n^{(m)}(z)$ is a two–point PA of type (n,n) for the pair $(z^{-m}Z^{(m)}(z), z^{-m}\hat{Z}^{(m)}(z))$ and $\hat{A}_n^{(m)}(z)/\hat{Q}_n^{(m)}(z)$ is a two–point PA of the same pair but of type $(n-1,n)$.*

$\square$

It is possible to obtain some other two–point PAs, not for the pair $(z^{-m}Z^{(m)}(z), z^{-m}\hat{Z}^{(m)}(z))$, but for other pairs that are also directly related to $F(z)$. Herefore we have to introduce some new polynomials that are also solutions of recurrence relation (3.6). We shall do this first.

Define the polynomials $U_n^{(m)}(z)$, $\hat{U}_n^{(m)}(z)$, $V_n^{(m)}(z)$ and $\hat{V}_n^{(m)}(z)$ all of degree n by

$$\begin{vmatrix} V_n^{(m)}(z) & \hat{V}_n^{(m)}(z) \\ zU_n^{(m)}(z) & z\hat{U}_n^{(m)}(z) \end{vmatrix} := \frac{1}{f_m} \begin{vmatrix} 1 & f_m' \\ -1 & f_m' \end{vmatrix} \begin{vmatrix} A_{n+1}^{(m)}(z) & \hat{A}_{n+1}^{(m)}(z) \\ Q_{n+1}^{(m)}(z) & \hat{Q}_{n+1}^{(m)}(z) \end{vmatrix}. \tag{4.13}$$

The polynomials in the rightmost matrix are as we defined them earlier in (3.1) and (4.3), $f_m' = \frac{1}{2}f_m$ is as in (4.2). Any linear combination of two polynomial solutions of (3.6) gives again a polynomial solution. Hence, the leftmost matrix contains polynomials satisfying (3.6). That these are indeed polynomials of the indicated degree n follows from the recursion (3.6) and the initial conditions

$$\begin{vmatrix} V_0^{(m)}(z) & \hat{V}_0^{(m)}(z) \\ U_0^{(m)}(z) & \hat{U}_0^{(m)}(z) \end{vmatrix} = \begin{vmatrix} 1 & -\hat{\alpha}_1^{(m)} \\ -\alpha_1^{(m)} & 1 \end{vmatrix}. \tag{4.14}$$

Note that we could, at least formally, replace (4.14) by

$$\begin{vmatrix} V_{-1}^{(m)} & \hat{V}_{-1}^{(m)} \\ zU_{-1}^{(m)} & z\hat{U}_{-1}^{(m)} \end{vmatrix} = \begin{vmatrix} 1 & 0 \\ 0 & 1 \end{vmatrix}.$$

Now we shall show how these polynomials may be used to construct two–point PAs. Insert between the two factors in the left–hand side of (4.6) the product

$$\begin{vmatrix} f_m' & -f_m' \\ 1 & 1 \end{vmatrix} \frac{1}{2f_m'} \begin{vmatrix} 1 & f_m' \\ -1 & f_m' \end{vmatrix} = \begin{vmatrix} 1 & 0 \\ 0 & 1 \end{vmatrix}$$

so that (4.6) becomes

$$\begin{vmatrix} -f'_m+z^{-m}Z^{(m)}(z) & f'_m+z^{-m}Z^{(m)}(z) \\ -\hat{f}'_m+z^{-m}\hat{Z}^{(m)}(z) & \hat{f}'_m+z^{-m}\hat{Z}^{(m)}(z) \end{vmatrix} \begin{vmatrix} V^{(m)}_{n-1}(z) & \hat{V}^{(m)}_{n-1}(z) \\ zU^{(m)}_{n-1}(z) & z\hat{U}^{(m)}_{n-1}(z) \end{vmatrix} =$$

$$= z^{-m} \begin{vmatrix} R^{(m)}_0(z) & \hat{R}^{(m)}_0(z) \\ -P^{(m)}_0(z) & -\hat{P}^{(m)}_0(z) \end{vmatrix} \begin{vmatrix} V^{(m)}_{n-1}(z) & \hat{V}^{(m)}_{n-1}(z) \\ zU^{(m)}_{n-1}(z) & z\hat{U}^{(m)}_{n-1}(z) \end{vmatrix}$$

$$= z^{-m} \begin{vmatrix} R^{(m)}_n(z) & \hat{R}^{(m)}_n(z) \\ -P^{(m)}_n(z) & -\hat{P}^{(m)}_n(z) \end{vmatrix} = \begin{vmatrix} O_+(z^{n+1}) & O_+(z^n) \\ O_-(z^0) & O_-(z^{-1}) \end{vmatrix}. \tag{4.15}$$

This implies, just like in previous theorem 4.6, that we have shown the following theorem:

THEOREM 4.7. *Let $m \in \mathbb{Z}$ and $n \in \mathbb{N}$. For $F(z)$, a normal fls, let the polynomials $U^{(m)}_n(z)$, $\hat{U}^{(m)}_n(z)$, $V^{(m)}_n(z)$ and $\hat{V}^{(m)}_n(z)$, all of dergree n, be defined by (4.13) and the series $P^{(m)}_0(z)$, $\hat{P}^{(m)}_0(z)$, $R^{(m)}_0(z)$ and $\hat{R}^{(m)}_0(z)$ be as defined in (3.7). Then $U^{(m)}_n(z)/V^{(m)}_n(z)$ is a (n,n) two-point PA for the pair $(-R^{(m)}_0(z)/(z\hat{R}^{(m)}_0(z)), -P^{(m)}_0(z)/(z\hat{P}^{(m)}_0(z)))$ and $\hat{U}^{(m)}_n(z)/\hat{V}^{(m)}_n(z)$ is a $(n-1,n)$ two-point PA for the same pair.*

PROOF. To show that we have two-point PAs, it remains to prove that the order relations in (4.15) are still as they should be after dividing out $z\hat{P}^{(m)}_0(z)$ or $z\hat{R}^{(m)}_0(z)$ and $V^{(m)}_n(z)$ or $\hat{V}^{(m)}_n(z)$. We illustrate this for only one of the four possible relations of (4.15), e.g. the (1,1) relation, which is, after augmenting n to $n+1$:

$$z^{-m}[R^{(m)}_0(z)V^{(m)}_n(z) + z\hat{R}^{(m)}_0(z)U^{(m)}_n(z)] = O_+(z^{n+2}).$$

After dividing out $z^{1-m}\hat{R}^{(m)}_0(z)$ we get:

$$\frac{R^{(m)}_0(z)}{z\hat{R}^{(m)}_0(z)} V^{(m)}_n(z) + U^{(m)}_n(z) = O_+(z^{n+1}).$$

The order is changed from $O_+(z^{n+2})$ to $O_+(z^{n+1})$ because

$$z^{1-m}\hat{R}^{(m)}_0(z) = \hat{v}^{(m)}_0 z + O_+(z^2)$$

with $\hat{v}^{(m)}_0 \neq 0$. (See chapter 2.) After dividing out $-V^{(m)}_n(z)$ we get:

$$-\frac{R^{(m)}_0(z)}{z\hat{R}^{(m)}_0(z)} - L_+(\frac{U^{(m)}_n(z)}{V^{(m)}_n(z)}) = O_+(z^{n+1})$$

because $V^{(m)}_n(0) \neq 0$ by corollary 3.2.

The other three relations of (4.15) are treated similarly.

□

Some examples illustrating the theorems of this chapter can be found in chapter 18.

The polynomials $A_n^{(m)}(z)$, $U_n^{(m)}(z)$, $V_n^{(m)}(z)$ and the Laurent polynomials $B(p)_n^{(m)}(z)$, as well as the corresponding expressions with a hat will be used throughout the rest of this volume. The symbols we used for them in this section will be reserved to have always the meaning they have in this section, even if it is not explicitly mentioned.

Chapter 5

Continued fractions

In the previous chapter we introduced a number of Padé approximants of different nature. The numerators and denominators of those approximants were all generated by the fundamental recursion (3.6). We have seen in chapters 3 and 4 that in (3.6) S_n can be replaced by one of P_n, Q_n, R_n, A_n, $B(p)_n$, zU_{n-1} or V_{n-1}, provided the appropriate initial conditions are used. It was explained in chapter 2 how Moebius transforms, like the one represented by (3.6), are related to continued fractions. We use this to show in this chapter how CFs can be obtained having for their successive convergents the different Padé-like approximants of chapter 4.

5.1 General observations

We compare the general relation (2.5) with recurrence (3.6). Note that the latter can be rewritten as

$$\begin{vmatrix} N_n^{(m)}(z) & \hat{N}_n^{(m)}(z) \\ Q_n^{(m)}(z) & \hat{Q}_n^{(m)}(z) \end{vmatrix} = \begin{vmatrix} N_{n-1}^{(m)}(z) & \hat{N}_{n-1}^{(m)}(z) \\ Q_{n-1}^{(m)}(z) & \hat{Q}_{n-1}^{(m)}(z) \end{vmatrix} \begin{vmatrix} 1 & -\hat{\alpha}_n^{(m)} \\ -z\alpha_n^{(m)} & z \end{vmatrix}, \ n \geqslant 1,$$

where N_n is one of P_n, R_n, $B(p)_n$, A_n, U_{n-1} or V_{n-1}. To transform (2.5) into (3.6), we have to make the following identifications between the parameters of (2.5) and the parameters of (3.6):

$$a_n = -\hat{\alpha}_n^{(m)}, \ b_n = z, \ c_n = 1, \ d_n = -z\alpha_n^{(m)} \quad \text{for } n \geqslant 1$$

and

$$a_0 = \hat{N}_0^{(m)}(z), \ b_0 = 1, \ c_0 = N_0^{(m)}(z), \ d_0 = 1.$$

The initial conditions for (3.6), i.e. $P_0^{(m)}(z)$, $\hat{P}_0^{(m)}(z)$, $R_0^{(m)}(z)$, $\hat{R}_0^{(m)}(z)$, $B(p)_0^{(m)}(z)$, $\hat{B}(p)_0^{(m)}(z)$, $A_0^{(m)}(z)$ and $\hat{A}_0^{(m)}(z)$ were given in previous chapter. They show that

$$\hat{N}_0^{(m)}(z) - N_0^{(m)}(z) = -f_m z^m$$

whenever N is one of P, $-R$, $B(p)$ or $z^m A$. In view of property 2.9, we find that the successive convergents of

$$N_0^{(m)}(z) + \cfrac{-f_m z^m}{\vert\quad 1\quad} + \cfrac{1}{\vert\;-\alpha_1^{(m)}z} + \cfrac{(1-\alpha_1^{(m)}\hat{\alpha}_1^{(m)})z}{\vert\quad -\hat{\alpha}_1^{(m)}} + \cdots$$

$$\cdots + \cfrac{1}{\vert\;-\alpha_n^{(m)}z} + \cfrac{(1-\alpha_n^{(m)}\hat{\alpha}_n^{(m)})z}{\vert\quad -\hat{\alpha}_n^{(m)}} + \cdots \qquad (5.1)$$

are

$$(N_0^{(m)}(z)/Q_0^{(m)}(z)),\ (\hat{N}_0^{(m)}(z)/\hat{Q}_0^{(m)}(z)),\ (N_1^{(m)}(z)/Q_1^{(m)}(z)),$$

$$(\hat{N}_1^{(m)}(z)/\hat{Q}_1^{(m)}(z)),...,$$

where N is P, $-R$, $B(p)$ or A.

For the sake of short notation we introduce

$$n_1^{(m)} := -f_m z^m \quad ; \quad m_1^{(m)} := 1 \qquad (5.2a)$$

and for $n = 1,2,3,...$:

$$n_{2n}^{(m)} := 1 \quad ; \quad n_{2n+1}^{(m)} := (1 - \alpha_n^{(m)}\hat{\alpha}_n^{(m)})z \qquad (5.2b)$$

and

$$m_{2n}^{(m)} := -\alpha_n^{(m)}z \quad ; \quad m_{2n+1}^{(m)} := -\hat{\alpha}_n^{(m)}. \qquad (5.2c)$$

Thus (5.1) is abbreviated to

$$N_0^{(m)}(z) + \sum_{n\geq 1} \cfrac{n_n^{(m)}}{\vert\; m_n^{(m)}}.$$

Now CF (5.1) can in its turn be rewritten as a sequence of Moebius transforms. Therefore use (2.15) with $A_{2n} = N_n^{(m)}(z)$, $B_{2n} = Q_n^{(m)}(z)$ for $n = 0,1,2,...$ and $A_{2n+1} = \hat{N}_n^{(m)}(z)$ and $B_{2n+1} = \hat{Q}_n^{(m)}(z)$ for $n = 0,1,2,....$ Thus we find

$$\begin{vmatrix} N_n^{(m)}(z) & \hat{N}_n^{(m)}(z) \\ Q_n^{(m)}(z) & \hat{Q}_n^{(m)}(z) \end{vmatrix} = \begin{vmatrix} \hat{N}_{n-1}^{(m)}(z) & N_n^{(m)}(z) \\ \hat{Q}_{n-1}^{(m)}(z) & Q_n^{(m)}(z) \end{vmatrix} \begin{bmatrix} 0 & n_{2n+1}^{(m)} \\ 1 & m_{2n+1}^{(m)} \end{bmatrix}, \quad n = 1,2,...$$

and

$$\begin{vmatrix} \hat{N}_n^{(m)}(z) & N_{n+1}^{(m)}(z) \\ \hat{Q}_n^{(m)}(z) & Q_{n+1}^{(m)}(z) \end{vmatrix} = \begin{vmatrix} N_n^{(m)}(z) & \hat{N}_n^{(m)}(z) \\ Q_n^{(m)}(z) & \hat{Q}_n^{(m)}(z) \end{vmatrix} \begin{bmatrix} 0 & n_{2n+2}^{(m)} \\ 1 & m_{2n+2}^{(m)} \end{bmatrix}, \quad n = 0,1,2,... .$$

The first of these recurrences can also start from $n = 0$ on if we set $\hat{N}_{-1}^{(m)} = 1$ and $\hat{Q}_{-1}^{(m)} = 0$. Property 2.5 shows that if we define for some $\Phi(z)$ and for

$n = 0,1,2,...$

$$S_n^{(m)}(z) := \Phi(z)Q_n^{(m)}(z) - N_n^{(m)}(z)$$

and

$$\hat{S}_n^{(m)}(z) := \Phi(z)\hat{Q}_n^{(m)}(z) - \hat{N}_n^{(m)}(z)$$

that then $\Phi(z)$ can be represented by a finite CF :

$$\Phi(z) = N_0^{(m)}(z) + \overset{2n+1}{\underset{k=1}{\Large\Sigma}} \frac{n_k^{(m)}}{|\, m_k^{(m)}} - \frac{\hat{S}_n^{(m)}(z)}{|\, S_n^{(m)}(z)}$$

or

$$\Phi(z) = N_0^{(m)}(z) + \overset{2n}{\underset{k=1}{\Large\Sigma}} \frac{n_k^{(m)}}{|\, m_k^{(m)}} - \frac{S_n^{(m)}(z)}{|\, \hat{S}_{n-1}^{(m)}(z)}.$$

5.2 Some special cases

As a special case of this general derivation, we can get CFs whose convergents are the Padé-like approximants, or elements thereof, derived in previous chapter. We shall see, in the form of theorems, what we get when we take $N = P$, $-R$, $B(p)$ or $z^m A$ and when an appropriate choice for $\Phi(z)$ is made. The proofs are omitted since they are only a special case of the derivation above. We first choose $N = P$ and $\Phi(z) = F(z)$. From the definitions (3.4) we get:

$$[R_n^{(m)}(z)\ \hat{R}_n^{(m)}(z)] = [-1\ \ F(z)] \begin{vmatrix} P_n^{(m)}(z) & \hat{P}_n^{(m)}(z) \\ Q_n^{(m)}(z) & \hat{Q}_n^{(m)}(z) \end{vmatrix} \tag{5.3}$$

This gives us the result:

THEOREM 5.1a. *Let $m \in \mathbb{Z}$ and $n \in \mathbb{N}$, let $F(z)$ be a normal s and let $\alpha_n^{(m)}$ and $\hat{\alpha}_n^{(m)}$ be its SS parameters. Suppose that the series $P_n^{(m)}(z)$, $\hat{P}_n^{(m)}(z)$, $R_n^{(m)}(z)$ and $\hat{R}_n^{(m)}(z)$ and the polynomials $Q_n^{(m)}(z)$ and $\hat{Q}_n^{(m)}(z)$ are related to $F(z)$ as in algorithms 1 and 2 and define $n_n^{(m)}$ and $m_n^{(m)}$ by (5.2). Then we have the (formal) CF expansions*

$$F(z) = P_0^{(m)}(z) + \overset{2n}{\underset{k=1}{\Large\Sigma}} \frac{n_k^{(m)}}{|\, m_k^{(m)}} - \frac{R_n^{(m)}(z)}{|\, \hat{R}_{n-1}^{(m)}(z)}\ ,\ \ n = 1,2,... \tag{5.4a}$$

$$= P_0^{(m)}(z) + \sum_{k=1}^{2n+1} \frac{n_k^{(m)}}{\mid m_k^{(m)}} - \frac{\hat{R}_n^{(m)}(z)}{\mid R_n^{(m)}(z)} \quad , \quad n = 0,1,2,.... \qquad (5.4b)$$

The convergents are

$$(P_n^{(m)}(z)/Q_n^{(m)}(z)) = P_0^{(m)}(z) + \sum_{k=1}^{2n} \frac{n_k^{(m)}}{\mid m_k^{(m)}}$$

and

$$(\hat{P}_n^{(m)}(z)/\hat{Q}_n^{(m)}(z)) = P_0^{(m)}(z) + \sum_{k=1}^{2n+1} \frac{n_k^{(m)}}{\mid m_k^{(m)}} .$$

$\square$

Remarks

1. (5.4a) is also true for $n = 0$ if we set by definition $\hat{R}_{-1}^{(m)} = -1$ and consider the sum ranging from 1 to 0 as nonexistent ($= 0$).
2. One has to be careful in the interpretation of the equality sign of (5.4). The so called forward evaluation scheme i.e. evaluating numerator and denominator of the k-th convergent for $k = 0,1,2,...$ by multiplying the matrices in (2.15) from left to right will give a problem in the last step of CF (5.4). Indeed the multiplications of

$$\begin{vmatrix} \hat{P}_{n-1}^{(m)}(z) & P_n^{(m)}(z) \\ \hat{Q}_{n-1}^{(m)}(z) & Q_n^{(m)}(z) \end{vmatrix} \begin{vmatrix} 0 & -R_n^{(m)}(z) \\ 1 & \hat{R}_{n-1}^{(m)}(z) \end{vmatrix}$$

   or

$$\begin{vmatrix} P_n^{(m)}(z) & \hat{P}_n^{(m)}(z) \\ Q_n^{(m)}(z) & \hat{Q}_n^{(m)}(z) \end{vmatrix} \begin{vmatrix} 0 & -\hat{R}_n^{(m)}(z) \\ 1 & R_n^{(m)}(z) \end{vmatrix}$$

   are not defined because $P_k^{(m)}(z)$ and $\hat{P}_k^{(m)}(z)$ have infinitely many negative powers of z while $R_k^{(m)}(z)$ and $\hat{R}_k^{(m)}(z)$ have infinitely many positive powers of z. The correct interpretation of (5.4) is that $F(z)-P_0^{(m)}(z)$ is a fls with finitely many negative powers of z and so is the L_+ expansion of the remaining part in the right hand side of (5.4). The equality sign means that these fls are equal.
3. It is clear that in (5.3) we can interchange the role of P and R. Taking the special choice of $n_1^{(m)} = -f_m z^m$ into account, it turns out that theorem 5.1a is also true if P is replaced by $-R$, R by $-P$ and F by $-F$.

4. The successive convergents of (5.4) are the Padé approximants that are found in the order of a horizontal sawtooth path alternating between row m and row $m-1$ of the Padé table for $F(z)$ (see theorem 4.1).

We next find a CF with convergents that are the elements appearing in the LPA expressions of theorem 4.3. Therefore take in the general derivation $N = B(p)$ and $\Phi(z) = Z^{(p)}(z)$ or $\hat{Z}^{(p)}(z)$. The analogue of (5.3) becomes :

$$\begin{vmatrix} R_n^{(m)}(z) & \hat{R}_n^{(m)}(z) \\ -P_n^{(m)}(z) & -\hat{P}_n^{(m)}(z) \end{vmatrix} = \begin{vmatrix} -1 & Z^{(p)}(z) \\ -1 & \hat{Z}^{(p)}(z) \end{vmatrix} \begin{vmatrix} B(p)_n^{(m)}(z) & \hat{B}(p)_n^{(m)}(z) \\ Q_n^{(m)}(z) & \hat{Q}_n^{(m)}(z) \end{vmatrix} \tag{5.5}$$

so that we get the next theorem :

THEOREM 5.1b. *Under the conditions of theorem 5.1a, define for $p \geqslant 0$, an integer, the Laurent polynomials $B(p)_n^{(m)}(z)$ and $\hat{B}(p)_n^{(m)}(z)$ as in (4.7) and the series $Z^{(p)}(z)$ and $\hat{Z}^{(p)}(z)$ as in (4.2). Then*

$$Z^{(p)}(z) = B(p)_0^{(m)}(z) + \sum_{k=1}^{2n} \frac{n_k^{(m)}}{\lceil m_k^{(m)}} - \frac{R_n^{(m)}(z)}{\lceil \hat{R}_{n-1}^{(m)}(z)} , \quad n = 1,2,... \tag{5.6a}$$

$$= B(p)_0^{(m)}(z) + \sum_{k=1}^{2n+1} \frac{n_k^{(m)}}{\lceil m_k^{(m)}} - \frac{\hat{R}_n^{(m)}(z)}{\lceil R_n^{(m)}(z)} , \quad n = 0,1,2,... \tag{5.6b}$$

and also

$$\hat{Z}^{(p)}(z) = B(p)_0^{(m)}(z) + \sum_{k=1}^{2n} \frac{n_k^{(m)}}{\lceil m_k^{(m)}} - \frac{-P_n^{(m)}(z)}{\lceil -\hat{P}_{n-1}^{(m)}(z)} , \quad n = 1,2,... \tag{5.7a}$$

$$= B(p)_0^{(m)}(z) + \sum_{k=1}^{2n+1} \frac{n_k^{(m)}}{\lceil m_k^{(m)}} - \frac{-\hat{P}_n^{(m)}(z)}{\lceil -P_n^{(m)}(z)} , \quad n = 0,1,2,... \tag{5.7b}$$

The successive convergents are

$$(B(p)_n^{(m)}(z)/Q_n^{(m)}(z)) = B(p)_0^{(m)}(z) + \sum_{k=1}^{2n} \frac{n_k^{(m)}}{\lceil m_k^{(m)}} , \quad n = 1,2,...$$

and

$$(\hat{B}(p)_n^{(m)}(z)/\hat{Q}_n^{(m)}(z)) = B(p)_0^{(m)}(z) + \sum_{k=1}^{2n+1} \frac{n_k^{(m)}}{\lceil m_k^{(m)}} , \quad n = 0,1,2,...$$

$\square$

Remarks similar to those made after theorem 5.1a can be made here too.

Since we have seen in previous chapter that $B(m)_n^{(m)}(z) = z^m A_n^{(m)}(z)$ and $\hat{B}(m)_n^{(m)}(z) = z^m \hat{A}_n^{(m)}(z)$, we get as a special case of previous theorem for $p = m$, and after dividing out z^m an expression involving the polynomials $A_n^{(m)}(z)$ and $\hat{A}_n^{(m)}(z)$. We omit the details.

Finally we can get expansions involving the polynomials $U_n^{(m)}(z)$, $\hat{U}_n^{(m)}(z)$, $V_n^{(m)}(z)$ and $\hat{V}_n^{(m)}(z)$. This result is formulated in the next theorem.

THEOREM 5.2. *Under the conditions of theorem 5.1a and with the polynomials* $U_n^{(m)}(z)$, $\hat{U}_n^{(m)}(z)$, $V_n^{(m)}(z)$ *and* $\hat{V}_n^{(m)}(z)$ *as defined in (4.13), we have*

$$(-z^{-m} R_0^{(m)}(z) / z^{-m} \hat{R}_0^{(m)}(z)) = m_2^{(m)} + \sum_{k=3}^{2n} \frac{n_k^{(m)}}{m_k^{(m)}} - \frac{R_n^{(m)}(z)}{\hat{R}_{n-1}^{(m)}(z)} \,, \quad n \geqslant 1^{(\dagger)} \quad (5.8a)$$

$$= m_2^{(m)} + \sum_{k=3}^{2n+1} \frac{n_k^{(m)}}{m_k^{(m)}} - \frac{\hat{R}_n^{(m)}(z)}{R_n^{(m)}(z)} \,, \quad n \geqslant 1 \quad (5.8b)$$

and

$$(-z^{-m} P_0^{(m)}(z) / z^{-m} \hat{P}_0^{(m)}(z)) = m_2^{(m)} + \sum_{k=3}^{2n} \frac{n_k^{(m)}}{m_k^{(m)}} - \frac{-P_n^{(m)}(z)}{-\hat{P}_{n-1}^{(m)}(z)} \,, \quad n \geqslant 2 \quad (5.9a)$$

$$= m_2^{(m)} + \sum_{k=3}^{2n+1} \frac{n_k^{(m)}}{m_k^{(m)}} - \frac{-\hat{P}_n^{(m)}(z)}{-P_n^{(m)}(z)} \,, \quad n \geqslant 1 \quad (5.9b)$$

The convergents are:

$$(zU_0^{(m)}(z) / V_0^{(m)}(z)), \ (z\hat{U}_0^{(m)}(z) / \hat{V}_0^{(m)}(z)), \ (zU_1^{(m)}(z) / V_1^{(m)}(z)),$$

$$(z\hat{U}_1^{(m)}(z) / \hat{V}_1^{(m)}(z)),\dots .$$

PROOF. (5.8a) can be shown as follows: rewrite (5.6a) for $p = m$ as

$$Z^{(m)}(z) - z^m A_0^{(m)}(z) = \frac{-f_m z^m}{1} + \frac{1}{m_2^{(m)}} + \sum_{k=3}^{2n} \frac{n_k^{(m)}}{m_k^{(m)}} - \frac{R_n^{(m)}(z)}{\hat{R}_{n-1}^{(m)}(z)} .$$

The left-hand side is $R_0^{(m)}(z)$ by definition. (Use (4.2), (4.3) and (3.4)). The right-hand side is transformed into the right-hand side of (5.8a) by performing

---

(†) For $n = 1$, the sum is supposed to be zero.

the next sequence of operations: (1) divide by $-f_m z^m$, (2) invert, (3) subtract 1 and (4) invert again. If you do these operations on the left-hand side, it becomes the left-hand side of (5.8a).

The other relations are similarly proved.

$\square$

Chapter 6

Moebius transforms

In this chapter we shall again look in more detail at the recurrence (3.6). Chapter 5 exhausted the interpretation of (3.6) in terms of CFs. Now we shall interpret (3.6) as a sequence of Moebius transforms for series. In this way we shall obtain an nonhomogeneous version of algorithm 2 and of an inverse for algorithm 1. In the special case that $F(z)$ for $z = \exp(i\theta)$ represents the Fourier expansion of a positive function, the reformulation of algorithm 2 will turn out to be the algorithm as originally formulated by Schur. The inverse of algorithm 1 as we shall formulate it, becomes the classical Schur-Cohn test to check if the zeros of a polynomial are inside the unit disc. These facts will be explained in chapter 17.

6.1 General observations

For $\alpha_n^{(m)}$ and $\hat{\alpha}_n^{(m)}$ as in (3.6), the SS parameters for $F(z)$, let's introduce the notations:

$$\theta_n^{(m)} := \begin{vmatrix} 1 & -\hat{\alpha}_n^{(m)} \\ -z\alpha_n^{(m)} & z \end{vmatrix} \tag{6.1}$$

and

$$\Theta_n^{(m)} := \theta_1^{(m)}\theta_2^{(m)} \cdots \theta_n^{(m)}. \tag{6.2}$$

Then (3.6) can be restated as

$$[S_n^{(m)}(z)\ \hat{S}_n^{(m)}(z)] = [S_{n-1}^{(m)}(z)\ \hat{S}_{n-1}^{(m)}(z)]\,\theta_n^{(m)}$$

$$= [S_0^{(m)}(z)\ \hat{S}_0^{(m)}(z)]\,\Theta_n^{(m)}, \tag{6.3a}$$

with S_n one of P_n, Q_n, R_n, $B(p)_n$, A_n, zU_{n-1} or V_{n-1}. The initial values are given in chapters 3 and 4. They are resumed in (6.3b–d):

$$\begin{vmatrix} Q_0^{(m)}(z) & \hat{Q}_0^{(m)}(z) \\ P_0^{(m)}(z) & \hat{P}_0^{(m)}(z) \\ R_0^{(m)}(z) & \hat{R}_0^{(m)}(z) \end{vmatrix} = \begin{vmatrix} 1 & 1 \\ \Pi_{-\infty:m}F(z) & \Pi_{-\infty:m-1}F(z) \\ \Pi_{m+1:\infty}F(z) & \Pi_{m:\infty}F(z) \end{vmatrix} \tag{6.3b}$$

$$\begin{vmatrix} A_0^{(m)}(z) & \hat{A}_0^{(m)}(z) \\ B(p)_0^{(m)}(z) & \hat{B}(p)_0^{(m)}(z) \end{vmatrix} = \begin{vmatrix} f'_m & -f'_m \\ Z^{(p)}(z)-R_0^{(m)}(z) & Z^{(p)}(z)-\hat{R}_0^{(m)}(z) \end{vmatrix} \tag{6.3c}$$

$$\begin{vmatrix} zU_{-1}^{(m)}(z) & z\hat{U}_{-1}^{(m)}(z) \\ V_{-1}^{(m)}(z) & \hat{V}_{-1}^{(m)}(z) \end{vmatrix} = \begin{vmatrix} 0 & 1 \\ 1 & 0 \end{vmatrix}. \tag{6.3d}$$

The flow graph representing the multiplication with $\theta_n^{(m)}$ in (6.3a) is given in fig. 6.1.

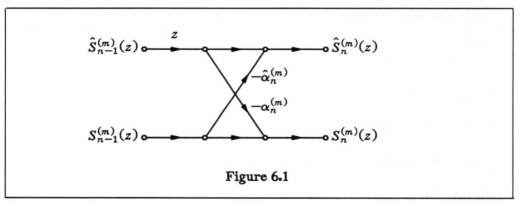

Figure 6.1

A possible Moebius transform that can be associated with $\theta_n^{(m)}$ is

$$t_n^{(m)}(w) := \frac{w-\alpha_n^{(m)}}{1-\hat{\alpha}_n^{(m)}w} \tag{6.4a}$$

and, as you can see from (6.3a):

$$\frac{S_n^{(m)}(z)}{\hat{S}_n^{(m)}(z)} = t_n^{(m)} \begin{vmatrix} S_{n-1}^{(m)}(z) \\ z\hat{S}_{n-1}^{(m)}(z) \end{vmatrix}. \tag{6.5a}$$

The flow graph for this is given in fig. 6.2.
The dual for (6.4a) in the sense of (2.8) is

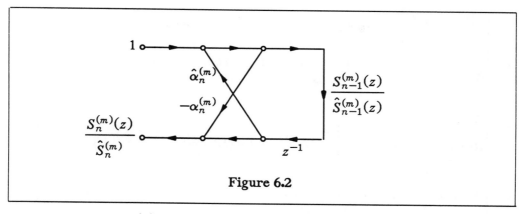

Figure 6.2

$$\hat{t}_n^{(m)}(w) := \frac{w - \hat{\alpha}_n^{(m)}}{1 - \alpha_n^{(m)} w}.$$

(6.4b)

I.e. simply interchange $\alpha_n^{(m)}$ and $\hat{\alpha}_n^{(m)}$.
It again follows easily from (6.3a) that

$$\frac{\hat{S}_n^{(m)}(z)}{S_n^{(m)}(z)} = \hat{t}_n^{(m)} \left| \frac{z\hat{S}_{n-1}^{(m)}(z)}{S_{n-1}^{(m)}(z)} \right|.$$

(6.5b)

6.2 Some special cases

We shall now take special choices for S in (6.5).

THEOREM 6.1. *Under the same conditions as theorem 4.1, suppose $t_n^{(m)}(\cdot)$ and $\hat{t}_n^{(m)}(\cdot)$ are the Moebius transforms of (6.4). Then we have the following sequence of relations:*
Define $\Pi_n^{(m)}(z) := L_-(Q_n^{(m)}(z)/\hat{Q}_n^{(m)}(z))$. Then

$$\Pi_n^{(m)}(z) = t_n^{(m)}(z^{-1} \, \Pi_{n-1}^{(m)}(z)).$$

(6.6a)

Define $\hat{\Pi}_n^{(m)}(z) := L_+(\hat{Q}_n^{(m)}(z)/Q_n^{(m)}(z))$. Then

$$\hat{\Pi}_n^{(m)}(z) = \hat{t}_n^{(m)}(z \, \hat{\Pi}_{n-1}^{(m)}(z)).$$

(6.6b)

Define $\Gamma_n^{(m)}(z) := R_n^{(m)}(z)/(z\hat{R}_n^{(m)}(z))$. Then

$$\Gamma_n^{(m)}(z) = z^{-1} t_n^{(m)}(\Gamma_{n-1}^{(m)}(z)).$$

(6.6c)

Define $\hat{\Gamma}_n^{(m)}(z) := z\hat{P}_n^{(m)}(z)/P_n^{(m)}(z)$. Then

$$\hat{\Gamma}_n^{(m)}(z) = z\hat{t}_n^{(m)}(\hat{\Gamma}_{n-1}^{(m)}(z)).$$ (6.6d)

PROOF. Take $S = Q$ in (6.5a,b) and you get (6.6a,b). Similarly, with $S = R$ in (6.5a) you get (6.6c) and with $S = P$ in (6.5b) you get (6.6d).

$\square$

Remark. For $Q_n^{(m)}(z)/\hat{Q}_n^{(m)}(z)$ we had to specify which series we wanted to associate with it: either the L_+ or the L_- expansion. In all other instances, the ratio of two series is uniquely defined and can only be understood in one possible way. $\Pi_n^{(m)}(z)$ and $\Gamma_n^{(m)}(z)$ are fps in z and $\hat{\Pi}_n^{(m)}(z)$ and $\hat{\Gamma}_n^{(m)}(z)$ are power series in z^{-1}. Note also that in each of these series, the constant term is not zero.

These relations give us a possibility to rewrite algorithm 2. Indeed from (3.5) and (3.2c) we can directly see that

$$\Gamma_n^{(m)}(0) = \frac{u_n^{(m)}}{v_n^{(m)}} = \alpha_{n+1}^{(m)} \quad \text{and} \quad \hat{\Gamma}_n^{(m)}(\infty) = \frac{\hat{u}_n^{(m)}}{\hat{v}_n^{(m)}} = \hat{\alpha}_{n+1}^{(m)}.$$ (6.7)

Thus (6.6c,d) and (6.7) together with the initial conditions

$$\Gamma_0^{(m)}(z) = \frac{z^{-m}Z^{(m)}(z)-f_m'}{(z^{-m}Z^{(m)}(z)+f_m')z} \quad \text{and} \quad \hat{\Gamma}_0^{(m)}(z) = \frac{(z^{-m}\hat{Z}^{(m)}(z)+f_m')z}{z^{-m}\hat{Z}^{(m)}(z)-f_m'}$$ (6.8)

give a reformulation of algorithm 2 which is displayed in fig. 6.3.

$$\Gamma_0^{(m)}(z) = \frac{z^{-m}Z^{(m)}(z)-f_m'}{(z^{-m}Z^{(m)}(z)+f_m')z}$$

$$\hat{\Gamma}_0^{(m)}(z) = \frac{(z^{-m}\hat{Z}^{(m)}(z)+f_m')z}{z^{-m}\hat{Z}^{(m)}(z)-f_m'}$$

for $n = 0,1,2,\ldots$

$$\alpha_{n+1}^{(m)} = \Gamma_n^{(m)}(0) \quad ; \quad \hat{\alpha}_{n+1}^{(m)} = \hat{\Gamma}_n^{(m)}(\infty)$$

$$\Gamma_{n+1}^{(m)}(z) = z^{-1}t_{n+1}^{(m)}(\Gamma_n^{(m)}(z))$$

$$\hat{\Gamma}_{n+1}^{(m)}(z) = z\hat{t}_{n+1}^{(m)}(\hat{\Gamma}_n^{(m)}(z))$$

Figure 6.3: Algorithm 2a

Remembering that $Q_n^{(m)}(z) = 1 + \cdots + (-\alpha_n^{(m)})z^n$ and $\hat{Q}_n^{(m)}(z) = (-\hat{\alpha}_n^{(m)}) + \cdots + z^n$, (see (3.2)), we also have

$$\Pi_n^{(m)}(\infty) = -\alpha_n^{(m)} \text{ and } \hat{\Pi}_n^{(m)}(0) = -\hat{\alpha}_n^{(m)}. \tag{6.9}$$

This however does not give a possibility to reformulate algorithm 1 since we need $\Pi_n^{(m)}(z)$ and $\hat{\Pi}_n^{(m)}(z)$ to find $\alpha_n^{(m)}$ and $\hat{\alpha}_n^{(m)}$ from (6.9), while at the same time these numbers are needed to generate $\Pi_n^{(m)}(z)$ and $\hat{\Pi}_n^{(m)}(z)$ from (6.6a,b). It is however possible to formulate a kind of inverse for algorithm 1. I.e. given $\Pi_n^{(m)}(z)$ and $\hat{\Pi}_n^{(m)}(z)$, or what is the same, from $Q_n^{(m)}(z)$ and $\hat{Q}_n^{(m)}(z)$, we can recover $\alpha_k^{(m)}$ and $\hat{\alpha}_k^{(m)}$ for $1 \leqslant k \leqslant n$, used to generate them. Indeed this is formulated in the next theorem, which is trivial to verify.

THEOREM 6.2. *For a normal fls $F(z)$, let the series $\Pi_n^{(m)}(z)$ and $\hat{\Pi}_n^{(m)}(z)$ be defined by (6.6) where $m \in \mathbb{Z}$ and $n \in \mathbb{N}$. Then the series $\Pi_k^{(m)}(z)$ and $\hat{\Pi}_k^{(m)}(z)$ and the SS parameters $\alpha_k^{(m)}$ and $\hat{\alpha}_k^{(m)}$, for $k = 0,1,...,n$ can be recovered from $Q_n^{(m)}(z)$ and $\hat{Q}_n^{(m)}(z)$ (defined by 3.1) by algorithm inverse 1a which is given in fig. 6.4.*

□

$$\Pi_n^{(m)}(z) = L_-(Q_n^{(m)}(z)/\hat{Q}_n^{(m)}(z))$$

$$\hat{\Pi}_n^{(m)}(z) = L_+(\hat{Q}_n^{(m)}(z)/Q_n^{(m)}(z))$$

for $k = n, n-1, ..., 1$

$$\alpha_k^{(m)} = -\Pi_k^{(m)}(\infty) \quad ; \quad \hat{\alpha}_k^{(m)} = -\hat{\Pi}_k^{(m)}(0)$$

$$\Pi_{k-1}^{(m)}(z) = z \frac{\Pi_k^{(m)}(z) + \alpha_k^{(m)}}{1 + \hat{\alpha}_k^{(m)} \Pi_k^{(m)}(z)} = z t_k^{(m)-1}(\Pi_k^{(m)}(z)) \tag{6.10a}$$

$$\hat{\Pi}_{k-1}^{(m)}(z) = z^{-1} \frac{\hat{\Pi}_k^{(m)}(z) + \hat{\alpha}_k^{(m)}}{1 + \alpha_k^{(m)}\hat{\Pi}_k^{(m)}(z)} = z^{-1} \hat{t}_k^{(m)-1}(\hat{\Pi}_k^{(m)}(z)) \tag{6.10b}$$

Figure 6.4: Algorithm inverse 1a

The transformations hidden in (6.2) are applied in (6.3a) from left to right, i.e. first $\theta_1^{(m)}$, then $\theta_2^{(m)}$ on the previous result etc. We could also use these transformations in opposite order, i.e. from right to left instead of from left to right. A result of this type is given in theorem 6.2. We can get some other results as well. This is done as follows: application of (6.3a) with the initial conditions for $S = U$ and $S = V$, given in (6.3d), leads to the following relation:

$$\begin{vmatrix} V_{n-1}^{(m)}(z) & \hat{V}_{n-1}^{(m)}(z) \\ zU_{n-1}^{(m)}(z) & z\hat{U}_{n-1}^{(m)}(z) \end{vmatrix} = \begin{vmatrix} 1 & 0 \\ 0 & 1 \end{vmatrix} \Theta_n^{(m)}$$

or

$$\begin{vmatrix} 1 & 0 \\ 0 & z \end{vmatrix} \begin{vmatrix} V_{n-1}^{(m)}(z) & \hat{V}_{n-1}^{(m)}(z) \\ U_{n-1}^{(m)}(z) & \hat{U}_{n-1}^{(m)}(z) \end{vmatrix} = \Theta_n^{(m)}. \tag{6.11}$$

Multiply (6.11) from the right with $[v\ u]^T$. The result in the right-hand side is computed from right to left, i.e. multiply $[v\ u]^T$ successively with $\theta_n^{(m)}$, $\theta_{n-1}^{(m)}$, $\cdots$ until $\theta_1^{(m)}$. This corresponds to a sequence of Moebius transformations so that we get

$$z\frac{u\hat{U}_{n-1}^{(m)}(z)+vU_{n-1}^{(m)}(z)}{u\hat{V}_{n-1}^{(m)}(z)+vV_{n-1}^{(m)}(z)} = \tau_1^{(m)} \circ \tau_2^{(m)} \circ \cdots \circ \tau_n^{(m)}\,(u/v) \tag{6.12}$$

where $\tau_k^{(m)}(\cdot) = zt_k^{(m)}(\cdot)$ and $t_k^{(m)}(\cdot)$ as in (6.4a).

For $u = 0$ and $v \neq 0$, we will obtain the two–point PA $U_{n-1}^{(m)}(z)/V_{n-1}^{(m)}(z)$ and for $v = 0$ and $u \neq 0$, we get after inverting the argument and the result of the transforms, (see property 2.3), $\hat{V}_{n-1}^{(m)}(z)/\hat{U}_{n-1}^{(m)}(z)$. The result is shown in the next theorem. The proof is by simple verification and therefore omitted.

THEOREM 6.3. *For $n \in \mathbb{N}$, $m \in \mathbb{Z}$ and a normal fls $F(z)$, define the polynomials $U_n^{(m)}(z)$ and $V_n^{(m)}(z)$, as well as the corresponding polynomials with a hat as in (4.13) and define the transformations $t_n^{(m)}(\cdot)$ and $\hat{t}_n^{(m)}(\cdot)$ by (6.4) where $\alpha_n^{(m)}$ and $\alpha_n^{(m)}$ are the SS parameters for $F(z)$. Then we have the following results:*
Set $\Sigma_n^{(m)}(z) := L_+(U_n^{(m)}(z)/V_n^{(m)}(z))$. Then

$$z\Sigma_n^{(m)}(z) = \tau_1^{(m)} \circ \tau_2^{(m)} \circ \cdots \circ \tau_{n+1}^{(m)}(0) \tag{6.13a}$$

with $\tau_k^{(m)}(w) := z(w-\alpha_k^{(m)})/(1-\hat{\alpha}_k^{(m)}w) = zt_k^{(m)}(w)$.

Set $\hat{\Sigma}_n^{(m)}(z) := L_-(\hat{V}_n^{(m)}(z)/\hat{U}_n^{(m)}(z))$. Then

$$z^{-1}\hat{\Sigma}_n^{(m)}(z) = \hat{\tau}_1^{(m)} \circ \hat{\tau}_2^{(m)} \circ \cdots \circ \hat{\tau}_{n+1}^{(m)}(0) \tag{6.13b}$$

with $\hat{\tau}_k^{(m)}(w) := z^{-1}(w-\hat{\alpha}_k^{(m)})/(1-\alpha_k^{(m)}w) = z^{-1}\hat{t}_k^{(m)}(w)$.

$\square$

It directly follows that we can derive from this theorem and (4.13), expressions for the other two–point PAs $A_n^{(m)}(z)/Q_n^{(m)}(z)$ and $\hat{A}_n^{(m)}(z)/\hat{Q}_n^{(m)}(z)$ that were obtained in chapter 4 (see theorem 4.6). This leads to the next results :

COROLLARY 6.4. *Under the conditions of theorem 4.6, define*

$$\Omega_{n+1}^{(m)}(z) := A_{n+1}^{(m)}/Q_{n+1}^{(m)}(z) \text{ and } \hat{\Omega}_{n+1}^{(m)}(z) := \hat{A}_{n+1}^{(m)}(z)/\hat{Q}_{n+1}^{(m)}(z) .$$

Then

$$\Omega_{n+1}^{(m)}(z) = \tau_0^{(m)}(z\Sigma_n^{(m)}(z)) = \tau_0^{(m)} \circ \tau_1^{(m)} \circ \cdots \circ \tau_{n+1}^{(m)}(0)$$

and

$$\hat{\Omega}_{n+1}^{(m)}(z) = \hat{\tau}_0^{(m)}(z^{-1}\hat{\Sigma}_n^{(m)}(z)) = \hat{\tau}_0^{(m)} \circ \hat{\tau}_1^{(m)} \circ \cdots \circ \hat{\tau}_{n+1}^{(m)}(0)$$

where $\tau_0^{(m)}(w) := (f_m')^{-1}(1-w)/(1+w)$, $\hat{\tau}_0^{(m)} := f_m'(w-1)/(w+1)$ *and the other transformations* $\tau_k^{(m)}$ *and* $\hat{\tau}_k^{(m)}$ *are given by* (6.13).

PROOF. To prove the first relation, we only have to verify that $\tau_0^{(m)}(z\Sigma_n^{(m)}(z)) = \Omega_{n+1}^{(m)}(z)$. Now,

$$\tau_0^{(m)}(z\Sigma_n^{(m)}(z)) = (f_m')^{-1} \frac{1 - zL_+(U_n^{(m)}(z)/V_n^{(m)}(z))}{1 + zL_+(U_n^{(m)}(z)/V_n^{(m)}(z))}$$

$$= (f_m')^{-1} L_+ \left| \frac{V_n^{(m)}(z) - zU_n^{(m)}(z)}{V_n^{(m)}(z) + zU_n^{(m)}(z)} \right| . \tag{6.14}$$

It follows from (4.13) that

$$A_{n+1}^{(m)}(z) = V_n^{(m)}(z) - zU_n^{(m)}(z)$$

and

$$Q_{n+1}^{(m)}(z) = f_m' (V_n^{(m)}(z) + zU_n^{(m)}(z)) .$$

Plug this into (6.14) and you get the result.
The second relation is to be shown similarly.

$\square$

Note that in theorem 6.3 and its corollary the operations in the right hand side of expression (6.12), are built up from right to left. Starting from a constant, numerator and denominator polynomials of increasing degree are generated. It is only after application of the final transformation $\tau_1^{(m)}(\cdot)$ that we get some U and V polynomials that we are already familiar with. In the sequel, the intermediate polynomials will also be of some importance. Therefore we shall reserve a special notation for them. Of course, each of these polynomials will depend on the starting point n. This justifies the notation we used in the following definition of these polynomials.

$$\begin{vmatrix} V_{k,n}^{(m)}(z) & \hat{V}_{k,n}^{(m)}(z) \\ zU_{k,n}^{(m)}(z) & z\hat{U}_{k,n}^{(m)}(z) \end{vmatrix} := \theta_{k+1}^{(m)}\theta_{k+2}^{(m)} \cdots \theta_{n+1}^{(m)}, \tag{6.15}$$

where $k = 0,1,...,n$. Clearly, each polynomial in the left-hand side matrix has to be of degree at most $n-k$. Note also that e.g. $V_{0,n}^{(m)}(z) \equiv V_n^{(m)}(z)$ with $V_n^{(m)}(z)$ as before and similar relations hold for the other polynomials.

They can be used to give another inverse for algorithm 1. This algorithm inverse 1b, given in fig. 6.5, computes the SS parameters $\alpha_k^{(m)}$ and $\hat{\alpha}_k^{(m)}$ from the series $\Sigma_n^{(m)}(z)$ and $\hat{\Sigma}_n^{(m)}(z)$, defined in theorem 6.3. This is shown in the next theorem.

$$\Pi_{0,n}^{(m)}(z) = \Sigma_n^{(m)}(z) \quad ; \quad \hat{\Pi}_{0,n}^{(m)}(z) = \hat{\Sigma}_n^{(m)}(z)$$

for $k = 0,1,...,n$

$$\alpha_{k+1}^{(m)} = -\Pi_{k,n}^{(m)}(0) \quad ; \quad \hat{\alpha}_{k+1}^{(m)} = -\hat{\Pi}_{k,n}^{(m)}(\infty)$$

$$z\Pi_{k+1,n}^{(m)}(z) = \tau_{k+1}^{(m)-1}(z\Pi_{k,n}^{(m)}(z)) = t_{k+1}^{(m)-1}(\Pi_{k,n}^{(m)}(z))$$

$$z^{-1}\hat{\Pi}_{k+1,n}^{(m)}(z) = \hat{\tau}_{k+1}^{(m)-1}(z^{-1}\hat{\Pi}_{k,n}^{(m)}(z)) = \hat{t}_{k+1}^{(m)-1}(\hat{\Pi}_{k,n}^{(m)}(z)).$$

Figure 6.5: Algorithm inverse 1b

THEOREM 6.5. *Let $\alpha_n^{(m)}$ and $\hat{\alpha}_n^{(m)}$ be the SS parameters for the normal fls $F(z)$ and let $\theta_n^{(m)}$ be as in (6.1). Define for given $n \in \mathbb{N}$ and $m \in \mathbb{Z}$ and for $k = 0,1,...,n$ the series*

$$\Pi_{k,n}^{(m)}(z) := L_+(U_{k,n}^{(m)}(z)/V_{k,n}^{(m)}(z)) \tag{6.16a}$$

and

$$\hat{\Pi}_{k,n}^{(m)}(z) := L_-(\hat{V}_{k,n}^{(m)}(z)/\hat{U}_{k,n}^{(m)}(z)) \tag{6.16b}$$

where the polynomials $U_{k,n}^{(m)}(z)$, $V_{k,n}^{(m)}(z)$, $\hat{U}_{k,n}^{(m)}(z)$ and $\hat{V}_{k,n}^{(m)}(z)$ are given by (6.15). The series $\Pi_{k,n}^{(m)}(z)$ and $\hat{\Pi}_{k,n}^{(m)}(z)$ can be found from $\Sigma_n^{(m)}(z)$ and $\hat{\Sigma}_n^{(m)}(z)$ (defined in theorem 6.3) by algorithm inverse 1b which is given in fig. 6.5. In the algorithm, $\tau_k^{(m)}(\cdot)$, $\hat{\tau}_k^{(m)}(\cdot)$, $t_k^{(m)}(\cdot)$ and $\hat{t}_k^{(m)}(\cdot)$ are the Moebius transforms defined in theorem 6.3.

PROOF. From the definition of $\Sigma_n^{(m)}(z)$ and $\Pi_{k,n}^{(m)}(z)$, it is clear that $\Pi_{0,n}^{(m)}(z) = \Sigma_n^{(m)}(z)$. (6.15) gives :

$$\begin{vmatrix} V_{k,n}^{(m)}(z) \\ U_{k,n}^{(m)}(z) \end{vmatrix} = \begin{vmatrix} 1 & 0 \\ 0 & z^{-1} \end{vmatrix} \theta_{k+1}^{(m)} \cdots \theta_{n+1}^{(m)} \begin{vmatrix} 1 \\ 0 \end{vmatrix}.$$

If we put $z = 0$ and work out, we get :

$$[V_{k,n}^{(m)}(0) \ \ U_{k,n}^{(m)}(0)]^T = [1 \ \ -\alpha_{k+1}^{(m)}]^T,$$

hence $\Pi_{k,n}^{(m)}(0) = -\alpha_{k+1}^{(m)}$.

From (6.15) we can also get :

$$\begin{vmatrix} z^{n-k} \hat{V}_{k,n}^{(m)}(z^{-1}) \\ z^{n-k} \hat{U}_{k,n}^{(m)}(z^{-1}) \end{vmatrix} = \begin{vmatrix} z^{-1} & 0 \\ 0 & 1 \end{vmatrix} \theta_{k+1}^{(m)*} \cdots \theta_{n+1}^{(m)*} \begin{vmatrix} 0 \\ 1 \end{vmatrix}$$

with $\theta_l^{(m)*} := \begin{vmatrix} z & -\hat{\alpha}_l^{(m)} z \\ -\alpha_l^{(m)} & 1 \end{vmatrix}$.

For $z = 0$ we get the highest degree coefficients of $\hat{V}_{k,n}^{(m)}(z)$ and $\hat{U}_{k,n}^{(m)}(z)$. They are $-\hat{\alpha}_{k+1}^{(m)}$ and 1 respectively, so that $\hat{\Pi}_{k,n}^{(m)}(\infty) = -\hat{\alpha}_{k+1}^{(m)}$.

Since

$$\begin{vmatrix} V_{k,n}^{(m)}(z) \\ zU_{k,n}^{(m)}(z) \end{vmatrix} = \theta_{k+1}^{(m)} \begin{vmatrix} V_{k+1,n}^{(m)}(z) \\ zU_{k+1,n}^{(m)}(z) \end{vmatrix},$$

or

$$\begin{vmatrix} V_{k,n}^{(m)}(z) = V_{k+1,n}^{(m)}(z) - z\hat{\alpha}_{k+1}^{(m)} U_{k+1,n}^{(m)}(z) \\ U_{k,n}^{(m)}(z) = -\alpha_{k+1}^{(m)} V_{k+1,n}^{(m)}(z) + zU_{k+1,n}^{(m)}(z) \end{vmatrix}$$

we get :

$$\Pi_{k,n}^{(m)}(z) = \frac{z\Pi_{k+1,n}^{(m)}(z) - \alpha_{k+1}^{(m)}}{1 - z\hat{\alpha}_{k+1}^{(m)} \Pi_{k+1,n}^{(m)}(z)} = z^{-1} \tau_{k+1}^{(m)}(z\Pi_{k+1,n}^{(m)}(z)).$$

Inverting this relation gives the first of the recurrence relations in algorithm inverse 1b.

The other one is similarly obtained.

$\square$

Note that algorithm inverse 1b ends after n steps because $\Pi_{k,n}^{(m)} = \hat{\Pi}_{k,n}^{(m)} = 0$ for $k > n$.

The algorithms of this chapter are illustrated for an example in chapter 18.

Chapter 7

Rhombus algorithms

After introducing algorithms of type 1 and 2 in chapter 3, we now give a third class of algorithms that are of rhombus type. This type of algorithm was first introduced by Rutishauser [RUT] and called the qd algorithm. We shall also give the variant of it which is in a sense more natural. It was introduced by Gragg [GR2] and called $\pi\zeta$ algorithm. A third type of rhombus algorithm which we shall consider was given by McCabe [MC1] (see also [JOT]). We shall call it the FG algorithm because of the notation used by Jones and his coworkers. The qd and $\pi\zeta$ algorithms are in a sense dual algorithms. This duality is the same duality as we have used for the quantities with and without a hat. To make this duality explicit, we shall not use the qd or $\pi\zeta$ notation, but use the notation ab and $\hat{ab}$ instead. Also the indexing of these numbers will be more adapted to our previous approach where the algorithms progressed along horizontal lines in a Padé table. At the end of this chapter we shall give explicit correspondences between our notation and the original notation for these algorithms. With these ab, $\hat{ab}$, FG and $\hat{FG}$ numbers, it will be possible to give a lot of recurrence relations between three neighbouring elements in a Padé table. These relations will also be given for further reference.

7.1 The ab parameters (sawtooth path)

It was shown in theorem 4.1 that $P_n^{(m)}(z)/Q_n^{(m)}(z)$ is the (m/n) PA and $\hat{P}_n^{(m)}(z)/\hat{Q}_n^{(m)}(z)$ is the $(m-1/n)$ PA for $F(z)$. By the algorithms of chapter 3, these approximants were computed for m fixed and for $n = 0,1,2,....$ Hence we traverse two adjacent rows in the Padé table of $F(z)$. Recall that these approximants have a different normalization. Indeed, in (3.1) we have chosen $q_{0,n}^{(m)} = 1$ and $\hat{q}_{n,n}^{(m)} = 1$. Therefore $Q_n^{(m)}(z)$ was of the form $Q_n^{(m)}(z) = 1 + \cdots + (-\alpha_n^{(m)})z^n$ and $\hat{Q}_n^{(m)}(z)$ had the form $\hat{Q}_n^{(m)}(z) = (-\hat{\alpha}_n^{(m)}) + \cdots + z^n$. So, $P_n^{(m-1)}(z)/Q_n^{(m-1)}(z)$ and $\hat{P}_n^{(m)}(z)/\hat{Q}_n^{(m)}(z)$ are both $(m-1/n)$ PAs for $F(z)$, their only difference being their normalization. This shows that $P_n^{(m-1)}(z) = -\hat{P}_n^{(m)}(z)/\hat{\alpha}_n^{(m)}$ and $Q_n^{(m-1)}(z) = -\hat{Q}_n^{(m)}(z)/\hat{\alpha}_n^{(m)}$ and conversely, $\hat{P}_n^{(m)}(z) = -P_n^{(m-1)}(z)/\alpha_n^{(m-1)}$ and $\hat{Q}_n^{(m)}(z) = -Q_n^{(m-1)}(z)/\alpha_n^{(m-1)}$. Similar relations will be valid for the residuals $R_n^{(m-1)}(z)$ and $\hat{R}_n^{(m)}(z)$ and after a look at the definitions (4.7) for the Laurent polynomials $B(p)_n^{(m-1)}(z)$ and $\hat{B}(p)_n^{(m)}(z)$ these relations will also hold for these. Note however that these relations don't work for the polynomials $A_n^{(m)}(z)$ (see definition (4.3)) and for the derived polynomials $U_n^{(m)}(z)$ and $V_n^{(m)}(z)$. If we divide e.g. the right hand side of (4.3b) by $-\hat{\alpha}_n^{(m)}$ then we do get $\hat{Z}^{(m)}(z)Q_n^{(m-1)}(z) + P_n^{(m-1)}(z)$ but this is not the definition of $z^{m-1}A_n^{(m-1)}(z)$. The problem being that $\hat{Z}^{(m)}(z)$ depends on m. For the Laurent polynomials $B(p)_n^{(m)}(z)$, this $\hat{Z}^{(m)}(z)$ has to be replaced by $\hat{Z}^{(p)}(z)$, so that the previous relations do work again. We can resume this by writing that

$$S_n^{(m-1)}(z) = -\hat{S}_n^{(m)}(z)/\hat{\alpha}_n^{(m)}, \tag{7.1a}$$
$$\hat{S}_n^{(m)}(z) = -S_n^{(m-1)}/\alpha_n^{(m-1)}, \tag{7.1b}$$

if $S = P,Q,R$ or $B(p)$ but not A,U or V. For $n = 0$ we set $\alpha_0^{(m)} = \hat{\alpha}_0^{(m)} = -1$ by definition. Thus (3.6) becomes

$$[S_{n+1}^{(m)}(z)\ S_{n+1}^{(m-1)}(z)] = [S_n^{(m)}(z)\ S_n^{(m-1)}(z)]\begin{vmatrix} 1 & 1 \\ z\alpha_{n+1}^{(m)}\hat{\alpha}_n^{(m)} & z\hat{\alpha}_n^{(m)}/\hat{\alpha}_{n+1}^{(m)} \end{vmatrix}; \tag{7.2}$$

as long as S is one of P,Q,R or $B(p)$.

The CF (5.1) was derived from the recurrence (3.6). The corresponding CF associated with (7.2) can be obtained by property 2.9. It takes the form of (7.3) (N is $P,B(p)$ or $-R$) which is equivalent with (5.1) in the sense of property 2.7.

$$N_0^{(m)}(z) + \cfrac{-f_m z^m}{1} + \cfrac{1}{\alpha_1^{(m)}\hat{\alpha}_0^{(m)}z} + \cfrac{z(1-\alpha_1^{(m)}\hat{\alpha}_1^{(m)})\hat{\alpha}_0^{(m)}/\hat{\alpha}_1^{(m)}}{1} + \cdots$$

$$\cdots + \cfrac{1}{\alpha_n^{(m)}\hat{\alpha}_{n-1}^{(m)}z} + \cfrac{z(1-\alpha_n^{(m)}\hat{\alpha}_n^{(m)})\hat{\alpha}_{n-1}^{(m)}/\hat{\alpha}_n^{(m)}}{1} + \cdots. \tag{7.3}$$

The convergents of this CF are of course

$$(N_0^{(m)}(z)/Q_0^{(m)}(z)),(N_0^{(m-1)}(z)/Q_0^{(m-1)}(z)),(N_1^{(m)}(z)/Q_1^{(m)}(z)),$$
$$(N_1^{(m-1)}(z)/Q_1^{(m-1)}(z)),\dots.$$

As you can see, the even convergents of this CF are on row m of the Padé table while the odd convergents are on row $m-1$. Tracing the positions of the successive convergents in the Padé table, you will get a sawtooth path oscillating between row $m-1$ and row m. Thus the odd convergents of (7.3) and the even convergents of the CF which is obtained by replacing m by $m-1$ in (7.3) will be the same. I.e. the successive elements of row $m-1$ in the Padé table. Our rhombus relations will be obtained by making this identification explicit.

To start, use property 2.8 to obtain the odd part of (7.3)

$$N_0^{(m-1)}(z) + \frac{f_m z^m}{\left| 1 + (a_2^{(m)} - b_1^{(m)})z \right.} + \sum_{k \geqslant 2} \frac{-a_k^{(m)} z}{\left| 1 + (a_{k+1}^{(m)} - b_k^{(m)})z \right.} \tag{7.4}$$

where we used the abbreviations

$$a_{n+1}^{(m)} = (1 - \alpha_n^{(m)} \hat{\alpha}_n^{(m)}) \hat{\alpha}_{n-1}^{(m)} / \hat{\alpha}_n^{(m)} \tag{7.5a}$$

and

$$b_n^{(m)} = -\alpha_n^{(m)} \hat{\alpha}_{n-1}^{(m)}. \tag{7.5b}$$

The convergents of (7.4) are $(N_k^{(m-1)}(z)/Q_k^{(m-1)}(z))$, $k = 0,1,2,\dots$.

Replace in (7.3) m by $m-1$ and take the even part of it (see property 2.8). This gives a CF of the form

$$N_0^{(m-1)}(z) + \frac{f_{m-1} z^m b_1^{(m-1)}}{\left| 1 - b_1^{(m-1)} z \right.} + \sum_{k \geqslant 2} \frac{-(b_{k-1}^{(m-1)})^{-1} a_k^{(m-1)} b_k^{(m-1)} z}{\left| 1 + (-b_k^{(m-1)} + (b_{k-1}^{(m)})^{-1} b_k^{(m-1)} a_k^{(m-1)})z \right.}. \tag{7.6}$$

This CF has the same convergents as (7.4) with the same normalisation. Therefore we can equate term by term so that

$$b_1^{(m-1)} = f_m / f_{m-1} \tag{7.7a}$$

$$a_1^{(m)} = 0 \tag{7.7b}$$

$$a_k^{(m)} b_{k-1}^{(m-1)} = a_k^{(m-1)} b_k^{(m-1)} \quad , \quad k \geqslant 2 \tag{7.7c}$$

$$a_{k+1}^{(m)} + b_k^{(m-1)} = a_k^{(m)} + b_k^{(m)} \quad , \quad k \geqslant 1 \tag{7.7d}$$

The relations in (7.7) give an algorithm to construct the table in fig. 7.1 column by column. The algorithm is called algorithm 3a and it is given in fig. 7.2.

Just like the SS parameters $\alpha_k^{(m)}$ and $\hat{\alpha}_k^{(m)}$ could be used to construct the polynomials $Q_n^{(m)}(z)$, we can now use the $a_k^{(m)}$ and $b_k^{(m)}$ for the same objective. If desired we can also reconstruct the $\alpha_n^{(m)}$ and $\hat{\alpha}_n^{(m)}$ from them by

$$\hat{\alpha}_0^{(m)} = -1 \tag{7.8a}$$

and for $n = 1,2,\dots$

$$\alpha_n^{(m)} = -b_n^{(m)} / \hat{\alpha}_{n-1}^{(m)} \tag{7.8b}$$

$$\hat{\alpha}_n^{(m)} = \hat{\alpha}_{n-1}^{(m)} / (a_{n+1}^{(m)} - b_n^{(m)}) = 1 / \alpha_n^{(m-1)}. \tag{7.8c}$$

The last of these equalities follows e.g. from (7.1b) if you take $s = Q$ and $z = 0$. For further reference, we shall call the numbers $a_n^{(m)}, b_n^{(m)}$ as they were here defined for a normal fls $F(z)$, the *ab parameters* of this fls. Thus we have proved the following theorem :

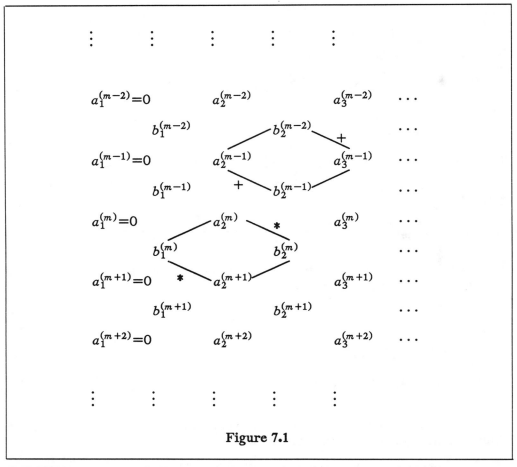

Figure 7.1

THEOREM 7.1. *Let $F(z) = \sum f_k z^k$ be a normal fls. Then its ab parameters satisfy the following rhombus rules :*

$$a_k^{(m)} b_{k-1}^{(m-1)} = a_k^{(m-1)} b_k^{(m-1)} \quad , \; k \geqslant 2$$

$$a_{k+1}^{(m)} + b_k^{(m-1)} = a_k^{(m)} + b_k^{(m)} \quad , \; k \geqslant 1.$$

The initial conditions are :

$$b_1^{(m-1)} = f_m / f_{m-1}$$

$$a_1^{(m)} = 0$$

where $m \in \mathbb{Z}$.

$\square$

---

for $m=0,\pm1,\pm2,\dots$

$$a_1^{(m)} = 0$$

$$b_1^{(m)} = f_{m+1}/f_m$$

for $n=1,2,\dots$

for $m=0,\pm1,\pm2,\dots$

$$a_{n+1}^{(m)} = a_n^{(m)} + b_n^{(m)} - b_n^{(m-1)}$$

for $m=0,\pm1,\pm2,\dots$

$$b_{n+1}^{(m)} = a_{n+1}^{(m+1)} b_n^{(m)} (a_{n+1}^{(m)})^{-1}$$

Figure 7.2: Algorithm 3a

The CF (7.3) gives us some recurrences for its successive convergents and others will be derived from it. Depending on n being odd or even, the forward recursion of the CF (7.3) corresponds to (see (2.15))

$$[S_{n-1}^{(m-1)}(z)\ S_n^{(m)}(z)] = [S_{n-1}^{(m)}(z)\ S_{n-1}^{(m-1)}(z)] \begin{vmatrix} 0 & 1 \\ 1 & -b_n^{(m)}z \end{vmatrix} \tag{7.9a}$$

or

$$[S_n^{(m)}(z)\ S_n^{(m-1)}(z)] = [S_{n-1}^{(m-1)}(z)\ S_n^{(m)}(z)] \begin{vmatrix} 0 & a_{n+1}^{(m)}z \\ 1 & 1 \end{vmatrix} \tag{7.9b}$$

where S is P,Q,R or $B(p)$.

The ladder graph in fig. 2.8 which corresponds to such a situation becomes in this case like in fig. 7.3. Using the relations of (7.9) or equivalently by taking a subgraph of fig. 7.3 we get a number of relations between neighbouring elements.

THEOREM 7.2. *Let $F(z)$ be a normal fls and $\{\alpha_n^{(m)}, \hat{\alpha}_n^{(m)}\}$ its SS parameters and $\{a_n^{(m)}, b_n^{(m)}\}$ its ab parameters. With S one of P,Q,R or $B(p)$ as generated by (6.3), we have the following recurrence relations :*

$$S_n^{(m-1)}(z) = S_n^{(m)}(z) + za_{n+1}^{(m)} S_{n-1}^{(m-1)}(z), \tag{7.10a}$$

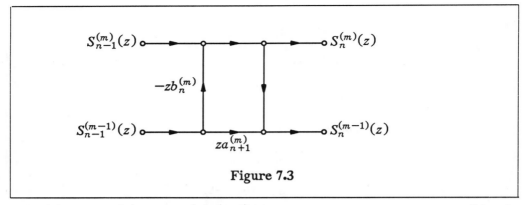

Figure 7.3

$$S_n^{(m)}(z) = S_{n-1}^{(m)}(z) - zb_n^{(m)}S_{n-1}^{(m-1)}(z), \tag{7.10b}$$

$$S_n^{(m-1)}(z) = S_n^{(m)}(z) + zG_n^{(m)}S_{n-1}^{(m-1)}(z) \quad ; \quad G_n^{(m)} = a_{n+1}^{(m)} - b_n^{(m)}, \tag{7.10c}$$

$$S_n^{(m)}(z) = \alpha_n^{(m)}\hat{\alpha}_n^{(m)}S_n^{(m-1)}(z) + (1 - \alpha_n^{(m)}\hat{\alpha}_n^{(m)})S_{n-1}^{(m)}(z), \tag{7.10d}$$

$$S_n^{(m+1)}(z) = (1 - zG_{n+1}^{(m+1)})S_n^{(m)}(z) - zb_{n+1}^{(m)}S_n^{(m-1)}(z) \tag{7.10e}$$

for all values of the indices that make sense.

PROOF. (7.10a,b) are very simple to verify from (7.9).
(7.10c) is obtained by eliminating $S_n^{(m)}(z)$ between (7.10a) and (7.10b).
For (7.10d) eliminate $S_{n-1}^{(m-1)}(z)$ from (7.10a) and (7.10b) to obtain

$$S_n^{(m-1)}(z) = (1 - a_{n+1}^{(m)}/b_n^{(m)})S_n^{(m)}(z) + S_{n-1}^{(m)}(z)a_{n+1}^{(m)}/b_n^{(m)}. \tag{7.11}$$

Use the definitions (7.5) of $a_{n+1}^{(m)}$ and $b_n^{(m)}$ to get

$$a_{n+1}^{(m)}/b_n^{(m)} = -(1 - \alpha_n^{(m)}\hat{\alpha}_n^{(m)})/(\alpha_n^{(m)}\hat{\alpha}_n^{(m)}). \tag{7.12}$$

(7.12) plugged into (7.11) gives (7.10d).
To prove (7.10e) take (7.10b) and rewrite (7.10c) for m replaced by $m+1$.
Eliminate $S_n^{(m)}(z)$ between these and you will obtain (7.10e) with n replaced by $n-1$.

$\square$

Relations (7.10b,c) are represented by figures 7.4. Linking these together we find figures 7.5a and b. The node value for node (j,k) is $S_k^{(j)}(z)$.

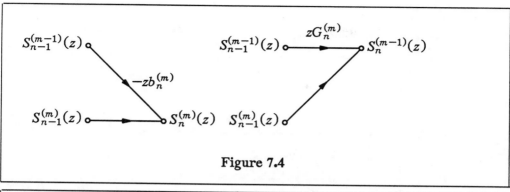

Figure 7.4

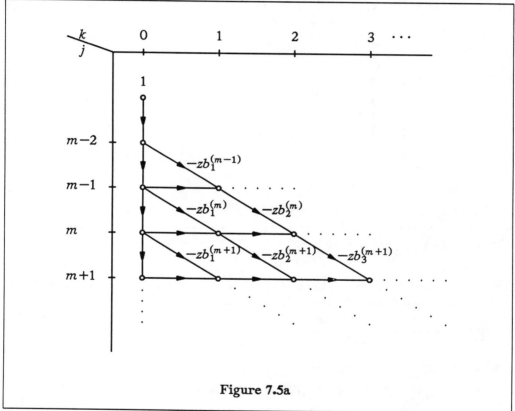

Figure 7.5a

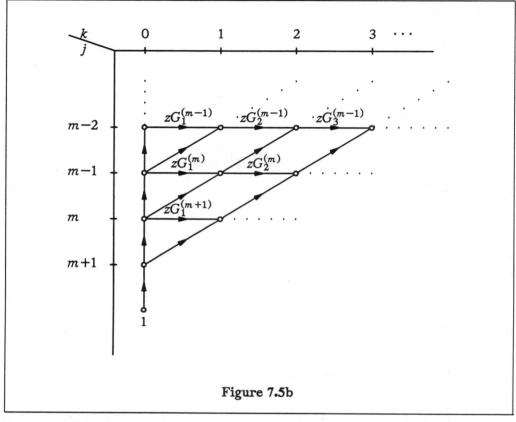

Figure 7.5b

7.2 The FG parameters (row path)

Recall that we had the sawtooth CF (7.3) and its contracted form (7.4) which describes a row. We rewrite it in the form

$$N_0^{(m-1)}(z) + \cfrac{f_m z^m}{\lfloor 1 + z G_1^{(m)}} + \sum_{k \geqslant 2} \cfrac{F_k^{(m)} z}{\lfloor 1 + z G_k^{(m)}} \quad (7.13)$$

where we used the abbreviations

$$G_k^{(m)} := a_{k+1}^{(m)} - b_k^{(m)} = \hat{\alpha}_{k-1}^{(m)} / \hat{\alpha}_k^{(m)} = \hat{\alpha}_{k-1}^{(m)} \alpha_k^{(m-1)} \quad (7.14a)$$

and

$$F_k^{(m)} := -a_k^{(m)} , \quad k \geqslant 1. \quad (7.14b)$$

These numbers form yet another set of parameters associated with $F(z)$. We shall call them the *FG parameters*. It is remarkable that the *FG* numbers also satisfy some rhombus rules that are quite similar to those of the *ab* numbers.

These are given in the next theorem.

THEOREM 7.3. *If $F(z) = \sum f_k z^k$ is a normal fls, then its FG numbers will satisfy the following rhombus rules for $k = 1, 2, \dots$ and $m \in \mathbb{Z}$*

$$F_{k+1}^{(m)} + G_k^{(m)} = F_k^{(m+1)} + G_k^{(m+1)} \tag{7.15a}$$

$$F_{k+1}^{(m)} G_{k+1}^{(m+1)} = F_{k+1}^{(m+1)} G_k^{(m)}. \tag{7.15b}$$

The initial conditions are

$$F_1^{(m)} = 0 \quad , \quad G_1^{(m)} = -f_m / f_{m-1} \tag{7.15c}$$

for all $m \in \mathbb{Z}$.

PROOF. Using the definitions (7.14) of the *FG* parameters, we get

$$F_{k+1}^{(m)} + G_k^{(m)} = -b_k^{(m)}$$

while similarly

$$F_k^{(m+1)} + G_k^{(m+1)} = a_{k+1}^{(m+1)} - a_k^{(m+1)} - b_k^{(m+1)}.$$

Because of the rhombus rule for the *ab* parameters, these expressions are the same, so that we get (7.15a).
In the same way we get

$$F_{k+1}^{(m)} G_{k+1}^{(m+1)} = a_{k+1}^{(m)} b_{k+1}^{(m+1)} - a_{k+1}^{(m)} a_{k+2}^{(m+1)}.$$

Replace $b_{k+1}^{(m+1)}$ by an expression we get from (7.7d) :

$$b_{k+1}^{(m+1)} = a_{k+2}^{(m+1)} + b_{k+1}^{(m)} - a_{k+1}^{(m+1)}$$

so that

$$F_{k+1}^{(m)} G_{k+1}^{(m+1)} = a_{k+1}^{(m)} b_{k+1}^{(m)} - a_{k+1}^{(m)} a_{k+1}^{(m+1)}.$$

Now by (7.7c) this may be replaced by

$$F_{k+1}^{(m)} G_{k+1}^{(m+1)} = a_{k+1}^{(m+1)} b_k^{(m)} - a_{k+1}^{(m)} a_{k+1}^{(m+1)}$$

where the right hand side is exactly $F_{k+1}^{(m+1)} G_k^{(m)}$.

□

For further study of the rhombus rules for *FG* parameters consult [MC2].

7.3 A staircase path

The *ab* table of fig. 7.1 also contains information about other CFs. We have derived (7.10a,b) from CF (7.3), but it is possible to go in the other direction and derive from the relations (7.10) some CFs. We give an example of a staircase path. From (7.10a,b) :

$$S_{k+1}^{(m)}(z) = S_k^{(m)}(z) - b_{k+1}^{(m)} z \, S_k^{(m-1)}(z)$$

$$S_k^{(m+1)}(z) = S_k^{(m)}(z) - a_{k+1}^{(m+1)} z \, S_{k-1}^{(m)}(z)$$

with S one of Q,P,R or $B(p)$. Consequently the convergents of

$$N_0^{(m)}(z) + \cfrac{f_{m+1} z^{m+1}}{1} - \cfrac{b_1^{(m+1)} z}{1} - \cfrac{a_2^{(m+2)} z}{1} - \cfrac{b_2^{(m+2)} z}{1} - \cdots \quad (7.16)$$

are

$$(N_0^{(m)}(z)/Q_0^{(m)}(z)),(N_0^{(m+1)}(z)/Q_0^{(m+1)}(z)),(N_1^{(m+1)}(z)/Q_1^{(m+1)}(z)),$$

$$(N_1^{(m+2)}(z)/Q_1^{(m+2)}(z)),...$$

with N one of $P,B(p)$ or $-R$. I.e. the elements on a descending staircase of an (m,n) table. The recursion can be represented by the graph of fig. 7.6 which shows the staircase structure clearly.

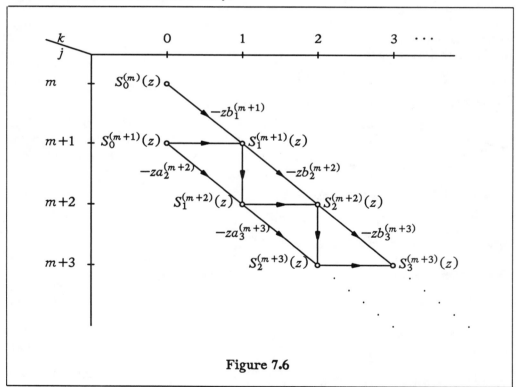

Figure 7.6

At node $(m+k,k)$ you find $S_k^{(m+k)}(z)$ and at node $(m+k+1,k)$ you find $S_k^{(m+k+1)}(z)$.

It turned out that the rhombus algorithm 3a didn't compute the SS parameters directly, but generated the *ab* parameters instead. It is however possible to generate these *ab* numbers by some algorithms that are of type 1 or type 2 like the algorithms of chapter 3. These correspond to classical algorithms for the generation of Padé approximants. These algorithms will not progress along two rows like algorithm 1 and algorithm 2, but their computations go along a staircase like the one of fig. 7.6. Therefore, the *ab* numbers are generated in the order $b_k^{(m+k)}$, $a_k^{(m+k)}$, $k = 0,1,...$ with m fixed. These algorithms are obtained as follows :

Using definition (3.2) of the SS parameters, i.e. $\alpha_{n+1}^{(m)} = u_n^{(m)}/v_n^{(m)}$ and $\hat{\alpha}_{n+1}^{(m)} = \hat{u}_n^{(m)}/\hat{v}_n^{(m)}$, and filling this into definition (7.5) of the *ab* numbers, you will find after some algebra that

$$a_{n+1}^{(m)} = u_n^{(m-1)}/u_{n-1}^{(m-1)} \quad \text{and} \quad b_{n+1}^{(m)} = u_n^{(m)}/u_n^{(m-1)}.$$

(This will also follow from theorem 9.2).

Now, there are two ways of computing these $u_n^{(m)}$ which will correspond to type 1 and type 2 algorithms. The first way is by an inner product $u_n^{(m)} = [f_{m+n+1} \cdots f_{m+1}]Q_n^{(m)}$ like in (3.2a). Therefore, you need the polynomials $Q_n^{(m)}(z)$ which can be generated by a scheme as represented by fig. 7.6 with $S = Q$. The polynomials $Q_n^{(m)}(z)$ are generated along a staircase, so they show up in the order $Q_0^{(m)}(z)$, $Q_0^{(m+1)}(z)$, $Q_1^{(m+1)}(z)$, $Q_1^{(m+2)}(z)$, $Q_2^{(m+2)}(z),...$. This gives us algorithm 4 of fig. 7.7.

To get a type 2 algorithm, we observe that $u_n^{(m)}$ is the first nonzero coefficient of in $R_n^{(m)}(z)$ (see (3.5)). So, in this type of algorithm, we should generate the residuals $R_n^{(m)}(z)$. These can again be obtained by a scheme like the one represented by fig. 7.6, but now with $S = R$. The corresponding type 2 algorithm is called algorithm 5 and is given in fig. 7.8.

7.4 $\rho\sigma$ paramaters (diagonal path)

In analogy with the sawtooth-to-row contraction we can also consider a staircase-to-diagonal contraction. Using property 2.8, we get the even part of (7.16) which is the diagonal CF

$$N_0^{(m)}(z) + \cfrac{f_{m+1}z^{m+1}}{1-z\sigma_1^{(m+1)}} + \sum_{k\geq2} \cfrac{-\rho_k^{(m+k-1)}z^2}{1-z\sigma_k^{(m+k)}} \tag{7.17}$$

where we used the abbreviations σ and ρ for the values of (7.7). I.e.

$$S_{-1} = S_0 = 1$$

$$u_{-1} = f_{m+1}$$

for $n = 0,1,2,...$

$$u_n = \Pi_{0:0}(z^{-m-n-2} F(z) S_n(z))$$

$$\{u_{2k} := u_k^{(m+k+1)} \text{ and } u_{2k+1} := u_{k+1}^{(m+k+1)}\}$$

$$c_n = u_n / u_{n-1}$$

$$\{c_{2k} := b_{k+1}^{(m+k+1)} \text{ and } c_{2k+1} := a_{k+2}^{(m+k+2)}\}$$

$$S_{n+1}(z) = S_n(z) - c_n z \, S_{n-1}(z)$$

$$\{S_{2k+1}(z) := Q_{k+1}^{(m+k+1)}(z) \text{ and } S_{2k+2}(z) := Q_{k+1}^{(m+k+2)}(z)\}$$

Figure 7.7: Algorithm 4

$$S_{-1}(z) = \Pi_{m+1:\infty} F(z) \; ; \; S_0(z) = \Pi_{m+2:\infty} F(z)$$

$$u_{-1} = f_{m+1}$$

for $n = 0,1,2,...$

$\{u_k$ and c_k are as in algorithm 4 while

$$S_{2k+1}(z) := R_{k+1}^{(m+k+1)}(z) \text{ and } S_{2k+2}(z) := R_{k+1}^{(m+k+2)}(z)\}$$

$$u_n = \Pi_{0:0} (z^{-m-n-2} S_n(z))$$

$$c_n = u_n / u_{n-1}$$

$$S_{n+1}(z) = S_n(z) - c_n z \, S_{n-1}(z)$$

Figure 7.8: Algorithm 5

$$\rho_k^{(m)} := a_k^{(m)} b_k^{(m)} = a_k^{(m+1)} b_{k-1}^{(m)} \quad , k \geqslant 2 \tag{7.18a}$$

$$\sigma_k^{(m)} := a_k^{(m)} + b_k^{(m)} = a_{k+1}^{(m)} + b_k^{(m-1)} \quad , k \geqslant 1. \tag{7.18b}$$

Note that it follows from (7.7b), (7.8a) and (7.8b) that

$$\sigma_1^{(m)} = b_1^{(m)} = \alpha_1^{(m)}. \tag{7.18c}$$

Although we don't need it for the moment, it will be convenient for later use to define also

$$\rho_1^{(m)} := a_1^{(m)} = 0. \tag{7.18d}$$

We shall refer to the numbers defined in (7.18) as the ρσ *parameters* for $F(z)$. The forward evaluation scheme of the diagonal CF (7.17) and of the row CF (7.13) give us two new recurrences for elements on a row and on a diagonal path respectively. We give them for further reference in theorem 7.4.

THEOREM 7.4. *Let* $F(z)$ *be a normal fls and suppose* $\{F_n^{(m)}, G_n^{(m)}\}$ *are its FG parameters and* $\{\rho_n^{(m)}, \sigma_n^{(m)}\}$ *are its ρσ parameters. Then with S one of P,Q,R or* $B(p)$ *as generated by* (6.3), *we shall have the following recurrence relations for* $n = 1,2,...$ *and* $m \in \mathbb{Z}$:

$$S_{n+1}^{(m-1)}(z) = (1 + G_{n+1}^{(m)} z) S_n^{(m-1)}(z) + F_{n+1}^{(m)} z \, S_{n-1}^{(m-1)}(z) \tag{7.19a}$$

and

$$S_{n+1}^{(m+1)}(z) = (1 - z\sigma_{n+1}^{(m+1)}) S_n^{(m)}(z) - z^2 \, \rho_{n+1}^{(m)} \, S_{n-1}^{(m-1)}(z). \tag{7.19b}$$

PROOF. (7.19) represent the forward recursion for the evaluation of CFs (7.13) and (7.17) respectively.

□

With all these relations between adjacent S elements, it will be clear that many CFs and eventually corresponding algorithms to compute them may be formulated. We shall not pursue this any further for the moment. We just mention that a number of CFs associated with the *ab* table may be found in [MC2].

7.5 Some dual results

To generate the rhombus rules for the *ab* parameters, we have normalized the $\hat{S}_n^{(m)}(z)$ and replaced them by $-S_n^{(m-1)}(z)/\alpha_n^{(m-1)} = -\hat{\alpha}_n^{(m)} S_n^{(m-1)}(z)$, where S was one of Q,P,R or $B(p)$. It is possible to give a completely dual derivation if $S_n^{(m)}(z)$ is eliminated and replaced by

$-\hat{S}_n^{(m+1)}(z)/\hat{\alpha}_n^{(m+1)} = -\alpha_n^{(m)}\hat{S}_n^{(m+1)}$. We shall not give all the details for the derivation of these dual results but give the definitions and theorems for further reference.

The CF which is the dual of the sawtooth CF (7.3) is another sawtooth CF which has the form

$$\hat{N}_0^{(m)}(z) + \cfrac{f_m z^m}{|\,1\,} + \cfrac{z}{|\,-\hat{b}_1^{(m)}\,} + \cfrac{\hat{a}_2^{(m)}}{|\,1\,} + \cfrac{z}{|\,-\hat{b}_2^{(m)}\,} + \cfrac{\hat{a}_3^{(m)}}{|\,1\,} + \cdots .\tag{7.20}$$

It is based on the $\hat{a}\hat{b}$ *parameters* for $F(z)$ defined as

$$\hat{a}_{n+1}^{(m)} := (1-\alpha_n^{(m)}\hat{\alpha}_n^{(m)})\alpha_{n-1}^{(m)}/\alpha_n^{(m)}$$

and

$$\hat{b}_n^{(m)} := -\hat{\alpha}_n^{(m)}\alpha_{n-1}^{(m)}$$

where $\alpha_n^{(m)}$ and $\hat{\alpha}_n^{(m)}$ are the SS parameters for $F(z)$. The convergents of (7.20) are

$$(\hat{N}_0^{(m)}(z)/\hat{Q}_0^{(m)}(z)),(\hat{N}_0^{(m+1)}(z)/\hat{Q}_0^{(m+1)}(z)),(\hat{N}_1^{(m)}(z)/\hat{Q}_1^{(m)}(z)),$$
$$(\hat{N}_1^{(m+1)}(z)/\hat{Q}_1^{(m+1)}(z)),\dots .$$

The rhombus rules for the $\hat{a}\hat{b}$ parameters are given in the next theorem.

THEOREM 7.5. *Let $F(z) = \sum f_k z^k$ be a normal fls. Then its $\hat{a}\hat{b}$ parameters satisfy the following rhombus rules for $m \in \mathbb{Z}$:*

$$\hat{a}_k^{(m)}\hat{b}_{k-1}^{(m+1)} = \hat{a}_k^{(m+1)}\hat{b}_k^{(m+1)} \quad , \; k\geq 2 \tag{7.21a}$$

$$\hat{a}_{k+1}^{(m)} + \hat{b}_k^{(m+1)} = \hat{a}_k^{(m)} + \hat{b}_k^{(m)} \quad , \; k\geq 1, \tag{7.21b}$$

with initial conditions

$$\hat{b}_1^{(m+1)} = f_m/f_{m+1} \quad and \quad \hat{a}_1^{(m)} = 0 \tag{7.21c}$$

for all $m \in \mathbb{Z}$.

$\square$

The table of fig. 7.1 becomes like in fig. 7.9. Algorithm 3a becomes algorithm 3b given in fig. 7.10. The $\hat{\rho}\hat{\sigma}$ *parameters* and the $\hat{F}\hat{G}$ *parameters* are defined by

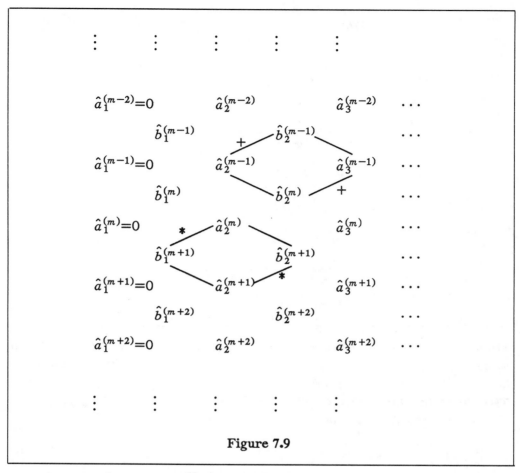

Figure 7.9

$$\hat{\rho}_n^{(m)} := \hat{a}_n^{(m)}\hat{b}_n^{(m)} = \hat{a}_n^{(m-1)}\hat{b}_{n-1}^{(m)} \quad , \quad n \geq 2 \tag{7.22a}$$

$$\hat{\sigma}_n^{(m)} := \hat{a}_n^{(m)} + \hat{b}_n^{(m)} = \hat{a}_{n+1}^{(m)} + \hat{b}_n^{(m+1)} \quad , \quad n \geq 1 \tag{7.22b}$$

$$\hat{\sigma}_1^{(m)} := \hat{b}_1^{(m)} = \hat{\alpha}_1^{(m)} \quad \text{and} \quad \hat{\rho}_1^{(m)} := \hat{a}_1^{(m)} = 0 \tag{7.22c}$$

and

$$\hat{F}_n^{(m)} := -\hat{a}_n^{(m)} \quad , \quad n \geq 1 \tag{7.23a}$$

$$\hat{G}_n^{(m)} := \hat{a}_{n+1}^{(m)} - \hat{b}_n^{(m)} = \alpha_{n-1}^{(m)}\hat{\alpha}_n^{(m+1)} \quad , \quad n \geq 1. \tag{7.23b}$$

The duals of the relations given in theorems 7.2 and 7.4 are summarized in theorem 7.6.

for $m = 0, \pm 1, \pm 2, \ldots$

$$\hat{a}_1^{(m)} = 0$$

$$\hat{b}_1^{(m)} = f_{m-1}/f_m$$

for $n = 1, 2, \ldots$

for $m = 0, \pm 1, \pm 2, \ldots$

$$\hat{a}_{n+1}^{(m)} = \hat{a}_n^{(m)} + \hat{b}_n^{(m)} - \hat{b}_n^{(m+1)}$$

for $m = 0, \pm 1, \pm 2, \ldots$

$$\hat{b}_{n+1}^{(m)} = \hat{a}_{n+1}^{(m-1)} \, \hat{b}_n^{(m)} \, (\hat{a}_{n+1}^{(m)})^{-1}$$

Figure 7.10: Algorithm 3b

THEOREM 7.6. *Let $F(z)$ be a normal fls with SS parameters $\{\alpha_n^{(m)}, \hat{\alpha}_n^{(m)}\}$, with $\hat{a}\hat{b}$ parameters $\{\hat{a}_n^{(m)}, \hat{b}_n^{(m)}\}$, with $\hat{F}\hat{G}$ parameters $\{\hat{F}_n^{(m)}, \hat{G}_n^{(m)}\}$, and with $\hat{\rho}\hat{\sigma}$ parameters $\{\hat{\rho}_n^{(m)}, \hat{\sigma}_n^{(m)}\}$. Then with S one of P, Q, R or $B(p)$ as generated by (6.3), we have the following relations for $n = 1, 2, \ldots$ and $m \in \mathbb{Z}$:*

$$\hat{S}_n^{(m+1)}(z) = \hat{S}_n^{(m)} + \hat{a}_{n+1}^{(m)} \hat{S}_{n-1}^{(m+1)}(z), \tag{7.24a}$$

$$\hat{S}_n^{(m)}(z) = -\hat{b}_n^{(m)} \hat{S}_{n-1}^{(m+1)}(z) + z \hat{S}_{n-1}^{(m)}(z), \tag{7.24b}$$

$$\hat{S}_n^{(m+1)}(z) = \hat{G}_n^{(m)} \hat{S}_{n-1}^{(m+1)}(z) + z \hat{S}_{n-1}^{(m)}(z), \tag{7.24c}$$

$$\hat{S}_n^{(m)}(z) = \alpha_n^{(m)} \hat{\alpha}_n^{(m)} \hat{S}_n^{(m+1)}(z) + z(1 - \alpha_n^{(m)} \hat{\alpha}_n^{(m)}) \hat{S}_{n-1}^{(m)}(z), \tag{7.24d}$$

$$z \hat{S}_n^{(m-1)}(z) = (z - \hat{G}_{n+1}^{(m-1)}) \hat{S}_n^{(m)}(z) - \hat{b}_{n+1}^{(m)} \hat{S}_n^{(m+1)}(z), \tag{7.24e}$$

$$\hat{S}_{n+1}^{(m+1)}(z) = (z + \hat{G}_{n+1}^{(m)}) \hat{S}_n^{(m+1)}(z) + \hat{F}_{n+1}^{(m)} z \, \hat{S}_{n-1}^{(m+1)}(z), \tag{7.24f}$$

$$\hat{S}_{n+1}^{(m-1)}(z) = (z - \hat{\sigma}_{n+1}^{(m-1)}) \hat{S}_n^{(m)}(z) - \hat{\rho}_{n+1}^{(m)} \hat{S}_{n-1}^{(m+1)}(z). \tag{7.24g}$$

$\square$

The rhombus rules for the $\hat{F}\hat{G}$ parameters are given in next theorem.

THEOREM 7.7. *Let* $F(z) = \sum f_k z^k$ *be a normal fls. Then its* $\hat{F}\hat{G}$ *parameters satisfy the following rhombus rules for* $k = 1,2,...$ *and* $m \in \mathbb{Z}$:

$$\hat{F}_{k+1}^{(m)} + \hat{G}_k^{(m)} = \hat{F}_k^{(m-1)} + \hat{G}_k^{(m-1)} \qquad (7.25a)$$

$$\hat{F}_{k+1}^{(m)} \hat{G}_{k+1}^{(m-1)} = \hat{F}_{k+1}^{(m-1)} \hat{G}_k^{(m)} \qquad (7.25b)$$

with initial conditions

$$\hat{F}_1^{(m)} = 0 \quad \text{and} \quad \hat{G}_1^{(m)} = -f_m/f_{m+1} \quad m \in \mathbb{Z}. \qquad (7.25c)$$

$\square$

From (7.24a) and (7.24b) we find in analogy with the staircase CF (7.17) another staircase CF of the form

$$\hat{N}_0^{(m)}(z) - \cfrac{f_m z^m}{\vert\,1\,\vert} - \cfrac{\hat{b}_1^{(m-1)}}{\vert\,z\,\vert} - \cfrac{\hat{a}_2^{(m-2)}}{\vert\,1\,\vert} - \cfrac{\hat{b}_2^{(m-2)}}{\vert\,z\,\vert} - \cfrac{\hat{a}_3^{(m-3)}}{\vert\,1\,\vert} \cdots$$

with convergents

$$(\hat{N}_0^{(m)}(z)/\hat{Q}_0^{(m)}(z)), (\hat{N}_0^{(m-1)}(z)/\hat{Q}_0^{(m-1)}(z)), (\hat{N}_1^{(m-1)}(z)/\hat{Q}_1^{(m-1)}(z)),$$

$$(\hat{N}_1^{(m-2)}(z)/\hat{Q}_1^{(m-2)}(z)),...$$

where N is again one of $P, B(p)$ or $-R$. These are elements on an ascending staircase like in fig. 7.11 which represents the graph corresponding to it. At node $(m-k,k)$ we find $\hat{S}_k^{(m-k)}(z)$ and at node $(m-k-1,k)$ we find $\hat{S}_k^{(m-k-1)}(z)$.

With some algebra one can show that

$$\hat{a}_{n+1}^{(m)} = \hat{u}_n^{(m+1)}/\hat{u}_{n-1}^{(m+1)} \quad \text{and} \quad \hat{b}_{n+1}^{(m)} = \hat{u}_n^{(m)}/\hat{u}_n^{(m+1)}.$$

Again type 1 and type 2 algorithms can be obtained as alternatives for the rhombus rules to compute the numbers $\hat{a}_n^{(m-n)}$, $\hat{b}_n^{(m-n)}$,$n = 1,2,...$. With $S = Q$ in fig. 7.7 and with a formula like (3.2a) you get a type 1 form and with $S = P$ and (3.5) you get a type 2 algorithm.

7.6 Relation with classical algorithms

The rhombus algorithms 3a and 3b for the ab and $\hat{a}\hat{b}$ paramaters correspond to algorithms that appeared in the literature.

The classical qd algorithm of Rutishauser [RUT], [HEN] associates with a fps $F(z)$ a table of numbers $e_k^{(m)}, q_k^{(m)}$ via relations like those in algorithm 3a. Both algorithms are the same if one sets

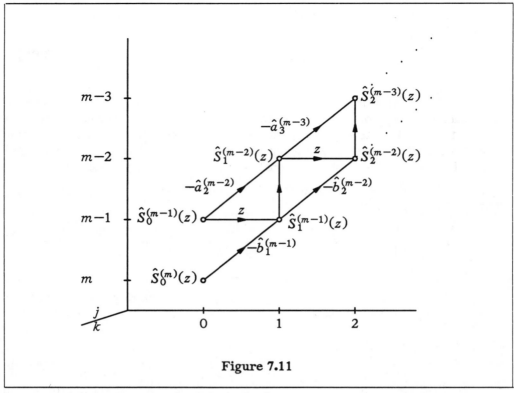

Figure 7.11

$$b_k^{(m)} = q_k^{(m-k+1)} \qquad q_k^{(m)} = b_k^{(m+k-1)}$$

or $\qquad\qquad\qquad\qquad\qquad$ (7.26)

$$a_k^{(m)} = e_{k-1}^{(m-k+1)} \qquad e_k^{(m)} = a_{k+1}^{(m+k)} \ .$$

In [GR2] Gragg gave a variant of this algorithm. This algorithm again associates with a fps some numbers $\pi_k^{(m)}$ and $\zeta_k^{(m)}$. It is the same as algorithm 3b if one sets

$$\hat{b}_k^{(m)} = \pi_k^{(m)} \qquad \pi_k^{(m)} = \hat{b}_k^{(m)}$$

or $\qquad\qquad\qquad\qquad\qquad$ (7.27)

$$\hat{a}_k^{(m)} = \zeta_{k-1}^{(m+1)} \qquad \zeta_k^{(m)} = \hat{a}_{k+1}^{(m-1)} \ .$$

The rhombus relations for the FG and the $\hat{F}\hat{G}$ parameters of theorem 7.4 and theorem 7.7 correspond to an algorithm due to McCabe [MC1,MC2,MCM] which was derived in connection with two–point Padé approximation. It is here described in the FG notation of [JOT].

Chapter 8

Biorthogonal polynomials, quadrature and reproducing kernels

The recurrence relations we have introduced so far can be interpreted as recurrence relations for polynomials that are orthogonal in a formal sense with respect to an indefinite bilinear form. Some of these orthogonalities and some other properties of these polynomials will be given in section 8.1. It is a well known fact that the zeros of orthogonal polynomials are very useful as abscissas for the construction of Gauss quadrature rules. Some ideas on this application will be given in section 8.2. In section 8.3 it is shown how some classical results on reproducing kernels in separable Hilbert spaces can be formally generalized to our situation. All this is developed in our viewpoint of the basic algorithms of chapter 3 that generated the polynomials of the first kind $Q_n^{(m)}(z)$ and $\hat{Q}_n^{(m)}(z)$ for m fixed and $n = 0,1,2,...$ which corresponds to a horizontal path in an (m,n) grid. In other works related to Padé approximation, a similar theory is given, but for polynomials on diagonals in an (m,n) grid. The most complete compilation in this area is probably given by Brezinski [BRE] and Draux [DRA]. Another way to show the difference between our approach and the more classical ones is that we started from algorithms of chapter 3 that are fundamental for the solution of Toeplitz systems, while in classical Padé approximation recurrence relations are related to the Euclidean algorithm and methods to solve Hankel systems. So ours is a "Toeplitz approach" while the more classical one is a "Hankel approach". In section 8.4 we shall briefly mention some results on the latter.

8.1 Biorthogonal polynomials

We shall start by introducing a bilinear form which is almost an indefinite inner product and for which the polynomials of the first kind $Q_n^{(m)}(z)$ and $\hat{Q}_n^{(m)}(z)$ (m fixed) will form a biorthogonal set of polynomials.

With a fls $F(z) = \sum f_k z^k$ we associate complex valued linear functionals $\lambda^{(m)}$ defined on the vector space of Laurent polynomials by

$$\lambda^{(m)}(z^k) := \Pi_{0:0}(z^{k-m} F(z)) = f_{m-k}.$$

m will be fixed throughout this section. For any series $G(z) = \sum g_k z^k$ we define $G_*(z)$ as the series $G_*(z) := \sum \bar{g}_k z^{-k}$ where the upper bar stands for complex conjugation, and for a polynomial $p(z)$ of degree n we define its *parahermitean conjugate* by $p^*(z) := z^n p_*(z)$. Next we introduce a bilinear form $<\cdot,\cdot>^{(m)}$

defined on the set of Laurent polynomials by

$$<P(z),Q(z)>^{(m)} := \lambda^{(m)}(P(z)Q_*(z)).$$

Recall that an inner product for a complex vector space X is a complex valued form $(\cdot,\cdot)$ with properties

(1) $(ax + by,z) = a(x,z) + b(y,z)$ $\forall x,y,z \in X; a,b \in \mathbb{C}$
     $(z,ax + by) = \bar{a}(z,x) + \bar{b}(z,y)$ (bilinear)
(2) $(x,y) = \overline{(y,x)}$ $\forall x,y \in X$ (symmetric)
(3) $(x,x) \geqslant 0$ $\forall x \in X$ (positive semidefinite)
(4) $(x,x) = 0$ iff $x = 0$ (nondegenerate)

If we drop the positivity condition (3), we have an indefinite inner product [BOG]. Our form $<\cdot,\cdot>^{(m)}$ is bilinear and if $F(z)$ is normal, it will be nondegenerate. It is therefore almost an indefinite inner product since the only property it does not satisfy is the symmetry relation (2). We have the symmetry relations

$$<P(z),Q(z)>^{(m)} = <Q_*(z),P_*(z)>^{(m)} = <Q^*(z),P^*(z)>^{(m)}$$

instead.

For further reading it will be useful to keep in mind that

$$<z^k,z^l>^{(m)} = f_{m+l-k}.$$

The fundamental ideas for the orthogonality of the polynomials $Q_n^{(m)}(z)$ and $\hat{Q}_n^{(m)}(z)$ are given in theorem 8.1.

THEOREM 8.1. *Let $F(z)$ be a normal fls and $n \in \mathbb{N}$, $m \in \mathbb{Z}$. Then, with the notation of chapter 3 we have the following :*

$$<\hat{Q}_n^{(m)}(z),z^k>^{(m)} = \Pi_{m+k:m+k}(\hat{P}_n^{(m)}(z)+\hat{R}_n^{(m)}(z)), k \in \mathbb{Z}$$

$$= \hat{u}_n^{(m)} \quad , k=-1$$

$$= 0 \quad , 0 \leqslant k \leqslant n-1 \qquad (8.1)$$

$$= \hat{v}_n^{(m)} \quad , k=n$$

$$<z^k,Q_n^{(m)*}(z)>^{(m)} = \Pi_{m+n-k:m+n-k}(P_n^{(m)}(z)+R_n^{(m)}(z)), k \in \mathbb{Z}$$

$$= u_n^{(m)} \quad , k=-1$$

$$= 0 \quad , 0 \leqslant k \leqslant n-1 \qquad (8.2)$$

$$= v_n^{(m)} \quad , k=n.$$

PROOF. This is trivial to verify since e.g.

$$<\hat{Q}_n^{(m)}(z),z^k>^{(m)} = \lambda^{(m)}(\hat{Q}_n^{(m)}(z)z^{-k}) = \Pi_{0:0}(F(z)\,\hat{Q}_n^{(m)}(z)\,z^{-m-k})$$

$$= \Pi_{m+k:m+k} \, (\hat{P}_n^{(m)}(z) + \hat{R}_n^{(m)}(z)).$$

The other three relations in (8.1) are special cases of this which are obvious because of the expressions (3.5).

The proof of (8.2) is completely analoguous and is left as an exercise.

$\square$

From theorem 8.1 we get immediately the biorthogonality relation we wanted to introduce.

COROLLARY 8.2. *Under the conditions of theorem 8.1 we have that*

(1) *The polynomials $\{\hat{Q}_n^{(m)}(z)\}$ and $\{Q_n^{(m)*}(z)\}$ are biorthogonal in the sense that*

$$<\hat{Q}_k^{(m)}(z), Q_l^{(m)*}(z)>^{(m)} = \delta_{kl} \, v_k^{(m)} \, , \quad k,l = 0,1,2,... \tag{8.3}$$

(2) *The numbers $u_n^{(m)}$ and $\hat{u}_n^{(m)}$ can be expressed as*

$$\hat{u}_n^{(m)} = <z\hat{Q}_n^{(m)}(z), Q_n^{(m)}(z)>^{(m)} \tag{8.4a}$$

$$u_n^{(m)} = <Q_n^{(m)}(z), z\hat{Q}_n^{(m)}(z)>^{(m)} \, . \tag{8.4b}$$

(3) *The SS parameters may be expressed as*

$$\alpha_{n+1}^{(m)} = \frac{<Q_n^{(m)}(z), z\hat{Q}_n^{(m)}(z)>^{(m)}}{<\hat{Q}_n^{(m)}(z), Q_n^{(m)*}(z)>^{(m)}} \tag{8.4c}$$

$$\hat{\alpha}_{n+1}^{(m)} = \frac{<z\hat{Q}_n^{(m)}(z), Q_n^{(m)}(z)>^{(m)}}{<\hat{Q}_n^{(m)}(z), Q_n^{(m)*}(z)>^{(m)}} . \tag{8.4d}$$

PROOF. The first part is trivial to prove with previous theorem. For the second part note that (3.3) gives

$$z\hat{Q}_n^{(m)}(z) = \hat{Q}_{n+1}^{(m)}(z) + \hat{\alpha}_{n+1}^{(m)} \hat{Q}_n^{(m)}(z).$$

Thus using the first part of this theorem and the relations of theorem 8.1 we get

$$<z\hat{Q}_n^{(m)}(z), Q_n^{(m)}(z)>^{(m)} = <\hat{Q}_{n+1}^{(m)}(z), Q_n^{(m)}(z)>^{(m)} + \hat{\alpha}_{n+1}^{(m)} <\hat{Q}_n^{(m)}(z), Q_n^{(m)}(z)>^{(m)}$$

$$= \hat{\alpha}_{n+1}^{(m)} <Q_n^{(m)*}(z), Q_n^{(m)*}(z)>^{(m)} = \hat{\alpha}_{n+1}^{(m)} v_n^{(m)} = \hat{u}_n^{(m)}$$

where the last equality follows from the definition (3.2) of the SS parameter $\hat{\alpha}_{n+1}^{(m)}$.

Similarly, if we use the symmetry relation $<P(z),Q(z)>^{(m)} = <P*(z),Q*(z)>^{(m)}$ for $<\cdot,\cdot>^{(m)}$ and the parahermitean conjugate of (3.3) :

$zQ_n^{(m)*}(z) = Q_{n+1}^{(m)*}(z) + \overline{\alpha_{n+1}^{(m)}}\hat{Q}_n^{(m)*}(z)$, then you get :

$$<Q_n^{(m)}(z), z\hat{Q}_n^{(m)}(z)>^{(m)} = <\hat{Q}_n^{(m)*}(z), zQ_n^{(m)*}(z)>^{(m)} =$$

$$= <\hat{Q}_n^{(m)*}(z), Q_{n+1}^{(m)*}(z)>^{(m)} + \alpha_{n+1}^{(m)} <\hat{Q}_n^{(m)*}(z), \hat{Q}_n^{(m)*}(z)>^{(m)}.$$

Using theorem 8.1, the symmetry relation for $<\cdot,\cdot>^{(m)}$ again and the definition (3.2) of $\alpha_{n+1}^{(m)}$, we get :

$$= \alpha_{n+1}^{(m)} <\hat{Q}_n^{(m)}(z), \hat{Q}_n^{(m)}(z)>^{(m)} = \alpha_{n+1}^{(m)}\hat{v}_n^{(m)} = u_n^{(m)},$$

which proves the second part of the theorem.

The third part of the theorem directly follows from this. E.g. the numerator of (8.4c) is $u_n^{(m)}$ while the denominator is $<Q_n^{(m)}(z), Q_n^{(m)*}(z)>^{(m)} = <z^n, Q_n^{(m)*}(z)>^{(m)} = v_n^{(m)}$ because of $Q_n^{(m)*}(z)$ being monic and relations (8.2) do the rest.

$\square$

The next theorem gives some formal expansions.

THEOREM 8.3. *Let $F(z) = \sum f_k z^k$ be a normal fls. Then for any $m \in \mathbb{Z}$ we have (1) and (2) below :*

(1) *If $\alpha_n^{(m)}$ and $\hat{\alpha}_n^{(m)}$ are the SS parameters of $F(z)$ and $Q_n^{(m)}(z)$ and $\hat{Q}_n^{(m)}(z)$ the biorthogonal polynomials of the first kind associated with it by (8.3). Then we have the following formal Fourier expansion*

$$z^{-1} = \sum_{k=0}^{\infty} \alpha_{k+1}^{(m)}\hat{Q}_k^{(m)}(z) = \sum_{k=0}^{\infty} \overline{\hat{\alpha}_{k+1}^{(m)}}Q_k^{(m)*}(z). \tag{8.5}$$

(2) *If $Z^{(m)}(z) = \tfrac{1}{2}f_m z^m + \sum_{k=1}^{\infty} f_{m+k} z^{m+k}$ and*

$\hat{Z}^{(m)}(z) = -\tfrac{1}{2}f_m z^m - \sum_{k=1}^{\infty} f_{m-k} z^{m-k}$ *as in (4.2).*

Then we have the following formal identities :

$$\frac{1}{2} <1, L_+(\frac{1+z\bar{y}}{1-z\bar{y}})>^{(m)} = y^{-m}Z^{(m)}(y) = \frac{1}{2} <L_-(\frac{z+y}{z-y}), 1>^{(m)} \tag{8.6a}$$

$$\frac{1}{2} <1, L_-(\frac{1+z\bar{y}}{1-z\bar{y}})>^{(m)} = y^{-m}\hat{Z}^{(m)}(y) = \frac{1}{2} <L_+(\frac{z+y}{z-y}), 1>^{(m)}. \tag{8.6b}$$

PROOF.

(1) Suppose $z^{-1} = \sum_{k=0}^{\infty} \beta_{k+1}^{(m)}\hat{Q}_k^{(m)}(z)$. Then multiplying from the right with $Q_l^{(m)*}(z)$ gives :

$$<z^{-1},Q_l^{(m)}*(z)>^{(m)} = \sum_{k=0}^{\infty} \beta_{k+1}^{(m)} <\hat{Q}_k^{(m)}(z),Q_l^{(m)}*(z)>^{(m)}.$$

By (8.2), we know that the left–hand side is $u_l^{(m)}$ and the right–hand side is $\beta_{l+1}^{(m)} v_l^{(m)}$, which gives

$$\beta_{l+1}^{(m)} = u_l^{(m)}/v_l^{(m)} = \alpha_{l+1}^{(m)}.$$

The other relation can be shown similarly.

(2)   We have $L_+(\dfrac{1+z\bar{y}}{1-z\bar{y}}) = 1+2 \sum_{k=1}^{\infty} (\bar{y}z)^k$. Thus if we fill this formal expansion into the left hand side of (8.6a) we get :

$$\frac{1}{2} <1, L_+(\frac{1+z\bar{y}}{1-z\bar{y}})>^{(m)} = \frac{1}{2} <1,1>^{(m)} + \sum_{k=1}^{\infty} y^k <1,z^k>^{(m)}$$

$$= \frac{1}{2} f_m + \sum_{k=1}^{\infty} f_{m+k} \, y^k = y^{-m} \, Z^{(m)}(y).$$

Similarly we have for (8.6b) :

$$\frac{1}{2} <L_-(\frac{z+y}{z-y}), 1>^{(m)} = \frac{1}{2} <1,1>^{(m)} + \sum_{k=1}^{\infty} y^k <z^{-k},1>^{(m)}$$

$$= \frac{1}{2} f_m + \sum_{k=1}^{\infty} f_{m+k} \, y^k = y^{-m} \, Z^{(m)}(y).$$

□

The polynomials of the second kind are given by the next theorem.

THEOREM 8.4. *Let* $F(z)$ *be a normal fls. Let* $Q_n^{(m)}(z)$ *and* $\hat{Q}_n^{(m)}(z)$ *be the polynomials of the first kind associated with it and let* $A_n^{(m)}(z)$ *and* $\hat{A}_n^{(m)}(z)$ *be the polynomials of the second kind, defined as in (4.3). Then for* $n > 0$ *and for any* $m \in \mathbb{Z}$:

$$\frac{1}{2} <\hat{Q}_n^{(m)}(y) - \hat{Q}_n^{(m)}(z), L_-(\frac{1+\bar{y}z}{1-\bar{y}z})>^{(m)} = \hat{A}_n^{(m)}(y) \tag{8.7a}$$

and

$$\frac{1}{2} <L_-(\frac{1+\bar{y}z}{1-\bar{y}z}), Q_n^{(m)}*(z) - Q_n^{(m)}*(y)>^{(m)} = \overline{A_n^{(m)}*(y)}. \tag{8.7b}$$

PROOF. With $\hat{Z}^{(m)}(z)$ as defined in (4.2), and using (8.6b) we get for the first term in the left hand side of (8.7a) :

$$\frac{1}{2} \hat{Q}_n^{(m)}(y) <1, \; L_-(\frac{1+\bar{y}z}{1-\bar{y}z})>^{(m)} = y^{-m}\hat{Q}_n^{(m)}(y)\, \hat{Z}^{(m)}(y).$$

The second part of the left hand side of (8.7a) is

$$-\frac{1}{2} <\hat{Q}_n^{(m)}(z), \; L_-(\frac{1+\bar{y}z}{1-\bar{y}z})>^{(m)}$$

$$= \frac{1}{2} <\hat{Q}_n^{(m)}(z), \; 1>^{(m)} + \sum_{k=1}^{\infty} y^{-k} <\hat{Q}_n^{(m)}(z), z^{-k}>^{(m)}.$$

By (8.1) the first term is zero. Using for the sum the definition of the form $<\cdot,\cdot>^{(m)}$ we get :

$$= y^{-m} \sum_{k=1}^{\infty} y^{m-k} \Pi_{m-k:m-k}\, (F(z)\hat{Q}_n^{(m)}(z))$$

which is in view of (3.4)

$$= y^{-m}\, \hat{P}_n^{(m)}(z).$$

Summing these equalities for the two parts shows that it equals $y^{-m}(\hat{Q}_n^{(m)}(y)\hat{Z}^{(m)}(y) + \hat{P}_n^{(m)}(y))$ which gives $\hat{A}_n^{(m)}(y)$ by definition (4.3b). The other relation is to be proved similarly.

□

Under the assumed normality condition for $F(z)$ we can show the following property concerning the zeros of the orthogonal polynomials of the first and second kind associated with it.

THEOREM 8.5. *Let $F(z)$ be a normal fls, $n \in \mathbb{N}$, $m \in \mathbb{Z}$ and let $Q_n^{(m)}(z)$ and $\hat{Q}_n^{(m)}(z)$ be the polynomials of the first kind and $A_n^{(m)}(z)$ and $\hat{A}_n^{(m)}(z)$ the polynomials of the second kind associated with it. Then the pairs of polynomials that are linked by a line in the following scheme can have no common zero.*

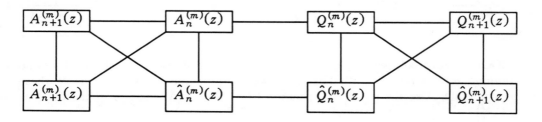

PROOF. Note that none of the polynomials can have a zero at $z_0 = 0$ since their constant term is nonzero. The existence of the lines forming the central square in the scheme is shown by recalling from chapter 4 that we had the determinant equality (2.7)

$$A_n^{(m)}(z)\hat{Q}_n^{(m)}(z) - \hat{A}_n^{(m)}(z)Q_n^{(m)}(z) = z^n v_n^{(m)}.$$

This indeed shows that the common zero cannot be $z_0 \neq 0$. The existence of the other lines follows from the recursions (3.6) :

$$S_{n+1}^{(m)}(z) = S_n^{(m)}(z) - z\alpha_{n+1}^{(m)}\, \hat{S}_n^{(m)}(z),$$

$$\hat{S}_{n+1}^{(m)}(z) = -\hat{\alpha}_{n+1}^{(m)}\, S_n^{(m)}(z) + z\, \hat{S}_n^{(m)}(z),$$

where S is A or Q. E.g. if $S_{n+1}^{(m)}(z)$ and $S_n^{(m)}(z)$ had a common zero $z_0 \neq 0$, then because of these relations, it would also be a zero of $\hat{S}_n^{(m)}(z)$ which is impossible by the first part of this proof etc.

□

We may replace A by $B(p)$ in the scheme of the previous theorem if we restrict ourselves to zeros in $0 < |z| < \infty$. The proof is the same.

A similar result can be obtained for the derived polynomials $U_n^{(m)}(z)$, $\hat{U}_n^{(m)}(z)$, $V_n^{(m)}(z)$ and $\hat{V}_n^{(m)}(z)$. This is given in theorem 8.6.

THEOREM 8.6. *Let* $F(z) = \sum f_k z^k$ *be a normal fls and associate with it the polynomials* $U_n^{(m)}(z)$, $\hat{U}_n^{(m)}(z)$, $V_n^{(m)}(z)$ *and* $\hat{V}_n^{(m)}(z)$, $n \in \mathbb{N}$, $m \in \mathbb{Z}$ *as in (4.13). Then the polynomials that are linked by a line in the following scheme can have no common zero.*

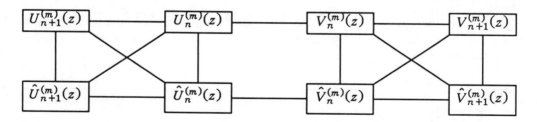

PROOF. The proof would be like the one of theorem 8.5 if we knew that the common zero is not $z_0 = 0$. Therefore we compute the constant terms of these polynomials. Use the recurrence relation (3.6) for $S = V$ and $S = zU$ so that we get.

$$\left| \begin{matrix} V_n^{(m)}(z) & \hat{V}_n^{(m)}(z) \\ zU_n^{(m)}(z) & z\hat{U}_n^{(m)}(z) \end{matrix} \right| = \left| \begin{matrix} 1 & 0 \\ 0 & 1 \end{matrix} \right| \left| \begin{matrix} 1 & -\hat{\alpha}_1^{(m)} \\ -\alpha_1^{(m)}z & z \end{matrix} \right| \cdots \left| \begin{matrix} 1 & -\hat{\alpha}_{n+1}^{(m)} \\ -\alpha_{n+1}^{(m)}z & z \end{matrix} \right|.$$

Now divide the second row by z and put then $z = 0$ and you will obtain :

$$\left| \begin{matrix} V_n^{(m)}(0) & \hat{V}_n^{(m)}(0) \\ U_n^{(m)}(0) & \hat{U}_n^{(m)}(0) \end{matrix} \right| = \left| \begin{matrix} 1 & -\hat{\alpha}_{n+1}^{(m)} \\ -\alpha_1^{(m)} & \alpha_1^{(m)}\hat{\alpha}_{n+1}^{(m)} \end{matrix} \right|.$$

All the constant terms are nonzero :

$$U_n^{(m)}(0) = -\alpha_1^{(m)} = -f_{m+1}/f_m \neq 0, \quad \text{(because } F(z) \text{ is~normal)}$$

while

$$\hat{U}_n^{(m)}(0) = -\hat{\alpha}_{n+1}^{(m)} \, U_n^{(m)}(0) \neq 0,$$

and

$$\hat{V}_n^{(m)}(0) = -\hat{\alpha}_{n+1}^{(m)} \neq 0$$

by theorem 3.1. All these are nonzero and the proof of the previous theorem can be copied mutatis mutandis.

$\square$

8.2 Interpolatory quadrature methods

Let us assume that n and m are fixed and let us denote the polynomial of degree n interpolating an arbitrary function $P(z)$ in the points $\{z_k\}_0^n$ by $L_P(z)$. I.e.

$$L_P(z) := \sum_{k=0}^{n} l_k(z) \, P(z_k)$$

with

$$l_k(z) := \prod_{\substack{j=0 \\ j \neq k}}^{n} (z - z_j) / \prod_{\substack{j=0 \\ j \neq k}}^{n} (z_k - z_j).$$

An approximation for $\lambda^{(m)}(z^{-p}P(z))$ given by

$$\lambda^{(m)}(z^{-p}P(z)) \approx \lambda^{(m)}(z^{-p}L_P(z)) =: \sum_{k=0}^{n} w_k \, P(z_k),$$

is called a *quadrature formula with weights*

$$w_k := \lambda^{(m+p)}(l_k(z))$$

and *abscissas* $\{z_k\}_0^n$.

It is obvious that if $P(z)$ is a polynomial of degree at most n, the quadrature approximation will be exact because the approximation $L_P(z)$ of $P(z)$ is exact. It is possible to make the quadrature formula exact for higher degree polynomials if we make a special choice for the abscissas $\{z_k\}_0^n$. Such results are given in theorems 8.7 and 8.8 below.

THEOREM 8.7. *Suppose $F(z)$ is a normal fls, $n \in \mathbb{N}$, $m,p \in \mathbb{Z}$ and let $\hat{Q}_n^{(m)}(z)$ be polynomials of the first kind that are associated with it as in (3.1). Suppose further that the zeros $\{z_k\}_0^n$ of $Q_{n+1}^{(m+p-n)}(z)$ are distinct. Let us associate with it the following quadrature formula :*

$$\lambda^{(m)}(z^{-p}P(z)) \approx \sum_{k=0}^n w_k P(z_k); \quad w_k = \lambda^{(m+p)}(l_k(z)).$$

Then it will be exact for any polynomial $P(z)$ of degree at most $2n+1$.

PROOF. We can always write $P(z)$ as

$$P(z) = q(z) \hat{Q}_{n+1}^{(m+p-n)}(z) + r(z)$$

with $q(z)$ and $r(z)$ polynomials of degree at most n. Hence

$$\lambda^{(m)}(z^{-p}P(z)) = \lambda^{(m+p-n)}(z^{-n}q(z) \hat{Q}_{n+1}^{(m+p-n)}(z)) + \lambda^{(m+p)}(r(z))$$

$$= <\hat{Q}_{n+1}^{(m+p-n)}(z), q^*(z)>^{(m+p-n)} + \lambda^{(m+p)}(r(z))$$

$$= \lambda^{(m+p)}(r(z))$$

because of the orthogonality.

If $\{z_k\}_0^n$ are the zeros of $\hat{Q}_n^{(m+p-n)}(z)$, then $P(z_k) = r(z_k)$ and thus

$$\lambda^{(m)}(z^{-p}P(z)) = \lambda^{(m)}(z^{-p}r(z)) = \sum_{k=0}^n w_k r(z_k) = \sum_{k=0}^n w_k P(z_k)$$

which proves the theorem.

$\square$

Remarks

(1) Without further restriction on $F(z)$ we cannot guarantee that the zeros of $\hat{Q}_{n+1}^{(m+p-n)}(z)$ are distinct in general.

(2) The name quadrature formula can be explained as follows. If we take $m=p=0$, and if $\sum_{-\infty}^{\infty} f_k e^{ik\theta}$ is the Fourier series of some weight function F,

then

$$\lambda^{(0)}(P(z)) = \frac{1}{2\pi} \int_0^{2\pi} P(e^{i\theta})F(e^{i\theta})d\theta \approx \sum_{k=0}^{n} w_k P(z_k),$$

with weights

$$w_k = \frac{1}{2\pi} \int_0^{2\pi} l_k(e^{i\theta})F(e^{i\theta})d\theta.$$

Another interesting choice for the interpolation points is given in the next theorem.

THEOREM 8.8. *Let $F(z)$ be a normal fls, $n \in \mathbb{N}$, $m,p \in \mathbb{Z}$ and let $Q_n^{(m)}(z)$ and $\hat{Q}_n^{(m)}(z)$ be the polynomials of the first kind that are associated with it as in (3.1). Suppose that $\{\alpha_n^{(m)}, \hat{\alpha}_n^{(m)}\}$ denote its SS parameters and that $\{z_k\}_0^n$ are the zeros of the polynomial*

$$\psi(z) := \hat{Q}_{n+1}^{(m+p-n)}(z) + \tau \, Q_{n+1}^{(m+p-n)}(z)$$

where $\tau \neq \hat{\alpha}_{n+1}^{(m+p-n+1)}$ and assume that these zeros are distinct. Then the following quadrature formula

$$\lambda^{(m)}(z^{-p}P(z)) \approx \sum_{k=0}^{n} w_k P(z_k); \qquad w_k = \lambda^{(m+p)}(l_k(z))$$

is exact for any polynomial $P(z)$ of degree at most $2n$.

PROOF. Recall that $\hat{Q}_{n+1}^{(m+p-n)}(z)$ is monic and that the highest degree coefficient of $Q_{n+1}^{(m+p-n)}(z)$ is $-\alpha_{n+1}^{(m+p-n)} = 1/\hat{\alpha}_{n+1}^{(m+p-n+1)}$. (See (7.8c).) Hence

$$\psi(z) = (1-\tau/\hat{\alpha}_{n+1}^{(m+p-n+1)})z^{n+1} + \cdots$$

which shows that $\psi(z)$ is a polynomial of strict degree $n+1$ if $\tau \neq \hat{\alpha}_{n+1}^{(m+p-n+1)}$. It cannot be guaranteed, even under the normality condition for $F(z)$, that the zeros of $\psi(z)$ are distinct in general. We suppose that they are.
We can always write $P(z)$ as $P(z) = q(z)\psi(z) + r(z)$ with $q(z)$ a polynomial of degree at most $n-1$ and $r(z)$ a polynomial of degree at most n. Hence

$$\lambda^{(m)}(z^{-p}P(z)) = \lambda^{(m+p-n)}(z^{-n}q(z)\hat{Q}_{n+1}^{(m+p-n)}(z))$$

$$+ \tau \, \lambda^{(m+p-n)}(z^{-n-1}zq(z)Q_{n+1}^{(m+p-n)}(z))$$

$$+ \lambda^{(m+p)}(r(z))$$

$$= <\hat{Q}_{n+1}^{(m+p-n)}(z), zq^*(z)>^{(m+p-n)}$$

$$+ \tau <zq(z), Q_{n+1}^{(m+p-n)*}(z)>^{(m+p-n)}$$

$$+ \lambda^{(m+p)}(r(z))$$

$$= \lambda^{(m+p)}(r(z)).$$

The last equality follows from the orthogonality relations. If $\{z_k\}_0^n$ are the zeros of $\psi(z)$, then $P(z_k) = r(z_k)$ and therefore

$$\lambda^{(m)}(z^{-p}P(z)) = \lambda^{(m)}(z^{-p}r(z)) = \sum_{k=0}^{n} w_k r(z_k) = \sum_{k=0}^{n} w_k P(z_k)$$

which proves the theorem.

$\square$

Remarks

(1) Another way to formulate theorem 8.8 for $p = n$ is the following: Substitute $z^{-n}P(z)$ by $\tilde{P}(z)$. Then the quadrature formula

$$\lambda^{(m)}(\tilde{P}(z)) \approx \sum_{k=0}^{n} \tilde{w}_k \tilde{P}(z_k); \quad \tilde{w}_k = \lambda^{(m)}(\tilde{l}_k(z))$$

with

$$\tilde{l}_k(z) := \prod_{\substack{j=0 \\ j \neq k}}^{n} (1 - z_j/z) / \prod_{\substack{j=0 \\ j \neq k}}^{n} (1 - z_j/z_k)$$

will be exact for all Laurent polynomials $\tilde{P}(z)$ of degree at most n if the abscissas z_k are as in theorem 8.8. Indeed after comparison with theorem 8.8 you see that

$$\tilde{w}_k = w_k z_k^n = z_k^n \lambda^{(m+n)}(l_k(z)) = \lambda^{(m)}(z_k^n z^{-n} l_k(z)) = \lambda^{(m)}(\tilde{l}_k(z))$$

(2) An interesting example, although for a nonnormal fls, is the following: If we take $F(z) \equiv 1$, and $m = p = 0$, then

$$\lambda^{(0)}(P(z)) = \frac{1}{2\pi} \int_0^{2\pi} P(e^{i\theta}) d\theta \approx \sum_{k=0}^{n} w_k P(z_k)$$

will be our quadrature formula. The orthogonal polynomials for $F(z) = 1$ are $\hat{Q}_{n+1}^{(0)}(z) = Q_{n+1}^{(0)*}(z) = z^{n+1}$ so that $\psi(z) = z^{n+1} + \tau$ and its zeros are the $(n+1)$st roots of τ. If $|\tau| = 1$, then these are equidistant on the unit circle.

This concludes our connection with quadrature. In the next subsection we give some ideas related to reproducing kernels.

8.3 Reproducing kernels

Given an orthogonal basis in a separable Hilbert space, it is easy to construct a reproducing kernel [ARO], [MES]. We don't have a Hilbert space, but our bilinear form $<\cdot,\cdot>^{(m)}$ is rich enough to generate a number of results on reproducing kernels and Christoffel–Darboux relations that generalize the classical results. See e.g. [KVM]. Let $F(z)$ be a normal fls and $Q_n^{(m)}(z)$ and $\hat{Q}_n^{(m)}(z)$ the biorthogonal polynomials of the first kind satisfying (8.3). We shall consider the expression

$$k_n^{(m)}(x,y) := \sum_{k=0}^{n} \frac{\hat{Q}_k^{(m)}(y)\overline{Q_k^{(m)*}(x)}}{v_k^{(m)}}. \tag{8.8}$$

This is called a *reproducing kernel associated with* $<\cdot,\cdot>^{(m)}$. The kernel is called reproducing because for all polynomials of degree at most n we have the following theorem.

THEOREM 8.9. *Let $F(z)$ be a normal fls, $n \in \mathbb{N}$, $m \in \mathbb{Z}$ and let $k_n^{(m)}(x,y)$ be its reproducing kernel associated with $<\cdot,\cdot>^{(m)}$. Then for any polynomial $P(z)$ of degree at most n we have*

$$<k_n^{(m)}(x,z),P(z)>^{(m)} = \overline{P(x)} \tag{8.9a}$$

$$<P(z),\overline{k_n^{(m)}(z,y)}>^{(m)} = P(y). \tag{8.9b}$$

PROOF. Since the polynomials $Q_k^{(m)*}(z)$ are of exact degree k we can use them as a basis for polynomials of degree n and thus e.g.

$$P(z) = \sum_{k=0}^{n} a_k Q_k^{(m)*}(z).$$

Therefore it is a matter of simple algebra to work out the left hand side of (8.9a) :

$$<k_n^{(m)}(x,z),P(z)>^{(m)} =$$

$$= \sum_{k,l=0}^{n} \bar{a}_k (v_l^{(m)})^{-1} \overline{Q_l^{(m)*}(x)} <\hat{Q}_l^{(m)}(z),Q_k^{(m)*}(z)>^{(m)}$$

$$= \sum_{k,l=0}^{n} \bar{a}_k (v_l^{(m)})^{-1} \overline{Q_l^{(m)*}(x)} \delta_{kl} v_k^{(m)} = \sum_{k=0}^{n} \bar{a}_k \overline{Q_k^{(m)*}(x)} = \overline{P(x)}.$$

For the second relation write $P(z)$ as

$$P(z) = \sum_{k=0}^{n} b_k \hat{Q}_k^{(m)}(z),$$

and proceed as above.

□

The following theorem gives *Christoffel-Darboux-type relations :*

THEOREM 8.10. *Let* $n \in \mathbb{N}$, $m \in \mathbb{Z}$ *and let* $F(z)$ *be a normal fls. Associate with it the bilinear form* $<\cdot,\cdot>^{(m)}$. *Let* $Q_n^{(m)}(z)$ *and* $\hat{Q}_n^{(m)}(z)$ *be the biorthogonal polynomials of the first kind for it and let* $k_n^{(m)}(x,y)$ *be its reproducing kernel. Then*

$$k_n^{(m)}(x,y) = \frac{Q_n^{(m)}(y)\overline{\hat{Q}_n^{(m)*}(x)} - \bar{x}y\hat{Q}_n^{(m)}(y)\overline{Q_n^{(m)*}(x)}}{v_n^{(m)} (1-\bar{x}y)} \tag{8.10a}$$

$$= \frac{Q_{n+1}^{(m)}(y)\overline{\hat{Q}_{n+1}^{(m)*}(x)} - \hat{Q}_{n+1}^{(m)}(y)\overline{Q_{n+1}^{(m)*}(x)}}{v_{n+1}^{(m)} (1-\bar{x}y)}, \tag{8.10b}$$

where

$$v_n^{(m)} = <\hat{Q}_n^{(m)}(z),Q_n^{(m)*}(z)>^{(m)}.$$

PROOF. (8.10a) is obviously true for $n=0$. The rest follows by induction. Indeed, let $l_n^{(m)}(x,y)$ be the right-hand side of (8.10a), then we have to show that (see (8.8))

$$l_n^{(m)}(x,y) - l_{n-1}^{(m)}(x,y) = \hat{Q}_n^{(m)}(y)\overline{Q_n^{(m)*}(x)}/v_n^{(m)}.$$

This difference equals $T/[v_n^{(m)}(1-\bar{x}y)]$ with (use (3.2c))

$$T = -\bar{x}y\hat{Q}_n^{(m)}(y)\overline{Q_n^{(m)*}(x)} + Q_n^{(m)}(y)\overline{\hat{Q}_n^{(m)*}(x)} - (1-\alpha_n^{(m)}\hat{\alpha}_n^{(m)}) \,.$$

$$\cdot [Q_{n-1}^{(m)}(y)\overline{\hat{Q}_{n-1}^{(m)*}(x)} - \bar{x}y\hat{Q}_{n-1}^{(m)}(y)\overline{Q_{n-1}^{(m)*}(x)}]. \tag{8.11}$$

Thus it remains to show that the last two terms together give $\hat{Q}_n^{(m)}(y)\overline{Q_n^{(m)*}(x)}$. This is most easily done by using the relations (3.3) and the associated

$$[Q_n^{(m)*}(z) \, \hat{Q}_n^{(m)*}(z)] = [Q_{n-1}^{(m)*}(z) \, \hat{Q}_{n-1}^{(m)*}(z)] \begin{vmatrix} z & -z\hat{\alpha}_n^{(m)} \\ -\alpha_n^{(m)} & 1 \end{vmatrix}$$

Substituting $Q_n^{(m)}(y)$ and $Q_n^{(m)*}(x)$ in (8.11) gives the result after some simple algebra.
Relation (8.10b) is similarly proved .

$\square$

Theorem 8.10 allows us to prove a number of properties for the reproducing kernel.

COROLLARY 8.11. *Under the conditions of theorem 8.10 we shall have the relations (1)–(4) below :*

(1) $k_n^{(m)}(x,y) = \bar{x}^n y^n k_n^{(m)}(1/\bar{y},1/\bar{x})$,

(2) $k_n^{(m)}(0,y) = Q_n^{(m)}(y)/v_n^{(m)}$,

(3) $k_n^{(m)}(x,0) = \overline{\hat{Q}_n^{(m)*}(x)}/v_n^{(m)}$,

(4) $k_n^{(m)}(0,0) = 1/v_n^{(m)}$.

PROOF. This is only a matter of simple algebra.

(1) You work out the right hand side using the right hand side of (8.10a) as an expression for $k_n^{(m)}(x,y)$. Make also use of the relation $\overline{P^*(z)} = P(1/\bar{z})\bar{z}^n$ which is valid for any polynomial $P(z)$ of degree n. The result will be the right hand side of (8.10a) which is $k_n^{(m)}(x,y)$. This proves (1).

(2) Set $x = 0$ in (8.10a) and you will get the result because $\hat{Q}_n^{(m)}(x)$ is monic and hence $\hat{Q}_n^{(m)*}(0) = 1$.

(3) This also follows from (8.10a) by setting $y = 0$ because $Q_n^{(m)}(0) = 1$.

(4) Set $y = 0$ in (2) of this theorem and you get the result.

$\square$

(2) of corollary 8.11 shows that $k_n^{(m)}(0,y)$ is in fact a renormalized orthogonal polynomial of the first kind. It is possible to generalize the recurrence relation (3.3) for these polynomials to a recurrence relation for the kernels. To give this relation, we have to introduce some generalizations of the SS parameters.

Recall that

$$Q_n^{(m)}(z) = 1 + \cdots + (-\alpha_n^{(m)})z^n \quad \text{and} \quad \hat{Q}_n^{(m)}(z) = (-\hat{\alpha}_n^{(m)}) + \cdots + z^n$$

so that the SS parameters are given by

$$\alpha_n^{(m)} = -\frac{\overline{Q_n^{(m)*}(0)}}{Q_n^{(m)}(0)} \quad \text{and} \quad \hat{\alpha}_n^{(m)} = -\frac{\hat{Q}_n^{(m)}(0)}{\hat{Q}_n^{(m)*}(0)}.$$

We now generalize this to

$$\alpha_n^{(m)}(x) := -\frac{\overline{Q_n^{(m)*}(x)}}{Q_n^{(m)}(x)} \quad \text{and} \quad \hat{\alpha}_n^{(m)}(x) := -\frac{\hat{Q}_n^{(m)}(x)}{\hat{Q}_n^{(m)*}(x)}. \tag{8.12}$$

The following theorem generalizes recursion (3.3).

THEOREM 8.12. *Let $F(z)$ be a normal fls and $k_n^{(m)}(x,y)$ its reproducing kernel (8.8) for $<\cdot,\cdot>^{(m)}$. Then we have the following recurrence relation for $n \in \mathbb{N}$ and $m \in \mathbb{Z}$*

$$(1-\alpha_{n+1}^{(m)}(x)\hat{\alpha}_{n+1}^{(m)}(x))[k_{n+1}^{(m)}(x,y)\,\hat{k}_{n+1}^{(m)}(x,y)] = [k_n^{(m)}(x,y)\,\hat{k}_n^{(m)}(x,y)]\,.$$

$$\cdot\begin{vmatrix} 1 & \bar{x}\hat{\alpha}_{n+1}^{(m)}(x) \\ x\alpha_{n+1}^{(m)}(x) & 1 \end{vmatrix}\begin{vmatrix} 1 & -\hat{\alpha}_{n+1}^{(m)}(x) \\ -y\alpha_{n+1}^{(m)}(x) & y \end{vmatrix} \tag{8.13}$$

where $\hat{k}_n^{(m)}(x,y) := y^n k_n^{(m)}(1/\bar{y},x)$ and $\alpha_n^{(m)}(x)$ and $\hat{\alpha}_n^{(m)}(x)$ are as in (8.12). If $x = 0$, this reduces to (3.3).

PROOF. We have by definition

$$k_{n+1}^{(m)}(x,y) - k_n^{(m)}(x,y) = \hat{Q}_{n+1}^{(m)}(y)\overline{Q_{n+1}^{(m)*}(x)}/v_{n+1}^{(m)}. \tag{8.14}$$

Substitute the right-hand side by the expression that you obtain for it when pulling it out of the Christoffel-Darboux relation (8.10b) and you will obtain :

$$k_{n+1}^{(m)}(x,y) - k_n^{(m)}(x,y) = \frac{Q_{n+1}^{(m)}(y)\overline{\hat{Q}_{n+1}^{(m)*}(x)}}{v_{n+1}^{(m)}} - (1-\bar{x}y)k_n^{(m)}(x,y). \tag{8.15}$$

Replace in (8.14) x by $1/\bar{y}$, y by x and multiply with y^{n+1} then you get :

$$\hat{k}_{n+1}^{(m)}(x,y) - y\hat{k}_n^{(m)}(x,y) = \hat{Q}_{n+1}^{(m)}(x)Q_{n+1}^{(m)}(y)/v_{n+1}^{(m)}. \tag{8.16}$$

Extract $Q_{n+1}^{(m)}(y)/v_{n+1}^{(m)}$ from it and substitute in (8.15) to get :

$$\hat{\alpha}_{n+1}^{(m)}(x)k_{n+1}^{(m)}(x,y) = y\hat{k}_n^{(m)}(x,y) - \hat{k}_{n+1}^{(m)}(x,y) + \hat{\alpha}_{n+1}^{(m)}(x)\,\bar{x}yk_n^{(m)}(x,y). \tag{8.17}$$

Take (8.15) and replace x by $1/\bar{y}$, y by x and multiply with y^{n+1}, then you get :

$$\hat{k}_{n+1}^{(m)}(x,y) - y\hat{k}_n^{(m)}(x,y) = \frac{Q_{n+1}^{(m)}(x)\hat{Q}_{n+1}^{(m)}(y)}{v_{n+1}^{(m)}} - (y-x)\hat{k}_n^{(m)}(x,y). \tag{8.18}$$

Get $\hat{Q}_{n+1}^{(m)}(y)/v_{n+1}^{(m)}$ from (8.14) and substitute in (8.18) to obtain

$$\alpha_{n+1}^{(m)}(x)\hat{k}_{n+1}^{(m)}(x,y) = k_n^{(m)}(x,y) - k_{n+1}^{(m)}(x,y) + x\alpha_{n+1}^{(m)}(x)\hat{k}_n^{(m)}(x,y). \tag{8.19}$$

A combination of (8.17) and (8.19) gives relation (8.13).

If we substitute $x = 0$ in (8.13) and take into account that

$$k_n^{(m)}(0,y) = Q_n^{(m)}(y)/v_n^{(m)} \text{ and } \hat{k}_n^{(m)}(0,y) = \hat{Q}_n^{(m)}(y)/v_n^{(m)},$$

then this recursion reduces to (3.3).

$\square$

8.4 Other orthogonality relations

As we have said in the introduction to this chapter, we have used the Toeplitz approach until now. I.e., we used the polynomials $Q_n^{(m)}(z)$ and $\hat{Q}_n^{(m)}(z)$ for m fixed and $n = 0,1,\dots$. I.e. we moved along rows in an (m,n) grid. In this subsection, we shall briefly mention the more classical Hankel approach like in [BRE] that uses the same polynomials, but now for indices that will move along a descending or an ascending diagonal in the same (m,n) grid. Therefore we shall have to introduce two other types of bilinear forms which will be much like $<\cdot,\cdot>^{(m)}$. The choice between both depends on whether we want to go along a descending or along an ascending diagonal. We shall start with the descending diagonal case. Therefore consider the following linear functional, associated with the normal fls $F(z)$ for some fixed integer m :

$$\hat{\lambda}^{(m+1)}(z^k) := \Pi_{0:0} (z^{-k-m-1}F(z)) = f_{k+m+1}.$$

A bilinear form $[\cdot,\cdot]^{(m)}$ is defined on the set of Laurent polynomials by

$$[P(z),Q(z)]^{(m)} := \hat{\lambda}^{(m+1)}(P(z)Q(z)).$$

This is again a form that is almost an indefinite inner product. It satisfies all the defining relations for it except that complex conjugation is left out at all instances. It will be helpful to remember that $[z^k,z^l]^{(m)} = f_{m+k+l+1}$.
The "Gram-matrix" with entries $[z^k,z^l]^{(m)}$ thus has a Hankel structure, as opposed to the Toeplitz structure of the "Gram-matrix" for the form $<\cdot,\cdot>^{(m)}$ whose entries are $<z^k,z^l>^{(m)} = f_{m+l-k}$. Because we have symmetry now, we shall not have a biorthogonality but a simple orthogonality property. The polynomials orthogonal with respect to $[\cdot,\cdot]^{(m)}$ will be the $Q_n^{(m+n)\times}(z)$ with $Q_n^{(m)}(z)$ polynomials of the first kind for $F(z)$ and where we introduced the notation $P^\times(z) = \overline{P*(\bar{z})}$ which is $z^n P(1/z)$ if $P(z)$ is a polynomial of degree n. The first step to this orthogonality is given in the next theorem which is the analogue of theorem 8.1.

THEOREM 8.13. *Let $F(z)$ be a normal fls. Then with the notation of chapter 3 we have for $n \in \mathbb{N}$ and $m \in \mathbb{Z}$:*

$$[Q_n^{(m+n)\times}(z),z^k]^{(m)} = \Pi_{m+n+k+1:m+n+k+1}(P_n^{(m+n)}(z)+R_n^{(m+n)}(z))$$

$$= v_n^{(m+n)} \quad , \quad k=-1$$

$$= 0 \qquad , \quad k=0,1,\dots,n-1$$

$$= u_n^{(m+n)} \quad , \quad k=n$$

PROOF. This immediatly follows from the definitions. Indeed, the left hand side is

$$[Q_n^{(m+n)\times}(z),z^k]^{(m)} = \hat{\lambda}^{(m+1)}(z^k Q_n^{(m+n)\times}(z))$$

$$= \hat{\lambda}^{(m+1)}(z^{n+k} Q_n^{(m+n)}(1/z))$$

$$= \hat{\lambda}^{(m+n+k+1)}(Q_n^{(m+n)}(1/z))$$

$$= \Pi_{m+n+k+1:m+n+k+1}(Q_n^{(m+n)}(z)F(z)),$$

which is equal to the right hand side by (3.4). The rest are special cases of this that directly follow from the relation (3.5).

$\square$

COROLLARY 8.14. *Under the conditions of theorem 8.13 we have the following two results :*

(1) *The polynomials $Q_n^{(m+n)\times}(z)$,$n = 0,1,...$ are orthogonal with respect to $[\cdot,\cdot]^{(m)}$: $[Q_k^{(m+k)\times}(z),Q_n^{(m+n)\times}(z)]^{(m)} = u_n^{(m+n)}\,\delta_{kn}$, $k,n = 0,1,2,...$.*

(2) *The $\rho\sigma$ parameters for $F(z)$ are given by :*

$$\sigma_{n+1}^{(m+n+1)} = \frac{[zQ_n^{(m+n)\times}(z),Q_n^{(m+n)\times}(z)]^{(m)}}{[Q_n^{(m+n)\times}(z),Q_n^{(m+n)\times}(z)]^{(m)}},$$

$$\rho_{n+1}^{(m+n)} = \frac{[zQ_n^{(m+n)\times}(z),Q_{n-1}^{(m+n-1)\times}(z)]^{(m)}}{[Q_{n-1}^{(m+n-1)\times}(z),Q_{n-1}^{(m+n-1)\times}(z)]^{(m)}} = \frac{u_n^{(m+n)}}{u_{n-1}^{(m+n-1)}}.$$

PROOF. The first part directly follows from the previous theorem. The second part follows from recursion (7.19b). Indeed, write down (7.19b) for $S = Q$ and replace m by $m+n$:

$$Q_{n+1}^{(m+n+1)}(z) = (1 - z\sigma_{n+1}^{(m+n+1)})Q_n^{(m+n)}(z) - z^2\rho_{n+1}^{(m+n)}Q_{n-1}^{(m+n-1)}(z).$$

Replace z by $1/z$ and multiply by z^{n+1} :

$$Q_{n+1}^{(m+n+1)\times}(z) = (z - \sigma_{n+1}^{(m+n+1)})Q_n^{(m+n)\times}(z) - \rho_{n+1}^{(m+n)}Q_{n-1}^{(m+n-1)\times}(z).$$

Multiply this with $Q_n^{(m+n)\times}(z)$:

$$[Q_{n+1}^{(m+n+1)\times}(z),Q_n^{(m+n)\times}(z)]^{(m)} = [zQ_n^{(m+n)\times}(z),Q_n^{(m+n)\times}(z)]^{(m)}$$

$$- \sigma_{n+1}^{(m+n+1)}[Q_n^{(m+n)\times}(z),Q_n^{(m+n)\times}(z)]^{(m)}$$

$$- \rho_{n+1}^{(m+n)}[Q_{n-1}^{(m+n-1)\times}(z),Q_n^{(m+n)\times}(z)]^{(m)}.$$

The left hand side and the last term in the right hand side are zero because of the first part of this theorem so that the expression for $\sigma_{n+1}^{(m+n+1)}$ follows. If we don't multiply with $Q_n^{(m+n)\times}(z)$ but with $Q_{n-1}^{(m+n-1)\times}(z)$ then we will find an expression for $\rho_{n+1}^{(m+n)}$ in a similar way.

$\square$

Because $\hat{Q}_n^{(m+n+1)}(z)$ is a constant multiple of $Q_n^{(m+n)}(z)$, the polynomials

$\hat{Q}_n^{(m+n+1)}(z)$, $n = 0,1,...$ will also be orthogonal .

The reproducing kernel for the bilinear form $[\cdot,\cdot]^{(m)}$ is given by the next theorem.

THEOREM 8.15. *Let $F(z)$ be a normal fls and let $Q_n^{(m)}(z)$ denote its polynomials of the first kind. Then the reproducing kernel for the bilinear form $[\cdot,\cdot]^{(m)}$ is given by*

$$l_n^{(m)}(x,y) = \sum_{k=0}^{n} \frac{Q_k^{(m+k)\times}(x)\, Q_k^{(m+k)\times}(y)}{u_k^{(m+k)}} \;,\quad n \in \mathbb{N},\ m \in \mathbb{Z},$$

with

$$u_k^{(m+k)} = [Q_k^{(m+k)\times}(z), Q_k^{(m+k)\times}(z)]^{(m)}.$$

It is a reproducing kernel in the sense that

$$[P(z), l_n^{(m)}(z,y)]^{(m)} = P(y)$$

for any polynomial $P(z)$ of degree at most n.

PROOF. This is not different from the proof for $<\cdot,\cdot>^{(m)}$ and we shall leave it as an exercise.

         □

The Christoffel–Darboux relations for the polynomials orthogonal with respect to $[\cdot,\cdot]^{(m)}$ are given in the next theorem.

THEOREM 8.16. *Let $F(z)$ be a normal fls. For some fixed $m \in \mathbb{Z}$, let $Q_n^{(m+n)\times}(z)$, $n = 0,1,2,...$ be the polynomials orthogonal with respect to the bilinear form $[\cdot,\cdot]^{(m)}$ and let $l_n^{(m)}(x,y)$ be the corresponding reproducing kernel. Then we have the following Christoffel-Darboux relations :*

$$l_n^{(m)}(x,y) = \frac{Q_{n+1}^{(m+n+1)\times}(x)Q_n^{(m+n)\times}(y) - Q_{n+1}^{(m+n+1)\times}(y)Q_n^{(m+n)\times}(x)}{u_n^{(m+n)}(x-y)}$$

$$= \frac{xQ_n^{(m+n+1)\times}(x)Q_n^{(m+n)\times}(y) - yQ_n^{(m+n+1)\times}(y)Q_n^{(m+n)\times}(x)}{u_n^{(m+n)}(x-y)}\;.$$

PROOF. This is similar to the proof for $<\cdot,\cdot>^{(m)}$ and it is left as an exercise. Hint : make use of $\rho_{n+1}^{(m+n)} = u_n^{(m+n)}/u_{n-1}^{(m+n-1)}$.

         □

Further results concerning polynomials of the second kind, the position of the zeros, interpolatory quadrature formulas and many other things in this context can be found in [BRE]. We shall not repeat them here. The interested reader should consult the references.

We shall conclude this chapter by giving some of the analog results for an ascending diagonal. The proofs are completely similar to those given before and we shall ommit all the details. So, yet another Hankel approach can be obtained by defining another bilinear form viz.

$$\{P(z),Q(z)\}^{(m)} := \lambda^{(m-1)}(P(z)Q(z))$$

where $\lambda^{(m)}$ is the same linear functional as defined at the beginning of this chapter. The Hankel nature of the bilinear form $\{\cdot,\cdot\}^{(m)}$ is shown by looking at the "Gram-matrix" with entry (k,l) equal to

$$\{z^k,z^l\}^{(m)} = f_{m-k-l-1},$$

so that it is another Hankel matrix. We have the following orthogonality relations for the polynomials $\hat{Q}_n^{(m-n)}(z)$, $n = 0,1,\dots$.

THEOREM 8.17. *Let $F(z)$ be a normal fls. Then with the notation of chapter 3 we have for $n \in \mathbb{N}$ and $m \in \mathbb{Z}$ the following relations for the bilinear form $\{\cdot,\cdot\}^{(m)}$ that we have just introduced :*

$$\{\hat{Q}_n^{(m-n)}(z),z^k\}^{(m)} = \Pi_{m-k-1:m-k-1} \left(\hat{P}_n^{(m-n)}(z) + \hat{R}_n^{(m-n)}(z)\right) ,k \in \mathbb{Z}$$

$$= \hat{u}_n^{(m-n)} \quad , \quad k=n$$

$$= 0 \qquad , \quad k=0,1,\dots,n-1$$

$$= \hat{v}_n^{(m-n)} \quad , \quad k=-1.$$

$$\square$$

COROLLARY 8.18. *Under the same conditions as theorem 8.17 we have that :*

(1) *The polynomials $\hat{Q}_n^{(m-n)}(z)$, $n = 0,1,\dots$ are orthogonal with respect to $\{\cdot,\cdot\}^{(m)}$ in the sense that $\{\hat{Q}_n^{(m-n)}(z),\hat{Q}_k^{(m-k)}(z)\}^{(m)} = \hat{u}_n^{(m-n)} \delta_{kn}$, $k,n = 0,1,\dots$.*

(2) *The $\hat{\rho}\hat{\sigma}$ parameters of $F(z)$ are given by :*

$$\hat{\sigma}_{n+1}^{(m-n-1)} = \frac{\{z\hat{Q}_n^{(m-n)}(z),\hat{Q}_n^{(m-n)}(z)\}^{(m)}}{\{\hat{Q}_n^{(m-n)}(z),\hat{Q}_n^{(m-n)}(z)\}^{(m)}}$$

$$\hat{\rho}_n^{(m-n)} = \frac{\{z\hat{Q}_{n-1}^{(m-n+1)}(z),\hat{Q}_n^{(m-n)}(z)\}^{(m)}}{\{\hat{Q}_{n-1}^{(m-n+1)}(z),\hat{Q}_{n-1}^{(m-n+1)}(z)\}^{(m)}} = \frac{\hat{u}_n^{(m-n)}}{\hat{u}_{n-1}^{(m-n+1)}} .$$

PROOF. This is analog to the proof of corollary 8.14. Hint : For (2) use the recursion (7.24g).

□

The reproducing kernel and the Christoffel–Darboux relations are given by

THEOREM 8.19. *Let $F(z)$ be a normal fls and let $\hat{Q}_n^{(m-n)}(z)$ be the polynomials of the first kind orthogonal with respect to $\{\cdot,\cdot\}^{(m)}$. Then for $n \in \mathbb{N}$ and $m \in \mathbb{Z}$:*

$$\hat{l}_n^{(m)}(x,y) := \sum_{k=0}^{n} \frac{\hat{Q}_k^{(m-k)}(x)\hat{Q}_k^{(m-k)}(y)}{\hat{u}_k^{(m-k)}}$$

with

$$\hat{u}_k^{(m-k)} := \{\hat{Q}_k^{(m-k)}(z),\hat{Q}_k^{(m-k)}(z)\}^{(m)}$$

is a reproducing kernel since

$$\{P(z),\hat{l}_n^{(m)}(z,y)\}^{(m)} = P(y)$$

for any polynomial $P(z)$ of degree at most n .
The Christoffel–Darboux relation is given by

$$\hat{l}_n^{(m)}(x,y) = \frac{\hat{Q}_{n+1}^{(m-n-1)}(x)\hat{Q}_n^{(m-n)}(y) - \hat{Q}_{n+1}^{(m-n-1)}(y)\hat{Q}_n^{(m-n)}(x)}{\hat{u}_n^{(m-n)}(x-y)}.$$

□

Chapter 9

Determinant expressions and matrix interpretations

In this chapter we go back to the origin of our basic algorithms of chapter 3. We started by formulating in (3.1) a problem of linear algebra wich was to solve recursively some nested Toeplitz systems of linear equations. This solution gave recurrence relation (3.6) which was the fundament of algorithms 1 and 2. In subsequent chapters we gave interpretations in terms of Padé approximants, continued fractions, Moebius transforms and orthogonal polynomials. In this chapter we shall come back to the linear algebra and show how the previous results may be interpreted in this environment.

Many of the quantities we have introduced so far can be most elegantly expressed in terms of determinants of Toeplitz matrices. Also the Q polynomials and the F and R series for the fls $F(z)$, which were denominators, numerators and residuals of Padé approximants can be expressed as determinants, which is a well known result for classical Padé approximation.

The determinant expressions will also allow for an easy derivation of some new recurrence relations between adjacent elements in an (m,n) grid of $S_n^{(m)}(z)$ elements where S is Q, P, R or $B(p)$ (see chapter 4). These relations are reformulations of the recurrences we already had in theorems 7.2, 7.4 and 7.6. All this is given in subsection 9.1. The other subsection treats matrix interpretations of algorithms 1 and 2. The coefficients of the polynomials of the first kind and the coefficients of the P and R series that go along with it can be arranged in triangular matrices that are factors of a Toeplitz or Hankel matrix or its inverse. Also triangular Hankel and Toeplitz matrices can be constructed from these. They will be used to give explicit inversion formulas for Toeplitz and Hankel matrices. These relations are all variants of the celebrated Gohberg-Semencul formula. Also ab, $\hat{a}\hat{b}$, $\rho\sigma$ and $\hat{\rho}\hat{\sigma}$ parameters will be used in an interpretation for Jacobi-type matrices.

9.1 Determinant expressions

Many of the numbers, polynomials and series that appeared in the previous theory can be most elegantly expressed in terms of Toeplitz or Hankel determinants associated with the fls $F(z) = \sum f_k z^k$. We introduce for these determinants the following notation

$$T_n^{(m)} := \det \mathbf{T}_n^{(m)} = \det \left(f_{m+i-j}\right)_{i,j=0}^n \tag{9.1a}$$

and

$$H_n^{(m)} := \det \mathbf{H}_n^{(m)} = \det \left(f_{m+i+j}\right)_{i,j=0}^n. \tag{9.1b}$$

We have a simple relation between both, given in the next lemma.

LEMMA 9.1. *The Toeplitz and Hankel determinants defined by (9.1) for some fls $F(z)$ are related by :*

$$H_n^{(m)} = (-1)^{(n+1)n/2} \, T_n^{(m+n)} \tag{9.2a}$$

$$T_n^{(m)} = (-1)^{(n+1)n/2} \, H_n^{(m-n)}. \tag{9.2b}$$

PROOF. Let $\mathbf{K}_n$ be the anti-unit matrix defined by $\mathbf{K}_n = [\delta_{i,n-j}]_{i,j=0}^n$. Then because $\mathbf{H}_n^{(m)} = \mathbf{T}_n^{(m+n)}\mathbf{K}_n$ and $\det \mathbf{K}_n = (-1)^{(n+1)n/2}$, (9.2a) follows. Similarly (9.2b) follows because $\mathbf{T}_n^{(m)} = \mathbf{H}_n^{(m-n)}\mathbf{K}_n$.

$\square$

Most of the parameters we have associated with a fls before can be expressed as a ratio of (a product of) Toeplitz or Hankel matrices. We give a survey of such results in the next theorem.

THEOREM 9.2. *Let $F(z) = \sum f_k z^k$ be a normal fls and for $n \in \mathbb{N}$ and $m \in \mathbb{Z}$ associate with it the Toeplitz and Hankel determinants (9.1). Then*
(1) The uv parameters defined in (3.1) and (3.2) can be expressed as

$$v_n^{(m)} = \hat{v}_n^{(m)} = \frac{T_n^{(m)}}{T_{n-1}^{(m)}} = (-1)^n \, \frac{H_n^{(m-n)}}{H_{n-1}^{(m-n+1)}}, \tag{9.3a}$$

$$u_n^{(m)} = (-1)^n \, \frac{T_n^{(m+1)}}{T_{n-1}^{(m)}} = \frac{H_n^{(m-n+1)}}{H_{n-1}^{(m-n+1)}}, \tag{9.3b}$$

$$\hat{u}_n^{(m)} = (-1)^n \, \frac{T_n^{(m-1)}}{T_{n-1}^{(m)}} = \frac{H_n^{(m-n-1)}}{H_{n-1}^{(m-n+1)}}, \tag{9.3c}$$

(2) the SS parameters $\alpha_{n+1}^{(m)}$ and $\hat{\alpha}_{n+1}^{(m)}$ can be expressed as

$$\alpha_{n+1}^{(m)} = (-1)^n \, \frac{T_n^{(m+1)}}{T_n^{(m)}} = (-1)^n \, \frac{H_n^{(m-n+1)}}{H_n^{(m-n)}}, \tag{9.3d}$$

$$\hat{\alpha}_{n+1}^{(m)} = (-1)^n \, \frac{T_n^{(m-1)}}{T_n^{(m)}} = (-1)^n \, \frac{H_n^{(m-n-1)}}{H_n^{(m-n)}}, \tag{9.3e}$$

(3) the ab and $\hat{ab}$ parameters can be expressed as

$$b_{n+1}^{(m)} = \frac{T_n^{(m+1)}T_{n-1}^{(m-1)}}{T_n^{(m)}T_{n-1}^{(m)}} = \frac{H_n^{(m-n+1)}H_{n-1}^{(m-n)}}{H_n^{(m-n)}H_{n-1}^{(m-n+1)}}, \tag{9.3f}$$

$$\hat{b}_{n+1}^{(m)} = \frac{T_n^{(m-1)}T_{n-1}^{(m+1)}}{T_n^{(m)}T_{n-1}^{(m)}} = \frac{H_n^{(m-n-1)}H_{n-1}^{(m-n+2)}}{H_n^{(m-n)}H_{n-1}^{(m-n+1)}}. \tag{9.3g}$$

$$a_{n+1}^{(m)} = -F_{n+1}^{(m)} = -\frac{T_{n-2}^{(m-1)}T_n^{(m)}}{T_{n-1}^{(m-1)}T_{n-1}^{(m)}} = \frac{H_{n-2}^{(m-n+1)}H_n^{(m-n)}}{H_{n-1}^{(m-n)}H_{n-1}^{(m-n+1)}}, \tag{9.3h}$$

$$\hat{a}_{n+1}^{(m)} = -\hat{F}_{n+1}^{(m)} = -\frac{T_{n-2}^{(m+1)}T_n^{(m)}}{T_{n-1}^{(m+1)}T_{n-1}^{(m)}} = \frac{H_{n-2}^{(m-n+3)}H_n^{(m-n)}}{H_{n-1}^{(m-n+2)}H_{n-1}^{(m-n+1)}}, \tag{9.3i}$$

(4) the G and $\hat{G}$ from the FG parameters can be expressed as

$$G_n^{(m)} = -\frac{T_{n-2}^{(m-1)}T_{n-1}^{(m)}}{T_{n-2}^{(m)}T_{n-1}^{(m-1)}} = -\frac{H_{n-2}^{(m-n+1)}H_{n-1}^{(m-n+1)}}{H_{n-2}^{(m-n+2)}H_{n-1}^{(m-n)}}, \tag{9.3j}$$

$$\hat{G}_n^{(m)} = -\frac{T_{n-2}^{(m+1)}T_{n-1}^{(m)}}{T_{n-2}^{(m)}T_{n-1}^{(m+1)}} = -\frac{H_{n-2}^{(m-n+3)}H_{n-1}^{(m-n+1)}}{H_{n-2}^{(m-n+2)}H_{n-1}^{(m-n+2)}}, \tag{9.3k}$$

(5) the ρ and $\hat{\rho}$ from the $\rho\sigma$ parameters can be expressed as

$$\rho_{n+1}^{(m)} = \frac{u_n^{(m)}}{u_{n-1}^{(m-1)}} = -\frac{T_{n-2}^{(m-1)}T_n^{(m+1)}}{(T_{n-1}^{(m)})^2} = \frac{H_{n-2}^{(m-n+1)}H_n^{(m-n+1)}}{(H_{n-1}^{(m-n+1)})^2}, \tag{9.3l}$$

$$\hat{\rho}_{n+1}^{(m)} = \frac{\hat{u}_n^{(m)}}{\hat{u}_{n-1}^{(m+1)}} = -\frac{T_{n-2}^{(m+1)}T_n^{(m-1)}}{(T_{n-1}^{(m)})^2} = \frac{H_{n-2}^{(m-n+3)}H_n^{(m-n-1)}}{(H_{n-1}^{(m-n+1)})^2}. \tag{9.3m}$$

PROOF. The expressions for $u_n^{(m)}$, $\hat{u}_n^{(m)}$, $v_n^{(m)}$ and $\hat{v}_n^{(m)}$ are easily found from (3.1) with Cramer's rule. The other relations all follow from these expressions. Sometimes the result can be simplified using Jacobi's identity for Toeplitz matrices (see e.g. [GR2])

$$(T_n^{(m)})^2 = T_n^{(m-1)}\,T_n^{(m+1)} + T_{n+1}^{(m)}\,T_{n-1}^{(m)}. \tag{9.4}$$

The algebra is straightforward and we gladly leave this to the reader.

$\square$

A simple corollarly which is directly verified from the expressions (9.3) is :

COROLLARY 9.3. *Under the conditions of theorem 9.2, the following equalities are valid :*

$$\frac{b_n^{(m)}}{\hat{b}_n^{(m)}} = \frac{a_{n+1}^{(m)}}{\hat{a}_{n+1}^{(m)}} = \frac{G_n^{(m)}}{\hat{G}_n^{(m)}} = \frac{F_{n+1}^{(m)}}{\hat{F}_{n+1}^{(m)}} = \frac{v_{n-2}^{(m+1)}}{\hat{v}_{n-2}^{(m-1)}}$$

$\square$

In theorems 7.1, 7.2 and 7.4 we gave a number of recurrence relations for neighbouring $S_n^{(m)}(z)$ series where S could be P, Q, R or $B(p)$. With the expressions of (9.3) in theorem 9.2, it is possible to transform all the relations given in those theorems into recurrence relations for renormalized series/polynomials defined as :

$$S'^{(m)}_n(z) := S_n^{(m)}(z)/u_n^{(m)} \quad \text{and} \quad \hat{S}'^{(m)}_n(z) := \hat{S}_n^{(m)}(z)/\hat{u}_n^{(m)}.$$

where $u_n^{(m)}$ and $\hat{u}_n^{(m)}$ are the u parameters introduced in (3.2a). If $F(z)$ is normal, then $u_n^{(m)}\hat{u}_n^{(m)} \neq 0$ and hence these primed objects are well defined. We shall need some of those relations for S' in later sections and we give them all in theorem 9.4 for the sake of completeness. All these relations and several others were generalized to the matrix case and they may be found in [BU5].

THEOREM 9.4. *Let $F(z)$ be a normal fls and $n \in \mathbb{N}$ and $m \in \mathbb{Z}$. Let $\{Q_n^{(m)}(z), \hat{Q}_n^{(m)}(z)\}$ be its Q polynomials, $\{P_n^{(m)}(z), \hat{P}_n^{(m)}(z)\}$ its P series and $\{R_n^{(m)}(z), \hat{R}_n^{(m)}(z)\}$ its R series. They are associated with $F(z)$ as in chapter 3. For $p \in \mathbb{Z}$, let $\{B(p)_n^{(m)}(z), \hat{B}(p)_n^{(m)}(z)\}$ be the Laurent polynomials associated with $F(z)$ as in (4.7). Furthermore define*

$$S'^{(m)}_n(z) := S_n^{(m)}(z)/u_n^{(m)} \quad \text{and} \quad \hat{S}'^{(m)}_n(z) := \hat{S}_n^{(m)}(z)/\hat{u}_n^{(m)}$$

where $u_n^{(m)}$ and $\hat{u}_n^{(m)}$ are defined in (3.2a) and where S is one of P, Q, R or $B(p)$. Then the following relations hold for $n = 1,2,...$ and $m \in \mathbb{Z}$:

$$S'^{(m-1)}_n(z) = b_{n+1}^{(m)}S'^{(m)}_n(z) + zS'^{(m-1)}_{n-1}(z), \tag{9.5a}$$

$$S'^{(m)}_{n-1}(z) = a_{n+1}^{(m+1)}S'^{(m)}_n(z) + zS'^{(m-1)}_{n-1}(z), \tag{9.5b}$$

$$zS'^{(m-1)}_{n-1}(z) = (1-\alpha_n^{(m)}\hat{\alpha}_n^{(m)})S'^{(m-1)}_n(z) + \alpha_n^{(m)}\hat{\alpha}_n^{(m)}S'^{(m)}_{n-1}(z), \tag{9.5c}$$

$$S'^{(m)}_{n-1}(z) = S'^{(m-1)}_n(z) + G_{n+1}^{(m+1)}S'^{(m)}_n(z), \tag{9.5d}$$

$$zS'^{(m-1)}_n(z) = (1-zG_{n+1}^{(m+1)})S'^{(m)}_n(z) - b_{n+1}^{(m+1)}S'^{(m+1)}_n(z), \tag{9.5e}$$

$$zS'^{(m-1)}_{n-1}(z) = (1+zG_{n+1}^{(m)})S'^{(m-1)}_n(z) + F_{n+2}^{(m)}S'^{(m+1)}_{n+1}(z), \tag{9.5f}$$

$$z^2S'^{(m-1)}_{n-1}(z) = (1-z\sigma_{n+1}^{(m+1)})S'^{(m)}_n(z) - \rho_{n+2}^{(m+1)}S'^{(m+1)}_{n+1}(z), \tag{9.5g}$$

and for the $\hat{S}'(z)$ series we have :

$$\hat{S}'^{(m+1)}_n(z) = \hat{b}_{n+1}^{(m)}\hat{S}'^{(m)}_n(z) + \hat{S}'^{(m+1)}_{n-1}(z), \tag{9.6a}$$

$$\hat{S}'^{(m+1)}_{n-1}(z) = -\hat{a}_{n+1}^{(m-1)}\hat{S}'^{(m)}_n(z) + z\hat{S}'^{(m)}_{n-1}(z), \tag{9.6b}$$

$$\hat{S}'^{(m+1)}_{n-1}(z) = (1-\alpha_n^{(m)}\hat{\alpha}_n^{(m)})\hat{S}'^{(m+1)}_n(z) + z\alpha_n^{(m)}\hat{\alpha}_n^{(m)}\hat{S}'^{(m)}_{n-1}(z), \tag{9.6c}$$

$$\hat{S}'^{(m+1)}_n(z) = z\hat{S}'^{(m)}_{n-1}(z) - \hat{G}^{(m-1)}_{n+1}\hat{S}'^{(m)}_n(z), \tag{9.6d}$$

$$\hat{S}'^{(m+1)}_n(z) = (z-\hat{G}^{(m-1)}_{n+1})\hat{S}'^{(m)}_n(z) - z\hat{b}^{(m-1)}_{n+1}\hat{S}'^{(m-1)}_n(z), \tag{9.6e}$$

$$z\hat{S}'^{(m+1)}_{n-1}(z) = (z+\hat{G}^{(m)}_{n+1})\hat{S}'^{(m+1)}_n(z) + \hat{F}^{(m)}_{n+2}\hat{S}'^{(m+1)}_{n+1}(z), \tag{9.6f}$$

$$\hat{S}'^{(m+1)}_{n-1}(z) = (z-\hat{\sigma}^{(m-1)}_{n+1})\hat{S}'^{(m)}_n(z) - \hat{\rho}^{(m-1)}_{n+2}\hat{S}'^{(m-1)}_{n+1}(z). \tag{9.6g}$$

PROOF. This is only a matter of straightforward algebra. We shall prove (9.5a) and (9.5g) as an example and leave the verification of the rest to the reader. (7.10a) is rewritten as

$$\frac{S^{(m-1)}_n(z)}{u^{(m-1)}_n} = \frac{S^{(m)}_n(z)}{u^{(m)}_n}\frac{u^{(m)}_n}{u^{(m-1)}_n} + za^{(m)}_{n+1}\frac{u^{(m-1)}_{n-1}}{u^{(m-1)}_n}\frac{S^{(m-1)}_{n-1}(z)}{u^{(m-1)}_{n-1}}$$

or

$$S'^{(m-1)}_n(z) = \frac{u^{(m)}_n}{u^{(m-1)}_n}S'^{(m-1)}_n(z) + za^{(m)}_{n+1}\frac{u^{(m-1)}_{n-1}}{u^{(m-1)}_n}S'^{(m-1)}_{n-1}(z).$$

By (9.3f) and (9.3b)

$$\frac{u^{(m)}_n}{u^{(m-1)}_n} = \frac{T^{(m+1)}_n T^{(m-1)}_{n-1}}{T^{(m)}_{n-1}T^{(m)}_n} = b^{(m)}_{n+1}$$

and by (9.3h) and (9.3b) :

$$a^{(m)}_{n+1}\frac{u^{(m-1)}_{n-1}}{u^{(m-1)}_n} = \frac{T^{(m-1)}_{n-2} T^{(m)}_n T^{(m)}_{n-1} T^{(m-1)}_{n-1}}{T^{(m-1)}_{n-1} T^{(m)}_{n-1} T^{(m-1)}_{n-2} T^{(m)}_n} = 1,$$

so that (9.5a) follows.
For (9.5g) we start from (7.19b) which we write as

$$\frac{S^{(m+1)}_{n+1}(z)}{u^{(m+1)}_{n+1}} = (1-z\sigma^{(m+1)}_{n+1})\frac{u^{(m)}_n}{u^{(m+1)}_{n+1}}\frac{S^{(m)}_n(z)}{u^{(m)}_n} - z^2\rho^{(m)}_{n+1}\frac{u^{(m-1)}_{n-1}}{u^{(m+1)}_{n+1}}\frac{S^{(m-1)}_{n-1}(z)}{u^{(m-1)}_{n-1}} \tag{9.7}$$

Now with (9.3l) we find :

$$\rho^{(m)}_{n+1}\frac{u^{(m-1)}_{n-1}}{u^{(m+1)}_{n+1}} = \frac{u^{(m)}_n}{u^{(m+1)}_{n+1}} = \frac{1}{\rho^{(m+1)}_{n+2}}.$$

Multiply (9.7) with $\rho^{(m+1)}_{n+2}$ to get :

$$\rho^{(m+1)}_{n+2}S'^{(m+1)}_{n+1}(z) = (1 - z\sigma^{(m+1)}_{n+1})\frac{u^{(m)}_n\rho^{(m+1)}_{n+2}}{u^{(m+1)}_{n+1}}S'^{(m)}_n(z) - z^2S'^{(m-1)}_{n-1}(z). \tag{9.8}$$

Now by (9.3l) again :

$$\frac{\rho_{n+2}^{(m+1)} u_n^{(m)}}{u_{n+1}^{(m+1)}} = 1,$$

so that (9.5g) has been proved.

□

As for classical Padé approximation (see e.g. [GR2]) it is possible to give a determinant form for some of the series or polynomials we introduced before. Such determinant expressions are given in the next three theorems.

THEOREM 9.5a. *With the normal fls $F(z)$ we associate the series $S_n^{(m)}(z)$ as in theorem 9.4, where S was P, Q, R or $B(p)$. Then with the Toeplitz determinants (9.1a) we have for $n \in \mathbb{N}$ and $m \in \mathbb{Z}$:*

$$S_n^{(m)}(z) = \det \begin{vmatrix} S_0^{(m+n)}(z) & zS_0^{(m+n-1)}(z) & \cdots & z^n S_0^{(m)}(z) \\ \hline f_{m+1} & & & \\ \vdots & & \mathbf{T}_{n-1}^{(m)} & \\ f_{m+n} & & & \end{vmatrix} / T_{n-1}^{(m)} \qquad (9.9a)$$

and

$$\hat{S}_n^{(m)}(z) = \det \begin{vmatrix} & \mathbf{T}_{n-1}^{(m)} & & f_{m-n} \\ & & & \vdots \\ & & & f_{m-1} \\ \hline \hat{S}_0^{(m+n)}(z) & \cdots & z^{n-1}\hat{S}_0^{(m+1)}(z) & z^n \hat{S}_0^{(m)} \end{vmatrix} / T_{n-1}^{(m)} . \qquad (9.9b)$$

PROOF. We shall prove (9.9a) as an example and leave (9.9b) to the reader. If we take $S = Q$, and use the fact that $Q_0^{(m)}(z) = 1$, then you can easily see that the coefficient of z^k in (9.9a) is the ratio of two determinants. This ratio is exactly the one you would obtain if you solved $q_{k,n}^{(m)}$ from (3.2a) by Cramer's rule. This proves (9.9a) for $S = Q$.

For $S = P$, we use the definition (3.4) :

$$P_n^{(m)}(z) = \Pi_{-\infty:m}(F(z)Q_n^{(m)}(z)) = \Pi_{-\infty:m+n}(F(z)Q_n^{(m)}(z))$$

where the last equality follows from (3.5c) and the relation

$$F(z)Q_n^{(m)}(z) = P_n^{(m)}(z) + R_n^{(m)}(z).$$

The multiplication with $F(z)$ and the projection $\Pi_{-\infty:m+n}$ applied to the determinant expression for $Q_n^{(m)}(z)$ is equivalent with an application of these operations to the elements in the first row. Thus the kth element in the first row becomes :

$$\Pi_{-\infty:m+n}(z^k F(z)) = z^k P_0^{(m+n-k)}(z)$$

by definition, so that the result follows for $S = P$.

For $S = R$, exactly the same technique can be used, but now with the projection $\Pi_{m+1:\infty}$ instead of $\Pi_{-\infty:m+n}$.

$\square$

It is a simple matter to transform the expressions in previous theorem into Hankel type expressions. They are given in the next theorem.

THEOREM 9.5b. *Under the same conditions as theorem 9.5a and with the Hankel notation of (9.1b) we have :*

$$z^n \overline{S_{n*}^{(m+n)}}(z) = \det \begin{vmatrix} & & & f_{m+n+1} \\ & H_{n-1}^{(m+1)} & & \vdots \\ & & & f_{m+2n} \\ \hline \overline{S_{0*}^{(m+n)}}(z) \ z\overline{S_{0*}^{(m+n+1)}}(z) & \cdots & z^n \overline{S_{0*}^{(m+2n)}}(z) \end{vmatrix} \Big/ H_{n-1}^{(m+1)} \quad (9.9c)$$

and

$$\hat{S}_n^{(m-n)}(z) = \det \begin{vmatrix} \hat{S}_0^{(m)}(z) \ \cdots \ z^{n-1}\hat{S}_0^{(m-n+1)}(z) \ z^n \hat{S}_0^{(m-n)}(z) \\ \hline & & & f_{m-n-1} \\ & H_{-n+1}^{(m-1)} & & \vdots \\ & & & f_{m-2n} \end{vmatrix} \Big/ H_{-n+1}^{(m-1)}. \quad (9.9d)$$

Remember that $\overline{G_*}(z) = G(1/z)$ for any fls $G(z)$.

PROOF. Again we only prove (9.9c) and leave (9.9d) as an exercise. From (9.9a) you find that

$$z^n \overline{S_{n*}^{(m+n)}}(z) = N/T_{n-1}^{(m+n)}$$

with

$$N := \det \begin{vmatrix} z^n \overline{S_{0*}^{(m+2n)}}(z) \ z^{n-1}\overline{S_{0*}^{(m+2n-1)}}(z) & \cdots & \overline{S_{0*}^{(m+n)}}(z) \\ f_{m+n+1} \\ \vdots & & T_{n-1}^{(m+n)} \\ f_{m+2n} \end{vmatrix}.$$

Multiply the numerator N with $\det K_n$ and the denominator with $\det K_{n-1}$ where K_n represents the anti unit matrix of lemma 9.1. This causes a sign change of $(-1)^{n(n+1)/2-n(n-1)/2} = (-1)^n$. Because the product of determinants is the

the numerator is almost equal to the numerator of (9.9c). We only have to move the first row to the last position. This again causes a sign change of $(-1)^n$ which compensates the sign change we introduced before and thus (9.9c) is proved.

$\square$

Another useful determinant expression for the polynomials of the first kind can be given in terms of Jacobi matrices. These are tridiagonal matrices containing the $\rho\sigma$ parameters. We give them in theorem 9.6.

THEOREM 9.6. *Let $F(z)$ be a normal fls, $n = 1,2,...$ and $m \in \mathbb{Z}$. Let $\{Q_n^{(m)}(z), \hat{Q}_n^{(m)}(z)\}$ be the polynomials of the first kind for $F(z)$ and let $\{\rho_n^{(m)}, \sigma_n^{(m)}\}$ and $\{\hat{\rho}_n^{(m)}, \hat{\sigma}_n^{(m)}\}$ be its $\rho\sigma$ parameters. Then*

$$Q_n^{(m)}(z) = \det(I_n - z\, J_n^{(m)}) \tag{9.10a}$$

with $J_n^{(m)} = \text{tridiag} \begin{vmatrix} \rho_n^{(m-1)} & \rho_{n-1}^{(m-2)} & \cdots & \rho_2^{(m-n+1)} \\ \sigma_n^{(m)} & \sigma_{n-1}^{(m-1)} & \cdots & \sigma_1^{(m-n+1)} \\ 1 & 1 & & 1 \end{vmatrix}$

and

$$\hat{Q}_n^{(m)}(z) = \det(zI_n - \hat{J}_n^{(m)}) \tag{9.10b}$$

with $\hat{J}_n^{(m)} = \text{tridiag} \begin{vmatrix} \hat{\rho}_n^{(m+1)} & \hat{\rho}_{n-1}^{(m+2)} & \cdots & \hat{\rho}_2^{(m+n-1)} \\ \hat{\sigma}_n^{(m)} & \hat{\sigma}_{n-1}^{(m+1)} & \cdots & \hat{\sigma}_1^{(m+n-1)} \\ 1 & 1 & & 1 \end{vmatrix}$

where I_n denotes the $n \times n$ unit matrix.

PROOF. The theorem is true for $n = 1$ since $Q_1^{(m)}(z) = 1 - \alpha_n^{(m)}z$ by recursion (3.3) and (9.10a) gives $Q_1^{(m)}(z) = 1 - z\sigma_n^{(m)}$. (7.18c) shows that these are the same. The rest follows by induction from the recurrence relations (7.19b) for a diagonal. Indeed, this recurrence relation is exactly the one you would obtain if the determinant in the right hand side of (9.10a) were expanded along its first row.

To prove (9.10b) you can proceed in exactly the same way if you use (7.24g) and (7.22c).

$\square$

In the proof of previous theorem we used the recurrence relation (7.19b). This is a diagonal relation generating $Q_{n+1}^{(m+1)}(z)$ from $Q_n^{(m)}(z)$ and $Q_{n-1}^{(m-1)}(z)$. As we have seen, this corresponds to an expansion of the determinant expression (9.10a) along its first row. We would find another recurrence relation to evaluate this determinant if we would expand it along its last column. We then generate a sequence of polynomials of an increasing degree that will end with $Q_n^{(m)}(z)$, but

the intermediate polynomials are not any of the polynomials of the first kind. We are in a situation that is much like in algorithm inverse 1b of fig. 6.5 where we used intermediate polynomials $U_{k,n}^{(m)}(z)$ and $V_{k,n}^{(m)}(z)$ as defined in (6.15). We denote the present intermediate polynomials by $Q_{k,n}^{(m)}(z)$ and $\hat{Q}_{k,n}^{(m)}(z)$ for $k = 0,1,...,n-1$. They are introduced as follows :
Define $J_{k,n}^{(m)}$ as the matrix $J_n^{(m)}$ where the last k rows and columns are deleted. Similarly $\hat{J}_{k,n}^{(m)}$ is $\hat{J}_n^{(m)}$ with the last k rows and columns deleted.

Define polynomials of degree $n-k$ for $n = 1,2,...;$ $k = 0,1,...,n-1$ and $m \in \mathbb{Z}$ by :

$$Q_{k,n}^{(m)}(z) := \det (I_{n-k} - zJ_{k,n}^{(m)})$$ (9.11a)

and

$$\hat{Q}_{k,n}^{(m)}(z) := \det (zI_{n-k} - \hat{J}_{k,n}^{(m)}).$$ (9.11b)

We shall also define these polynomials for $k = n$ and $k = n+1$ since these will be useful as initial conditions for the recurrences. These are given by :

$$Q_{n,n}^{(m)}(z) = \hat{Q}_{n,n}^{(m)}(z) := 1 \quad \text{and} \quad Q_{n+1,n}^{(m)}(z) = \hat{Q}_{n+1,n}^{(m)}(z) := 0.$$ (9.11c)

Note however that a relation like

$$[Q_{n+1}^{(m)}(z)\,\hat{Q}_{n+1}^{(m)}(z)] = [1 \;\; 1] \begin{vmatrix} V_n^{(m)}(z) & \hat{V}_n^{(m)}(z) \\ zU_n^{(m)}(z) & z\hat{U}_n^{(m)}(z) \end{vmatrix}$$

is not true anymore if you repace a subscript n by k,n.
These intermediate polynomials satisfy some recurrence relations we have announced before. They are given in theorem 9.7.

THEOREM 9.7. *Let $F(z)$ be a normal fls with po parameters $\{\rho_n^{(m)}, \sigma_n^{(m)}\}$ and $\{\hat{\rho}_n^{(m)}, \hat{\sigma}_n^{(m)}\}$. Associate with it the polynomials $Q_{k,n}^{(m)}(z)$ and $\hat{Q}_{k,n}^{(m)}(z)$ as in (9.11). Then for $m \in \mathbb{Z}$, $n = 1,2,...$ and $0 \leqslant k < n$ we have*

$$Q_{k,n}^{(m)}(z) = (1 - z\sigma_n^{(m)})Q_{k,n-1}^{(m-1)}(z) - z^2\rho_n^{(m-1)}Q_{k,n-2}^{(m-2)}(z)$$ (9.12a)

with initial conditions $Q_{k,k}^{(m-n+k)}(z) = 1$ and $Q_{k,k-1}^{(m-n+k-1)}(z) = 0$,

and

$$Q_{k,n}^{(m)}(z) = (1 - z\sigma_{k+1}^{(m-n+k+1)})Q_{k+1,n}^{(m)}(z) - z^2\rho_{k+2}^{(m-n+k+1)}Q_{k+2,n}^{(m)}(z)$$ (9.12b)

with initial conditions $Q_{n,n}^{(m)}(z) = 1$ and $Q_{n+1,n}^{(m)}(z) = 0$.

Similarly

$$\hat{Q}_{k,n}^{(m)}(z) = (z - \hat{\sigma}_n^{(m)})\hat{Q}_{k,n-1}^{(m+1)}(z) - \hat{\rho}_n^{(m+1)}\hat{Q}_{k,n-2}^{(m+2)}(z)$$ (9.13a)

with initial conditions $Q_{k,k}^{(m+n-k)}(z) = 1$ and $Q_{k,k-1}^{(m+n-k+1)}(z) = 0$

and

$$\hat{Q}_{k,n}^{(m)}(z) = (z - \hat{\sigma}_{k+1}^{(m+n-k-1)})\hat{Q}_{k+1,n}^{(m)}(z) - \hat{\rho}_{k+2}^{(m+n-k-1)}\hat{Q}_{k+2,n}^{(m)}(z) \qquad (9.13b)$$

with initial conditions $\hat{Q}_{n,n}^{(m)}(z) = 1$ and $\hat{Q}_{n+1,n}^{(m)} = 0$.

PROOF. (9.12a) and (9.13a) immediately follow from the defining determinant expressions (9.11) if you expand the determinants along their first column. (9.12b) and (9.13b) follow similarly by expansion along the last column.

□

9.2 Matrix interpretations

     In this subsection we give the matrix factorization interpretation of algorithms 1 and 2. These algorithms contain all the ingredients to set up triangular factors for Toeplitz matrices and their inverses. These factorizations are given in theorems 9.8–9.10. With these relations it will be easy to derive a determinant expression for the reproducing kernel which will be given in theorem 9.11. The Chistoffel-Darboux relations allow us to give explicit inversion formulas for Toeplitz matrices among which is the well known Gohberg-Semencul formula (Theorems 9.12, 9.13 and 9.19).

     Similar results for Hankel matrices are given in theorems 9.14–9.19. Finally, some results on tridiagonal Jacobi matrices are given in theorem 9.20. Many of these matrix interpretations for classical Padé approximation were given by Gragg [GR3] and in [BU7] for the matrix case. We shall begin with the results related to Toeplitz matrices.

9.2.1 Toeplitz matrices

     We start with the introduction of some triangular matrices whose entries are the coefficients of Q polynomials or P or R series associated with the normal fls $F(z)$. So, if $Q_n^{(m)}(z) = \sum_{k=0}^{n} q_{k,n}^{(m)}z^k$ and $\hat{Q}_n^{(m)}(z) = \sum_{k=0}^{n} \hat{q}_{k,n}^{(m)}z^k$ are the polynomials of the first kind, then define the triangular matrices

$$
\mathbf{Q}_n^{(m)} :=
\begin{vmatrix}
q_{0,0}^{(m)} & q_{1,1}^{(m)} & \cdots & q_{n,n}^{(m)} \\
0 & q_{0,1}^{(m)} & \cdots & q_{n-1,n}^{(m)} \\
0 & 0 & & q_{n-2,n}^{(m)} \\
\vdots & \vdots & & \vdots \\
0 & 0 & \cdots & q_{0,n}^{(m)}
\end{vmatrix}
\tag{9.14}
$$

and

$$
\hat{\mathbf{Q}}_n^{(m)} :=
\begin{vmatrix}
\hat{q}_{0,0}^{(m)} & \hat{q}_{0,1}^{(m)} & \cdots & \hat{q}_{0,n}^{(m)} \\
0 & \hat{q}_{1,1}^{(m)} & \cdots & \hat{q}_{1,n}^{(m)} \\
0 & 0 & & \hat{q}_{2,n}^{(m)} \\
\vdots & \vdots & & \vdots \\
0 & 0 & \cdots & \hat{q}_{n,n}^{(m)}
\end{vmatrix} .
\tag{9.15}
$$

Let the P series associated with it be given by

$$
P_n^{(m)}(z) = \sum_{k=-\infty}^{m} p_{k,n}^{(m)} z^k \quad \text{with} \quad p_{m,n}^{(m)} = v_n^{(m)} ,
\tag{9.16a}
$$

and let the $\hat{R}$ series be given by

$$
\hat{R}_n^{(m)}(z) = \sum_{k=m+n}^{\infty} \hat{r}_{k,n}^{(m)} z^k \quad \text{with} \quad \hat{r}_{m+n}^{(m)} = \hat{v}_n^{(m)} .
\tag{9.16b}
$$

Then define the triangular matrices

$$
\mathbf{P}_n^{(m)} :=
\begin{vmatrix}
p_{m,0}^{(m)} & \cdots & 0 & 0 \\
\vdots & & \vdots & \vdots \\
p_{m-n+2,0}^{(m)} & & 0 & 0 \\
p_{m-n+1,0}^{(m)} & \cdots & p_{m,n-1}^{(m)} & 0 \\
p_{m-n,0}^{(m)} & \cdots & p_{m-1,n-1}^{(m)} & p_{m,n}^{(m)}
\end{vmatrix}
\tag{9.17}
$$

and

$$
\hat{R}_n^{(m)} := \begin{vmatrix} \hat{r}_{m,0}^{(m)} & \cdots & 0 & 0 \\ \vdots & & \vdots & \vdots \\ \hat{r}_{m+n-2,0}^{(m)} & 0 & 0 \\ \hat{r}_{m+n-1,0}^{(m)} & \cdots & \hat{r}_{m+n-1,n-1}^{(m)} & 0 \\ \hat{r}_{m+n,0}^{(m)} & \cdots & \hat{r}_{m+n,n-1}^{(m)} & \hat{r}_{m+n,n}^{(m)} \end{vmatrix}. \tag{9.18}
$$

Observe that $Q_n^{(m)}$ and $\hat{Q}_n^{(m)}$ are upper unit triangular (i.e. with diagonal elements equal to 1 because $q_{0,k}^{(m)} = \hat{q}_{k,k}^{(m)} = 1$) and $\hat{R}_n^{(m)}$ and $P_n^{(m)}$ are lower triangular with diagonal elements $v_k^{(m)} = \hat{v}_k^{(m)}$.

Finally define as before the anti unit matrix $K_n = [\delta_{i,n-j}]_{i,j=0}^n$.

With this notation we can formulate the following factorization theorem :

THEOREM 9.8. *Let $F(z)$ be a normal fls, $n \in \mathbb{N}$ and $m \in \mathbb{Z}$. Let $T_n^{(m)}$ be the Toeplitz matrices associated with $F(z)$ as in (9.1a) and let the upper triangular matrices $Q_n^{(m)}$ and $\hat{Q}_n^{(m)}$ be defined as in (9.14) and (9.15). Then we have the following factorization :*

$$
[Q_n^{(m)}]^T \, T_n^{(m)} \, [\hat{Q}_n^{(m)}] = D_n^{(m)} \tag{9.19}
$$

$$
\text{with } D_n^{(m)} = \text{diag}\,(v_0^{(m)}, v_1^{(m)}, \cdots, v_n^{(m)}) \tag{9.20}
$$

where $v_k^{(m)}$ is the leading coefficient of $P_k^{(m)}(z)$ (see 9.16a).

PROOF. It follows from the defining relations (3.4) of $P_n^{(m)}(z)$ and $\hat{R}_n^{(m)}(z)$ that

$$
T_n^{(m)} \, \hat{Q}_n^{(m)} = \hat{R}_n^{(m)} \quad \text{and} \quad K_n T_n^{(m)} K_n Q_n^{(m)} = P_n^{(m)}. \tag{9.21a}
$$

Because the Toeplitz matrix $T_n^{(m)}$ is persymmetric, i.e. $K_n T_n^{(m)} K_n = [T_n^{(m)}]^T$, we may write the second relation as :

$$
[Q_n^{(m)}]^T \, T_n^{(m)} = [P_n^{(m)}]^T \tag{9.21b}
$$

and hence

$$
[Q_n^{(m)}]^T T_n^{(m)} [\hat{Q}_n^{(m)}] = [P_n^{(m)}]^T [\hat{Q}_n^{(m)}] = [Q_n^{(m)}]^T [\hat{R}_n^{(m)}].
$$

Note that $[P_n^{(m)}]^T$ and $\hat{Q}_n^{(m)}$ are upper triangular, while $[Q_n^{(m)}]^T$ and $\hat{R}_n^{(m)}$ are lower triangular. Thus the expression in the left-hand side of (9.19) must be simultaneously upper and lower triangular, i.e. it is a diagonal matrix. Because the diagonal elements of $P_n^{(m)}$ are exactly $v_k^{(m)}$ and the diagonal elements of $Q_n^{(m)}$ are all 1, we have the result stated.

□

From (9.19) we find that

$$[T_n^{(m)}]^{-1} = [\hat{Q}_n^{(m)}] [D_n^{(m)}]^{-1} [Q_n^{(m)}]^T \tag{9.22}$$

is a UDL (i.e. Upper unit triangular - Diagonal - Lower unit triangular) factorization of $[T_n^{(m)}]^{-1}$. Thus algorithm 1, which generated in the kth step the polynomials $Q_k^{(m)}(z)$ and $\hat{Q}_k^{(m)}(z)$ and the numbers $v_k^{(m)}$, can be considered as an algorithm to compute the UDL factorization of $[T_n^{(m)}]^{-1}$.

If a matrix M is persymmetric, then its inverse will be persymmetric too. Indeed, $K_n M K_n = M^T$ implies $K_n M^{-1} K_n = M^{-T}$ because $K_n^{-1} = K_n$. Hence, multiplying (9.22) from the left and from the right with K_n and taking the transpose gives :

$$[T_n^{(m)}]^{-1} = [K_n Q_n^{(m)} K_n] [K_n (D_n^{(m)})^{-1} K_n] [K_n \hat{Q}_n^{(m)} K_n]^T \tag{9.23}$$

which is an LDU (Lower unit triangular - Diagonal - Upper unit triangular) factorization of $[T_n^{(m)}]^{-1}$.

From the previous results, we can easily derive some relations between the triangular factors we have introduced. This is given in corollary 9.9.

COROLLARY 9.9. *Under the conditions of theorem 9.8 and with the notations of (9.14),(9.16) and (9.18) we have :*

$$\hat{R}_n^{(m)}[D_n^{(m)}]^{-1} = [Q_n^{(m)}]^{-T} \text{ and this is unit lower triangular,}$$

$$[D_n^{(m)}]^{-1}[P_n^{(m)}]^T = [\hat{Q}_n^{(m)}]^{-1} \text{ and this is unit upper triangular,}$$

and thus

$$T_n^{(m)} = [\hat{R}_n^{(m)}(D_n^{(m)})^{-1}] D_n^{(m)} [(D_n^{(m)})^{-1}(P_n^{(m)})^T] \tag{9.24}$$

is an LDU (Lower unit triangular - Diagonal - Upper unit triangular) factorization of $T_n^{(m)}$.

PROOF. From (9.19) we find :

$$T_n^{(m)}\hat{Q}_n^{(m)}[D_n^{(m)}]^{-1} = [Q_n^{(m)}]^{-T}$$

while (9.21a) gives :

$$T_n^{(m)}\hat{Q}_n^{(m)}[D_n^{(m)}]^{-1} = \hat{R}_n^{(m)}[D_n^{(m)}]^{-1} .$$

So, the first relation follows.
The second relation follows similarly from (9.19) and (9.21b). Substituting these relations into the inverse of (9.22) gives (9.24).

$$\square$$

Corollary 9.9 and especially (9.24) means that algorithm 2, which computes in the kth step the $P_k^{(m)}(z)$ and $\hat{R}_k^{(m)}(z)$ and hence also the $v_k^{(m)} = \hat{v}_k^{(m)}$ (their leading coefficients), can be considered as a method to compute the LDU factorization of $T_n^{(m)}$.

Completely similar to this we also have factorizations related to $T_n^{(m+1)}$ and $T_n^{(m-1)}$. Therefore we need some new triangular matrices. With the same notation for the $Q_n^{(m)}(z)$, $\hat{Q}_n^{(m)}(z)$ polynomials as we had before in (9.14) and (9.15) and for the $P_n^{(m)}(z)$ and $\hat{R}_n^{(m)}(z)$ series we use a notation similar to the one used in (9.16), these triangular matrices are defined by the following relations:

$$
\mathbf{U}_n^{(m)} := \begin{vmatrix}
q_{0,0}^{(m)} & q_{0,1}^{(m)} & \cdots & q_{0,n}^{(m)} \\
0 & q_{1,1}^{(m)} & \cdots & q_{1,n}^{(m)} \\
0 & 0 & & q_{2,n}^{(m)} \\
\vdots & \vdots & & \vdots \\
0 & 0 & \cdots & q_{n,n}^{(m)}
\end{vmatrix}, \tag{9.25}
$$

$$
\hat{\mathbf{U}}_n^{(m)} := \begin{vmatrix}
\hat{q}_{0,n}^{(m)} & \cdots & 0 & 0 \\
\vdots & & \vdots & \vdots \\
\hat{q}_{n-2,n}^{(m)} & & 0 & 0 \\
\hat{q}_{n-1,n}^{(m)} & \cdots & \hat{q}_{0,1}^{(m)} & 0 \\
\hat{q}_{n,n}^{(m)} & \cdots & \hat{q}_{1,1}^{(m)} & \hat{q}_{0,0}^{(m)}
\end{vmatrix}, \tag{9.26}
$$

$$
\mathbf{R}_n^{(m)} := \begin{vmatrix}
r_{m+1,0}^{(m)} & \cdots & 0 & 0 \\
\vdots & & \vdots & \vdots \\
r_{m+n-1,0}^{(m)} & & 0 & 0 \\
r_{m+n,0}^{(m)} & \cdots & r_{m+n,n-1}^{(m)} & 0 \\
r_{m+n+1,0}^{(m)} & \cdots & r_{m+n+1,n-1}^{(m)} & r_{m+n+1,n}^{(m)}
\end{vmatrix}, \tag{9.27}
$$

and

$$
\hat{\mathbf{P}}_n^{(m)} := \begin{vmatrix}
\hat{p}_{m-1,n}^{(m)} & \hat{p}_{m-2,n-1}^{(m)} & \cdots & \hat{p}_{m-n-1,0}^{(m)} \\
0 & \hat{p}_{m-1,n-1}^{(m)} & \cdots & \hat{p}_{m-n,0}^{(m)} \\
0 & 0 & & \hat{p}_{m-n+1,0}^{(m)} \\
\vdots & \vdots & & \vdots \\
0 & 0 & \cdots & \hat{p}_{m-1,0}^{(m)}
\end{vmatrix}. \tag{9.28}
$$

With these matrices we can give the following factorizations:

THEOREM 9.10. *Under the same conditions as in theorem 9.8 and with the notations (9.25-28) we have :*

$$T_n^{(m+1)} U_n^{(m)} = R_n^{(m)} \qquad (9.29)$$

and

$$T_n^{(m-1)} \hat{U}_n^{(m)} = \hat{P}_n^{(m)}. \qquad (9.30)$$

PROOF. Recall relations (7.1) :

$$\hat{S}_k^{(m)}(z) = S_k^{(m-1)}(z)/(-\alpha_k^{(m-1)}) \quad \text{and} \quad S_k^{(m-1)}(z) = \hat{S}_k^{(m)}(z)/(-\hat{\alpha}_k^{(m)})$$

for S one of Q, R or P. Thus if we multiply $\hat{S}_n^{(m)}$ from the right with the inverse of $-$ diag $(\hat{\alpha}_0^{(m)} \, \hat{\alpha}_1^{(m)} \, \cdots \, \hat{\alpha}_n^{(m)})$ to get a renormalization you will end up with $S_n^{(m-1)}$ where in this case S is Q or R. By the operations just described, you can find (9.29) (with m replaced by $m-1$) from the first relation in (9.21a). Similarly, we rewrite the second relation in (9.21b) as

$$T_n^{(m)} K_n Q_n^{(m)} = K_n P_n^{(m)} .$$

Now we multiply this from the right with K_n and with the inverse of $-$ diag $(\alpha_0^{(m)} \, \alpha_1^{(m)} \, \cdots \, \alpha_n^{(m)})$. The diagonal matrix will get you the proper renormalisation and the matrices K_n will give the appropriate reordering so that you will find (9.30) for m replaced by $m+1$.

□

Thus algorithm 1, which computes the entries of $U_n^{(m)}$ and $\hat{U}_n^{(m)}$ column by column, also gives the upper triangular factor $U_n^{(m)}$ in an UL (Upper triangular – Lower triangular) factorization

$$[T_n^{(m+1)}]^{-1} = [U_n^{(m)}][R_n^{(m)}]^{-1} \qquad (9.31)$$

of $[T_n^{(m+1)}]^{-1}$ and the lower triangular factor $\hat{U}_n^{(m)}$ in an LU (Lower triangular – Upper triangular) factorization

$$[T_n^{(m-1)}]^{-1} = [\hat{U}_n^{(m)}][\hat{P}_n^{(m)}]^{-1} \qquad (9.32)$$

of $[T_n^{(m-1)}]^{-1}$ while algorithm 2, wich computes also the entries of the factors $R_n^{(m)}$ and $\hat{P}_n^{(m)}$ column by column, gives the lower triangular factor $R_n^{(m)}$ in the LU factorization

$$T_n^{(m+1)} = [R_n^{(m)}][U_n^{(m)}]^{-1} \qquad (9.33)$$

of $T_n^{(m+1)}$ and the upper triangular factor $\hat{P}_n^{(m)}$ in the UL factorization

$$T_n^{(m-1)} = [\hat{P}_n^{(m)}][\hat{U}_n^{(m)}]^{-1} \qquad (9.34)$$

of $T_n^{(m-1)}$. The triangular factors $U_n^{(m)}$ and $\hat{U}_n^{(m)}$ are not unit triangular in this case but the can easily be made unit triangular by normalization.

Relation (9.19) is a matrix notation for the biorthogonality relation (8.3) of the polynomials of the first kind with respect to the bilinear form $<\cdot,\cdot>^{(m)}$ defined in section 8.1. Indeed, $T_n^{(m)}$ is the "Gram-matrix"

$$T_n^{(m)} = [<z^k,z^l>^{(m)}]_{k,l=0}^n.$$

Algorithm 1 diagonalizes this matrix and is thus a sort of Gram-Schmidt procedure. Because it uses only $O(n^2)$ arithmetic operations, it is called a *fast Gram-Schmidt procedure* for Toeplitz matrices. If $T_n^{(m)}$ were symmetric and positive definite, the factors in (9.22) would be exactly the factors that would have been found by a rational Cholesky procedure for the inverse $[T_n^{(m)}]^{-1}$. Therefore, algorithm 1 is sometimes referred to as an *inverse Cholesky procedure* for Toeplitz matrices. For the similar reasons (see (9.24)), algorithm 2 is sometimes called a *fast Cholesky procedure* for Toeplitz matrices.

We shall now use the matrix relations we have just found to derive a determinant expression for the reproducing kernel $k_n^{(m)}(x,y)$ of (8.8), associated with $<\cdot,\cdot>^{(m)}$. With the previous definitions of $Q_n^{(m)}$, $\hat{Q}_n^{(m)}$ and $D_n^{(m)}$, we can rewrite definition (8.8) of the reproducing kernel $k_n^{(m)}(x,y)$ as

$$k_n^{(m)}(x,y) = [1 \; y \; \cdots \; y^n][\hat{Q}_n^{(m)}][D_n^{(m)}]^{-1}[Q_n^{(m)}]^T[1 \; x \; \cdots \; x^n]^H, \tag{9.35}$$

where the superscript ^{H} means complex conjugate transpose.
By (9.22) we can rewrite this as

$$k_n^{(m)}(x,y) = [1 \; y \; \cdots \; y^n][T_n^{(m)}]^{-1}[1 \; x \; \cdots \; x^n]^H.$$

With this formula the following theorem is easy to verify.

THEOREM 9.11. *Let $F(z)$ be a normal fls, $n \in \mathbb{N}$ and $m \in \mathbb{Z}$. Let $k_n^{(m)}(x,y)$ be the reproducing kernel (8.8) associated with the bilinear form $<\cdot,\cdot>^{(m)}$. Then, with the Toeplitz notation (9.1a) we have the following determinant expression for $k_n^{(m)}(x,y)$:*

$$k_n^{(m)}(x,y) = -\det \begin{vmatrix} 0 & 1 \; y \; \cdots \; y^n \\ 1 & \\ \bar{x} & \quad T_n^{(m)} \\ \vdots & \\ \bar{x}^n & \end{vmatrix} \Big/ T_n^{(m)} \tag{9.36}$$

PROOF. The coefficient of $\bar{x}^k y^l$ in the expansion of this determinant is exactly the (l,k)th element of $[T_n^{(m)}]^{-1}$. Indeed, it is the ratio of the cofactor of the (k,l) entry of $T_n^{(m)}$ over $T_n^{(m)}$ with an appropriate sign.

□

We shall now work towards explicit inversion formulas for Toeplitz matrices. We shall derive them from the Chistoffel-Darboux relations of theorem 8.10. A first step in that direction is given in the next theorem.

THEOREM 9.12. *Let $F(z)$ be a normal fls, $n \in \mathbb{N}$ and $m \in \mathbb{Z}$. Let $Q_n^{(m)}(z)$ and $\hat{Q}_n^{(m)}(z)$ be the polynomials of the first kind and $v_n^{(m)}$ the v parameters of (3.1). Denote as before the coefficients of the polynomials by $Q_n^{(m)}(y) = \sum_{k=0}^{n} q_{k,n}^{(m)} y^k$ and $\hat{Q}_n^{(m)}(x) = \sum_{k=0}^{n} \hat{q}_{k,n}^{(m)} x^k$. Then we can express entry $(i+1,j+1)$ of $[T_n^{(m)}]^{-1}$ in terms of entry (i,j) and the coefficients of $Q_n^{(m)}(z)$ and $\hat{Q}_n^{(m)}(z)$ as follows :*

$$[(T_n^{(m)})^{-1}]_{i+1,j+1} = [(T_n^{(m)})^{-1}]_{i,j} + (v_n^{(m)})^{-1}(q_{i+1,n}^{(m)} \hat{q}_{n-j-1,n}^{(m)} - \hat{q}_{i,n}^{(m)} q_{n-j,n}^{(m)})$$

$$i,j = 0,1,...,n-1, \qquad\qquad (9.37a)$$

and

$$[(T_n^{(m)})^{-1}]_{i+1,j+1} =$$

$$[(T_n^{(m)})^{-1}]_{i,j} + (v_{n+1}^{(m)})^{-1}(q_{i+1,n+1}^{(m)} \hat{q}_{n-j,n+1}^{(m)} - \hat{q}_{i+1,n+1}^{(m)} q_{n-j,n+1}^{(m)}).$$

$$i,j = 0,1,...,n-1. \qquad\qquad (9.37b)$$

PROOF. The Christoffel-Darboux relation (8.10a) was

$$(1-\bar{x}y)k_n^{(m)}(x,y) = (v_n^{(m)})^{-1}\{Q_n^{(m)}(y)\overline{\hat{Q}_n^{(m)*}(x)} - \bar{x}y\hat{Q}_n^{(m)}(y)\overline{Q_n^{(m)*}(x)}\}$$

which can be rewritten with $X^H := [1 \ x \ \cdots \ x^{n+1}]$ and $Y^T := [1 \ y \ \cdots \ y^{n+1}]$ as (use (9.35))

$$Y^T\left\{ \begin{vmatrix} & & 0 \\ [T_n^{(m)}]^{-1} & & \vdots \\ & & \\ 0 & \cdots & 0 \end{vmatrix} - \begin{vmatrix} 0 & \cdots & 0 \\ \vdots & & \\ & [T_n^{(m)}]^{-1} & \\ 0 & & \end{vmatrix} \right\} X =$$

$$Y^T\left\{(v_n^{(m)})^{-1}\begin{vmatrix} Q_n^{(m)} \\ 0 \end{vmatrix}[(\hat{Q}_n^{(m)*})^H \ 0] - (v_n^{(m)})^{-1}\begin{vmatrix} 0 \\ \hat{Q}_n^{(m)} \end{vmatrix}[0 \ (Q_n^{(m)*})^H]\right\}X$$

Equate the coefficients of $y^{i+1}\bar{x}^{j+1}$ for the left and the right hand side and this will give (9.37a). (9.37b) can be proved similarly starting from the relation

(8.10b).

$\square$

From this theorem we can derive the inversion formulas for Toeplitz matrices. Before we can give this result, we need some triangular Toeplitz matrices we shall introduce now.

If Y is a column vector with entries $Y^T = [y_0 \cdots y_n]$, then $\mathbb{L}(Y)$ will denote a lower triangular Toeplitz matrix with first column the entries of Y :

$$\mathbb{L}(Y) := \begin{vmatrix} y_0 & \cdots & 0 & 0 \\ \vdots & & \vdots & \vdots \\ y_{n-2} & & 0 & 0 \\ y_{n-1} & \cdots & y_0 & 0 \\ y_n & \cdots & y_1 & y_0 \end{vmatrix}. \tag{9.38}$$

Let $Q_n^{(m)}(z) = \sum\limits_{k=0}^{n} q_{k,n}^{(m)} z^k$ and $\hat{Q}_n^{(m)}(z) = \sum\limits_{k=0}^{n} \hat{q}_{k,n}^{(m)} z^k$ be the polynomials of the first kind associated with a fls $F(z)$. Then define the triangular Toeplitz matrices :

$$\mathbf{X}_n^{(m)} := \mathbb{L}([q_{0,n}^{(m)} \cdots q_{n,n}^{(m)}]^T) \quad \text{and} \quad \mathbf{Y}_n^{(m)} := \mathbb{L}([\hat{q}_{n,n}^{(m)} \cdots \hat{q}_{0,n}^{(m)}]^T), \tag{9.39a}$$

$$\hat{\mathbf{X}}_n^{(m)} := \mathbb{L}([0\ q_{n,n}^{(m)} \cdots q_{1,n}^{(m)}]^T) \quad \text{and} \quad \hat{\mathbf{Y}}_n^{(m)} := \mathbb{L}([0\ \hat{q}_{0,n}^{(m)} \cdots \hat{q}_{n-1,n}^{(m)}]^T), \tag{9.39b}$$

$$\mathbf{V}_n^{(m)} := \mathbb{L}([q_{0,n+1}^{(m)} \cdots q_{n,n+1}^{(m)}]^T) \text{ and } \hat{\mathbf{V}}_n^{(m)} := \mathbb{L}([q_{n+1,n+1}^{(m)} \cdots q_{1,n+1}^{(m)}]^T) \tag{9.39c}$$

and finally

$$\mathbf{W}_n^{(m)} := \mathbb{L}([\hat{q}_{n+1,n+1}^{(m)} \cdots \hat{q}_{1,n+1}^{(m)}]) \quad \text{and} \quad \hat{\mathbf{W}}_n^{(m)} := \mathbb{L}([\hat{q}_{0,n+1}^{(m)} \cdots \hat{q}_{n,n+1}^{(m)}]) \tag{9.39d}$$

With these notations, we can give the following formulation for the inversion theorem.

THEOREM 9.13. *Let $F(z) = \sum f_k z^k$ be a normal fls. Associate with it the Toeplitz matrices $\mathbf{T}_n^{(m)}$ as in (9.1a). Then for $n \in \mathbb{N}$ and $m \in \mathbb{Z}$, we have the inversion formula*

$$(\mathbf{T}_n^{(m)})^{-1} = (v_n^{(m)})^{-1}\{ (\mathbf{X}_n^{(m)})\ (\mathbf{Y}_n^{(m)})^T - (\hat{\mathbf{Y}}_n^{(m)})\ (\hat{\mathbf{X}}_n^{(m)})^T\} \tag{9.40a}$$

$$= (v_{n+1}^{(m)})^{-1}\{ (\mathbf{V}_n^{(m)})\ (\mathbf{W}_n^{(m)})^T - (\hat{\mathbf{W}}_n^{(m)})\ (\hat{\mathbf{V}}_n^{(m)})^T\} \tag{9.40b}$$

where the $v_n^{(m)}$ are the v parameters defined in (3.1) and the matrices in the right *hand side are given in (9.39).*

PROOF. The first column of $[T_n^{(m)}]^{-1}$ is $(v_n^{(m)})^{-1}Q_n^{(m)}$ as you can see from (3.1). The first row can be found as follows : From (3.1) we get :

$$K_n T_n^{(m)} K_n K_n \hat{Q}_n^{(m)} = K_n [0 \cdots 0 \, \hat{v}_n^{(m)}]^T$$

where K_n is the anti unit matrix as before. Because $T_n^{(m)}$ is persymmetric, this may be rewritten as

$$[T_n^{(m)}]^T K_n \hat{Q}_n^{(m)} = [\hat{v}_n^{(m)} \, 0 \cdots 0]^T = [v_n^{(m)} \, 0 \cdots 0]^T$$

or

$$\hat{Q}_n^{(m)^T} K_n = [v_n^{(m)} \, 0 \cdots 0][T_n^{(m)}]^{-1} .$$

The entries of the first row of $[T_n^{(m)}]^{-1}$ are therefore the entries of $(v_n^{(m)})^{-1}\hat{Q}_n^{(m)^T}$ but in opposite order. Because $\hat{Y}_n^{(m)}$ and $\hat{X}_n^{(m)}$ have zero diagonal elements, we find that the first row and the first column in the right hand side of (9.40a) are precisely these first row and column of $[T_n^{(m)}]^{-1}$ as we have just described them. The other entries of (9.40a) are shown to be $[T_n^{(m)}]^{-1}$ entries by induction. Indeed, the $(i+1, j+1)$ entry of the right hand side of (9.40a) is

$$(v_n^{(m)})^{-1}\{[q_{i+1,n}^{(m)} \cdots q_{0,n}^{(m)} \, 0 \cdots 0][\hat{q}_{n-j-1,n}^{(m)} \cdots \hat{q}_{n,n}^{(m)} \, 0 \cdots 0]^T$$

$$- [\hat{q}_{i,n}^{(m)} \cdots \hat{q}_{0,n}^{(m)} \, 0 \cdots 0][q_{n-j,n}^{(m)} \cdots q_{n,n}^{(m)} \, 0 \cdots 0]^T\}$$

and this can be split up as

$$(v_n^{(m)})^{-1}\{[q_{i,n}^{(m)} \cdots q_{0,n}^{(m)} \, 0 \cdots 0][\hat{q}_{n-j,n}^{(m)} \cdots \hat{q}_{n,n}^{(m)} \, 0 \cdots 0]^T$$

$$- [\hat{q}_{i+1,n}^{(m)} \cdots \hat{q}_{0,n} \, 0 \cdots 0][q_{n-j-1,n}^{(m)} \cdots q_{n,n}^{(m)} \, 0 \cdots 0]^T\}$$

$$+ (v_n^{(m)})^{-1}\{q_{i+1,n}^{(m)}\hat{q}_{n-j-1,n}^{(m)} - \hat{q}_{i,n}^{(m)} q_{n-j,n}^{(m)}\}$$

By induction hypothesis, the first part equals $[(T_n^{(m)})^{-1}]_{i,j}$ and (9.37a) shows that the total is then the $(i+1, j+1)$ entry of $(T_n^{(m)})^{-1}$.
The proof of (9.40b) is similar to the previous one and is left as an exercise.

□

Relation (9.40a) is known as the Gohberg – Semencul formula (see [KVM] , [GOF]).

As you can see from algorithm 1 or relations (3.1), $Q_{n+1}^{(m)}$ and $\hat{Q}_{n+1}^{(m)}$ will depend upon f_{m+n+1} and f_{m-n-1}. Hence, also the right hand side of (9.40b) will depend upon f_{m+n+1} and f_{m-n-1} while the left hand side doesn't. These two f coefficients appear as parameters in this formula. It remains true whatever value you give them, provided $T_{n+1}^{(m)}$ is not singular, because then $v_{n+1}^{(m)}$ would be zero.

9.2.2 Hankel matrices

The previous treatment was mainly based on the quantities $S_n^{(m)}(z)$ for some fixed m while $n = 0, 1, \ldots$, i.e. on a row in the Padé table and the related bi-orthogonality with respect to $\langle \cdot, \cdot \rangle^{(m)}$. We can similarly derive results concerning a more Hankel oriented approach in connection with a descending diagonal and the related $[\cdot, \cdot]^{(m)}$ or an ascending diagonal and the related $\{\cdot, \cdot\}^{(m)}$. We give the results for a descending diagonal only. For an ascending diagonal, the results are similar. We use the same notation as in section 9.2.1 but with a different meaning. We now define the matrices $Q_n^{(m)}$ and $R_n^{(m)}$ as follows :

$$
Q_n^{(m)} := \begin{vmatrix}
q_{0,0}^{(m)} & q_{1,1}^{(m+1)} & \cdots & q_{n,n}^{(m+n)} \\
0 & q_{0,1}^{(m+1)} & \cdots & q_{n-1,n}^{(m+n)} \\
0 & 0 & & q_{n-2,n}^{(m+n)} \\
\vdots & \vdots & & \vdots \\
0 & 0 & \cdots & q_{0,n}^{(m+n)}
\end{vmatrix}
\tag{9.41a}
$$

and

$$
R_n^{(m)} := \begin{vmatrix}
r_{m+1,0}^{(m)} & \cdots & & 0 & & 0 \\
\vdots & & & \vdots & & \vdots \\
r_{m+n-1,0}^{(m)} & & & 0 & & 0 \\
r_{m+n,0}^{(m)} & \cdots & r_{m+n,n-1}^{(m+n-1)} & & 0 \\
r_{m+n+1,0}^{(m)} & \cdots & r_{m+n+1,n-1}^{(m+n-1)} & r_{m+n+1,n}^{(m+n)}
\end{vmatrix}.
\tag{9.41b}
$$

$Q_n^{(m)}$ is unit upper triangular and $R_n^{(m)}$ is lower triangular.

When as before $H_n^{(m)} = [f_{m+i+j}]_{i,j=0}^n$ and $K_n = [\delta_{i,n-j}]_{i,j=0}^n$, we have in analogy with theorem 9.8 the following theorem :

THEOREM 9.14. *Let* $F(z) = \sum f_k z^k$ *be a normal fls,* $n \in \mathbb{N}$ *and* $m \in \mathbb{Z}$. *Associate with it the Hankel matrices* $H_n^{(m)}$ *as in (9.1b). Then with the notation (9.41) we have the following relation :*

$$
Q_n^{(m)T} H_n^{(m+1)} Q_n^{(m)} = D_n^{(m)}
\tag{9.42}
$$

with $D_n^{(m)} = \mathrm{diag}(u_0^{(m)}, u_1^{(m+1)}, \ldots, u_n^{(m+n)})$ *where the* $u_k^{(m+k)}$ *are the u parameters of (3.2a).*

PROOF. From the definitions (3.1) and (3.4) of $Q_n^{(m+n)}(z)$ and $R_n^{(m+n)}(z)$ we get

$$
T_n^{(m+n+1)} K_n Q_n^{(m)} = R_n^{(m)}
$$

where K_n is the anti unit matrix. Thus, since $T_n^{(m+n+1)} K_n = H_n^{(m+1)}$ we find

$$H_n^{(m+1)} Q_n^{(m)} = R_n^{(m)}. \tag{9.43}$$

Because the Hankel matrix $H_n^{(m+1)}$ is symmetric we find by multiplying this relation from the left with $[Q_n^{(m)}]^T$ the first equality below. Similarly we can take the transpose of (9.43) and then multiply it from the right with $Q_n^{(m)}$. Then we find the second equality below.

$$[Q_n^{(m)}]^T H_n^{(m+1)} Q_n^{(m)} = [Q_n^{(m)}]^T R_n^{(m)} = [R_n^{(m)}]^T Q_n^{(m)} = D_n^{(m)}.$$

The last equality follows from the fact that $[Q_n^{(m)}]^T R_n^{(m)}$ is the product of lower triangular factors, hence it is lower triangular itself, while $[R_n^{(m)}]^T Q_n^{(m)}$ is the product of upper triangular factors, hence it is also upper triangular. Since they are equal, this must be diagonal. Because the diagonal elements of $R_n^{(m)}$ are $u_k^{(m+k)}$ and the diagonal elements of $Q_n^{(m)}$ are all 1, this diagonal must be $D_n^{(m)}$. This proves (9.42).

□

From this theorem we directly get the UDL factorization of $[H_n^{(m+1)}]^{-1}$ and the LDU factorization of $H_n^{(m+1)}$. These are given in the next theorem.

THEOREM 9.15. *Under the same conditions as in theorem 9.14 we have that*

$$[H_n^{(m+1)}]^{-1} = [Q_n^{(m)}][D_n^{(m)}]^{-1}[Q_n^{(m)}]^T \tag{9.44}$$

is a UDL factorization of $[H_n^{(m+1)}]^{-1}$ *, while*

$$H_n^{(m+1)} = [R_n^{(m)}(D_n^{(m)})^{-1}][D_n^{(m)}][(D_n^{(m)})^{-1}(R_n^{(m)})^T] \tag{9.45}$$

is a LDU factorization of $H_n^{(m+1)}$. *Of course, the relation between both factorizations is*

$$[Q_n^{(m)}]^{-1} = (D_n^{(m)})^{-1}(R_n^{(m)})^T. \tag{9.46}$$

PROOF. (9.44) follows from (9.42) after inversion and multiplication from the left with $Q_n^{(m)}$ and from the right with $[Q_n^{(m)}]^T$. Multiplication of (9.42) from the left with $[Q_n^{(m)}]^{-T}$ gives

$$H_n^{(m+1)}Q_n^{(m)} = [Q_n^{(m)}]^{-T}D_n^{(m)} \tag{9.47}$$

and comparison with (9.43) gives (9.46). Multiplying (9.47) from the right with $[Q_n^{(m)}]^{-1}$ finally gives (9.45).

□

This means that algorithm 4 of fig.7.7 for a descending staircase which computes in the kth step the kth column of $Q_n^{(m)}$ and of $Q_n^{(m+1)}$ will actually give the UDL factorizations (9.44) of $[H_n^{(m+1)}]^{-1}$ and $[H_n^{(m+2)}]^{-1}$ while algorithm 5 of fig.7.8 which computes in the kth step the kth column of $R_n^{(m)}$ and $R_n^{(m+1)}$ will produce the LDU factorization (9.45) of $H_n^{(m+1)}$ and $H_n^{(m+2)}$.

As for the Toeplitz case, we can see in (9.42) a matrix formulation for the orthogonality of the polynomials $Q_k^{(m+k)\times}(z)$ with respect to $[\cdot,\cdot]^{(m)}$ as in corollary

8.14. The corresponding reproducing kernel $l_n^{(m)}(x,y)$ of theorem 8.15 for this bilinear form can be expressed as in (9.48):

$$l_n^{(m)}(x,y) = [1 \ y \ \cdots \ y^n][Q_n^{(m)}][D_n^{(m)}]^{-1}[Q_n^{(m)}]^T[1 \ x \ \cdots \ x^n]^T$$

$$= [1 \ y \ \cdots \ y^n][H_n^{(m+1)}]^{-1}[1 \ x \ \cdots \ x^n]^T, \tag{9.48}$$

just like (9.35) gave the kernel $k_n^{(m)}(x,y)$. In analogy with theorem 9.11, we can derive from this the determinant expression for $l_n^{(m)}(x,y)$. The proof of it is similar to the one of theorem 9.11 and we leave it as an exercise. The result is given in the next theorem.

THEOREM 9.16. *Let $F(z)$ be a normal fls, $n \in \mathbb{N}$ and $m \in \mathbb{Z}$. Let $l_n^{(m)}(x,y)$ be the reproducing kernel with respect to the bilinear form $[\cdot,\cdot]^{(m)}$ as in theorem 8.15. Then, with the Hankel notation of (9.1b), we can express it as*

$$l_n^{(m)}(x,y) = - \det \begin{vmatrix} 0 & 1 & y & \cdots y^n \\ 1 & & & \\ \vdots & & H_n^{(m+1)} & \\ x^n & & & \end{vmatrix} / H_n^{(m+1)}. \tag{9.49}$$

$\square$

Using the Cristoffel – Darboux relations like in theorem 9.12, we may obtain explicit inversion formulas for the Hankel matrix $H_n^{(m+1)}$. The proof of these formulas is along the same lines as the proof of theorems 9.12-13. We shall not repeat it here. For their formulation we shall need triangular Hankel and Toeplitz matrices. To introduce them we shall use the following notation : Let

$$Q_n^{(m)}(z) = \sum_{k=0}^n q_{k,n}^{(m)} z^k \quad \text{and} \quad \hat{Q}_n^{(m)}(z) = \sum_{k=0}^n \hat{q}_{k,n}^{(m)} z^k$$

denote the polynomials of the first kind, associated with the normal fls $F(z)$. With the notation (9.38) for lower triangular Toeplitz matrices we define for $n \in \mathbb{N}$ and $m \in \mathbb{Z}$

$$X_n^{(m)} := \mathbb{L}([q_{n,n}^{(m+n)} \ \cdots \ q_{0,n}^{(m+n)}]^T) \tag{9.50a}$$

and

$$V_n^{(m)} := \mathbb{L}([q_{n,n+1}^{(m+n+1)} \ \cdots \ q_{1,n+1}^{(m+n+1)}]^T). \tag{9.50b}$$

Furthermore, define the "upper triangular" Hankel matrices

$$\mathbf{Y}_n^{(m)} := \begin{vmatrix} q_{n,n+1}^{(m+n+1)} & \cdots & q_{1,n+1}^{(m+n+1)} & q_{0,n+1}^{(m+n+1)} \\ q_{n-1,n+1}^{(m+n+1)} & \cdots & q_{0,n+1}^{(m+n+1)} & 0 \\ q_{n-2,n+1}^{(m+n+1)} & & 0 & 0 \\ \vdots & & \vdots & \vdots \\ q_{0,n+1}^{(m+n+1)} & \cdots & 0 & 0 \end{vmatrix} \tag{9.51a}$$

and

$$\mathbf{W}_n^{(m)} := \begin{vmatrix} q_{n-1,n}^{(m+n)} & \cdots & q_{0,n}^{(m+n)} & 0 \\ q_{n-2,n}^{(m+n)} & \cdots & 0 & 0 \\ \vdots & & \vdots & \vdots \\ q_{0,n}^{(m+n)} & & 0 & 0 \\ 0 & \cdots & 0 & 0 \end{vmatrix}. \tag{9.51b}$$

With this notation we can give the following inversion formula for the Hankel matrix $\mathbf{H}_n^{(m+1)}$ as it can be found from the first Christoffel–Darboux relation of theorem 8.15.

THEOREM 9.17. *Let* $F(z) = \sum f_k z^k$ *be a normal fls,* $n \in \mathbb{N}$ *and* $m \in \mathbb{Z}$. *Then with the notation of (9.50-51) we have for the Hankel matrices (9.1b) the inversion formula*

$$(\mathbf{H}_n^{(m+1)})^{-1} = (u_n^{(m+n)})^{-1}\{ (\mathbf{X}_n^{(m)})\ (\mathbf{Y}_n^{(m)})^T - (\mathbf{V}_n^{(m)})\ (\mathbf{W}_n^{(m)})^T\} \tag{9.52a}$$

or by taking the transpose

$$(\mathbf{H}_n^{(m+1)})^{-1} = (u_n^{(m+n)})^{-1}\{ (\mathbf{Y}_n^{(m)})\ (\mathbf{X}_n^{(m)})^T - (\mathbf{W}_n^{(m)})\ (\mathbf{V}_n^{(m)})^T\} \tag{9.52b}$$

where $u_k^{(m+k)}$ *denote the u parameters of (3.22).*

                                                               □

Of course, we can transform a Toeplitz matrix into a Hankel matrix by reversing the row or column order. Therefore it is possible to translate the inversion formulas (9.40) for Toeplitz matrices into inversion formulas for Hankel matrices. This will give us yet some other inversion formulas that are given in the next theorem.

THEOREM 9.18. *Let $F(z) = \sum f_k z^k$ be a normal fls, $n \in \mathbb{N}$ and $m \in \mathbb{Z}$. Then with the notation of (9.39) and with $\mathbf{K}_n$ the $(n+1)\times(n+1)$ anti unit matrix, we have for the Hankel matrices of (9.1b)*

$$(\mathbf{H}_n^{(m+1)})^{-1} =$$
$$(v_n^{(m+n+1)})^{-1}\{(\mathbf{K}_n \mathbf{X}_n^{(m+n+1)})(\mathbf{Y}_n^{(m+n+1)})^T - (\mathbf{K}_n \hat{\mathbf{Y}}_n^{(m+n+1)})(\hat{\mathbf{X}}_n^{(m+n+1)})^T\} \quad (9.52c)$$

$$(\mathbf{H}_n^{(m+1)})^{-1} =$$
$$(v_{n+1}^{(m+n+1)})^{-1}\{(\mathbf{K}_n \mathbf{V}_n^{(m+n+1)})(\mathbf{W}_n^{(m+n+1)})^T - (\mathbf{K}_n \hat{\mathbf{W}}_n^{(m+n+1)})(\hat{\mathbf{V}}_n^{(m+n+1)})^T\}, \quad (9.52d)$$

where $v_n^{(m)}$ represents the v parameter of (3.1).

PROOF. Take the formulas (9.40) for m replaced by $m+n+1$ and multiply from the right with $\mathbf{K}_n$. Use then

$$\mathbf{K}_n[\mathbf{T}_n^{(m+n+1)}]^{-1} = [\mathbf{T}_n^{(m+n+1)}\mathbf{K}_n]^{-1} = [\mathbf{H}_n^{(m+1)}]^{-1}$$

and you get the result.

□

We could of course do the reverse operation to go from the Hankel inversion formulas (9.52a,b) to Toeplitz inversion formulas. Then we get the formulas given in the next theorem.

THEOREM 9.19. *Let $F(z) = \sum f_k z^k$ be a normal fls, $n \in \mathbb{N}$ and $m \in \mathbb{Z}$. Then with the notation (9.50-51), used in theorem 9.17, we get for the Toeplitz matrices (9.1a) associated with $F(z)$ the formulas*

$$(T_n^{(m)})^{-1} =$$

$$(u_n^{(m-1)})^{-1}\{(K_n X_n^{(m-n-1)})(Y_n^{(m-n-1)}) - (K_n V_n^{(m-n-1)})(W_n^{(m-n-1)})\} \quad (9.53a)$$

and

$$(T_n^{(m)})^{-1} =$$

$$(u_n^{(m-1)})^{-1}\{(K_n Y_n^{(m-n-1)})(X_n^{(m-n-1)})^T - (K_n W_n^{(m-n-1)})(V_n^{(m-n-1)})^T\}, (9.53b)$$

where K_n is the $(n+1)\times(n+1)$ anti unit matrix and $u_n^{(m)}$ are the u parameters of (3.2a).

PROOF. Write down the formulas (9.52a,b) for m replaced by $m-n-1$ and multiply from the left with K_n and you will get the result if you use

$$K_n[H_n^{(m-n)}]^{-1} = [H_n^{(m-n)}K_n]^{-1} = [T_n^{(m)}]^{-1}.$$

□

Like in (9.40b), the elements f_m and f_{m+2n+2} that are implicit in the right hand sides of (9.52c,d) appear as parameters as long as they don't make $H_n^{(m+1)}$ singular. A similar remark concerning the parameter f_m in (9.52a,b) and the parameter f_{m+n+1} in (9.53a,b) can be made.

More on inversion formulas for Hankel and Toeplitz matrices is found in [HER].

9.2.3 Tridiagonal matrices

Also concerning the *ab* parameters and the $\hat{ab}$ parameters appearing in the rhombus algorithms 3 we can give some matrix relations involving these parameters. Therefore define the following bidiagonal matrices :

$$A_n^{(m)} := \begin{vmatrix} 1 & a_n^{(m)} & & & \\ & 1 & a_{n-1}^{(m-1)} & & \\ & & \cdot & \cdot & \\ & & & \cdot & a_2^{(m-n+2)} \\ & & & & 1 \end{vmatrix}, \quad (9.54a)$$

$$
\mathbf{B}_n^{(m)} := \begin{vmatrix} b_n^{(m)} & & & \\ 1 & b_{n-1}^{(m-1)} & & \\ & \cdot & \cdot & \\ & & \cdot & \cdot \\ & & 1 & b_1^{(m+n-1)} \end{vmatrix},
$$
(9.54b)

$$
\hat{\mathbf{A}}_n^{(m)} := \begin{vmatrix} 1 & \hat{a}_n^{(m)} & & & \\ & 1 & \hat{a}_{n-1}^{(m+1)} & & \\ & & \cdot & \cdot & \\ & & & \cdot & \hat{a}_2^{(m+n-2)} \\ & & & & 1 \end{vmatrix},
$$
(9.54c)

$$
\hat{\mathbf{B}}_n^{(m)} := \begin{vmatrix} \hat{b}_n^{(m)} & & & \\ 1 & \hat{b}_{n-1}^{(m+1)} & & \\ & \cdot & \cdot & \\ & & \cdot & \cdot \\ & & 1 & \hat{b}_1^{(m+n-1)} \end{vmatrix}.
$$
(9.54d)

Then with the matrices $\mathbf{J}_n^{(m)}$ and $\hat{\mathbf{J}}_n^{(m)}$ as defined in (9.10) we have the next theorem :

THEOREM 9.20. *Let* $F(z)$ *be a normal fls,* $n \in \mathbb{N}$ *and* $m \in \mathbb{Z}$. *For the ab parameters and the* $\hat{a}\hat{b}$ *parameters associated with it, define the bidiagonal matrices (9.54) as above. Let the matrices* $\mathbf{J}_n^{(m)}$ *and* $\hat{\mathbf{J}}_n^{(m)}$ *be associated with its* $\rho\sigma$ *and* $\hat{\rho}\hat{\sigma}$ *parameters as in (9.10). Then we have the following relations:*

$$
\mathbf{J}_n^{(m)} = \mathbf{A}_n^{(m)} \mathbf{B}_n^{(m)},
$$
(9.55a)

$$
\hat{\mathbf{J}}_n^{(m)} = \hat{\mathbf{A}}_n^{(m)} \hat{\mathbf{B}}_n^{(m)},
$$
(9.55b)

and

$$
\mathbf{B}_n^{(m)} \mathbf{A}_n^{(m)} = \mathbf{J}_n^{(m+1)} - a_{n+1}^{(m+1)} E_0 E_0^T
$$
(9.56a)

$$
\hat{\mathbf{B}}_n^{(m)} \hat{\mathbf{A}}_n^{(m)} = \hat{\mathbf{J}}_n^{(m-1)} - \hat{a}_{n+1}^{(m-1)} E_0 E_0^T,
$$
(9.56b)

with $E_0^T = [1 \ 0 \ 0 \ \cdots \ 0]$.

PROOF. The results are easily obtained if you compute the elements of the matrix products and use the rhombus relations.

□

Chapter 10

Symmetry Properties

With a fls $F(z) = \sum f_k z^k$ we have associated a lot of mathematical objects like uv parameters, SS parameters, ab parameters, FG parameters and $\rho\sigma$ parameters, polynomials $Q_n^{(m)}(z)$ the first kind, polynomials $A_n^{(m)}(z)$ of the second kind, Laurent polynomials $B(p)_n^{(m)}(z)$, other polynomials like $U_{k,n}^{(m)}(z)$, $V_{k,n}^{(m)}(z)$, $Q_{k,n}^{(m)}$ and series $P_n^{(m)}(z)$, $R_n^{(m)}(z)$, $\Pi_n^{(m)}(z)$, $\Gamma_n^{(m)}(z)$, $\Sigma_n^{(m)}(z)$, $\Omega_n^{(m)}(z)$ and $\Pi_{k,n}^{(m)}(z)$.

Now we shall consider the series $\hat{F}(z) = F(1/z)$ which is the fls $F(z)$ where f_k is replaced by f_{-k}. With $\hat{F}(z)$ we can again associate these mathematical objects. It will be shown in this chapter how they can be easily derived from the corresponding objects for $F(z)$. This will introduce a certain symmetry with respect to $m=0$ for the tables of the above mentioned parameters for $F(z)$ and $\hat{F}(z)$ as given in theorem 10.2. Corresponding symmetries for polynomials and series are given in theorem 10.3.

We shall also consider the case where $F(z)$ is a fps (i.e. $f_k = 0$ for $k < 0$). If the fps $F(z)$ is normal, then $f_0 \neq 0$ and its formal inverse $G(z) = 1/F(z)$ will exist as a fps. If $F(z)$ was a fls, the above mentioned objects were defined for $m \in \mathbb{Z}$ and $n \in \mathbb{N}$. Now that $F(z)$ is a fps, they will only be defined for m and $n \in \mathbb{N}$. By comparing the tables of parameters for $F(z)$ and the corresponding tables for $G(z)$, we will find that essentially the role of m and n are interchanged so that we more or less get a symmetry with respect to the diagonal $m=n$. This symmetry is derived in theorems 10.4–6.

10.1 Symmetry for $F(z)$ and $\hat{F}(z) = F(1/z)$

We shall first look at the relations between mathematical objects related to a fls $F(z) = \sum f_k z^k$ and those related to the dual series $\hat{F}(z) = F(1/z)$ $= \sum f_{-k} z^k$. We shall give an extra argument F or $\hat{F}$ to distinguish between quantities related to F and $\hat{F}$ respectively. The basic lemma concerns the Toeplitz determinants associated with them.

LEMMA 10.1. *Let $F(z) = \sum f_k z^k$ be a normal fls. For $m \in \mathbb{Z}$ and $n \in \mathbb{N}$, associate with it the Toeplitz determinants $T_n^{(m)}(F)$ of (9.1a). Similarly, $T_n^{(m)}(\hat{F})$ are the Toeplitz determinants associated with $\hat{F}(z)$. Then we have the following relation :*

$$T_n^{(m)}(\hat{F}) = T_{-n}^{(-m)}(F) = T_n^{(-m)}(F).$$

PROOF. Since $\hat{F}(z) = \sum f_{-k} z^k$, we have by definition :

$$T_n^{(m)}(\hat{F}) = \det \begin{vmatrix} f_{-m} & f_{-m+1} & \cdots & f_{-m+n} \\ f_{-m-1} & f_{-m} & \cdots & f_{-m+n-1} \\ \vdots & \vdots & & \vdots \\ f_{-m-n} & f_{-m-n+1} & \cdots & f_{-m} \end{vmatrix},$$

which is by definition $T_{-n}^{(-m)}(F)$ and if we transpose the above matrix we get $T_n^{(-m)}(F)$.

□

This lemma and the expressions of theorem 9.2 immediately give the next theorem.

THEOREM 10.2. *Let $F(z)$ be a normal fls and $\hat{F}(z) = F(1/z)$. Associate with these series the uv parameters as in (3.1) and (3.2a), the SS parameters as in (3.2b), the ab parameters as in (7.5) and (7.20), the $\rho\sigma$ parameters as in (7.18) and (7.22) and the FG parameters as in (7.14) and (7.23). Then*

$$s_n^{(-m)}(\hat{F}) = \hat{s}_n^{(m)}(F) \tag{10.1}$$

with s one of the symbols $u, v, \alpha, a, b, F, G, \rho$ or σ.

PROOF. This is easily verified with the expressions of theorem 9.2 and lemma 10.1. Take for example $v_n^{(-m)}(\hat{F})$. By (9.3a) it equals

$$v_n^{(-m)}(\hat{F}) = \frac{T_n^{(-m)}(\hat{F})}{T_{n-1}^{(-m)}(\hat{F})}.$$

If we use lemma 10.1 on this expression we get

$$v_n^{(-m)}(\hat{F}) = \frac{T_n^{(m)}(F)}{T_{n-1}^{(m)}(F)} = v_n^{(m)}(F) = \hat{v}_n^{(m)}(F).$$

The other relations can be verified in the same way.

□

With this result and the recurrence relations used before we also find that a number of correspondences exist as given in theorem 10.3.

THEOREM 10.3. *Let $F(z)$ be a normal fls and $\hat{F}(z) = F(1/z)$.*
- *For $m \in \mathbb{Z}$ and $n \in \mathbb{N}$ associate with these series*
  - *the P and R series as in (3.4)*
  - *the Q polynomials of the first kind as in (3.1)*
  - *the A polynomials of the second kind as in (4.3).*

Then we have

$$R_n^{(-m)}(z;\hat{F}) = z^n \hat{P}_n^{(m)}(1/z;F), \tag{10.2a}$$

$$P_n^{(-m)}(z;\hat{F}) = z^n \hat{R}_n^{(m)}(1/z;F), \tag{10.2b}$$

$$Q_n^{(-m)}(z;\hat{F}) = z^n \hat{Q}_n^{(m)}(1/z;F), \tag{10.2c}$$

$$A_n^{(-m)}(z;\hat{F}) = -z^n \hat{A}_n^{(m)}(1/z;F). \tag{10.2d}$$

- *For m and $p \in \mathbb{Z}$ and $n \in \mathbb{N}$ associate with these series the Laurent polynomials*
  - *$B(p)_n^{(m)}(z)$ as in (4.7),*
  - *$L(p)_n^{(m)}(z)$ as in (4.10).*

Then we have

$$B(p)_n^{(-m)}(z;\hat{F}) = -z^n \hat{B}(-p)_n^{(m)}(1/z;F), \tag{10.2e}$$

$$L(p)_n^{(-m)}(z;\hat{F}) = -\hat{L}(-p)_n^{(m)}(1/z;F). \tag{10.2f}$$

- *For $m \in \mathbb{Z}$ and $n \in \mathbb{N}$ associate with these series the LPA's $K(0)_n^{(m)}(z)$ as in (4.9) for $p=0$. Then*

$$K(0)_n^{(-m)}(z;\hat{F}) = -\hat{K}(0)_n^{(m)}(1/z;F). \tag{10.2g}$$

- *For $m \in \mathbb{Z}$ and $n \in \mathbb{N}$ associate with these series*
  - *the θ matrices as in (6.1)*
  - *the Moebius transforms $t(\cdot)$ as in (6.4).*

Then

$$\theta_n^{(-m)}(z;\hat{F}) = z\mathbf{K}_1\theta_n^{(m)}(1/z;F)\mathbf{K}_1 \quad \text{with } \mathbf{K}_1 = \begin{vmatrix} 0 & 1 \\ 1 & 0 \end{vmatrix}, \tag{10.2h}$$

$$t_n^{(-m)}(\cdot;\hat{F}) = \hat{t}_n^{(m)}(\cdot;F). \tag{10.2i}$$

- *For $m \in \mathbb{Z}$ and $n \in \mathbb{N}$ associate with these series*
  - *the Π series as in (6.6),*
  - *the Γ series as in (6.6),*

— the Σ series as in (6.13),
— the Ω series as in Corollary 6.4.

Then

$$\Pi_n^{(-m)}(z;\hat{F}) = \hat{\Pi}_n^{(m)}(1/z;F), \tag{10.2j}$$

$$\Gamma_n^{(-m)}(z;\hat{F}) = \hat{\Gamma}_n^{(m)}(1/z;F), \tag{10.2k}$$

$$\Sigma_n^{(-m)}(z;\hat{F}) = \hat{\Sigma}_n^{(m)}(1/z;F), \tag{10.2l}$$

$$\Omega_n^{(-m)}(z;\hat{F}) = -\hat{\Omega}_n^{(m)}(1/z;F), \tag{10.2m}$$

• For $m \in \mathbb{Z}$, $n \in \mathbb{N}$ and $k = 0,1,\ldots,n$ associate with these series
— the $U_{k,n}^{(m)}(z)$ polynomials as in (6.15),
— the $V_{k,n}^{(m)}(z)$ polynomials as in (6.15),
— the $\Pi_{k,n}^{(m)}(z)$ series as in (6.16),
— the $Q_{k,n}^{(m)}(z)$ polynomials as in (9.11).

Then

$$U_{k,n}^{(m)}(z;\hat{F}) = z^{n-k}\hat{V}_{k,n}^{(m)}(1/z;F), \tag{10.2n}$$

$$V_{k,n}^{(m)}(z;\hat{F}) = z^{n-k}\hat{U}_{k,n}^{(m)}(1/z;F), \tag{10.2o}$$

$$\Pi_{k,n}^{(-m)}(z;\hat{F}) = \hat{\Pi}_{k,n}^{(m)}(1/z;F). \tag{10.2p}$$

$$Q_{k,n}^{(-m)}(z;\hat{F}) = z^{n-k}\hat{Q}_{k,n}^{(m)}(1/z;F). \tag{10.2q}$$

PROOF. Practically all of these ralations can be proved by induction on n by using the recurrences that exist for them. All these recurrences use the parameters of theorem 10.2 for which a symmetry relation has been shown to exist.

Take for example $(10.2c)$. Certainly

$$Q_0^{(-m)}(z;\hat{F}) = \hat{Q}_0^{(-m)}(1/z;F)$$

since both are equal to 1. By (3.3) we have for the induction step

$$[Q_{n+1}^{(-m)}(z;\hat{F})\ \hat{Q}_{n+1}^{(-m)}(z;\hat{F})] = [Q_n^{(-m)}(z;\hat{F})\ \hat{Q}_n^{(-m)}(z;\hat{F})] \begin{vmatrix} 1 & -\hat{\alpha}_{n+1}^{(-m)}(\hat{F}) \\ -z\alpha_{n+1}^{(-m)}(\hat{F}) & z \end{vmatrix}$$

$$= [z^n\hat{Q}_n^{(m)}(1/z;F)\ z^nQ_n^{(m)}(1/z;F)] \begin{vmatrix} 1 & -\alpha_{n+1}^{(m)}(F) \\ -z\hat{\alpha}_{n+1}^{(m)}(F) & z \end{vmatrix}.$$

The right hand side equals

$$z^{n+1}[\hat{Q}_n^{(m)}(1/z;F)\ Q_n^{(m)}(1/z;F)] \begin{vmatrix} z^{-1} & -z^{-1}\alpha_{n+1}^{(m)}(F) \\ -\hat{\alpha}_{n+1}^{(m)}(F) & 1 \end{vmatrix}.$$

Introduce before and after the 2×2 factor in this expression the identity $K_1K_1 = I$ with K_1 the 2×2 anti unit matrix and you get :

$$z^{n+1}[Q_n^{(m)}(1/z;F)\ \hat{Q}_n^{(m)}(1/z;F)] \begin{vmatrix} 1 & -\hat{\alpha}_{n+1}^{(m)}(F) \\ -z^{-1}\alpha_{n+1}^{(m)}(F) & z^{-1} \end{vmatrix} K_1$$

which is the same as

$$z^{n+1}[Q_{n+1}^{(m)}(1/z;F)\ \hat{Q}_{n+1}^{(m)}(1/z;F)]K_1 = [z^{n+1}\hat{Q}_{n+1}^{(m)}(1/z;F)\ z^{n+1}Q_{n+1}^{(m)}(1/z;F)].$$

This proves (10.2c). The same technique can be used for all the other polynomials and series that satisfy the recurrence (3.6). This allows us to prove (10.2a-e). The minus sign in (10.2d) originates from the initial condition

$$A_0^{(-m)}(z;\hat{F}) = f_m' = -A_0^{(m)}(1/z;F).$$

In (10.2e) p gets a minus sign because the initial condition gives (see 4.8).

$$B(p)_0^{(-m)}(z;\hat{F}) = -\hat{B}(-p)_0^{(m)}(1/z;F).$$

Relation (10.2f-g) then follow from the definitions (4.9-10) and the relations proved above.

(10.2h) has been obtained as a side result in the beginning of this proof and it directly gives (10.2i).

If these are used in combination with the recurrences of theorem 6.1, theorem 6.3 and corollary 6.4, you can also prove (10.2j-m). sp 0 (10.2n-o) follow from the definition (6.15) and (10.2h). The recurrence relation of algorithm inverse 1b can be used together with (10.2i) to prove (10.2p) and finally, recurrence (9.12) together with theorem 10.2 can be used to prove (10.2q).

□

Note that the duality between $F(z) = \sum f_k z^k$ and $\hat{F}(z) = \sum f_{-k}z^k$ can be brought to a duality between $F(z)$ and $F_*(z) = \sum \bar{f}_{-k}z^k$ (see chapter 8). This is only a matter of taking the complex conjugate of the coefficients. Symmetry relations for this duality can be easily found from the previous results if you take the complex conjugate of the right-hand sides in lemma 10.1 and 10.2 and similarly for theorem 10.3 : If $(z;\hat{F})$ in the left-hand side is replaced by $(z;F_*)$, then you must replace $(1/z;F)$ in the right-hand side by $_*(z;F)$.

10.2 Symmetry for $F(z)$ and $G(z) = 1/F(z)$

As it was already anounced, there will also be some symmetry relations for a fps $F(z)$ and its formal inverse $G(z) = 1/F(z)$. We shall only treat the case of $F(z)$ being a fps in z. Of course, similar relations may be obtained when $F(z)$ is a fps in z^{-1}. Before we shall give the symmetry relations we shall first prove a theorem which gives the initial conditions for the ab parameters of $F(z)$ in terms of $G(z)$.

THEOREM 10.4. *Let* $F(z) = \sum_0^\infty f_k z^k$, $f_0 \neq 0$ *be a normal fps and* $G(z) = \sum_0^\infty g_k z^k$ *its formal inverse. Then the ab parameters for $F(z)$ viz.* $a_k^{(m+1)}(F)$ *and* $b_k^{(m)}(F)$ *from chapter 7 are only defined for $m \geq 0$ and $k \geq 1$ and we have*

$$a_k^{(1)}(F) = g_k/g_{k-1}, \quad k \geq 2 \quad , a_1^{(1)}(F) = 0, \tag{10.3a}$$
$$b_k^{(0)}(F) = 0 \qquad , \quad k \geq 2 \quad , b_1^{(0)}(F) = -g_1/g_0. \tag{10.3b}$$

Similarly $\hat{a}_k^{(m)}(F)$ and $\hat{b}_k^{(m)}(F)$ are defined for $m \geq 0$, $k \geq 1$ and

$$\hat{a}_{k+1}^{(0)}(F) = g_{k-1}/g_k \quad , \quad k \geq 1 \quad , \quad \hat{a}_1^{(0)}(F) = 0, \tag{10.3c}$$
$$\hat{b}_k^{(0)}(F) = 0 \qquad , \quad k \geq 1. \tag{10.3d}$$

PROOF. Since $f_k=0$ for $k < 0$, the defining relations (3.1) give $\hat{Q}_n^{(0)}(z;F) = z^n$ and thus $\hat{Q}_n^{(0)}(0;F) = -\hat{a}_n^{(0)}(F) = 0$ for $n \geq 1$, $\hat{a}_0^{(0)}(F) = -1$. From the definition (3.4) we obtain

$$F(z)Q_n^{(0)}(z;F) - P_n^{(0)}(z;F) = 0_+(z^{n+1}).$$

Thus $P_n^{(0)}(z;F) = f_0$. Multiply with $G(z)$ to get

$$Q_n^{(0)}(z;F) - G(z)f_0 = 0_+(z^{n+1}).$$

The coefficient of z^n gives $-\alpha_n^{(0)}(F) - g_n f_0 = 0$ or $\alpha_n^{(0)}(F) = -f_0 g_n$, $n \geq 0$. Consequently, because $f_0 = 1/g_0$:

$$b_n^{(0)}(F) = -\alpha_n^{(0)}(F)\hat{\alpha}_n^{(0)}(F) = 0 \qquad , n \geq 2$$
$$= -g_1/g_0 , n=1.$$

This proves (10.3b). We also found, using the definition of $\hat{b}(F)_n^{(0)}$, that

$$\hat{b}_n^{(0)}(F) = -\hat{\alpha}_n^{(0)}(F)\alpha_{n-1}^{(0)}(F) = 0 \qquad , n \geq 1,$$

which proves (10.3d).

From (7.24a): $\hat{Q}_n^{(1)}(z;F) = \hat{Q}_n^{(0)}(z;F) + \hat{a}_{n+1}^{(0)}(F)\hat{Q}_{n-1}^{(1)}(z;F)$. The constant term gives (use $\hat{\alpha}_n^{(m)} = 1/\alpha_{n-1}^{(m-1)}$ and $\hat{\alpha}_n^{(0)} = 0$)

$$\hat{a}_{n+1}^{(0)}(F) = \hat{\alpha}_n^{(1)}(F)/\hat{\alpha}_{n+1}^{(1)}(F) = \alpha_{n-1}^{(0)}(F)/\alpha_n^{(0)}(F) = g_{n-1}/g_n , n \geq 1.$$

Because by (7.21d) $\hat{a}_1^{(m)} = 0$, we have proved (10.3c). From (7.19a): $Q_{n+1}^{(0)}(z;F) = (1+zG_{n+1}^{(1)}(F))Q_n^{(0)}(z;F) + zF_{n+1}^{(1)}(F)Q_{n-1}^{(0)}(z;F)$. The coefficient of z^{n+1} gives

$$G_{n+1}^{(1)}(F) = \alpha_{n+1}^{(0)}(F)/\alpha_n^{(0)}(F) = g_{n+1}/g_n ,$$
$$n \geq 1$$

and with (7.14) and (7.7d)

$$G_{n+1}^{(1)}(F) = a_{n+2}^{(1)}(F) - b_{n+1}^{(1)}(F) = a_{n+1}^{(1)}(F) - b_{n+1}^{(0)}(F) = a_{n+1}^{(1)}(F) = g_{n+1}/g_n , n \geq 1.$$

Furthermore $a_1^{(1)}(F) = 0$ by (7.7b). This proves (10.3a).

□

From the preceding theorem we can derive the following symmetry properties.

THEOREM 10.5. *Let $F(z) = \sum_0^\infty f_k z^k$ be a normal fps and $G(z) = 1/F(z) = \sum_0^\infty g_k z^k$ its formal inverse. Then the ab parameters satisfy the following symmetry relations for $n \geq 1$ and $m \geq 0$:*

$$a_n^{(m)}(F) = b_m^{(n-1)}(G), \quad \forall m,n \geq 1 , \tag{10.4a}$$

except for $m=n=1$ where we have

$$b_1^{(0)}(F) = -b_1^{(0)}(G) = f_1/f_0 = -g_1/g_0, \tag{10.4b}$$
$$a_1^{(1)}(F) = a_1^{(1)}(G) = 0. \tag{10.4c}$$

Also

$$\hat{a}_{n+1}^{(m)}(F) = \hat{b}_{n+1}^{(m)}(G) \text{ for all } m,n \geq 0. \tag{10.4d}$$

PROOF. This follows from the initial conditions given in previous theorem and the rules (7.7) and (7.21). Indeed because of (10.3a) is $a_1^{(1)}(F) = 0 = a_1^{(1)}(G)$ which proves (10.4c). By (10.3b) we have $b_1^{(0)}(F) = -g_1/g_0$ and by (7.7a): $-b_1^{(0)}(G) = -g_1/g_0$ and $b_1^{(0)}(F) = f_1/f_0$. This proves (10.4b). The relation (10.4a) is shown by induction. By (7.7c) we have

$$a_n^{(m)}(F) = a_n^{(m-1)}(F)b_n^{(m-1)}(F)/b_{n-1}^{(m-1)}(F).$$

By induction hypothesis this equals

$$a_n^{(m)}(F) = b_{m-1}^{(n-1)}(G)a_m^{(n)}(G)/a_m^{(n-1)}(G).$$

When using (7.7c) again we find that the right hand side is equal to $b_m^{(n-1)}(G)$. This proves (10.4a).

The other relations are proved similarly.

$\square$

The symmetry of previous theorem is depicted in figures 10.1a and 10.1b.

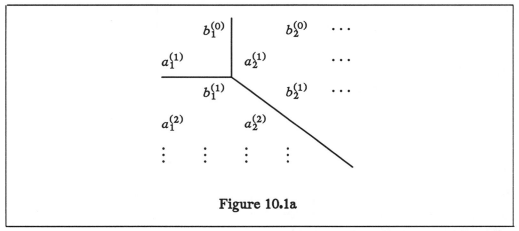

Figure 10.1a

If these tables are associated with $F(z)$, then by a reflection in the indicated diagonals (with an exception for $a_1^{(1)}$ and $b_1^{(0)}$) you will obtain the corresponding tables for $G(z) = 1/F(z)$.

The symmetry property of the above theorem also implies the symmetry relations given in theorem 10.6.

THEOREM 10.6. *Let $F(z) = \sum_0^\infty f_k z^k$ be a normal fps and $G(z) = 1/F(z) = \sum_0^\infty g_k z^k$ its formal inverse. Associate with these two fps*
  — the G parameters as in (7.14) and (7.23b),
  — the $\rho\sigma$ parameters as in (7.18) and (7.22),
  — the Q polynomials of the first kind as in (3.1),
  — the P and R series as in (3.4).

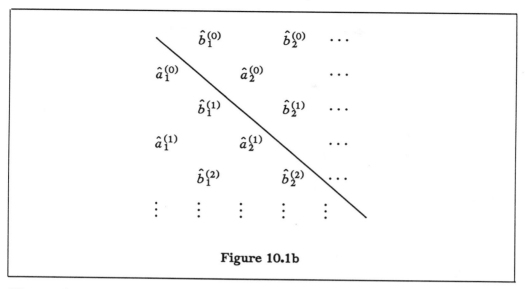

Figure 10.1b

Then we have the following relations :

$$G_n^{(m)}(F) = -G_n^{(m)}(G) \quad ; \quad \hat{G}_n^{(m)}(F) = -\hat{G}_{m+1}^{(n-1)}(G);$$

$$\rho_n^{(m)}(F) = \rho_{m+1}^{(n-1)}(G) \quad ; \quad \hat{\rho}_n^{(m)}(F) = \hat{\rho}_{m+1}^{(n-1)}(G);$$

$$\sigma_n^{(m)}(F) = \sigma_m^{(n)}(G) \quad ; \quad \hat{\sigma}_n^{(m)}(F) = \hat{\sigma}_{m+1}^{(n-1)}(G);$$

$$Q_n^{(m)}(z;G) = g_0 P_n^{(m)}(z;F) \quad ; \quad \hat{Q}_{m-1}^{(n+1)}(z;G) = \hat{P'}_n^{(m)}(z;F);$$

$$P_n^{(m)}(z:G) = g_0 Q_n^{(m)}(z;F) \quad ; \quad \hat{P}_{m-1}^{(n+1)}(z;G) = \hat{Q'}_n^{(m)}(z;F),$$

with as in theorem 9.4 $\hat{S'}_n^{(m)}(z) := \hat{S}_n^{(m)}(z)/\hat{u}_n^{(m)}$ for $S = P$ or Q.

PROOF. The first 6 relations can be obtained by expressing everything in terms of a and b or $\hat{a}$ and $\hat{b}$ parameters and using the previous theorem. For the last 4 relations note that if $F(z)$ is a fps then e.g. $P_n^{(m)}(z)$ is a polynomial of degree m. Then transform

$$F(z)Q_n^{(m)}(z;F) - P_n^{(m)}(z;F) = O_+(z^{m+n+1})$$

into

$$G(z)P_n^{(m)}(z;F) - Q_n^{(m)}(z;F) = O_+(z^{m+n+1}).$$

Thus $P_n^{(m)}(z;F)$ and $Q_n^{(m)}(z;F)$ satisfy the defining relations for $Q_m^{(n)}(z;G)$ and $P_m^{(n)}(z;G)$ respectively. g_0 serves to obtain the appropriate normalization. The relations with a hat are obtained in a similar way.

□

Chapter 11

Block structures

Until now we supposed that the fls $F(z)$ was normal which implies that $S_n^{(m)}(z)$ and $\hat{S}_n^{(m)}(z)$ where S is one of A, Q, P, $B(p)$, R existed for all $m = 0, \pm 1, \pm 2, \ldots$ and $n = 0, 1, 2, \ldots$. All the PAs $P_n^{(m)}(z)/Q_n^{(m)}(z)$ and $\hat{P}_n^{(m)}(z)/\hat{Q}_n^{(m)}(z)$, all the two–point PAs $A_n^{(m)}(z)/Q_n^{(m)}(z)$ and $\hat{A}_n^{(m)}(z)/\hat{Q}_n^{(m)}(z)$ and all LPAs $K_n^{(m)}(z)$ and $\hat{K}_n^{(m)}(z)$ existed and were unique for each value of m and n. We shall investigate what happens if $F(z)$ is not normal, i.e. if the Toeplitz determinants $T_n^{(m)}$ are not all nonzero. It is well known that for a fps $F(z)$, the table with (m,n)th entry $T_n^{(m)}$ has a so called block structure. This means that zero entries in the T-table show up in square blocks. The block structure of the T-table also introduces a block structure in the table of Padé approximants, of Laurent-Padé approximants and two–point Padé approximants. In fact, if the fls is not normal, some of these approximants do not exist. However, Padé forms, Laurent-Padé forms and two–point Padé forms will always exist according to our definitions of section 2.5. In chapter 4 we have seen how these approximants could be obtained from the algorithms of chapter 3. More precisely, we have found these approximants in terms of the quantities $Q_n^{(m)}(z)$, $A_n^{(m)}(z)$, $B(p)_n^{(m)}(z)$ that appeared in the algorithms of chapter 3. However they were defined under the conditions that $F(z)$ were a normal fls. Since now $F(z)$ is not normal any more, we shall redefine these polynomials and also the series $P_n^{(m)}(z)$ and $R_n^{(m)}(z)$ in a weaker form. This will be treated in section 11.1. It will be shown that these weaker definitions allow us to find Padé forms (PF), Laurent-Padé forms (LPF) and two–point Padé forms for the nonnormal fls $F(z)$. The exact $+$ and/or $-$ orders of $Q_n^{(m)}(z)$, $P_n^{(m)}(z)$ and $R_n^{(m)}(z)$ will give the block structure of the T-table which is treated in section 11.2. This structure will then be used in section 11.3 to give the (block) structure of the Padé table, the Laurent-Padé table and the two–point Padé table. Our approach is as in [GR2].

11.1 Pade forms, Laurent-Pade forms and two-point Pade forms

The polynomials $Q_n^{(m)}(z)$ and $\hat{Q}_n^{(m)}(z)$ are central. The defining equations (3.1) can be reformulated as :

$$\Pi_{m+1:m+n}(F(z)Q_n^{(m)}(z)) = 0 \text{ and } \Pi_{m:m+n-1}(F(z)\hat{Q}_n^{(m)}(z)) = 0. \qquad (11.1a)$$

If however $F(z)$ is not normal any more, then we shall not be able to keep the conditions that

$$Q_n^{(m)}(z) = \sum_{k=0}^{n} q_{k,n}^{(m)} z^k \quad \text{with} \quad q_{0,n}^{(m)} = 1$$

and

$$\hat{Q}_n^{(m)}(z) = \sum_{k=0}^{n} \hat{q}_{k,n}^{(m)} z^k \quad \text{with} \quad \hat{q}_{n,n}^{(m)} = 1.$$

We shall relax these conditions to

if $q_{0,n}^{(m)} = q_{1,n}^{(m)} = \cdots = q_{l-1,n}^{(m)} = 0$ and $q_{l,n}^m \neq 0$ then we require $q_{l,n}^{(m)}$ to be 1

and   (11.1b)

if $\hat{q}_{n,n}^{(m)} = \hat{q}_{n-1,n}^{(m)} = \cdots = \hat{q}_{k+1,n}^{(m)} = 0$ and $\hat{q}_{k,n}^{(m)} \neq 0$ then we require $\hat{q}_{k,n}^{(m)}$ to be 1.

Apart from that, $Q_n^{(m)}(z)$ and $\hat{Q}_n^{(m)}(z)$ represent any nontrivial solution of (11.1). Associate with these polynomials the series $P_n^{(m)}(z)$, $\hat{P}_n^{(m)}(z)$, $R_n^{(m)}(z)$ and $\hat{R}_n^{(m)}(z)$ as in (3.4). I.e.

$$P_n^{(m)}(z) = \Pi_{-\infty:m}(F(z)Q_n^{(m)}(z)); \quad \hat{P}_n^{(m)}(z) = \Pi_{-\infty:m-1}(F(z)\hat{Q}_n^{(m)}(z)) \qquad (11.2a)$$

and

$$R_n^{(m)}(z) = \Pi_{m+1:\infty}(F(z)Q_n^{(m)}(z)); \quad \hat{R}_n^{(m)}(z) = \Pi_{m:\infty}(F(z)\hat{Q}_n^{(m)}(z)). \qquad (11.2b)$$

For $B(p)_n^{(m)}(z)$ and $\hat{B}(p)_n^{(m)}(z)$, we shall simplify the notation and the development by taking $p=0$ in (4.7). So we define

$$B_n^{(m)}(z) := \Pi_{\min(0,m+n+1):\max(m,n)}(Z^{(0)}(z)Q_n^{(m)}(z)) \qquad (11.3a)$$

and

$$\hat{B}_n^{(m)}(z) := \Pi_{\min(0,m+n):\max(m-1,n)}(\hat{Z}^{(0)}(z)\hat{Q}_n^{(m)}(z)). \qquad (11.3b)$$

In the normal case $B_n^{(m)}(z)$ and $\hat{B}_n^{(m)}(z)$ coincide with $B(0)_n^{(m)}(z)$ and $\hat{B}(0)_n^{(m)}$ of chapter 4. It is a simple matter to verify that these quantities still satisfy the determinant expression (9.9) if only $T_{n-1}^{(m)} \neq 0$. The polynomials $A_n^{(m)}(z)$ and $\hat{A}_n^{(m)}(z)$ are introduced by relations (4.3). I.e.

$$z^m A_n^{(m)}(z) := Z^{(m)}(z)Q_n^{(m)}(z) - R_n^{(m)}(z) = \hat{Z}^{(m)}(z)Q_n^{(m)}(z) + P_n^{(m)}(z)$$

and   (11.4a)

$$z^{(m)}\hat{A}_n^{(m)}(z) := Z^{(m)}(z)\hat{Q}_n^{(m)}(z) - \hat{R}_n^{(m)}(z) = \hat{Z}^{(m)}(z)\hat{Q}_n^{(m)}(z) + \hat{P}_n^{(m)}(z)$$

where $Z^{(m)}(z) = \frac{1}{2} f_m z^m + f_{m+1} z^{m+1} + \cdots$ and $\hat{Z}^{(m)} = -\frac{1}{2} f_m z^m$ $- f_{m-1} z^{m-1} - \cdots$. Finally we introduce the couples $K_n^{(m)}(z)$ and $\hat{K}_n^{(m)}(z)$

conform to (4.9) with $p = 0$ as

$$K_n^{(m)}(z) := (B_n^{(m)}(z)/S_n^{(m)}(z), -z^{-n}\hat{B}_n^{(-m)}(z)/z^{-n}\hat{Q}_n^{(-m)}(z))$$

and   (11.4b)

$$\hat{K}_n^{(m)}(z) := (\hat{B}_n^{(m)}(z)/\hat{Q}_n^{(m)}(z), -z^{-n}B_n^{(-m)}(z)/z^{-n}Q_n^{(-m)}(z)).$$

With the quantities thus introduced we can give expressions for PFs, LPFs and two-points PFs.

THEOREM 11.1. *Let $F(z)$ be a fls and for $m \in \mathbb{Z}$ and $n \in \mathbb{N}$. Associate with it the polynomials of the first kind $Q_n^{(m)}(z)$ and $\hat{Q}_n^{(m)}(z)$ as in (11.1), the series $P_n^{(m)}(z)$, $\hat{P}_n^{(m)}(z)$, $R_n^{(m)}(z)$ and $\hat{R}_n^{(m)}(z)$ as in (11.2), the Laurent polynomials $B_n^{(m)}(z)$ and $\hat{B}_n^{(m)}(z)$ as in (11.3), the polynomials of the second kind $A_n^{(m)}(z)$ and $\hat{A}_n^{(m)}(z)$ as in (11.4a) and the couples $K_n^{(m)}(z)$ and $\hat{K}_n^{(m)}(z)$ as in (11.4b). Then, according to the definitions of section 2.5 :*

(1) *$(P_n^{(m)}(z)/Q_n^{(m)}(z))$ is a (m/n) PF and $(\hat{P}_n^{(m)}(z)/\hat{Q}_n^{(m)}(z))$ is a $(m-1/n)$ PF for the fls $F(z)$.*

(2) *$(\dfrac{A_n^{(m)}(z)}{Q_n^{(m)}(z)}, -\dfrac{z^{-n}\hat{A}_n^{(m)}(z)}{z^{-n}\hat{Q}_n^{(m)}(z)})$ is a $(0/n)$ LPF for $z^{-m} F(z)$.*

(3) *$K_n^{(m)}(z) = (\dfrac{B_n^{(m)}(z)}{Q_n^{(m)}(z)}, -\dfrac{z^{-n}\hat{B}_n^{(-m)}(z)}{z^{-n}\hat{Q}_n^{(-m)}(z)})$ is a (m/n) LPF for $F(z)$ if $m \geqslant 0$*

and

$\hat{K}_n^{(m)}(z) = (\dfrac{\hat{B}_n^{(m)}(z)}{\hat{Q}_n^{(m)}(z)}, -\dfrac{z^{-n}B_n^{(-m)}(z)}{z^{-n}Q_n^{(-m)}(z)})$ is a $(m-1/n)$ LPF for $F(z)$ if $m > 0$.

(4) *$A_n^{(m)}(z)/Q_n^{(m)}(z)$ is a two-point PF of type (n,n) and $\hat{A}_n^{(m)}(z)/\hat{Q}_n^{(m)}(z)$ is a two-point PF of type $(n-1,n)$ for the pair $(z^{-m}Z^{(m)}(z), z^{-m}\hat{Z}^{(m)}(z))$.*

PROOF. This essentially repeats the corresponding proofs of chapter 4 for the normal case. We do not repeat them here.

□

11.2 The T-table

A PF for a fps, which is the pair of polynomials $(P_n^{(m)}(z)/Q_n^{(m)}(z))$ may be reducible. I.e. $P_n^{(m)}(z)$ and $Q_n^{(m)}(z)$ may have a common factor which can be divided out to give a reduced ratio which is still the same function as the one defined by the unreduced form. For a fls, this is somewhat more complicated since $Q_n^{(m)}(z)$ is a polynomial, but $P_n^{(m)}(z)$ is a series. We shall now introduce a reduced solution which simulates the previous reduction via a reduction of $(B_n^{(m)}(z)/Q_n^{(m)}(z))$. Suppose the quadruple $S_n^{(m)}(z) = (B_n^{(m)}(z), Q_n^{(m)}(z), P_n^{(m)}(z), R_n^{(m)}(z))$ is as defined in section 11.1 by (11.1-3). I.e. as a solution of equations

$$\Pi_{m+1:m+n} (F(z)Q_n^{(m)}(z)) = 0 \tag{11.5a}$$

$$P_n^{(m)}(z) = \Pi_{-\infty:m} (F(z)Q_n^{(m)}(z)) \tag{11.5b}$$

$$R_n^{(m)}(z) = \Pi_{m+1:\infty} (F(z)Q_n^{(m)}(z)) \tag{11.5c}$$

$$B_n^{(m)}(z) = \Pi_{\min(0,m+n+1):\max(m,n)} (Z^{(0)}(z)Q_n^{(m)}(z)) \tag{11.5d}$$

where $Q_n^{(m)}(z)$ is a nontrivial polynomial of degree at most n and of the form $Q_n^{(m)}(z) = z^r + O_+(z^{r+1})$ with $r = \text{ord}_+(Q_n^{(m)}(z))$.

We shall reduce this solution to a simpler form by eliminating common factors. This goes as follows. Define

$$k(m,n) := \min(0,m+n+1)$$

and set

$$\tilde{B}_n^{(m)}(z) := z^{-k(m,n)} B_n^{(m)}(z)$$

so that $\tilde{B}_n^{(m)}(z)$ is a genuine polynomial of degree at most $\max(m,n)-k(m,n)$. Let $\tilde{B}(z)/Q(z)$ be the unique reduced form of $\tilde{B}_n^{(m)}(z)/Q_n^{(m)}(z)$ with the same normalization for $Q(z)$ as we introduced for $Q_n^{(m)}(z)$. Set further

$$B(z) := z^{k(m,n)} \tilde{B}(z) \tag{11.6a}$$

$$P(z) := -\hat{Z}^{(0)}(z)Q(z) + B(z) \tag{11.6b}$$

$$R(z) := Z^{(0)}(z)Q(z) - B(z). \tag{11.6c}$$

Then we call $S(z) = (B(z),Q(z),P(z),R(z))$ the *reduced solution* of (11.5). Because of the normalizing condition on $Q(z)$, such a reduced solution will be unique. We have the following lemma concerning this reduced solution.

LEMMA 11.2. Let $F(z) \neq 0$ be a fls, $m \in \mathbb{Z}$ and $n \in \mathbb{N}$.

Let $S_n^{(m)}(z) = (B_n^{(m)}(z), Q_n^{(m)}(z), P_n^{(m)}(z), R_n^{(m)}(z))$ be a solution of (11.5) and let $S(z) = (B(z),Q(z),P(z),R(z))$ be its reduced form as defined above. Suppose

$$Q_n^{(m)}(z) = z^\lambda D(z)Q(z) \tag{11.7a}$$

with $D(z) = d_0+d_1z + \cdots + d_\delta z^\delta$, $d_0 d_\delta \neq 0$. Then

$$S_n^{(m)}(z) = z^\lambda D(z)S(z)$$ (11.7b)

and if we define the polynomial $A_n^{(m)}(z)$ by (11.4a), i.e.

$$z^m A_n^{(m)}(z) = Z^{(m)}(z)Q_n^{(m)}(z) - R_n^{(m)}(z)$$

and the polynomial $A(z)$ by

$$z^m A(z) := Z^{(m)}(z)Q(z) - R(z),$$ (11.6d)

then

$$A_n^{(m)}(z) = z^\lambda D(z)A(z).$$ (11.7c)

PROOF. It suffices to observe that $z^\lambda D(z)$ is the greatest common divisor of $\tilde{B}_n^{(m)}(z)$ and $Q_n^{(m)}(z)$. Therefore $B_n^{(m)}(z) = z^\lambda D(z)B(z)$ and $Q_n^{(m)}(z) = z^\lambda D(z)Q(z)$. From the defining relations (11.6b–d) all the other relations follow. $\square$

This reduced solution will be the instrument to obtain the block structure of the T-table. As in the classical Padé case, ord$_-P(z)$ and ord$_+R(z)$ will be used to define the top row, respectively the bottom row of blocks in the T-table. In the classical case, ord$_-P(z)$ will always be nonnegative, but now ord$_-P(z)$ may be $-\infty$. Therefore a block is in general not defined by its top row and its size κ because the bottom row is not defined by ord$_-P(z)+\kappa$ if ord$_-P(z)$ and consequently $\kappa=\infty$. This justifies our introduction of top row and bottom row of the blocks separately. Theorem 3.2 in [GR2] gives the block structure of the T-table for a fps. We now give its generalization for a fls in the next theorem.

THEOREM 11.3. *Let $F(z)$ be a fls which is not zero. Let $\mu^+ = \text{ord}_+F(z)$ and $\mu^- = \text{ord}_-F(z)$ (μ^+ and μ^- may be infinite). Let $S(z)=(B(z),Q(z),P(z),R(z))$ be the reduced solution of equations (11.5) for some $n \geqslant 0$ and $\mu^+ \leqslant m \leqslant \mu^-$ and let*

$$\text{ord}_-Q(z) = \nu, \quad \text{ord}_-P(z) = \mu, \quad \text{ord}_+R(z) = \hat{\mu}+\nu+1.$$ (11.8)

Define $\kappa = \hat{\mu}-\mu$. Then the following is true
(1) $\kappa \geqslant 0$.
(2) $S(z) = (B(z),Q(z),P(z),R(z))$ is the reduced solution of equations (11.5) if and only if

$$\mu \leqslant m \leqslant \hat{\mu} \quad \text{and} \quad \nu \leqslant n \leqslant \nu + \kappa.$$ (11.9)

(3) For (m,n) satisfying (11.9): $S_n^{(m)}(z) = (B_n^{(m)}(z),Q_n^{(m)}(z),P_n^{(m)}(z),R_n^{(m)}(z))$ is a solution of (11.5) if and only if $S_n^{(m)}(z) = z^{\lambda_n^{(m)}} D(z)S(z)$ with

$$\lambda_n^{(m)} = \max\{0, (m-\mu)+(n-\nu)-\kappa\} \quad \text{if } \mu > -\infty \tag{11.10a}$$

$$= \max\{0, (m-\hat{\mu})+(n-\nu)\} \quad \text{if } \hat{\mu} < \infty \tag{11.10b}$$

and $D(z)$ is a nonzero polynomial of degree at most

$$\delta_n^{(m)} = n - \text{rank}[f_{m+l-j}]_{j=0,1,\ldots,n}^{l=1,2,\ldots,n}. \tag{11.11}$$

(4) *Define $T_{-1}^{(m)} = 1$. Then we have the following block structure properties for the Toeplitz determinants $T_n^{(m)}$ associated with $F(z)$:*

$$T_{\nu-1}^{(m)} \neq 0, \quad \mu \leqslant m \leqslant \hat{\mu},$$

$$T_{n-1}^{(m)} \neq 0, \quad \nu \leqslant n \leqslant \nu+\kappa, \quad \text{if } \mu > -\infty,$$

$$T_{n-1}^{(\hat{\mu}+1)} \neq 0, \quad \nu \leqslant n \leqslant \nu+\kappa, \quad \text{if } \hat{\mu} < \infty,$$

$$T_{\nu+\kappa}^{(m)} \neq 0, \quad \mu \leqslant m \leqslant \hat{\mu} \quad , \quad \text{if } \hat{\kappa} < \infty,$$

$$T_{n-1}^{(m)} = 0, \quad \mu < m \leqslant \hat{\mu} \quad \text{and } \nu < n \leqslant \nu+\kappa.$$

Remarks

(1) The cases $\mu > -\infty$ and $\hat{\mu} < \infty$ are covered separately. They cannot occur simultaneously if $F(z) \neq 0$. Indeed it would follow from $F(z)Q(z) = P(z)+R(z)$ that then $F(z)Q(z) = 0$. Since $Q(z) \neq 0$ we would have $F(z)=0$.

(2) This theorem was proved in [GR2] if $F(z) = \sum_0^\infty f_k z^k$ is a fps with $f_0 \neq 0$ i.e. if $\text{ord}_+ F(z) = 0$. Of course, this result can be easily generalized to the case that $\text{ord}_+ F(z) = \mu^+ > -\infty$. Indeed, except for a shift over μ^+ rows, the block structure of the T-table is as described in Gragg's theorem. Similarly with the transformation $z \rightarrow 1/z$, the case $\text{ord}_- F(z) = \mu^- < \infty$ is covered by it. Obviously a nonzero determinant $T_n^{(m)}$ can only occur in the region $\mu^+ \leqslant m \leqslant \mu^-$ and $n \geqslant 0$. In the proof of the theorem we therefore exclude the trivial cases $m < \mu^+$ and $m > \mu^-$.

PROOF. We shall give the proof for $\mu > -\infty$ only. In that case $\hat{\mu} = \mu+\kappa$. If $\mu = -\infty$, then $\hat{\mu}$ is finite and we can repeat the proof with μ replaced by $\hat{\mu}-\kappa$. If λ and δ are defined as in lemma 11.2. It is obvious that

$$\delta \geqslant 0 \quad \text{and} \quad \lambda \geqslant 0 \tag{11.12a}$$

and from (11.7a,b) it we easily see that

$$\delta + \lambda + \mu \leqslant m \quad \text{and} \quad \delta + \lambda + \nu \leqslant n. \tag{11.12b}$$

It also follows that

$$z^\lambda D(z)R(z) = R_n^{(m)}(z).$$

The left hand side has $+$ order which is exactly $\hat\mu + \nu + 1 + \lambda$ while the $+$ order of the right hand side is at least $m + n + 1$. Therefore

$$m + n \leqslant \hat\mu + \nu + \lambda = \mu + \kappa + \nu + \lambda. \tag{11.12c}$$

Now it can be easily verified that the system of unequalities (11.12) is equivalent with the following system (11.13).

$$\begin{aligned} &\delta \geqslant 0, \\ &\lambda \geqslant \max\{0,(m-\mu)+(n-\nu)-\kappa\}, \\ &\delta + \lambda \leqslant \min\{m-\mu,n-\nu\}. \end{aligned} \tag{11.13}$$

Conversely, let $S(z)=(B(z),Q(z),P(z),R(z))$ satisfy (11.5) with (m,n) replaced by (μ,ν) and suppose $Q(0)=0$, $\mathrm{ord\_}Q(z)=n$, $\mathrm{ord\_}P(z)=m$ and $\mathrm{ord}_+R(z) = m+n+k+1$. Then for λ and δ solutions of (11.13) and for an arbitrary polynomial $D(z)=d_0+d_1+...+d_\delta z^\delta$, $d_0 d_\delta \neq 0$, $S_n^{(m)}(z)$ given by (11.7b) will be a solution of (11.5). Now we know that $S(z)$ is the reduced solution of (11.5). Thus there must exist integers δ,λ,m,n satisfying (11.13). Hence

$$\kappa \geqslant (m-\mu)+(n-\nu)- \kappa \geqslant 2\delta+\lambda \geqslant 0.$$

This proves (1). Furthermore (11.13) can only have a solution if

$$\max\{0,(m-\mu)+(n-\nu)-\kappa\} \leqslant \min\{m-\mu,n-\nu\}. \tag{11.14}$$

This is equivalent with (11.9) so that also (2) is proved. To prove (3) we note that the most general solution of (11.5) is obtained by putting as many degrees of freedom in the factor $z^\lambda D(z)$ of (11.7) as is possible. I.e. by choosing λ as small as possible and δ as large as possible among the solutions of (11.13). It can be verified that $\lambda_n^{(m)}$ as defined in (11.10) and $\delta_n^{(m)}$ as defined in (11.11) are these extremal values for λ and δ. Indeed, $\delta_n^{(m)}$ is exactly the number of degrees of freedom that we have in the choice of a solution for $Q_n^{(m)}(z)$ in (11.1a). (Remember that we fixed one coefficient by normalization). This proves (3). We know that $T_{n-1}^{(m)} = 0$ if and only if (11.1a) has a nontrivial solution for $Q_n^{(m)}(z)$ with $Q_n^{(m)}(0) = 0$, i.e. with $\lambda > 0$. Because of (11.13), this occurs if and only if $\min(m-\mu,n-\nu) > 0$ and (11.14) is satisfied. This is equivalent with statement (4) of the theorem.

$\square$

It will be clear from the previous that the numbers μ, $\hat\mu$, ν and $\hat\nu$ as they were related to the unique reduced solution of (11.5), depend for a given $F(z)$ only on m and n. Including the zero determinants treated in remark (2) concerning theorem 11.3 we may define with the preceding notation

$$\nu_n^{(m)} := 0 \qquad \text{if } m < \mu^+ \text{ or } m > \mu^- \tag{11.15}$$
$$\phantom{\nu_n^{(m)}} := \nu \qquad \text{otherwise,}$$

$$\kappa_n^{(m)} := \infty \qquad \text{if } m < \mu^+ \text{ or } m > \mu^- \tag{11.16}$$
$$\phantom{\kappa_n^{(m)}} := \kappa \qquad \text{otherwise,}$$

$$\mu_n^{(m)} := -\infty \qquad \text{if } m < \mu^+ \tag{11.17}$$
$$\phantom{\mu_n^{(m)}} := \mu^- \qquad \text{if } m > \mu^-$$
$$\phantom{\mu_n^{(m)}} := \mu \qquad \text{otherwise,}$$

$$\hat{\mu}_n^{(m)} := \mu^+ + 1 \quad \text{if } m < \mu^+ \tag{11.18}$$
$$\phantom{\hat{\mu}_n^{(m)}} := \infty \qquad \text{if } m > \mu^-$$
$$\phantom{\hat{\mu}_n^{(m)}} := \hat{\mu} \qquad \text{otherwise.}$$

With this extended definition we have e.g. that $\kappa_n^{(m)} = \infty$ if and only if $\mu_n^{(m)} = -\infty$ or $\hat{\mu}_n^{(m)} = \infty$. Also $\hat{\mu}_n^{(m)} = \mu_n^{(m)} + \kappa_n^{(m)}$ if $\mu_n^{(m)} > -\infty$ and $\mu_n^{(m)} = \hat{\mu}_n^{(m)} - \kappa_n^{(m)}$ if $\hat{\mu}_n^{(m)} < \infty$. With these numbers we associate the square blocks

$$\mathbb{B}_n^{(m)} := \{(p,q): \mu_n^{(m)} \leqslant p \leqslant \hat{\mu}_n^{(m)}, \ \nu_n^{(m)} \leqslant q \leqslant \nu_n^{(m)} + \kappa_n^{(m)}\} \tag{11.19}$$

and by deleting the first row and the last column

$$\mathbb{b}_n^{(m)} := \{(p,q): \mu_n^{(m)} < p \leqslant \hat{\mu}_n^{(m)}, \ \nu_n^{(m)} \leqslant q < \nu_n^{(m)} + \kappa_n^{(m)}\}. \tag{11.20}$$

See fig 11.1

Part (4) of theorem 11.3 says that $T_q^{(p)} = 0$ for all $(p,q) \in \mathbb{b}_n^{(m)}$ and for all finite couples (p,q) bordering $\mathbb{b}_n^{(m)}$, $T_q^{(p)}$ will be nonzero. The blocks $\mathbb{B}_n^{(m)}$ correspond to the blocks as they were defined for the classical Padé case. It is clear that the blocks $\mathbb{B}_n^{(m)}$ do not overlap and give a complete tiling of the grid $\{(p,q): p \in \mathbb{Z}, q \in \mathbb{N}\}$. Furthermore, it is easly verified that the following are equivalent

(1) $\mu_q^{(p)} = \mu_n^{(m)}$ and $\nu_q^{(p)} = \nu_n^{(m)}$

(2) $\hat{\mu}_q^{(p)} = \hat{\mu}_n^{(m)}$ and $\nu_q^{(p)} = \nu_n^{(m)}$ (11.21)

(3) $(p,q) \in \mathbb{B}_n^{(m)}$.

Similarly

(1) $\mu_n^{(m)} = \mu_n^{(p)}$,

(2) $\hat{\mu}_n^{(m)} = \hat{\mu}_n^{(p)}$,   (11.22)

(3) $(p,n) \in \mathbb{B}_n^{(m)}$

are all equivalent and so are

(1) $\nu_n^{(m)} = \nu_q^{(m)}$,   (11.23a)

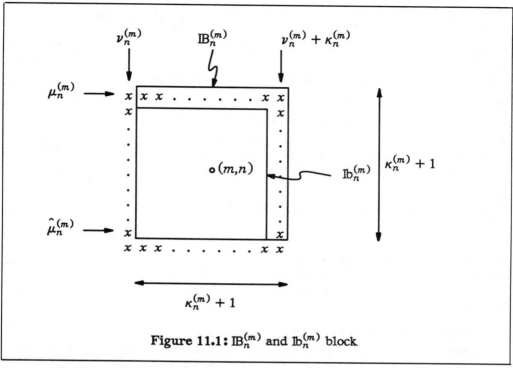

Figure 11.1: $\mathbb{B}_n^{(m)}$ and $\mathbb{b}_n^{(m)}$ block

(2) $(m,q) \in \mathbb{B}_n^{(m)}$. (11.23b)

11.3 The Pade, Laurent-Pade, and two-point Pade tables

If we fill up a table with (m,n)th entry some (m,n) Padé forms from theorem 11.1(1), then this table has square blocks where the entries are equivalent pairs. Those in the left top triangular part are PAs in the strict sense. This left top triangle is

$$\mathbb{L}_n^{(m)} = \{(p,q) \in \mathbb{B}_n^{(m)} : p+q \leqslant \hat{\mu}_n^{(m)}+\nu_n^{(m)}\}. \qquad (11.24)$$

This is stated more precisely in the next theorem.

THEOREM 11.4. *Let $F(z) \neq 0$ be a fls and let $(P_q^{(p)}(z)/Q_q^{(p)}(z))$ be some (p,q) PF of $F(z)$ for $p \in \mathbb{Z}$ and $q \in \mathbb{N}$ as defined in theorem 11.1. Suppose $\mathbb{B}_n^{(m)}$ and $\mathbb{L}_n^{(m)}$ are the set of points as defined in (11.19) and (11.24). Then*

(1) *$(P_n^{(m)}(z)/Q_n^{(m)}(z))$ is equivalent with $(P_\nu^{(\mu)}(z)/Q_\nu^{(\mu)}(z))$ if and only if $(m,n) \in \mathbb{B}_\nu^{(\mu)}$.*

(2) $(P_n^{(m)}(z)/Q_n^{(m)}(z))$ is the (m/n) PA of $F(z)$ if and only if $(m,n) \in \mathbb{L}_n^{(m)}$.

PROOF. From theorem 11.3(3) we know that all $(P_\nu^{(\mu)}(z)/Q_\nu^{(\mu)}(z))$ with $(\mu,\nu) \in \mathbb{B}_n^{(m)}$ are equivalent with $(P(z)/Q(z))$ where $P(z)$ and $Q(z)$ are taken from the reduced solution of (11.5). Since the reduced form is unique, this proves the first part. $(P_n^{(m)}(z)/Q_n^{(m)}(z))$ is a PA if and only if $Q_n^{(m)}(0) \neq 0$, i.e. $\lambda_n^{(m)} = 0$. From (11.10) it follows that this is precisely when $(m,n) \in \mathbb{L}_n^{(m)}$.

$\square$

For the other PFs a similar result holds. I.e. the PF $(\hat{P}_n^{(m)}(z)/\hat{Q}_n^{(m)}(z))$ is equivalent with $(\hat{P}_\nu^{(\mu)}(z)/\hat{Q}_\nu^{(\mu)}(z))$ if and only if (m,n) belongs to the shifted grid block

$$(1,0) + \mathbb{B}_\nu^{(\mu-1)} := \{(p+1,q):(p,q) \in \mathbb{B}_\nu^{(\mu-1)}\}. \tag{11.25}$$

This follows from the fact that, up to a normalization $\hat{Q}_n^{(m)}(z) = Q_n^{(m-1)}(z)$ and consequently a similar relation holds for $\hat{P}_n^{(m)}(z)$ etc. Again the entries in the left upper triangular part of this shifted block are PAs in a strict sense.
The blocks $\mathbb{B}_n^{(m)}$ also characterise the equivalent entries in the table of two–point Padé forms.

THEOREM 11.5. *Let $F(z)$ be a fls and let $A_n^{(m)}(z)/Q_n^{(m)}(z)$ represent the (m,n) two–point PFs for $F(z)$ as in theorem 11.1. Suppose the sets $\mathbb{B}_n^{(m)}$ and $\mathbb{L}_n^{(m)}$ are as defined in (11.19) and (11.24). Then $(A_n^{(m)}(z)/Q_n^{(m)}(z))$ is equivalent with $(A_\nu^{(\mu)}(z)/Q_\nu^{(\mu)}(z))$ if and only if $(m,n) \in \mathbb{B}_\nu^{(\mu)}$. $(A_n^{(m)}(z)/Q_n^{(m)}(z))$ is a two–point PA if and only if $(m,n) \in \mathbb{L}_n^{(m)} \cap \tilde{\mathbb{L}}_n^{(m)}$ with $\tilde{\mathbb{L}}_n^{(m)} = \{(p,q) \in \mathbb{B}_n^{(m)} : p-q \leqslant \mu_n^{(m)}-\nu_n^{(m)}\}$ (see fig 11.2).*

PROOF. The equivalence of the two–point PFs in $\mathbb{B}_\nu^{(\mu)}$ is shown as in the previous theorem. A two–point PF is also a two–point PA if $\mathrm{ord}_+Q_n^{(m)}(z) = 0$ and $\mathrm{ord}_-Q_n^{(m)}(z) = n$. We know that $\mathrm{ord}_+Q_n^{(m)}(z) = 0$ for $(m,n) \in \mathbb{L}_n^{(m)}$. Now $\mathrm{ord}_-Q_n^{(m)}(z) = n$ iff $\mathrm{ord}_+(z^n Q_n^{(m)}(1/z)) = 0$. From the symmetry property 10.3 we know that $z^n Q_n^{(m)}(1/z;F)$ is the same as the polynomial $\hat{Q}_n^{(-m)}(z;\hat{F})$ belonging to $\hat{F}(z) = F(1/z)$. The blocks of $\hat{F}$ and F are related by

$$\mathbb{B}_n^{(-m)}(\hat{F}) = \{(p,q):(-p,q) \in (1,0)+\mathbb{B}_n^{(m-1)}(F)\}. \tag{11.26}$$

This means that the T–blocks for $\hat{F}$ are obtained by reflecting the T–blocks of F in the line $m=-\frac{1}{2}$. We know that $\mathrm{ord}_+\hat{Q}_n^{(-m)}(z;\hat{F}) = 0$ in the left upper triangular part of $(1,0) + \mathbb{B}_n^{(-m-1)}(\hat{F})$. Reflecting this back gives that $\mathrm{ord}_-Q_n^{(m)}(z;F) = n$ in the left lower triangular part of $\mathbb{B}_n^{(m)}(F)$ which is $\tilde{\mathbb{L}}_n^{(m)}$. Thus $(A_n^{(m)}(z)/Q_n^{(m)}(z))$ will be a two–point PA iff $(m,n) \in \mathbb{L}_n^{(m)} \cap \tilde{\mathbb{L}}_n^{(m)}$ and this

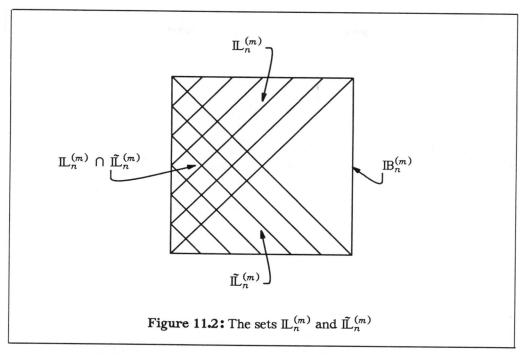

Figure 11.2: The sets $\mathbb{L}_n^{(m)}$ and $\tilde{\mathbb{L}}_n^{(m)}$

proves the theorem.

□

For the LPFs, the situation is a bit more complicated. We know from theorem 11.3 that $(B_n^{(m)}(z)/Q_n^{(m)}(z))$ is equivalent with $(B_\nu^{(\mu)}(z)/Q_\nu^{(\mu)}(z))$ if and only if $(m,n) \in \mathbb{B}_\nu^{(\mu)}$ and $(\hat{B}_n^{(-m)}(z)/\hat{Q}_n^{(-m)}(z))$ is equivalent with $(\hat{B}_\nu^{(-\mu)}(z)/\hat{Q}_\nu^{(-\mu)}(z))$ if and only if $(-m,n) \in (1,0) + \mathbb{B}_\nu^{(-\mu-1)}$. Combining this we find the result of the following theorem.

THEOREM 11.6. *Let $F(z) \neq 0$ be a fls. For $m \in \mathbb{Z}$ and $n \in \mathbb{N}$, let $K_n^{(m)}(z) :=$*
$(B_n^{(m)}(z)/Q_n^{(m)}(z), -z^{-n}\hat{B}_n^{(-m)}(z)/z^{-n}\hat{Q}_n^{(-m)}(z))$ be a (m,n) LPF of $F(z)$ as in theorem 11.1 and let $\mathbb{B}_n^{(m)}$ denote the block (11.19). The the two components of LPF $K_n^{(m)}(z)$ are equivalent with the two components of some other LPF $K_\nu^{(\mu)}(z)$ if and only if

$$(m,n) \in \mathbb{D}_\nu^{(\mu)} = \mathbb{B}_\nu^{(\mu)} \cap \hat{\mathbb{B}}_\nu^{(\mu)}$$

where

$$\hat{\mathbb{B}}_\nu^{(\mu)} := \{(p,q):(-p,q) \in (1,0) + \mathbb{B}_\nu^{(-\mu-1)}\}. \tag{11.27}$$

□

The rectangular blocks $\mathbb{D}_\nu^{(\mu)}$ are constructed as follows. (See fig. 11.3.)

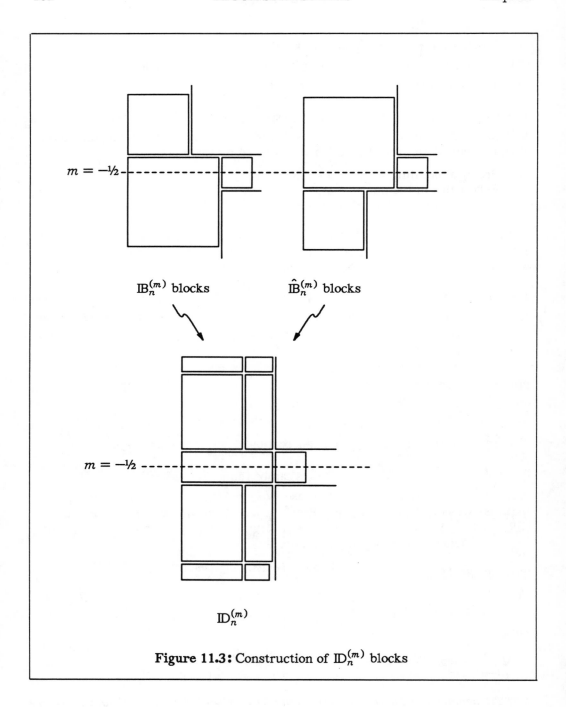

Figure 11.3: Construction of $\mathbb{D}_n^{(m)}$ blocks

(1) Produce a plot of the square blocks $\mathbb{B}_n^{(m)}$.
(2) Reflect this tiling in the line $m = -\frac{1}{2}$ to obtain the blocks $\hat{\mathbb{B}}_n^{(m)}$.
(3) Take the intersections of the tilings $\mathbb{B}_n^{(m)}$ and $\hat{\mathbb{B}}_n^{(m)}$.

The $\mathbb{D}_n^{(m)}$ tiling is symmetric with respect to $m = -\frac{1}{2}$. For the other LPFs $\hat{K}_n^{(m)}(z)$ of theorem 11.1, a similar result can be obtained. The rectangular blocks of equivalent entries for these LPFs are obtained by the procedure

(1) Produce the tiling with blocks $(1,0) + \mathbb{B}_n^{(m)}$.
(2) Reflect this in the line $m = \frac{1}{2}$.
(3) Take the intersection of these tilings.

Unlike in the situation of PFs or two-point PFs, it may happen that none of the entries in the blocks of the LPF table is a LPA. It is explained in the next theorem when an LPF is an LPA.

THEOREM 11.7. Let $F(z) \neq 0$ be a fls and let $K_n^{(m)}(z)$ be an (m/n) LPF. Then $K_n^{(m)}(z)$ is a LPA iff $(m,n) \in \mathbb{L}_n^{(m)} \cap \hat{\mathbb{L}}_n^{(m)}$, where $\hat{\mathbb{L}}_n^{(m)}$ is the left upper triangular part of $\hat{\mathbb{B}}_n^{(m)}$ defined in (11.27) and $\mathbb{L}_n^{(m)}$ is as in (11.24). Note that $\mathbb{L}_n^{(m)} \cap \hat{\mathbb{L}}_n^{(m)}$ may be empty.

PROOF. The LPF $K_n^{(m)}(z)$ will be a LPA iff $\mathrm{ord}_+ Q_n^{(m)}(z) = 0$ and $\mathrm{ord}_- Q_n^{(-m)}(z) = n$. We know that $\mathrm{ord}_+ Q_n^{(m)}(z) = 0$ iff $(m,n) \in \mathbb{L}_n^{(m)}$. With the techniques used in the proof of theorem 11.5 we can show that $\mathrm{ord}_- \hat{Q}_n^{(-m)}(z) = n$ iff (m,n) is in the left upper triangular part of $\hat{\mathbb{B}}_n^{(m)}(F) = \mathbb{B}_n^{(-m)}(\hat{F})$.

$\square$

Examples giving some block structures can be found in chapter 18.

It has some interest to consider the case $F(z) = \hat{F}(z)$. i.e. $f_k = f_{-k}$ for all k. In that case we may replace "Laurent-Padé" by "Chebyshev-Padé" in the previous text [GR1,GRJ]. The symmetry properties of chapter 10 give without any difficulty the block structure for the Chebyshev-Padé table.

THEOREM 11.8. Let $F(z) \neq 0$ be a fls for $m \in \mathbb{Z}$ and $n \in \mathbb{N}$, associate with it the polynomials $Q_n^{(m)}(z)$ as in (11.1a), the series $P_n^{(m)}(z)$, $R_n^{(m)}(z)$, $\hat{P}_n^{(m)}(z)$ and $\hat{R}_n^{(m)}(z)$ as in (11.2) and the Laurent polynomials $B_n^{(m)}(z)$ and $\hat{B}_n^{(m)}(z)$ as in (11.3). Then

$$Q_n^{(-m)}(z) = z^n \hat{Q}_n^{(m)}(1/z) \quad ; \quad P_n^{(-m)}(z) = z^n \hat{R}_n^{(m)}(1/z),$$
$$R_n^{(-m)}(z) = z^n \hat{P}_n^{(m)}(1/z) \quad \text{and} \quad B_n^{(-m)}(z) = z^n \hat{B}_n^{(m)}(1/z).$$

If $T_n^{(m)}$ denotes the Toeplitz determinants (9.1), then $T_n^{(-m)} = T_n^{(m)}$ and therefore $\mathbb{B}_n^{(m)} = \hat{\mathbb{B}}_n^{(m)} = \mathbb{D}_n^{(m)}$ when these denote the blocks of fig. 11.3. In the square

blocks $\mathbb{D}_n^{(m)}$,   all   the   Chebyshev-Padé   forms $(B_n^{(m)}(z)/Q_n^{(m)}(z)$,
$-B_n^{(m)}(1/z)/Q_n^{(m)}(1/z))$ are equivalent and in the left upper triangular part $\mathbb{L}_n^{(m)}$
they are Chebyshev-Padé approximants in a strict sense.

PROOF.   If $\hat{F}(z) = F(1/z)$,   then   we   know   from   theorem   10.3   that
$Q_n^{(-m)}(z;\hat{F}) = z^n \hat{Q}_n^{(m)}(1/z;F)$. Because $\hat{F}(z) = F(z)$ we find that $Q_n^{(-m)}(z;F) =$
$z^n \hat{Q}_n^{(m)}(1/z;F)$. The relations for the other series follow similarly. Also the
result for the Toeplitz determinants follows similarly from lemma 10.1. The
equivalence of the Chebyshev-Padé forms and the existence of Chebyshev-Padé
approximants follow from the previous two theorems on Laurent-Padé forms.

□

We recall that our treatment is still purely formal. In the case that $F(z)$
represents a function in some annular region of the complex plane one should be
more careful and take the pole positions of the approximants into account as was
done for the Chebyshev-Padé case in [GED]. In the next chapters we shall leave
the formal concept and require that $F(z)$ is a meromorphic function. Another
thing to remember is that all the recursive relations given in previous chapters
were derived under the normality assumption for $F(z)$. They remain valid as
long as we do not enter a block. Inside a block they will break down as can be
seen from the determinant expressions of section 9.1.

Chapter 12

Meromorphic functions and asymptotic behaviour

Asymptotic expressions for determinants of infinite Toeplitz matrices have been the subject of much research. An extensive treatment of the topic was recently given by Böttcher and Silbermann [BOT2]. Toeplitz operators occur in many applications like physics, orthogonal polynomials, random walk, prediction theory, stationary Gaussian processes, informations and control theory, integral equations, Wiener-Hopf factorization and probably many others.
In these studies, the entries of the Toeplitz matrices are Fourier coefficients of some function $F(e^{i\theta})$ which is the symbol of the Toeplitz operator. In our contect we are particularly interested in asymptotic expressions that contain the zeros of the symbol, which is supposed to be meromorphic in a certain region of the complex plane. Under certain conditions, such an expression was given by Day [DAY] for a rational symbol. We shall generalize these results for the meromorphic case.

12.1 The function $F(z)$

Of course we shall have to leave the formal treatment we used up to now and we suppose that the Laurent series $F(z) = \sum_{-\infty}^{\infty} f_k z^k$ converges in some annular region $\mathbb{E} := \{z : r < |z| < R\}$ of the complex plane to a function which will also be denoted by $F(z)$. It is supposed that $F(z)$ is analytically continuable to a meromorphic function in $\mathbb{D} := \{z : 0 < |z| < \infty\}$. Thus $F(z)$ can have at most a countable number of zeros and poles with 0 and ∞ as the only possible accumulation points. Thus there can only be a finite number of zeros in $\mathbb{D}$. We shall suppose that $\mathbb{E}$ is restricted such that it contains no zeros of $F(z)$. The zeros ζ_k, $-Z^- \leqslant k \leqslant Z^+$ and the poles π_k, $-P^- \leqslant k \leqslant P^+$ of $F(z)$ are supposed to be numbered such that

$$0 \leqslant \cdots \leqslant |\pi_{-1}| \leqslant |\pi_0| \leqslant r < \rho < R \leqslant |\pi_1| \leqslant |\pi_2| \leqslant \cdots \leqslant \infty \quad (12.1a)$$
$$0 \leqslant \cdots \leqslant |\zeta_{-1}| \leqslant |\zeta_0| \leqslant r < \rho < R \leqslant |\zeta_1| \leqslant |\zeta_2| \leqslant \cdots \leqslant \infty \quad (12.1b)$$

ρ is an arbitrary number between r and R. Each of these is repeated as many times as indicated by its multiplicity. If Z^+ is infinite, then ∞ is an accumulation point of the $|\zeta_k|$, but every ζ_k with finite k is finite. If Z^+ is finite, we introduce the artificial number ζ_{Z^++1} such that $\max(R, |\zeta_{Z^+}|) < \zeta_{Z^++1} < \infty$. Similar observations are valid for Z^-, P^+ and P^-. Any such function can be written in the form (see [GOF], chapter I, section 5)

$$F(z) = G_\rho(\tilde{F})F_+(z)F_-(z)z^\kappa. \tag{12.2}$$

For some number ρ such that $r < \rho < R$ the factors are defined as follows : κ is the winding number

$$\kappa := \kappa_\rho := \text{ind}_\rho(F) = \frac{1}{2\pi}[\arg F(\rho e^{i\theta})]_{\theta=0}^{2\pi}. \tag{12.3}$$

This implies that the function

$$\tilde{F}(z) = z^{-\kappa}F(z) \tag{12.4}$$

has winding number equal to zero : $\text{ind}_\rho(\tilde{F}) = 0$. The zeros and poles of $F(z)$ are distributed over the factors $F_+(z)$ and $F_-(z)$ such that the zeros and poles in $|z| > \rho$ are given to $F_+(z)$ and the zeros and poles in $|z| < \rho$ are given to $F_-(z)$. Note that $F_+(z)$ and its inverse are analytic in $|z| \leqslant \rho$ and $F_-(z)$ and its inverse are analytic in $|z| \geqslant \rho$. The constant factor $G_\rho(\tilde{F})$ is used for normalization. We can chose it such that $F_+(0) = F_-(\infty) = 1$. The definitions and notations introduced in this section will be used in the following chapters too. Instead of the multiplicative splitting (12.2), we could introduce as before the additive splitting of $F(z) = \sum\limits_{k=-\infty}^{\infty} f_k z^k$ viz. :

$$F(z) = Z^{(\kappa)}(z) - \hat{Z}^{(\kappa)}(z) \tag{12.5}$$

with, conform to our previous notation,

$$Z^{(\kappa)}(z) := (\tfrac{1}{2}f_\kappa + \sum_{k=1}^{\infty} f_{\kappa+k}z^k)z^\kappa \tag{12.6a}$$

and

$$\hat{Z}^{(\kappa)}(z) := -(\tfrac{1}{2}f_\kappa + \sum_{k=1}^{\infty} f_{\kappa-k}z^{-k})z^\kappa. \tag{12.6b}$$

The series (12.6a) converges in $\{z : 0 < |z| < R\}$ and represents a function which is analytically continuable to a meromorphic function in $\mathbb{D}$. Its poles in $\mathbb{D}$ are $\{\pi_k : k = 1, 2, \ldots, P^+\}$. Similarly (12.6b) converges in $\{z : r < |z| < \infty\}$ and represents a function analytically continuable to a meromorphic function in $\mathbb{D}$ with its poles in $\mathbb{D}$ being $\{\pi_{-k} : k = 0, 1, \ldots, P^-\}$.

12.2 Asymptotics for finite Toeplitz determinants

With the meromorphic function $F(z)$ as described in previous section and with Laurent series $\sum_{-\infty}^{\infty} f_k z^k$, $z \in A$, we associate the Toeplitz determinants

$T_n^{(m)}$, $m \in \mathbb{Z}$, $n \in \mathbb{N}$ as in (9.1a). I.e.

$$T_n^{(m)} := \det \mathbf{T}_n^{(m)} := \det (f_{m+i-j})_{i,j=0}^n. \tag{12.7}$$

We shall first look at the asymptotics of these determinants for $m \to \infty$ or $m \to -\infty$. It is clear that for $m \to \infty$, $T_n^{(m)}$ will only depend on $Z^{(\kappa)}(z)$ and for $m \to -\infty$ only on $\hat{Z}^{(\kappa)}(z)$. Now $Z^{(\kappa)}(z)$ is up to a shift in the powers of z, the Taylor series around $z=0$ of a meromorphic function. Asymptotic expressions for $T_n^{(m)}$ as $m \to \infty$ where the entries in $T_n^{(m)}$ are the McLaurin coefficients of a meromorphic function analytic at the origin are classical. We quote these results for further reference.

THEOREM 12.1. *Let $F(z) = \sum_0^\infty f_k z^k$ be the McLaurin series of a meromorphic function analytic at the origin with poles*

$$0 < |\pi_1| \leqslant |\pi_2| \leqslant \cdots \leqslant |\pi_N|.$$

If N is finite, define $\pi_{N+1} = \infty$ and define $f_k := 0$ for $k < 0$. Then the Toeplitz determinants $T_n^{(m)} := \det (f_{m+i-j})_{i,j=0}^n$ satisfy

$$T_{n-1}^{(m)} = C_n(\pi_1 \cdots \pi_n)^{-m}[1+O(|\pi_n/\pi_{n+1}^{(m)}|)], \quad m \to \infty$$

on condition that $0 < n < N+1$. $C_n \neq 0$ is a constant which does not depend on m.

PROOF. This result was proved in [GR2,p.45] under the condition that all the poles π_k are simple. Under the condition that $|\pi_n| < |\pi_{n+1}|$ a similar result was proved in [HEN;p.599]. In the latter a method of confluence was used to remove the condition that all poles have to be simple. In fact Henrici's result was formulated in terms of Hankel determinants, but lemma 9.1 allows us to reformulate this for Toeplitz determinants as we did. The method of confluence can also be applied to Gragg's results for simple poles. It was shown by Gragg that the constant C_n should be taken to be

$$C_n = (-1)^{n(n+1)/2} \mu_2 \mu_2 \cdots \mu_n \, v(\pi_1, \pi_2, \ldots, \pi_n)^2 (\pi_1 \pi_2 \cdots \pi_n)^{-n}$$

where

$$\sum_{k=1}^n \frac{\mu_k}{z-\pi_k}$$

are the principal parts of $F(z)$ for the simple poles $\pi_1, \ldots, \pi_n$ and $v(\pi_1, \pi_2, \ldots, \pi_n)$ is a Vandermonde determinant :

$$v(\pi_1, \ldots, \pi_n) = \det [\pi_j^{i-1}]_{i,j=1}^n = \prod_{i<j} (\pi_j - \pi_i).$$

The method of confluence consists in replacing a multiple pole

$$\pi_{k+1} = \pi_{k+2} = \cdots = \pi_{k+l}$$

by

$$\pi_{k+1}(\epsilon) = \pi_{k+1} + \epsilon w, \; \pi_{k+2}(\epsilon) = \pi_{k+2} + \epsilon w^2, \ldots, \pi_{k+l} = \pi_{k+l} + \epsilon w^l$$

where $w = \exp(2\pi i / l)$ and $\epsilon > 0$ is a small number.
The principal part for this multiple pole is

$$p(z) := \sum_{j=1}^{l} \frac{\nu_j}{(z - \pi_{k+1})^j}$$

and with the ϵ-perturbations, this is replaced by

$$p(z;\epsilon) := \sum_{i=1}^{l} \frac{\mu_j(\epsilon)}{z - \pi_{k+j}(\epsilon)}$$

where

$$\mu_j(\epsilon) := \frac{1}{l} \sum_{j=1}^{l} (\epsilon w^j)^{1-i} \nu_i, \quad j = 1, 2, \ldots, l.$$

Note that $\lim_{\epsilon \to 0} p(z;\epsilon) = p(z)$ uniformly on any compact set not containing π_{k+1}.
If $F(z;\epsilon)$ is the function $F(z)$ where the principle parts of the multiple poles π_{k+1} are replaced by the principal parts of the simple poles $\pi_{k+j}(\epsilon)$ and if $\{f_k(\epsilon)\}_0^{\infty}$ are its McLaurin coefficients, then also $\lim_{\epsilon \to 0} f_k(\epsilon) = f_k$. Hence, using Gragg's proof for simple poles we find that

$$T_{n-1}^{(m)}(\epsilon) = C_n(\epsilon) (\pi_1(\epsilon) \cdots \pi_n(\epsilon))^{-m} [1 + O(|\pi_n(\epsilon)/\pi_{n+1}(\epsilon)|^m], \quad m \to \infty$$

where for simple poles of $F(z)$ we have set $\pi_j(\epsilon) := \pi_j$, $\mu_j(\epsilon) := \nu_j$ and where

$$C_n(\epsilon) = (-1)^{n(n+1)/2} \mu_1(\epsilon) \ldots \mu_n(\epsilon) v(\pi_1(\epsilon), \ldots, \pi_n(\epsilon))^2 (\pi_1(\epsilon) \ldots \pi_n(\epsilon))^{-n}.$$

Now for the part of $C_n(\epsilon)$ related to the multiple pole π_{k+1} we find

$$\mu_{k+1}(\epsilon) \cdots \mu_{k+l}(\epsilon) = \prod_{j=1}^{l} \frac{1}{l} \sum_{i=1}^{l} (\epsilon w^j)^{1-i} \nu_i$$

which goes to infinity as $\epsilon \to 0$ since it contains $\epsilon^{(1-l)l}$ as most negative power of ϵ. However $v(\pi_1(\epsilon) \cdots \pi_n(\epsilon))$ contains factors of the form $\pi_j(\epsilon) - \pi_i(\epsilon)$ which is ϵw^{j-i} if $k+1 \le i < j \le k+l$. Therefore $v(\pi_1(\epsilon) \cdots \pi_n(\epsilon))^2$ contains the factor $\epsilon^{l(l-1)}$ and other factors that may depend on ϵ but which give a finite nonzero result as $\epsilon \to 0$. This shows that $C_n(\epsilon)$ will be a finite nonzero constant as $\epsilon \to 0$, so that our theorem is proved since $\lim_{\epsilon \to 0} \pi_j(\epsilon) = \pi_j$.

$\square$

From this theorem we can immediately find the asymptotics for the Toeplitz determinants $T_n^{(m)}$ for a Laurent series of a meromorphic function as $m \to \pm \infty$. This is given in the next theorem.

THEOREM 12.2. *Let $F(z)$ be a meromorphic function as described in section 12.1 and let $T_n^{(m)}$ denote the Toeplitz determinants associated with it. Then for each n, $0 \leqslant n < P^+$ we have*

$$T_n^{(m)} = c_n(\pi_1\pi_2\cdots\pi_{n+1})^{-m}(1+O(|\pi_{n+1}/\pi_{n+2}|^m)), \quad m \to \infty \tag{12.8}$$

and for each n, $0 \leqslant n \leqslant P^-$ we have

$$T_n^{(-m)} = c_n(\pi_0\pi_{-1}\cdots\pi_{-n})^m(1+O(|\pi_{-n}/\pi_{-n-1}|^{-m})), \quad m \to \infty, \tag{12.9}$$

where c_n is a constant not depending on m.

PROOF. The Toeplitz determinants $T_n^{(m)}$ for $n \geqslant 0$ and $m \geqslant 1$ depend only on f_{m+k}, $-n \leqslant k \leqslant n$. Hence, if m is large enough, $T_n^{(m)}$ for $F(z)$ will be the same as $T_n^{(m)}$ for $Z^{(\kappa)}(z)$. Since $Z^{(\kappa)}(z)$ is a McLaurin series of a meromorphic function with poles π_k, $k \geqslant 1$ such that $\rho < |\pi_1| \leqslant |\pi_2| \leqslant \cdots$, the previous theorem can be applied which gives (12.8). The asymptotic expression (12.9) can be derived similarly by using the transformation $z \to 1/z$. Indeed

$$T_n^{(-m)}(F) = T_n^{(-m)}(\hat{Z}^{(\kappa)})$$

if m is large enough. Now, with $\hat{\hat{Z}}^{(\kappa)}(z) = \hat{Z}^{(\kappa)}(1/z)$,

$$T_n^{(-m)}(\hat{Z}^{(\kappa)}) = T_{-n}^{(m)}(\hat{\hat{Z}}^{(\kappa)}) = T_n^{(m)}(\hat{\hat{Z}}^{(\kappa)}).$$

Since $\hat{\hat{Z}}^{(\kappa)}(z)$ is a McLaurin series of a meromorphic function with poles $(\pi_{-k})^{-1}$, $k \geqslant 0$ such that $\rho^{-1} < |\pi_0|^{-1} \leqslant |\pi_{-1}|^{-1} \leqslant \cdots$ the previous theorem can again be applied to give

$$T_n^{(m)}(\hat{\hat{Z}}^{(\kappa)}) = c_n(\pi_0^{-1}\pi_{-1}^{-1}\cdots\pi_{-n}^{-1})^{-m}(1+O(|\pi_{-n}^{-1}/\pi_{-n-1}^{-1}|^m)), \quad m \to \infty.$$

Hence (12.9) follows.

$\square$

12.3 Asymptotics for infinite Toeplitz determinants

What we shall need in our further development are asymptotic expressions for $T_n^{(m)}$ as $n \to \infty$. This was treated in [BU1]. The analysis is based on a theorem of Böttcher [BOT1] and the multiplicative splitting (12.2). We shall first give the analysis for a function $F(z)$ as described in section 12.1 with $\kappa = 0$, $\rho = 1$ and $G_1(F) = 1$. It will be shown later that these parameters can be brought into the problem by some simple transformations. We first quote a theorem of Böttcher which was proved in a more general context in [BOT1]. For our case it reads as follows :

THEOREM 12.3. *Let $F(z)$ be as described in section 11.1, with $\rho = 1$, $G_1(F) = 1$ and $\kappa = \mathrm{ind}_1(F) = 0$. Then as $n \to \infty$ we have for the Toeplitz determinants $T_n^{(m)}(F)$ that are associated with it :*

$$T_n^{(m)}(F) = c_m[1 + o(1)], \quad m = 0 \tag{12.10a}$$

$$T_n^{(m)}(F) = c_m(-1)^{(n+m)m}[T_{m-1}^{(n+1)}(F_+^{-1}) + o(1)], \quad m > 0 \tag{12.10b}$$

$$T_n^{(-m)}(F) = c_m(-1)^{(n+m)m}[T_{m-1}^{(-n-1)}(F_+/F_-) + o(1)], \quad m > 0 \tag{12.10c}$$

with c_m is a nonzero constant which does not depend on n.

PROOF. see [BOT1].

$\square$

It is clear from this theorem that we need asymptotic expressions for $T_{m-1}^{(n+1)}(F_+^{-1})$ and $T_{m-1}^{(-n-1)}(F_+/F_-)$ as $n \to \infty$. But these are finite Toeplitz determinants and thus we can use the results of previous section. This is done in the next lemma.

LEMMA 12.4. *Let $F(z)$ be as described in section 12.1 with $\rho = 1$, $G_1(F) = 1$ and $\kappa = \mathrm{ind}_1(F) = 0$. Then we have the following asymptotic expressions for Toeplitz determinants associated with the factor $1/F_+(z)$ and with $F_+(z)/F_-(z)$:*

$$T_{m-1}^{(n+1)}(1/F_+) = c_m(\zeta_1\zeta_2 \cdots \zeta_m)^{-n-1} [1 + O(|\zeta_m/\zeta_{m+1}|^{n+1})], \quad n \to \infty$$

and

$$T_{m-1}^{(-n-1)}(F_+/F_-) = c_m(\zeta_0\zeta_{-1} \cdots \zeta_{-m-1})^{n+1} [1 + O(|\zeta_{m-1}/\zeta_m|^{-(n+1)})], \quad n \to \infty$$

where c_m is a nonzero constant which is independent of n.

PROOF. $1/F_+(z)$ is meromorphic with poles ζ_k, $k \geq 1$ such that $\rho < |\zeta_1| \leq |\zeta_2| \leq \cdots$, and therefore we can apply theorem 12.1 to give the first result.
On the other hand, $F_+(z)/F_-(z)$ is also meromorphic, and its poles in $|z| < \rho$ are only given by the zeros ζ_{-k}, $k \geq 0$ of $F_-(z)$, which satisfy $\cdots \leq |\zeta_{-2}| \leq |\zeta_{-1}| \leq |\zeta_0| < \rho$. Hence we can apply (12.9) of theorem 12.2 to get the second result.

$\square$

We could now give a combination of theorem 12.3 and lemma 12.4 to obtain the result we were after in the case $\rho = 1$, $G_1(F) = 1$ and $\kappa = \mathrm{ind}_1(F) = 0$. We can directly give the result for the general situation if we use the transformations of the next lemmas.

LEMMA 12.5. *If* $F(z) = \sum_{-\infty}^{\infty} f_k z^k$ *and* $T_n^{(m)}(F)$ *are the Toeplitz determinants associated with it, then*

$$T_n^{(m)}(cF) = c^{n+1} T_n^{(m)}(F)$$

for any constant $c \neq 0$.

PROOF. This is trivial since all entries in the Toeplitz determinant are multiplied with c and the dimension is $n+1$.

□

LEMMA 12.6. *Let* $F(z)$ *be as described in section 12.1 and let* $\tilde{F}(z)$ *be defined by* (12.4). *Define*

$$H(z) := \tilde{F}(\rho z) = \sum_{k=-\infty}^{\infty} h_k z^k$$

for $r' < |z| < R'$ *with* $h_k = \rho^k f_{k+\kappa}$, $r' = r/\rho < 1$ *and* $R' = R/\rho > 1$.
Then we have :
(1) $G_\rho(\tilde{F}) = G_1(H)$
(2) $T_n^{(m)}(F) = T_n^{(m-\kappa)}(\tilde{F}) = \rho^{-(m-\kappa)n} T_n^{(m-\kappa)}(H)$
(3) *If* τ *is a pole (zero) of* $F(z)$, *then* τ/ρ *is a pole (zero) of* $H(z)$.

PROOF. To prove (1), note that $G_\rho(\tilde{F})$ is the geometric mean

$$G_\rho(\tilde{F}) = \exp\left[\frac{1}{2\pi} \int_0^{2\pi} \log \tilde{F}(\rho e^{i\theta}) d\theta\right]. \tag{12.11}$$

Since $\text{ind}_1(H) = 0$, $G_1(H)$ will be given by

$$G_1(H) = \exp\left[\frac{1}{2\pi} \int_0^{2\pi} \log H(e^{i\theta}) d\theta\right]$$

which is of course the same because $H(e^{i\theta}) = \tilde{F}(\rho e^{i\theta})$ by definition. The Laurent coefficients of $\tilde{F}(z)$ in $r < |z| < R$ are the same as the Laurent coefficients $F(z)$ in the same annulus but shifted over κ units. This gives the first equality of (2). the second equality follows from the fact that

$$T_n^{(m-\kappa)}(\tilde{F}) = \det(f_{m+i-j})_{i,j=0}^n = \det(\rho^{-m+\kappa-i+j} h_{m-\kappa+i-j})_{i,j=0}^n$$
$$= \det[\rho^{\kappa-m} D(\rho^{-1}) T_n^{(m-\kappa)}(H) D(\rho)]$$

with $D(\alpha) := \text{diag}(1, \alpha, \ldots, \alpha^n)$. Hence

$$T_n^{(m)}(F) = T_n^{(m-\kappa)}(\tilde{F}) = \rho^{(\kappa-m)n} T_n^{(m-\kappa)}(H).$$

This proves (2).

Statement (3) is trivial to verify.

$\square$

We are now ready to give the asymptotics for infinite Toeplitz determinants in the general case.

THEOREM 12.7. *Let $F(z)$ be as described in section 12.1 and let c_m be nonzero constants not depending on n. Then for $n \to \infty$ we have*

$$T_n^{(m)} = c_m[G_\rho(\tilde{F})]^{n+1}\{1 + o(1)\} \quad \text{for } m = \kappa, \tag{12.12a}$$

$$T_n^{(m)} = c_m[G_\rho(\tilde{F})]^{n+1}[(-\zeta_1)(-\zeta_2) \cdots (-\zeta_{m-\kappa})]^{-n}\{1 + O(|\zeta_{m-\kappa}/\zeta_{m-\kappa+1}|^n)\}, \tag{12.12b}$$

if $0 < m - \kappa < Z^+ + 1$, and

$$T_n^{(m)} = c_m[G_\rho(\tilde{F})]^{n+1}[(-\zeta_0)(-\zeta_{-1}) \cdots (-\zeta_{m-\kappa+1})]^n\{1 + O(|\zeta_{m-\kappa}/\zeta_{m-\kappa+1}|^n)\}, \tag{12.12c}$$

if $0 < \kappa - m < Z^- + 2$.

PROOF. If you plug the result of lemma 12.4 into the formulas of theorem 12.3 you will get the above results for $\rho = 1$, $G_1(\tilde{F}) = 1$ and $\kappa = \kappa(F) = \text{ind}_1(F) = 0$. If $\kappa = \kappa(F)$ is not 0 you have to introduce a shift over κ in the index m because of lemma 12.6 (2). If $G_1(\tilde{F}) \neq 1$ you have to introduce a factor $[G_1(\tilde{F})]^{n+1}$ by lemma 12.5 and finally, if $\rho \neq 1$ we need an extra factor $\rho^{(m-\kappa)n}$ by lemma 12.6 (2). This extra factor is 1 for (12.12a). For (12.12b–c) we have to replace ζ_k by ζ_k/ρ by lemma 12.6 (3) which gives a factor $\rho^{(m-\kappa)n} \rho^{-(m-\kappa)n} = 1$ in those cases too. This proves the theorem.

$\square$

Before we leave this section we give one more result that will be useful for the following chapters.

THEOREM 12.8. *Let $F(z)$ be as described in section 12.1. Then there exist constants c_m and λ only depending on F such that for $m \geqslant \kappa$*

$$T_n^{(m)}(F) = c_m \lambda^{n+1} T_n^{(m-\kappa)}(F_+)\{1 + o(1)\} \quad \text{as } n \to \infty \tag{12.13a}$$

and for $m \leqslant \kappa$:

$$T_n^{(m)}(F) = c_m \lambda^{n+1} T_n^{(m-\kappa)}(F_-)\{1 + o(1)\} \quad \text{as } n \to \infty. \tag{12.13b}$$

PROOF. Using the techniques of theorem 12.7 we derive from theorem 12.3 that for $m \geqslant \kappa$

$$T_n^{(m)}(F) = T_n^{(m-\kappa)}(\tilde{F})$$
$$= c_m(\tilde{F})[G_\rho(\tilde{F})]^{n+1}(-1)^{(n+m-\kappa)(m-\kappa)}\{T_{m-1-\kappa}^{(n+1)}(F_+^{-1})+o(1)\} \ , \ n \to \infty$$

where $\tilde{F}(z) = z^{-\kappa}F(z)$ and also

$$T_n^{(m-\kappa)}(F_+) = c_m(F_+)[G_\rho(F_+)]^{n+1}(-1)^{(n+m-\kappa)(m-\kappa)}\{T_{m-1-\kappa}^{(n+1)}(F_+^{-1})+o(1)\},$$
$$n \to \infty.$$

Hence the first part of the theorem is true if we take $c_m = c_m(\tilde{F})/c_m(F_+)$ and $\lambda = G_\rho(\tilde{F})/G_\rho(F_+)$. For the second part, note that if $\hat{F}(z) = F(1/z)$, then

$$\hat{F}(z) = G_\rho(\tilde{F})\hat{F}_+(z)\hat{F}_-(z)\hat{z}^{\hat{\kappa}}$$

with

$$\hat{\kappa} := -\kappa$$
$$\hat{F}_+(z) := F_-(1/z) \text{ with poles and zeros in } |z| > \hat{\rho} = 1/\rho$$
$$\hat{F}_-(z) := F_+(1/z) \text{ with poles and zeros in } |z| < \hat{\rho} = 1/\rho.$$

We can now apply (12.13a) to the right hand side of

$$T_n^{(m)}(F) = T_n^{(-m)}(\hat{F})$$

to find $(m \leqslant \kappa \Longleftrightarrow -m \geqslant \hat{\kappa})$

$$T_n^{(-m)}(\hat{F}) = c_m\lambda^{n+1}T_n^{(-m-\hat{\kappa})}(\hat{F}_+)\{1+o(1)\}, \ n \to \infty$$
$$= c_m\lambda^{n+1}T_n^{(m-\kappa)}(F_-)\{1+o(1)\}, \ n \to \infty$$

which gives (12.13b).

$$\square$$

12.4 Consequences for the T-table

The previous theorems can give us some information about the borders at infinity of the T-table. E.g. if two successive poles separate in modulus, then this implies a nonzero Toeplitz determinant at the border $m = -\infty$, while the separation in modulus of two successive zeros implies a nonzero Toeplitz determinant at the border $n = \infty$ of the T-table. Also, if the numbers Z^+ and P^+ of zeros, respectively poles in $|z| > \rho$ is finite, we will have an infinite block of zero determinants in the T-table. P^+ defines the left border and $\kappa + Z^+$ defines the upper border of the block. Similarly, if P^- and Z^- are finite we will have an infinite block of zero Toeplitz determinants in the right upper corner of the T-table. These results are formulated in the next two theorems:

THEOREM 12.9. *Let $T_n^{(m)}$ be the Toeplitz determinants associated with the Laurent series of $F(z) \neq 0$, which is as described in section 12.1. Then for m sufficiently large we have*

$$T_n^{(m)} \neq 0 \text{ if } 0 \leqslant n < P^+ \text{ and } |\pi_{n+1}| < |\pi_{n+2}|, \tag{12.14a}$$
$$T_n^{(-m)} \neq 0 \text{ if } 0 \leqslant n < P^-+1 \text{ and } |\pi_{-n-1}| < |\pi_{-n}|\$. \tag{12.14b}$$

For n sufficiently large we have

$$T_n^{(m)} \neq 0 \text{ if } -Z^--1 \leqslant m-\kappa < Z^++1 \text{ and } |\zeta_{m-\kappa}| < |\zeta_{m-\kappa+1}|. \tag{12.14c}$$

PROOF. This directly follows from the asymptotic expressions we have given before. E.g. (12.14a) follows from (12.8) since the correction term will vanish as $m \to \infty$. (12.14b) follows from (12.9) in exactly the same way. For (12.14c) you need one of the formulas (12.12), depending on the value of $m-\kappa$.

□

We shall now show the existence of infinite blocks at the right top or left bottom of the T-table if there is only a finite number of poles and zeros. See fig 12.1.

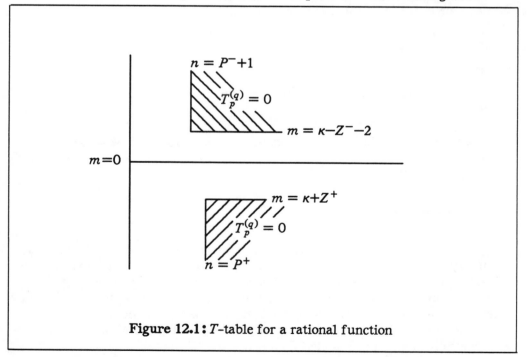

Figure 12.1: T-table for a rational function

THEOREM 12.10. *Let $F(z) \neq 0$ be as described in section 12.1 and let $T_n^{(m)}$ denote the associated Toeplitz determinants. P^+ (Z^+) is the number of poles (zeros) in $|z| > \rho$ and $Z^- + 1$ ($P^- + 1$) is the number of poles (zeros) in $|z| < \rho$. If P^+ and Z^+ are finite, then*

$$\{(p,q) : \kappa + Z^+ < p \leqslant \infty, \ P^+ \leqslant q \leqslant \infty\} \tag{12.15}$$

defines an infinite T-block of zero entries in the right bottom corner of the T-table and if P^- and Z^- are finite, then

$$\{(p,q) : -\infty \leqslant p \leqslant \kappa - Z^- - 2, \ P^- + 1 \leqslant q \leqslant \infty\} \tag{12.16}$$

defines an infinite T-block of zero entries in the right upper corner of the T-table.

PROOF. Theorem 7.e in [HEN,I,p.603] says that if $f(z)$ is a rational function analytic in $z = 0$ with Taylor series $\sum_0^\infty f_k z^k$ and if P is the sum of the orders of the finite poles π_k and h is the order of the pole at infinity, then

$$H_n^{(m)} = 0 \quad \text{for } m > h \text{ and } n \geqslant P$$

where $H_n^{(m)}$ is the Hankel matrix $(f_{m+i+j})_{i,j=0}^n$ as in section 9. In our situation where P^+ is finite, $\tilde{Z}^{(\kappa)}(z) := z^{-\kappa} Z^{(\kappa)}(z)$ (see (12.6)) is such a function. The poles of $\tilde{Z}^{(\kappa)}(z)$ are in $|z| > \rho$ and they are the same as the poles of $F(z)$ in this region. The order of the pole at infinity is $Z^+ - P^+$. Thus

$$H_n^{(m)}(\tilde{Z}^{(\kappa)}) = 0 \quad \text{for } m > Z^+ - P^+, \ n \geqslant P^+.$$

With lemma 9.1 we obtain for appropriate m and n

$$H_n^{(m)}(\tilde{Z}^{(\kappa)}) = H_n^{(m+\kappa)}(Z^{(\kappa)}) = (-1)^{(n+1)n/2} T_n^{(m+\kappa+n)}(F)$$
$$= (-1)^{(n+1)n/2} T_n^{(\kappa+Z^+ - P^+ + k + n)}(F) \quad \text{if } m = Z^+ - P^+ + k.$$

This proves the existence of an infinite block in the right bottom corner. The left border has column index at most P^+ and the top border has row index at most $\kappa + Z^+$. That P^+ and $\kappa + Z^+$ are indeed the borders of the block follows from theorem 12.9 since we have by definition $|\pi_{P^+}| < |\pi_{P^+ + 1}|$ and thus $T_{P^+ - 1}^{(m)} \neq 0$ for m sufficiently large. Similarly $|\zeta_{Z^+}| < |\zeta_{Z^+ + 1}|$ by definition so that $T_n^{(Z^+ + \kappa)} \neq 0$ for n sufficiently large.

(12.16) can be proved in a similar way.

$\square$

Chapter 13

Montessus de Ballore theorem for Laurent-Padé approximants

In this text we derived a number of quantities depending on n and m that were associated with a Laurent series in much the same way as was done for the classical Padé case for a Taylor series. As in the previous chapter, taking the limits of these for m going to $+\infty$ or $-\infty$ can be reduced to the classical Padé result.

The Montessus de Ballore theorem gives the convergence for m going to infinity of an (m/n) PA of a meromorphic function $F(z)$ which is analytic in the origin and which is given by its McLaurin series. In this chapter we shall generalize this result for the convergence for m going to infinity of an (m/n) LPA of a meromorphic function as described in section 12.1 which is analytic in an annular region and given by its Laurent series.

13.1 Semi infinite Laurent series

We first give the result for a Laurent series with finite $+$ or finite $-$ order. This means that without loss of generality, we can as well consider meromorphic functions as described in section 12.1 with $F_+(z) = 1$ or $F_-(z) = 1$. We shall first consider the asymptotic behaviour of the Q-polynomials of the first kind. Up to a normalization, they are also known under the name of *Hankel polynomials* or *Hadamard polynomials*. This is formulated in theorem 13.1. The next theorem then gives the classical Montessus de Ballore theorem for McLaurin series of a meromorphic function together with an adaptation for a series around infinity. Finally, in the next section, we shall give in theorem 13.3 the generalization of this theorem giving the convergence of Laurent-Padé approximants uniformly in compact subsets of the complex plane.

THEOREM 13.1.

(1) *Let $F(z)$ be the Laurent series of a meromorphic function as described in section 12.1 with $F_-(z) = 1$ (i.e. $Z^- = P^- = -1$). Then, for $0 \leqslant n \leqslant P^+$, and $z \neq \pi_k$, $0 < k \leqslant n$, the polynomials $Q_n^{(m)}(z)$ and $\hat{Q}_n^{(m)}(z)$ of the first kind satisfy for m sufficiently large*

$$Q_n^{(m)}(z) = (1-z/\pi_1)(1-z/\pi_2)\cdots(1-z/\pi_n)\{1+O(|\pi_n/\pi_{n+1}|^m)\},$$

$$m \to \infty, \qquad (13.1)$$

and

$$\hat{Q}_n^{(m)}(z) = (z-\pi_1)(z-\pi_2) \cdots (z-\pi_n)\{1+O(|\pi_n/\pi_{n+1}|^m)\},$$

$$m \to \infty. \qquad (13.2)$$

(2) Similarly, if $F(z)$ is the Laurent series of a meromorphic function as described in section 12.1 with $F_+(z) = 1$ (i.e. $Z^+ = P^+ = 0$). Then, for $0 \leqslant n \leqslant P^-+1$, and $z \neq \pi_{-k}$, $0 \leqslant k < n$ the polynomials $Q_n^{(m)}(z)$ and $\hat{Q}_n^{(m)}(z)$ of the first kind satisfy for $-m$ sufficiently large

$$\hat{Q}_n^{(m)}(z) = (z-\pi_0)(z-\pi_{-1}) \cdots (z-\pi_{-n+1})\{1+O(|\pi_{-n}/\pi_{-n+1}|^m)\},$$

$$m \to -\infty, \qquad (13.3)$$

and

$$Q_n^{(m)}(z) = (1-z/\pi_0)(1-z/\pi_{-1}) \cdots (1-z/\pi_{-n+1})$$

$$\{1+O(|\pi_{-n}/\pi_{-n+1}|^m)\}, m \to -\infty. \qquad (13.4)$$

These relations are valid uniformly for any z in a compact subset of $\mathbb{C}$.

PROOF. We make the following observations :

(1) The polynomials $Q_n^{(m)}(z)$ and $\hat{Q}_n^{(m)}(z)$ are well defined by the determinant expressions (9.9) since in case (1) of this theorem we must have by theorem 12.9 that $T_{n+1}^{(m)} \neq 0$ for m sufficiently large.

(2) We can take the winding number κ of $F(z)$ equal to zero without loss of generality because a nonzero κ only causes a shift in the index k of f_k, but for sufficiently large m, $Q_n^{(m)}(z)$ or $\hat{Q}_n^{(m)}(z)$ do not depend on the initial terms in the Laurent series as can be seen from (9.9).

Modulo some trivial transformation, the proof of (13.1) for $\kappa = 0$ and for $|\pi_n| < |\pi_{n+1}|$ can be found in [HEN,theorem 7.7b]. The proof for $\kappa = 0$ without the condition that $|\pi_n| < |\pi_{n+1}|$ can be found in [GR2,p44] but here the poles are supposed to be simple. The method of confluence which was used in [HEN] can be applied to this result to find that it is generally true. Indeed what is shown in theorem 8.2(b) of [GR2] is that some polynomial, which corresponds in our notation to $S_n^{(m)}(z) := T_{n-1}^m Q_n^{(m)}(z)$, satisfies for $m \to \infty$:

$$S_n^{(m)}(z) = (-1)^{n(n+1)/2} \mu_1\mu_2 \cdots \mu_n v(\pi_1\pi_2 \cdots \pi_n)^2.(\pi_1\pi_2 \cdots \pi_n)^{-m-n}$$
$$(1-z/\pi_1)(1-z/\pi_2) \cdots (1-z/\pi_n) \{1+O(|\pi_n/\pi_{n+1}|)^m)\}$$

on condition that the poles of $F(z)$ are simple. The above formula gives for $z = 0$ the result (12.8). Hence the factor on the first line is induced by the presence of $T_{n-1}^{(m)}$. Thus if we divide out this factor $T_{n-1}^{(m)}$ then the result (13.1) follows for simple poles. When using the method of confluence as in theorem 12.2, the factor on the first line has to be replaced by some nonzero constant which is still induced by the presence of $T_{n-1}^{(m)}$. In the other factor π_j has to be replaced by a slight perturbation $\pi_j(\epsilon)$ if π_j is a multiple pole. Letting $\epsilon \to 0$, the result follows as for simple poles.

To prove (13.2) note that, up to a normalizing constant factor, $Q_n^{(m)}(z)$ and $\hat{Q}_n^{(m+1)}(z)$ are the same. This factor is such that $Q_n^{(m)}(z)$ is co-monic, while $\hat{Q}_n^{(m+1)}(z)$ is monic. Hence also (13.2) will follow.

The second case of the theorem is shown by the transformation $z \to 1/z$. It is left as an exercise to the reader.

□

Theorem 13.1 is the key to a proof for the classical convergence theorem of Motessus de Ballore which proves the convergence of classical Padé approximants. It can be formulated as follows :

THEOREM 13.2. Let $F(z) = \sum f_k z^k$ be a meromorphic function as described in section 12.1. Associate with it $P_n^{(m)}(z)$, $\hat{P}_n^{(m)}(z)$, $Q_n^{(m)}(z)$, $\hat{Q}_n^{(m)}(z)$ as they are defined in (9.9) whenever this makes sense. Then we have the following two results

(1) Let $F(z)$ be as in case (1) of theorem 13.1 and $\kappa = 0$. Then for $0 \leqslant n \leqslant P^+$ and $|\pi_n| < |\pi_{n+1}|$:

$$\lim_{m \to \infty} P_n^{(m)}(z)/Q_n^{(m)}(z) = \lim_{m \to \infty} \hat{P}_n^{(m)}(z)/\hat{Q}_n^{(m)}(z) = F(z)$$

uniformly on compact subsets of its n-th pointed disc of convergence (around $z = 0$) :

$$\mathbb{D}_n := \{z : 0 < |z| < |\pi_{n+1}|, z \neq \pi_k, 1 \leqslant k \leqslant n\}.$$

(2) Let $F(z)$ be as in case (2) of theorem 13.1 and $\kappa = 0$. Then for $0 \leqslant n \leqslant P^- + 1$ and $|\pi_{-n}| < |\pi_{-n+1}|$:

$$\lim_{m \to -\infty} P_n^{(m)}(z)/Q_n^{(m)}(z) = \lim_{m \to -\infty} \hat{P}_n^{(m)}(z)/\hat{Q}_n^{(m)}(z) = F(z)$$

uniformly on compact subsets of its n-th pointed disc of convergence (around $z = \infty$) :

$$\hat{\mathbb{D}}_n := \{z : \infty > |z| > |\pi_{-n}|, z \neq \pi_{-k}, 0 \leqslant k \leqslant n-1\}.$$

PROOF. It is easy to derive the result in case (2) of the theorem from the result in case (1) by making the transformation $z \to 1/z$. Case (1) is a classical result and many different proofs for it can be found in the literature on Padé approximation. Again the proof is straightforward, although somewhat involving, if it is assumed that all the poles are simple. For multiple poles, a number of technicalities should be coped with. In [GR2] a proof can be found if all the poles are assumed to be simple. In [BGM] a proof is given for the general case.

□

13.2 Bi-infinite Laurent series

The two cases in theorem 13.2 can be combined to find a generalization of the theorem of Montessus de Ballore for Laurent-Padé approximants which is given in theorem 13.3.

THEOREM 13.3. *Let $F(z)$ be a meromorphic funtion as described in section 12.1. Define the LPFs of $F(z)$ as in section (11.4) i.e. for $n,m \in \mathbb{N}$:*

$$K_n^{(m)}(z) = (B_n^{(m)}(z)/Q_n^{(m)}(z), -\hat{B}_n^{(-m)}(z)/\hat{Q}_n^{(-m)}(z)).$$

Suppose $n \leqslant \min\{P^+, P^- + 1\}$ and $|\pi_n| < |\pi_{n+1}|$ and $|\pi_{-n}| < |\pi_{-n+1}|$. Then

$$\lim_{m \to \infty} K_n^{(m)}(z) \begin{vmatrix} 1 \\ 1 \end{vmatrix} = F(z)$$

uniformly on compact subsets of the n-th pointed annulus of convergence (in the neighbourhood of $|z| = \rho$) :

$$\mathbb{E}_n := \{z : |\pi_{-n}| < |z| < |\pi_{n+1}|, z \neq \pi_k, -n+1 \leqslant k \leqslant n\}$$

PROOF. Since $m \to \infty$ we may suppose that $m > n$ and that $K_n^{(m)}$ exists by the definitions (11.4b) because $T_{n-1}^{(m)}$ and $T_{n-1}^{(-m)}$ are nonzero for m sufficiently large and n satisfying the conditions of the theorem. More precisely, it follows from the definitions that $B_n^{(m)}(z)/Q_n^{(m)}(z)$ is an ordinary (m/n) PF for $Z(z) = \frac{1}{2} f_0 + \sum_1^\infty f_k z^k$ (see definition (12.6a)) if $m > n$. It then follows from theorem 13.2 that

$$\lim_{m \to \infty} B_n^{(m)}(z)/Q_n^{(m)}(z) = Z(z)$$

uniformly in compact subsets of

$$\mathbb{D}_n = \{z : 0 < |z| < |\pi_{n+1}|, z \neq \pi_k, 1 \leqslant k \leqslant n\}.$$

Similarly

$$\lim_{m \to \infty} \hat{B}_n^{(-m)}(z)/\hat{Q}_n^{(-m)}(z) = -\hat{Z}(z)$$

uniformly in compact subsets of

$$\hat{\mathbb{D}}_n := \{z : \infty > |z| > |\pi_{-n}|, z \neq \pi_{-k}, 0 \leqslant k \leqslant n-1\}$$

where $\hat{Z}(z)$ is as defined in (12.6b), i.e. $\hat{Z}(z) = -(\frac{1}{2} f_0 + \sum_1^\infty f_{-k} z^{-k})$. This proves the theorem since

$$K_n^{(m)}(z) \begin{bmatrix} 1 \\ 1 \end{bmatrix} = \frac{B_n^{(m)}(z)}{Q_n^{(m)}(z)} - \frac{\hat{B}_n^{(-m)}(z)}{\hat{Q}_n^{(-m)}(z)}$$

and this converges to $Z(z) - \hat{Z}(z) = F(z)$ in $\mathbb{D}_n \cap \hat{\mathbb{D}}_n = \mathbb{E}_n$.

$\square$

Chapter 14

Determination of poles

The purpose of this chapter is to find the poles of a meromorphic function from its Laurent series expansion in some annular region $\mathbb{K}$. Again this problem is solved for a McLaurin series of a meromorphic function. The problem is simple if some pole is separated in modules from the moduli of the neighbouring poles. In that case, the pole can be found as the limit of some $\hat{b}_n^{(m)}$ parameter for $m \to \infty$ or $m \to -\infty$. This could be shown by expressing $\hat{b}_n^{(m)}$ in terms of Toeplitz determinants as in (9.3g) and using the asymptotics of Toeplitz determinants of chapter 12. If the poles do not separate in modulus, a more complicated situation occurs where Rutishauser polynomials are needed. Again, when m goes to $\pm \infty$, these Rutishauser polynomials will converge to some polynomials whose zeros give a number of the poles of the given meromorphic function. This generalizes the results of theorem 13.1. Similar results for zeros will be derived in the next chapter.

14.1 Rutishauser polynomials of type 1 and type 2

We shall start by introducing the Rutishauser polynomials. Let $F(z)$ be a meromorphic function as described in section 12.1. Its Laurent series in $F(z) = \sum_{-\infty}^{\infty} f_k z^k$, $z \in \mathbb{E}$. If this series is normal, all polynomials $Q_n^{(m)}(z)$ do exist for $m \in \mathbb{Z}$ and $n \in \mathbb{N}$ and so do all the b-parameters $b_n^{(m)}$. We know from (7.10b) that the polynomials of the first kind satisfy the recurrence

$$Q_k^{(m)}(z) = Q_{k-1}^{(m)}(z) - z b_k^{(m)} Q_{k-1}^{(m-1)}(z) ; \quad Q_0^{(m)} = 1. \tag{14.1}$$

Type 1 Rutishauser polynomials are introduced by the recurrence ($m \in \mathbb{Z}$; $n,k \in \mathbb{N}$)

$$Q_{n,n+k}^{(m)}(z) = Q_{n,n+k-1}^{(m)}(z) - z b_{n+k}^{(m)} Q_{n,n+k-1}^{(m-1)}(z) ; \quad Q_{n,n}^{(m)} = 1 , \quad k \geqslant 1. \tag{14.2a}$$

This is the same recurrence as given in (14.1) but with a shift over n for the subscript of $b_k^{(m)}$. Note that these polynomials are found as the node values of the graph in fig. 7.5a if the first $n-1$ columns are deleted and the input is injected in column n. See fig. 14.1. In fig. 14.1 we find $Q_{n,n+k}^{(m)}(z)$ at node $(m,n+k)$. For $n=0$ we obtain again the polynomials $Q_k^{(m)}(z)$. I.e.

$$Q_{0,k}^{(m)}(z) = Q_k^{(m)}(z).$$

We could also define *type 2 Rutishauser polynomials* by the recurrence ($m \in \mathbb{Z}$;

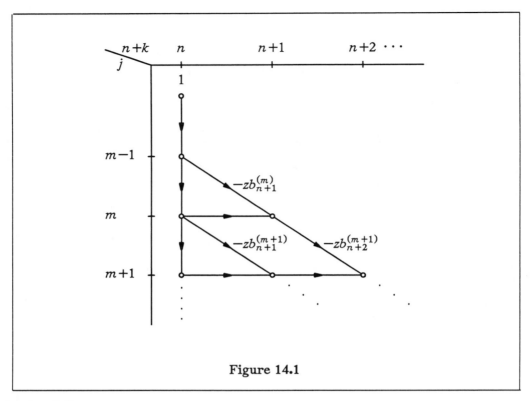

Figure 14.1

$n,k \in \mathbb{N}$)

$$Q_{n,n+k}^{(m-1)}(z) = Q_{n,n+k-1}^{(m)}(z) + zG_{k+n}^{(m)} Q_{n,n+k-1}^{(m-1)}(z); \quad Q_{n,n}^{(m)} = 1, \; k \geqslant 1. \quad (14.2b)$$

(Compare with (7.10c).) The $G_n^{(m)}$ are the G parameters associated with $F(z)$. We have again that $Q_{0,k}^{(m)}(z) = Q_k^{(m)}(z)$. $Q_{n,n+k}^{(m)}(z)$ is the value at node $(m,n+k)$ of the graph in fig. 14.2. Type 1 and type 2 Rutishauser polynomials are related to the Q polynomials of the first kind as indicated in the next lemma.

LEMMA 14.1. *Let* $F(z) = \sum_{-\infty}^{\infty} f_k z^k$ *be a normal fls. Its Q polynomials of the first kind are denoted as* $Q_n^{(m)}(z)$. *Suppose the type 1 Rutishauser polynomials are defined by (14.2a) and suppose* $Q_{n,n+k}^{(m)}(z)$ *is given by*

$$Q_{n,n+k}^{(m)}(z) = \sum_{i=0}^{k} q_i \, z^i.$$

Then

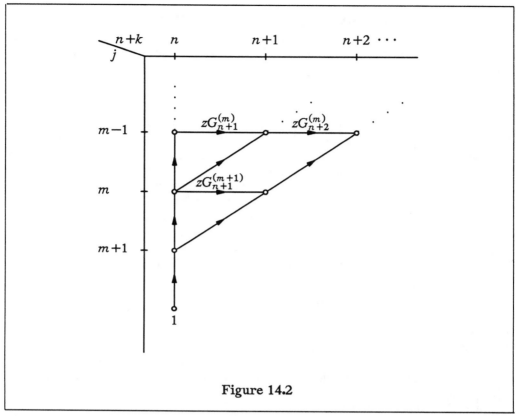

Figure 14.2

$$Q_{n+k}^{(m)}(z) = Q_{0,n+k}^{(m)}(z) = \sum_{i=0}^{k} q_i z^i Q_{0,n}^{(m-i)}(z). \tag{14.3a}$$

Suppose the type 2 Rutishauser polynomials are defined by (14.2b) and suppose $Q_{n,n+k}^{(m)}(z)$ *is given by*

$$Q_{n,n+k}^{(m)}(z) = \sum_{i=0}^{k} q_i z^i.$$

Then

$$Q_{n+k}^{(m)}(z) = Q_{0,n+k}^{(m)}(z) = \sum_{i=0}^{k} q_i z^i \, Q_{0,n}^{(m+k-i)}(z). \tag{14.3b}$$

PROOF. Relation (14.3a) is clearly true for $k=0$. For $k > 0$, the proof follows readily from figure 14.1. If at every node of column n we inject 1 as input, we obtain at node $(m,n+k)$ the Rutishauser polynomial $Q_{n,n+k}^{(m)}(z)$ by definition. If however the input at node (m,n) is $Q_n^{(m)}(z) = Q_{0,n}^{(m)}(z)$ for $m \in \mathbb{Z}$, then you get at node $(m,n+k)$ the node value $Q_{n+k}^{(m)}(z)$ by definition. By the linearity of the flow graph, you can easily check that if the node value at $(m-i,n)$ is multiplied by S, then the coefficient of z^i in the node value at $(m,n+k)$ will be multiplied with S too. In this way (14.3a) can be proved. The same technique can be used to prove (14.3b).

$\square$

We shall now try to find out how these Rutishauser polynomials behave as $m \to \infty$. Since we introduced them for a normal fls, we should answer the question whether they always exist in the nonnormal case. It is not possible to define them by the recurrence relations we used in the normal case because these may break down. So the question remains how we should define them when $F(z)$ is not normal. Lemma 14.1 will help us to give a definition in the nonnormal case if m is sufficiently large. Indeed if $F(z)$ is as described in section 12.1 and if $|\pi_n| < |\pi_{n+1}|$, for some n such that $1 \leqslant n \leqslant P^+$, then $T_{n-1}^{(m)} \neq 0$ for m sufficiently large (theorem 12.9). From the determinant expression (9.9a) we can then conclude that $Q_n^{(m)}(z)$ will be well defined for m sufficiently large. Thus the polynomials $Q_{0,n}^{(m-i)}(z)$ in the right hand side of (14.3a) are well defined. If also $|\pi_{n+k}| < |\pi_{n+k+1}|$, for some n and k such that $1 \leqslant n < n+k \leqslant P^+$, then $Q_{n+k}^{(m)}(z) = Q_{0,n+k}^{(m)}(z)$, which is the left hand side of (14.3a), will also be well defined. Hence (14.3a) will define the coefficients q_i, $i = 0,1,\ldots,k$ uniquely and therefore also the polynomials $Q_{n,n+k}^{(m)}(z)$ which are the type 1 Rutishauser polynomials. Hence in such a situation we shall consider (14.3a) as a definition of these Rutishauser polynomials. It is obvious that in the same circumstances, (14.3b) may be used to define the type 2 Rutishauser polynomials. With these definitions we should be able to find results on the pole positions of $F(z)$ that are in $|z| > \rho$. They are found as downward limits, i.e. as $m \to \infty$. For the pole positions in $|z| < \rho$, we shall need limits for $m \to -\infty$. The existence of Rutishauser polynomials $Q_{n,n+k}^{(m)}(z)$ for $m \to -\infty$ will depend on pole positions in $|z| < \rho$. With theorem 12.9 we can find as before that the Rutishauser polynomials are defined by (14.3) for m a sufficiently large negative number if $|\pi_{-n}| < |\pi_{-n+1}|$ and $|\pi_{-n-k}| < |\pi_{-n-k+1}|$ where $0 \leqslant n < n+k \leqslant P^-+1$.

Our definitions of Rutishauser polynomials introduced them as co-monic polynomials, i.e. with constant term equal to 1. It is also possible to renormalize them as monic polynomials.

These monic *type 1 Rutishauser polynomials* are defined in the normal case as $(m \in \mathbb{Z}; n,k \in \mathbb{N}, k \geqslant 1)$

$$\hat{Q}_{n,n+k}^{(m)}(z) = z \, \hat{Q}_{n,n+k-1}^{(m)}(z) - \hat{b}_{n+k}^{(m)} \, \hat{Q}_{n,n+k-1}^{(m+1)}(z) \, ; \quad \hat{Q}_{n,n}^{(m)} = 1 \qquad (14.4a)$$

and the monic *type 2 Rutishauser polynomials* by

$$\hat{Q}_{n,n+k}^{(m+1)}(z) = \hat{G}_{n+k}^{(m)} \, \hat{Q}_{n,n+k-1}^{(m+1)}(z) + z \, \hat{Q}_{n,n+k-1}^{(m)}(z) \, ; \quad \hat{Q}_{n,n}^{(m)} = 1. \tag{14.4b}$$

For the nonnormal case one can show that if the monic type 1 Ruthauser polynomial $\hat{Q}_{n,n+k}^{(m)}(z)$ is given by

$$\hat{Q}_{n,n+k}^{(m)}(z) = \sum_{i=0}^{k} \hat{q}_i z^i,$$

then it is related to the $\hat{Q}_n^{(m)}(z) = \hat{Q}_{0,n}^{(m)}(z)$ polynomials of the first kind by

$$\hat{Q}_{n+k}^{(m)}(z) = \hat{Q}_{0,n+k}^{(m)}(z) = \sum_{i=0}^{k} \hat{q}_i z^i \, \hat{Q}_{0,n}^{(m+k-i)}(z) \tag{14.5a}$$

so that under appropriate conditions (14.5a) can be used as a definition of the $\hat{q}_i$ for $\pm m$ sufficiently large. Similar observations are valid for the type 2 polynomials. We are now ready to prove the Rutishauser rules which generalize the results of theorem 13.1. A recent proof of them was given by Seewald [SEE].

THEOREM 14.2. *Let* $F(z)$ *be a meromorphic function as described in section 12.1 with* $F_-(z) = 1$. *Define for* $0 \leqslant n < n+h \leqslant P^+$ *the polynomials* $Q_{n,n+h}(z)$ *by*

$$Q_{n,n+h}(z) = (1-z/\pi_{n+1})(1-z/\pi_{n+2}) \cdots (1-z/\pi_{n+h}). \tag{14.6}$$

Suppose $|\pi_n| < |\pi_{n+1}|$ *and* $|\pi_{n+h}| < |\pi_{n+h+1}|$. *Then :*

$$|Q_{n,n+h}^{(m)}(z) - Q_{n,n+h}(z)| \leqslant C \, \lambda^m \, , \quad \forall z \in \mathbb{K} \tag{14.7}$$

where $\mathbb{K}$ *is a compact subset of the complex plane,* C *is a positive constant,*

$$1 > \lambda > \max\left(|\pi_n/\pi_{n+1}|, \, |\pi_{n+h}/\pi_{n+h+1}|\right).$$

and $Q_{n,n+h}^{(m)}(z)$ *denote type 1 or type 2 Rutishauser polynomials.*

PROOF. Again, without loss of generality we can suppose that the winding number $\kappa = 0$. First observe that the theorem is true for $n=0$. This was shown in theorem 13.1. Hence we have

$$|Q_{0,n}(z) - Q_{0,n}^{(m)}(z)| \leqslant C_1 \lambda^m$$

and

$$|Q_{0,n+h}(z) - Q_{0,n+h}^{(m)}(z)| \leqslant C_2 \lambda^m$$

for positive constants C_1 and C_2 and $z \in \mathbb{K}$, a compact subset of $\mathbb{C}$. The main tric of Seewald's proof is to make the observation which we formulated as lemma 14.1. Using this we get with $Q_{n,n+h}^{(m)}(z) = \sum_{i=0}^{h} q_i^{(m)} z^i$:

$$Q_{0,n}(z)Q^{(m)}_{n,n+h}(z) - Q^{(m)}_{0,n+h}(z) = \sum_{i=0}^{h} q_i^{(m)} z^i (Q_{0,n}(z) - Q_{0,n}^{(m+h-i)}(z)).$$

Hence,

$$|Q_{0,n}(z)Q^{(m)}_{n,n+h}(z) - Q^{(m)}_{0,n+h}(z)| \leq c_1 \sum_{i=0}^{h} |q_i^{(m)}| \, |z|^i \, \lambda^m.$$

Similarly :

$$|Q_{0,n}(z)Q^{(m)}_{n,n+h}(z) - Q_{0,n+h}(z)|$$

$$\leq |Q_{0,n}(z)Q^{(m)}_{n,n+h}(z) - Q^{(m)}_{0,n+h}(z)| + |Q^{(m)}_{0,n+h}(z) - Q_{0,n+h}(z)|$$

$$\leq [\sum_{i=0}^{h} |q_i^{(m)}| c_1 |z|^i + c_2] \lambda^m.$$

Now, set $Q_{n,n+h}(z) = \sum_0^h q_i z^i$ and suppose that β_m is a sequence of numbers such that $|q_i^{(m)} - q_i| \leq \beta_m$. Then we may use $|q_i^{(m)}| \leq |q_i| + \beta_m$ to get that the previous expression is bounded by

$$\leq [\sum_{i=0}^{h} (|q_i| + \beta_m) c_1 |z|^i + c_2] \lambda^m \leq c_0 (1 + \beta_m) \lambda^m$$

where c_0 is some appropriate constant. Because $Q_{0,n}(z)$ which is bounded in $\mathbb{K}'$ which is $\mathbb{K}$ minus some small neighbourhoods of the points π_k, $k = 1, 2, \ldots, n$ and because the ratio $Q_{0,n+h}(z)/Q_{0,n}(z)$ equals $Q_{n,n+h}(z)$ by definition, we get after dividing the previous relation by $Q_{0,n}(z)$

$$|Q^{(m)}_{n,n+h}(z) - Q_{n,n+h}(z)| \leq c_3 (1 + \beta_m) \lambda^m$$

with $c_3 > 0$ and z in $\mathbb{K}'$. Because the left hand side are just polynomials, this relation will be valid in $\mathbb{K}$ itself. Because this bound is uniform it is also valid coefficientwise. I.e. there exists a constant $c_4 > 0$ such that

$$|q_i^{(m)} - q_i| \leq c_4 (1 + \beta_m) \lambda^m, \text{ for } i = 0, 1, \ldots, h.$$

If we specify now β_m as

$$\beta_m := \max_{0 \leq i \leq h} |q_i^{(m)} - q_i|$$

then

$$\beta_m \leq c_4 (1 + \beta_m) \lambda^m$$

or

$$\beta_m (1 - c_4 \lambda^m) \leq c_4 \lambda^m.$$

This shows that β_m can be bounded by e.g.

$$\beta_m \leqslant 2c_4 \lambda^m$$

if m is sufficiently large whence β_m goes to zero because $\lambda < 1$. This proves the coefficientwise convergence of the type 1 Rutishauser polynomials.

$\square$

Seewald gave his proof for type 1 Rutishauser polynomials only when they are defined by the recurrence (14.2a). We have shown that this proof remains valid for type 2 Rutishauser polynomials and also in the nonnormal case where recurrence (14.2a) may break down. It is left as an exercise for the reader to prove similar results for the monic Rutishauser polynomials $\hat{Q}^{(m)}_{n,n+h}(z)$. Using the transformation $z \rightarrow 1/z$ appropriate results can be formulated for m going to $-\infty$.

14.2 Rutishauser polynomials of type 3

There is a third possibility to define Rutishauser polynomials having the same behaviour as those of type 1 and type 2. We call them *type 3 Rutishauser polynomials*. As the notation already suggested, they are defined by recurrences (9.12) or (9.13) or by the determinant expressions (9.11). I.e.

$$Q^{(m)}_{n,n+k}(z) = \det (\mathbf{I}_k - z\, \mathbf{J}^{(m)}_{n,n+k}) \tag{14.8a}$$

which are the co-monic ones and the monic ones are

$$\hat{Q}^{(m)}_{n,n+k}(z) = \det (z\, \mathbf{I}_k - \hat{\mathbf{J}}^{(m)}_{n,n+k}) \tag{14.8b}$$

where $\mathbf{J}^{(m)}_{n,n+k}$ and $\hat{\mathbf{J}}^{(m)}_{n,n+k}$ are the tridiagonal matrices

$$\mathbf{J}^{(m)}_{n,n+k} = \mathrm{tridiag} \begin{pmatrix} \rho^{(m-1)}_{n+k} & \cdots & \rho^{(m-k+1)}_{n+2} \\ \sigma^{(m)}_{n+k} & \cdots & \sigma^{(m-k+1)}_{n+1} \\ 1 & \cdots & 1 \end{pmatrix}$$

and

$$\hat{\mathbf{J}}^{(m)}_{n,n+k} = \mathrm{tridiag} \begin{pmatrix} \hat{\rho}^{(m+1)}_{n+k} & \cdots & \hat{\rho}^{(m+k-1)}_{n+2} \\ \hat{\sigma}^{(m)}_{n+k} & \cdots & \hat{\sigma}^{(m+k-1)}_{n+1} \\ 1 & \cdots & 1 \end{pmatrix}.$$

It was shown by Gragg [GR2,p.56] that theorem 14.2 is also true if $Q^{(m)}_{n,n+h}(z)$ or $\hat{Q}^{(m)}_{n,n+h}(z)$ are type 3 Rutishauser polynomials. His proof goes as follows. Note that

$$\det B = \det \begin{vmatrix} B_{11} & B_{12} \\ B_{21} & B_{22} \end{vmatrix} = \det \begin{vmatrix} A_{11} & B_{12} \\ O & B_{22} \end{vmatrix} = \det A_{11} \det B_{22}$$

where $A_{11} := B_{11} - B_{12} B_{22}^{-1} B_{21}$ and B_{22} nonsingular.

Apply this to the matrix $B = I_{n+h} - z\, J_{0,n+h}^{(m)}$ with $B_{22} = I_n - z\, J_{0,n}^{(m-h)}$. Clearly

$$\det B = Q_{0,n+h}^{(m)}(z) \quad \text{and} \quad \det B_{22} = Q_{0,n}^{(m-h)}(z).$$

Thus you get

$$\det A_{11} = Q_{0,n+h}^{(m)}(z)/Q_{0,n}^{(m)}(z).$$

Now,

$$A_{11} = B_{11} - \begin{vmatrix} 0 & 0 & \cdots & 0 \\ \vdots & & & \\ 0 & & & \\ \rho_{n+1}^{(m-h)} & 0 & \cdots & 0 \end{vmatrix} B_{22}^{-1} \begin{vmatrix} 0 & \cdots & 0 & 1 \\ & & & 0 \\ & & & \vdots \\ 0 & \cdots & 0 & 0 \end{vmatrix}.$$

The second term gives only one nonzero element at the (n,n) position of the matrix and it equals $\rho_{n+1}^{(m-h)}$ times the cofactor of the $(1,1)$ element of B_{22} divided by $\det B_{22}$. Thus

$$A_{11} = I_h - z\, J_{n,n+h}^{(m)} - \mu_m E_h E_h^T$$

where

$$E_h^T = [0\ 0\ \cdots\ 0\ 1]$$

and

$$\mu_m := \rho_{n+1}^{(m-h)} Q_{0,n-1}^{(m-h-1)}(z)/Q_{0,n}^{(m-h)}(z).$$

Now by (9.31) and theorem 12.2 we have

$$\rho_{n+1}^{(m-h)} = -\frac{T_{n-2}^{(m-h-1)} T_n^{(m-h+1)}}{(T_{n-1}^{(m-h)})^2} = \frac{O(\pi_1 \cdots \pi_{n-1})^{-m}\, O(\pi_1 \cdots \pi_{n+1})^{-m}}{O(\pi_1 \cdots \pi_n)^{-2m}}$$

$$= O(|\pi_{n+1}/\pi_n|^{-m}) \to 0 \text{ as } m \to \infty \tag{14.9}$$

if $|\pi_n| < |\pi_{n+1}|$. Furthermore, by theorem 13.1, $Q_{0,n-1}^{(m-h-1)}(z)/Q_{0,n}^{(m)}(z)$ will tend to $Q_{n,n+h}(z)$. The speed of convergence will be determined by $\max\,(|\pi_n/\pi_{n+1}|,\ |\pi_{n+h}/\pi_{n+h+1}|)$. Putting this together we find from

$$Q_{0,n+h}^{(m)}(z)/Q_{0,n}^{(m)}(z) = \det A_{11}$$

as $m \to \infty$ that the left hand side goes to $Q_{n,n+h}(z)$ and the right hand side to $\det\,[I_h - z\, J_{n,n+h}^{(m)}] = Q_{n,n+h}^{(m)}(z)$, provided $z \neq \pi_1, \ldots, \pi_n$. But since these are polynomials this will be valid for unrestricted values of z in a compact subset of $\mathbb{C}$.

$\square$

14.3 Rutishauser polynomials and Laurent series

Note that the three possibilities proposed for the definitions of $Q^{(m)}_{n,n+h}(z)$ give different polynomials, unless $n=0$, in which case $Q^{(m)}_{0,h}(z) = Q^{(m)}_{h}(z)$. All of them however have the same asymptotic behaviour if $m \to \infty$. They approximate $Q_{n,n+h}(z)$ uniformly on compact subsets of the complex plane.

We supposed that κ was zero in the expression for $F(z)$. If it were not zero, this would give a shift over κ in the superscript but since m tends to infinity, this does not affect the result.
It is an easy exercise to adapt the previous proofs for a power series in $1/z$, representing a meromorphic function, analytic at ∞ . Also dual results could be obtained for monic polynomials $\hat{Q}^{(m)}_{n,n+k}(z)$. A combination of all this is given in theorem 14.3.

THEOREM 14.3. *Let $F(z)$ be a meromorphic function as described in section 12.1. Then we have (1) and (2) below.*

(1) Define for $|\pi_n| < |\pi_{n+1}|$ and $|\pi_{n+h}| < |\pi_{n+h+1}|; 0 \leqslant n < n+h \leqslant P^+$

$$Q_{n,n+h}(z) = (1-z/\pi_{n+1})(1-z/\pi_{n+2}) \cdots (1-z/\pi_{n+h}) \qquad (14.10a)$$

and

$$\hat{Q}_{n,n+h}(z) = (z-\pi_{n+1})(z-\pi_{n+2}) \cdots (z-\pi_{n+h}). \qquad (14.10b)$$

Then

$$|Q^{(m)}_{n,n+h}(z) - Q_{n,n+h}(z)| \leqslant C \lambda^m , \qquad \forall z \in \mathbb{K} , \; m \text{ large} \qquad (14.11a)$$

and

$$|\hat{Q}^{(m)}_{n,n+h}(z) - \hat{Q}_{n,n+h}(z)| \leqslant C \lambda^m , \qquad \forall z \in \mathbb{K} , \; m \text{ large} \qquad (14.11b)$$

where C is a positive constant, $\mathbb{K}$ is a compact subset of $\{z : 0 \leqslant |z| < \infty\}$,

$$1 > \lambda > \max(|\pi_n/\pi_{n+1}|, |\pi_{n+h}/\pi_{n+h+1}|) \qquad (14.12)$$

and where the co-monic Rutishauser polynomials $Q^{(m)}_{n,n+k}(z)$ of type 1, 2 or 3 are defined by

$$Q^{(m)}_{n,n+k+1}(z) = Q^{(m)}_{n,n+k}(z) - zb^{(m)}_{n+k+1} Q^{(m-1)}_{n,n+k}(z) ; \quad Q^{(m)}_{n,n} = 1 \qquad (14.13a)$$

$$Q^{(m-1)}_{n,n+k+1}(z) = Q^{(m)}_{n,n+k}(z) + zG^{(m)}_{n+k+1} \, Q^{(m-1)}_{n,n+k}(z) \,; \quad Q^{(m)}_{n,n} = 1 \qquad (14.13b)$$

$$Q^{(m)}_{n,n+k+1}(z) = (1-z\sigma^{(m)}_{n+k-1}) \, Q^{(m-1)}_{n,n+k}(z) - z^2 \rho^{(m-1)}_{n+k+1} \, Q^{(m-2)}_{n,n+k-1}(z);$$

$$Q^{(m)}_{n,n} = 1, \quad Q^{(m)}_{n,n-1} = 0 \qquad (14.13c)$$

respectively or by an appropriate adaptation if these recurrences break down (see (14.3), (14.8a)) and the monic Rutishauser polynomials $\hat{Q}^{(m)}_{n,n+k}(z)$ *of type 1, 2 and 3 are defined by*

$$\hat{Q}^{(m)}_{n,n+k+1}(z) = z\hat{Q}^{(m)}_{n,n+k}(z) - \hat{b}^{(m)}_{n+k+1} \, \hat{Q}^{(m+1)}_{n,n+k}(z)\,; \quad \hat{Q}^{(m)}_{n,n} = 1 \qquad (14.14a)$$

$$\hat{Q}^{(m+1)}_{n,n+k+1}(z) = \hat{G}^{(m)}_{n+k+1} \, \hat{Q}^{(m+1)}_{n,n+k}(z) + z\hat{Q}^{(m)}_{n,n+k}(z)\,; \quad \hat{Q}^{(m)}_{n,n} = 1 \qquad (14.14b)$$

$$\hat{Q}^{(m)}_{n,n+k+1}(z) = (z-\hat{\sigma}^{(m)}_{n+k+1}) \, \hat{Q}^{(m+1)}_{n,n+k}(z) - \hat{\rho}^{(m+1)}_{n+k+1} \, \hat{Q}^{(m+2)}_{n,n+k-1}(z);$$

$$\hat{Q}^{(m)}_{n,n} = 1, \quad \hat{Q}^{(m)}_{n,n-1} = 0 \qquad (14.14c)$$

respectively or by an appropriate modification if these recurrences break down (see (14.5), (14.8b)).

(2) *Define for* $|\pi_{-n}| < |\pi_{-n+1}|$ *and* $|\pi_{-n-h}| < |\pi_{-n-h+1}|$, $0 \leqslant n < n+h \leqslant P^- + 1$:

$$Q_{n,n+h}(z) = (1-z/\pi_{-n})(1-z/\pi_{-n-1}) \cdots (1-z/\pi_{-n-h+1}), \qquad (14.15a)$$

$$\hat{Q}_{n,n+h}(z) = (z-\pi_{-n})(z-\pi_{-n-1}) \cdots (z-\pi_{-n-h+1}). \qquad (14.15b)$$

Then

$$|Q^{(-m)}_{n,n+h}(z) - Q_{n,n+h}(z)| \leqslant C \, \lambda^m, \; z \in \mathbb{K} \,, \; m \; large \qquad (14.16a)$$

and

$$|\hat{Q}^{(-m)}_{n,n+h}(z) - \hat{Q}_{n,n+h}(z)| \leqslant C \, \lambda^m, \; z \in \mathbb{K} \,, \; m \; large \qquad (14.16b)$$

where C is a positive constant, $\mathbb{K}$ *is a compact subset of* $\{z : 0 \leqslant |z| < \infty\}$,

$$1 > \lambda > \max(|\pi_{-n}/\pi_{-n+1}|, \; |\pi_{-n-h}/\pi_{-n-h+1}|) \qquad (14.17)$$

and where the polynomials $Q^{(-m)}_{n,n+k}(z)$ *and* $\hat{Q}^{(-m)}_{n,n+k}(z)$ *are defined as in case (1).*

PROOF. All these results can be obtained as before if the Rutishauser polynomials are defined in terms of the McLaurin coefficients of $F(z)$ around $z=0$ or around $z=\infty$. If they are defined in terms of Laurent coefficients of $F(z)$, we can remark that the Rutishauser polynomials $Q^{(m)}_{n,n+h}(z)$ will not depend on f_k, $k \leqslant 0$ as long as m is large enough. Thus the Rutishauser polynomials for $F(z) = \sum^{\infty}_{-\infty} f_k z^k$ and for $Z(z) = \frac{1}{2}f_0 + \sum^{\infty}_1 f_k z^k$ are the same if m is large enough. Thus we can apply the previous results to the meromorphic function $Z(z)$, which has the same poles as $F(z)$, viz. π_k, $1 \leqslant k \leqslant P^+$ in $|z| > \rho$. If m goes to $-\infty$, we can apply the same technique but for the function $\hat{Z}(z) = -(\frac{1}{2}f_0 + \sum^{\infty}_1 f_{-k}z^{-k})$.

The details are left to the reader.

□

Note that it is sufficient that

$$Z(z) = \tfrac{1}{2}f_0 + \sum_{k=1}^{\infty} f_k z^k$$

converges to a meromorphic function in a neighborhood of $z=0$ while

$$\hat{Z}(z) = -\left(\tfrac{1}{2}f_0 + \sum_{k=1}^{\infty} f_{-k}z^{-k}\right)$$

converges to a meromorphic function in a neighborhood of $z = \infty$. The convergence regions need not overlap so that $\sum_{-\infty}^{\infty} f_k z^k$ is not necessarily a Laurent series of a meromorphic function. This means that we can easily reformulate the previous theorem for two–point PAs. This was done e.g. in [JOM].

14.4 Convergence of parameters

The previous results allow us to formulate a number of convergence results for the parameters associated with a Laurent series of a meromorphic function. (E.g. SS parameters, FG parameters, ab parameters, and $\rho\sigma$ parameters) if their superscript m tends to $\pm \infty$. This convergence depends on the pole positions of $F(z)$. Convergence will only occur if the poles separate in modulus. For $m \to \infty$, the poles in $|z| > \rho$ are important and for $m \to -\infty$, the poles in $|z| < \rho$ will be important. If a pole is separated in modulus from its neighbouring poles, it can be found as the limit of some of these parameters (see case (2) and (5) in the next corollary). If poles do not separate in modulus, we shall need the convergence of the Rutishauser polynomials. The coefficients of these Rutishauser polynomials are made up of sums of products of these parameters and although the parameters do not converge individually, their combinations that make up the coefficients of these polynomials do converge and give sums of products of the poles as given by the Vieta formulas (see case (3) and (6) in the next theorem). Some examples illustrating these results are given in the next corollary.

COROLLARY 14.4. *Let $F(z)$ be a meromorphic function as described in section 12.1. Associate with its Laurent series the SS parameters $\alpha_n^{(m)}$, $\hat{\alpha}_n^{(m)}$, the ab parameters, the FG parameters and the $\rho\sigma$ parameters whenever they exist as in theorem 9.2. Then we have the convergence results $(1) - (6)$ below. (By $\lim$ we mean the limit for $m \to \infty$) For the downward limits we have :*

(1) If $|\pi_n| < |\pi_{n+1}|$, $0 \leqslant n \leqslant P^+$, then

$$\lim a_{n+1}^{(m)} = \lim F_{n+1}^{(m)} = \lim \rho_{n+1}^{(m)} = 0, \tag{14.18a}$$

$$\lim \hat{a}_{n+1}^{(m)} = \lim \hat{F}_{n+1}^{(m)} = \lim \hat{\rho}_{n+1}^{(m)} = 0, \tag{14.18b}$$

$$\lim \hat{\alpha}_n^{(m)} = \lim 1/\alpha_n^{(m)} = (-1)^{n+1} \pi_1 \pi_2 \cdots \pi_n. \tag{14.18c}$$

(2) If $|\pi_n| < |\pi_{n+1}| < |\pi_{n+2}|$, $0 \leqslant n \leqslant P^+ -1$, then

$$\lim b_{n+1}^{(m)} = \lim \sigma_{n+1}^{(m)} = -\lim G_{n+1}^{(m)} = -\lim \hat{a}_n^{(m)}\alpha_{n+1}^{(m)} = 1/\pi_{n+1}, \tag{14.19a}$$

$$\lim \hat{b}_{n+1}^{(m)} = \lim \hat{\sigma}_{n+1}^{(m)} = -\lim \hat{G}_{n+1}^{(m)} = -\lim \alpha_n^{(m)}\hat{a}_{n+1}^{(m)} = \pi_{n+1}. \tag{14.19b}$$

(3) If $|\pi_n| < |\pi_{n+1}| \leqslant |\pi_{n+2}| < |\pi_{n+3}|$, $0 \leqslant n \leqslant P^+ - 2$, then

$$\lim (b_{n+1}^{(m)}+b_{n+2}^{(m)}) = -\lim (G_{n+1}^{(m+1)}+G_{n+2}^{(m)}) = 1/\pi_{n+1}+1/\pi_{n+2}, \tag{14.20a}$$

$$\lim b_{n+1}^{(m-1)}b_{n+2}^{(m)} = \lim G_{n+1}^{(m)}G_{n+2}^{(m)} = 1/(\pi_{n+1}\pi_{n+2}), \tag{14.20b}$$

$$\lim (\hat{b}_{n+1}^{(m)}+\hat{b}_{n+2}^{(m)}) = -\lim (\hat{G}_{n+1}^{(m-1)}+\hat{G}_{n+2}^{(m)}) = \pi_{n+1}+\pi_{n+2}, \tag{14.20c}$$

$$\lim \hat{b}_{n+1}^{(m+1)}\hat{b}_{n+2}^{(m)} = \lim \hat{G}_{n+1}^{(m)}\hat{G}_{n+2}^{(m)} = \pi_{n+1}\pi_{n+2}. \tag{14.20d}$$

For the upward limits we have similarly :

(4) If $|\pi_{-n}| < |\pi_{-n+1}|$, $0 \leqslant n \leqslant P^- + 1$, then

$$\lim a_{n+1}^{(-m)} = \lim F_{n+1}^{(-m)} = \lim \rho_{n+1}^{(-m)} = 0, \tag{14.21a}$$

$$\lim \hat{a}_{n+1}^{(-m)} = \lim \hat{F}_{n+1}^{(-m)} = \lim \hat{\rho}_{n+1}^{(-m)} = 0, \tag{14.21b}$$

$$\lim \alpha_n^{(-m)} = \lim 1/\hat{\alpha}_n^{(-m)} = (-1)^{n+1} \pi_0 \pi_{-1} \cdots \pi_{-n+1}. \tag{14.21c}$$

(5) If $|\pi_{-n-1}| < |\pi_{-n}| < |\pi_{-n+1}|$, $0 \leqslant n \leqslant P^-$, then

$$\lim b_{n+1}^{(-m)} = \lim \sigma_{n+1}^{(-m)} = -\lim G_{n+1}^{(-m)}$$
$$= -\lim \hat{\alpha}_n^{(-m)}\alpha_{n+1}^{(-m)} = \pi_{-n}, \tag{14.22a}$$

$$\lim \hat{b}_{n+1}^{(-m)} = \lim \hat{\sigma}_{n+1}^{(-m)} = -\lim \hat{G}_{n+1}^{(-m)}$$
$$= -\lim \alpha_n^{(-m)}\hat{\alpha}_{n+1}^{(-m)} = 1/\pi_{-n}. \tag{14.22b}$$

(6) If $|\pi_{-n-2}| < |\pi_{-n-1}| \leqslant |\pi_{-n}| < |\pi_{-n+1}|$, $0 \leqslant n \leqslant P^- -1$, then

$$\lim (b_{n+1}^{(-m)}+b_{n+2}^{(-m)}) = -\lim (G_{n+1}^{(-m+1)}+G_{n+2}^{(-m)}) = \pi_{-n}+\pi_{-n-1}, \tag{14.23a}$$

$$\lim b_{n+1}^{(-m-1)}b_{n+2}^{(-m)} = \lim G_{n+1}^{(-m)}G_{n+2}^{(-m)} = \pi_{-n}\pi_{-n-1}, \tag{14.23b}$$

$$\lim (\hat{b}_{n+1}^{(-m)}+\hat{b}_{n+2}^{(-m)})=-\lim (\hat{G}_{n+1}^{(-m-1)}+\hat{G}_{n+2}^{(-m)})= 1/\pi_{-n}+1/\pi_{-n-1}, \tag{14.23c}$$

$$\lim \hat{b}_{n+1}^{(-m+1)}\hat{b}_{n+2}^{(-m)} = \lim \hat{G}_{n+1}^{(-m)}\hat{G}_{n+2}^{(-m)} = 1/(\pi_{-n}\pi_{-n-1}). \tag{14.23d}$$

PROOF.

(1) The easiest way to prove (14.18) is by taking the determinant expressions (9.3) in combination with the asymptotics (12.8), which directly gives (14.18). E.g. $\lim \rho_{n+1}^{(m)} = 0$ was found as (14.9).

(2) To show (14.19) use theorem 14.3 with $h=1$ in combination with (14.13a) which says that $Q_{n,n+1}^{(m)}(z) = 1-zb_{n+1}^{(m)}$. Because $Q_{n,n+1}^{(m)}(z)$ converges to $Q_{n,n+1}(z) = 1-z/\pi_{n+1}$ uniformly on compacts, hence coefficient wise, we have $\lim b_{n+1}^{(m)} = 1/\pi_{n+1}$. Because $b_{n+1}^{(m)} = -\alpha_{n+1}^{(m)}\hat{\alpha}_n^{(m)}$ (see 7.5b), also $-\lim \hat{\alpha}_n^{(m)}\alpha_{n+1}^{(m)} = 1/\pi_{n+1}$. Using polynomials (14.13b) and (14.13c), the rest of (14.19a) follows in essentially the same way. (14.19b) is shown by duality.

(3) The proof of (14.20) is similar to the proof in (2), but now with $h=2$.

(4), (5) and (6) are derived from (1), (2) and (3) with the symmetry relations of section 10.1. An example : if we set $\hat{F}(z) := F(1/z)$, then the poles π_{-k} of $F(z)$ are transformed into the poles $1/\pi_k$ of $\hat{F}(z)$ and they satisfy $\cdots |\pi_{-1}| \leqslant |\pi_0| < \rho$ and $1/\rho < |1/\pi_0| \leqslant |1/\pi_1| \leqslant \cdots$ respectively. We also have $b_{n+1}^{(m)}(\hat{F}) = \hat{b}_{n+1}^{(m)}(F)$. Hence by (14.19a) we may conclude that $\lim b_{n+1}^{(m)}(\hat{F}) = 1/\pi_{-n}$ if $|1/\pi_{-n+1}| < |1/\pi_{-n}| < |1/\pi_{-n-1}|$ which is the same as $\lim \hat{b}_{n+1}^{(-m)}(F) = 1/\pi_{-n}$ if $|\pi_{-n-1}| < |\pi_{-n}| < |\pi_{-n+1}|$.

$\square$

Chapter 15

Determination of zeros

In the previous chapter we have shown how to find the poles of a meromorphic function from its Laurent series coefficients. In this chapter we shall give similar results for its zeros. As we have seen, the theory used in the previous chapter was essentially the theory which worked for a power series in z or $1/z$. In the classical theory for power series, the computation of zeros is easily derived from the theory for its poles with the symmetry properties of chapter 10 for a power series $F(z)$ and its inverse $1/F(z)$. In this way poles are turned into zeros and the result follows immediately. If $F(z)$ is given by its Laurent series, we could use in the previous chapter the additive splitting of $F(z)$ as $Z(z) - \hat{Z}(z)$. The poles of $Z(z)$ and $\hat{Z}(z)$ made up the poles of $F(z)$, but this is not true anymore for its zeros. So, the inversion of $Z(z)$ and $\hat{Z}(z)$ doesn't help in this case. What we need now is the multiplicative splitting of $F(z)$ which contained the factors $F_+(z)$ and $F_-(z)$. Then the zeros of $F(z)$ are distributed over these factors and inverting them turns zeros into poles. How these zeros can then be computed is shown in theorem 15.1. The Rutishauser polynomials related to the poles of $1/F_+(z)$ will be the dual Rutishauser polynomials related to the zeros of $F_+(z)$. Next we have to relate the parameters associated with the power series of $F_+(z)$ (and $F_-(z)$) with the parameters associated with the Laurent coefficients of $F(z)$. This result is given in Lemma 15.2. Because the coefficients of the dual Rutishauser polynomials are made up of combinations of these parameters, also the dual Rutishauser polynomials of $F(z)$ and $F_+(z)$ (and $F_-(z)$) will be related (corollary 15.3). From this we shall be able to derive the convergence of the dual Rutishauser polynomials for $F(z)$ (theorem 15.4) and the convergence results concerning the zeros of $F(z)$.

15.1 Dual Rutishauser polynomials and semi-infinite series

The symmetry relations given in section 10.2 allow us to translate theorem 14.3 into theorem 15.1 below.

THEOREM 15.1. *Let $F(z)$ be as described in section 12.1 with $F_-(z) = 1$ and $\kappa = 0$. Define for $|\zeta_m| < |\zeta_{m+1}|$ and $|\zeta_{m+h}| < |\zeta_{m+h+1}|, 0 \leqslant m < m+h \leqslant Z^+$*

$$P^{(m,m+h)}(z) = (1 - z/\zeta_{m+1})(1 - z/\zeta_{m+2}) \cdots (1 - z/\zeta_{m+h}) \tag{15.1a}$$

and

$$\hat{P}^{(m,m+h)}(z) = (z - \zeta_{m+1})(z - \zeta_{m+2}) \cdots (z - \zeta_{m+h}).$$ (15.1b)

Then

$$|P_n^{(m,m+h)}(z) - P^{(m,m+h)}(z)| \leqslant C \lambda^n, \ \forall z \in \mathbb{K}, \ n \ large,$$ (15.2a)

and

$$|\hat{P}_n^{(m,m+h)}(z) - \hat{P}^{(m,m+h)}(z)| \leqslant C \lambda^n, \ \forall z \in \mathbb{K}, \ n \ large,$$ (15.2b)

where C is a positive constant, $\mathbb{K}$ a compact subset of $\{z : 0 \leqslant |z| < \infty\}$,

$$1 > \lambda > \max \left(|\zeta_m/\zeta_{m+1}|, \ |\zeta_{m+h}/\zeta_{m+h+1}|\right),$$

and where the dual co-monic Rutishauser polynomials $P_n^{(m,m+k)}(z)$ of type 1,2 or 3 are defined by

$$P_n^{(m,m+k+1)}(z) = P_n^{(m,m+k)}(z) - za_{n+1}^{(m+k+1)} P_{n-1}^{(m,m+k)}(z); \ P_n^{(m,m)} = 1,$$ (15.3a)

$$P_{n-1}^{(m,m+k+1)}(z) = P_n^{(m,m+k)}(z) - zG_{n+1}^{(m+k+1)} P_{n-1}^{(m,m+k)}(z); \ P_n^{(m,m)} = 1,$$ (15.3b)

$$P_n^{(m,m+k+1)}(z) = (1 - z\sigma_n^{(m+k+1)}) P_{n-1}^{(m,m+k)}(z) - z^2 \rho_n^{(m+k)} P_{n-2}^{(m,m+k-1)}(z),$$

$$P_n^{(m,m)} = 1, \ P_n^{(m,m-1)} = 0,$$ (15.3c)

respectively or an appropriate modification if these recursions break down. The dual monic Rutishauser polynomials $\hat{P}_n^{(m,m+k)}(z)$ of type 1,2 or 3 are defined by

$$\hat{P}_n^{(m,m+k+1)}(z) = z\hat{P}_n^{(m,m+k)}(z) - \hat{a}_{n+1}^{(m+k)} \hat{P}_n^{(m,m+k)}(z); \ \hat{P}_n^{(m,m)} = 1,$$ (15.4a)

$$\hat{P}_{n+1}^{(m,m+k+1)}(z) = -\hat{G}_{n+1}^{(m+k)} \hat{P}_{n+1}^{(m,m+k)}(z) + z\hat{P}_n^{(m,m+k)}(z); \ \hat{P}_n^{(m,m)} = 1,$$ (15.4b)

$$\hat{P}_n^{(m,m+k+1)}(z) = (z - \hat{\sigma}_{n+1}^{(m+k)}) \hat{P}_{n+1}^{(m,m+k)}(z) - \hat{\rho}_{n+2}^{(m+k)} \hat{P}_{n+2}^{(m,m+k-1)}(z);$$

$$\hat{P}_n^{(m,m)} = 1, \ \hat{P}_n^{(m,m-1)} = 0,$$ (15.4c)

respectively or an appropriate modification if these recursions break down.

PROOF. Let us denote $G(z) := 1/F(z) = 1/F_+(z)$. The poles of $G(z)$ are ζ_k, $1 \leqslant k \leqslant Z^+$ with $\rho < |\zeta_1| \leqslant |\zeta_2| \leqslant \cdots$. Let $Q_{n,n+k}^{(m)}(z;G)$ be the Rutishauser polynomials of type 1 for $G(z)$. They satisfy the recurrence (14.13a), i.e.

$$Q_{m,m+k+1}^{(n)}(z;G) = Q_{m,m+k}^{(n)}(z;G) - zb_{m+k+1}^{(n)}(G)Q_{m,m+k}^{(n-1)}(z;G); \ Q_{m,m}^{(n)}(z;G) = 1.$$

By (10.4a) we may replace $b_{m+k+1}^{(n)}(G)$ by $a_{n+1}^{(m+k+1)}(F)$ if $m+k \geqslant 0, n \geqslant 0$. Thus

$$Q_{m,m+k+1}^{(n)}(z;G) = Q_{m,m+k}^{(n)}(z;G) - za_{n+1}^{(m+k+1)}(F)Q_{m,m+k}^{(n-1)}(z;G)$$

and if we define

$$P_n^{(m,m+k+1)}(z;F) := Q_{m,m+k+1}^{(n)}(z;G),$$

then

$$P_n^{(m,m+k+1)}(z;F) = P_n^{(m,m+k)}(z;F) - za_{n+1}^{(m+k+1)}(F)P_{n-1}^{(m,m+k)}(z;F),$$

with initial condition

$$P_n^{(m,m)}(z;F) = 1$$

and this is recurrence (15.3a). These polynomials $P_n^{(m,m+k)}(z)$ are called *dual type 1 comonic Rutishauser polynomials* for $F(z)$.

Now theorem 14.3 for $G(z)$ says that

$$|Q_{m,m+h}^{(n)}(z;G) - Q_{m,m+h}(z;G)| \leqslant C\lambda^n, \forall z \in \mathbb{K}, n \text{ large}$$

if

$$Q_{m,m+h}(z;G) = (1 - z/\zeta_{m+1}) \cdots (1 - z/\zeta_{m+h}),$$

$C > 0$ is a constant, $\mathbb{K}$ a compact subset of $\{z : 0 \leqslant |z| < \infty\}$, $|\zeta_m| < |\zeta_{m+1}|$, $|\zeta_{m+h}| < |\zeta_{m+h+1}|$ and $1 > \lambda > \max(|\zeta_m/\zeta_{m+1}|, |\zeta_{m+h}/\zeta_{m+h+1}|)$.   Since $P_n^{(m,m+h)}(z;F) = Q_{m,m+h}^{(n)}(z;G)$ and $P^{(m,m+h)}(z;F) = Q_{m,m+h}(z;G)$, this proves (15.2a) for the dual type 1 comonic Rutishauser polynomials.

The proof for all the other cases is completely similar.

$\square$

Of course a similar result could be formulated for a power series in $1/z$. The condition $\kappa = 0$ is not essential because $\kappa \neq 0$ causes only a shift in the index m of the previous formulation.

If in (15.3) we take $m = 0$, then we obtain the recursions (7.10a), (7.10c) and (7.10b) respectively where S has to be replaced by P. Taking into account the initial conditions we may conclude that $P_n^{(0,k)}(z) \equiv P_n^{(k)}(z)/f_0$. If in (15.4) we take $m = 0$, then we obtain the recursions (9.6b), (9.6d) and (9.6g) for S replaced by P. With the initial conditions from above we have $\hat{P}_n^{(0,k)}(z) = \hat{P}'_{n-1}^{(k+1)}(z)$ the latter being defined in theorem 9.4.

15.2 From semi-infine to bi-infinite series

We shall now show how the case of a general Laurent series can be brought back to the case above. We start by the following lemma.

LEMMA 15.2. *For a meromorphic function $F(z)$ as defined in section 12.1 we have for $0 \leqslant m - \kappa \leqslant Z^+ + 1$*

$$s_{n+1}^{(m)}(F) = s_{n+1}^{(m-\kappa)}(F_+) \{1+o(1)\} \text{ for } n \to \infty, \tag{15.5a}$$

where s is one of the $\alpha, \hat{\alpha}, b, \hat{b}, a, \hat{a}, G, \hat{G}, \rho, \hat{\rho}, \sigma$ or $\hat{\sigma}$ parameters that can be associated with the Laurent series of $F(z)$ or the McLaurin series of $F_+(z)$.

PROOF. It is sufficient to give the proof for $s = \alpha$ because the others are completely similar. From (9.3d) we have for n sufficiently large and for m within the bounds indicated :

$$\alpha_{n+1}^{(m)} = (-1)^n T_n^{(m+1)}(F)/T_n^{(m)}(F).$$

By theorem 12.8 we may replace $T_n^{(m+1)}(F)$ by $C\lambda^{n+1} T_n^{(m+1-\kappa)}(F_+) \{1+o(1)\}$ and similarly for $T_n^{(m)}(F)$ if $n \to \infty$. Thus

$$\alpha_{n+1}^{(m)}(F) = (-1)^n T_n^{(m+1-\kappa)}(F_+)/T_n^{(m-\kappa)}(F_+) \{1+o(1)\}$$
$$= \alpha_{n+1}^{(m-\kappa)}(F_+) \{1+o(1)\}, \quad n \to \infty .$$

$\square$

Of course similar results may be obtained for $m \leqslant \kappa$. E.g. by using the duality between $F(z)$ and $\hat{F}(z) = F(1/z)$ we would find

$$s_n^{(m)}(F) = s_n^{(\kappa-m)}(F_-) \{1+o(1)\} \quad \text{as } n \to \infty \tag{15.5b}$$

where again s is one of the elements enumerated in lemma 15.2. This gives us directly the following corollary.

COROLLARY 15.3. *Let $F(z)$ be a meromorphic function as described in section 12.1. For the dual Rutishauser polynomials that can be associated with the Laurent series of $F(z)$ or with the McLaurin series of its factor $F_+(z)$ as in the definitions (15.3) and (15.4) we have for $n \to \infty$ and $0 \leqslant m- \kappa \leqslant m-\kappa+k \leqslant Z^+$*

$$P_n^{(m,m+k)}(z;F) = P_n^{(m-\kappa,m-\kappa+k)}(z;F_+) \{1+o(1)\} \tag{15.6a}$$

$$\hat{P}_n^{(m,m+k)}(z;F) = \hat{P}_n^{(m-\kappa,m-\kappa+k)}(z;F_+) \{1+o(1)\}. \tag{15.6b}$$

PROOF. The theorem is true for $k = 0$ since e.g. $P_n^{(m,m)}(z;F) = P_n^{(m-\kappa,m-\kappa)}(z;F_+) = 1$. The rest follows by a simple induction argument with recurrence relations (15.3) and the previous lemma.

$\square$

We are now ready to give the convergence results for the dual Rutishauser polynomials. They are given in the next theorem.

THEOREM 15.4. *Let $F(z)$ be a meromorphic function as described in section 12.1. Then we have (1) and (2) below.*

(1) *Define for $|\zeta_{m-\kappa}| < |\zeta_{m-\kappa+1}|$ and $|\zeta_{m-\kappa+h}| < |\zeta_{m-\kappa+h+1}|$, where $0 \leqslant m-\kappa < m-\kappa+h \leqslant Z^+$, the polynomials*

$$P^{(m,m+h)}(z) := (1-z/\zeta_{m-\kappa+1})(1-z/\zeta_{m-\kappa+2}) \cdots (1-z/\zeta_{m-\kappa+h}) \quad (15.7a)$$

and

$$\hat{P}^{(m,m+h)}(z) := (z - \zeta_{m-\kappa+1})(z - \zeta_{m-\kappa+2}) \cdots (z - \zeta_{m-\kappa+h}). \quad (15.7b)$$

Let the comonic dual Rutishauser polynomials $P_n^{(m,m+k)}(z)$ be defined by one of (15.3) and the monic Rutishauser polynomials $\hat{P}_n^{(m,m+k)}(z)$ by one of (15.4). Then

$$|P_n^{(m,m+h)}(z) - P^{(m,m+h)}(z)| \leqslant C\,\lambda^n\,, \quad \forall z \in \mathbb{K}, \ n \text{ large}, \quad (15.8a)$$

and

$$|\hat{P}_n^{(m,m+h)}(z) - \hat{P}^{(m,m+h)}(z)| \leqslant C\,\lambda^n\,, \quad \forall z \in \mathbb{K}, \ n \text{ large}, \quad (15.8b)$$

where $C > 0$ is a constant, $\mathbb{K}$ a compact subset of $\{z : 0 \leqslant |z| < \infty\}$ and

$$1 > \lambda > \max\left(|\zeta_{m-\kappa}/\zeta_{m-\kappa+1}|, |\zeta_{m-\kappa+h}/\zeta_{m-\kappa+h+1}|\right). \quad (15.9)$$

(2) *For $|\zeta_{m-\kappa}| < |\zeta_{m-\kappa+1}|$ and $|\zeta_{m-\kappa-h}| < |\zeta_{m-\kappa-h+1}|$, where $0 \geqslant m-\kappa > m-\kappa-h \geqslant -Z^- -1$, define the polynomials*

$$P^{(m,m-h)}(z) := (1-z/\zeta_{m-\kappa})(1-z/\zeta_{m-\kappa-1}) \cdots (1-z/\zeta_{m-\kappa-h+1}) \quad (15.10a)$$

and

$$\hat{P}^{(m,m-h)}(z) := (z - \zeta_{m-\kappa})(z - \zeta_{m-\kappa-1}) \cdots (z - \zeta_{m-\kappa-h+1}). \quad (15.10b)$$

Let the monic dual Rutishauser polynomials $\hat{P}_n^{(m,m-k)}(z)$ be defined by one of

$$\hat{P}_n^{(m,m-k-1)}(z) = z\hat{P}_n^{(m,m-k)}(z) - \hat{a}_{n+1}^{(m-k-1)}\hat{P}_{n-1}^{(m,m-k)}(z);$$

$$\hat{P}_n^{(m,m)} = 1, \quad (15.11a)$$

$$\hat{P}_{n-1}^{(m,m-k-1)}(z) = z\hat{P}_n^{(m,m-k)}(z) - \hat{G}_n^{(m-k-1)}\hat{P}_{n-1}^{(m,m-k)}(z);$$

$$\hat{P}_n^{(m,m)} = 1, \quad (15.11b)$$

$$\hat{P}_n^{(m,m-k-1)}(z) = (z - \hat{\sigma}_n^{(m-k-1)})\hat{P}_{n-1}^{(m,m-k)}(z) - \hat{\rho}_n^{(m-k)}\hat{P}_{n-2}^{(m,m-k+1)}(z);$$

$$\hat{P}_n^{(m,m)} = 1, \ \hat{P}_n^{(m,m+1)} = 0, \quad (15.11c)$$

and the comonic dual Rutishauser polynomials $P_n^{(m,m-k)}(z)$ are defined by one of

$$P_n^{(m,m-k-1)}(z) = P_n^{(m,m-k)}(z) - za_{n+1}^{(m-k)}P_{n+1}^{(m,m-k)}(z),$$

$$P_n^{(m,m)} = 1, \qquad (15.12a)$$

$$P_{n+1}^{(m,m-k-1)}(z) = P_n^{(m,m-k)}(z) - zG_n^{(m-k)}P_{n+1}^{(m,m-k)}(z),$$

$$P_n^{(m,m)} = 1, \qquad (15.12b)$$

$$P_n^{(m,m-k-1)}(z) = (1 - z\sigma_{n+1}^{(m-k)})P_{n+1}^{(m,m-k)}(z) - z^2\rho_{n+2}^{(m-k)}P_{n+2}^{(m,m-k+1)}(z),$$

$$P_n^{(m,m)} = 1, \; P_n^{(m,m+1)} = 0. \qquad (15.12c)$$

Then

$$|P_n^{(m,m-h)}(z) - P^{(m,m-h)}(z)| \leqslant C \lambda^n, \quad z \in \mathbb{K}, \; n \; large, \qquad (15.13a)$$

$$|\hat{P}_n^{(m,m-h)}(z) - \hat{P}^{(m,m-h)}(z)| \leqslant C \lambda^n, \quad z \in \mathbb{K}, \; n \; large, \qquad (15.13b)$$

where C is a positive constant, $\mathbb{K}$ a compact subset of $\{z: 0 \leqslant |z| < \infty\}$ and

$$1 > \lambda > \max (|\zeta_{m-\kappa}/\zeta_{m-\kappa+1}|, |\zeta_{m-\kappa-h}/\zeta_{m-\kappa-h+1}|). \qquad (15.14)$$

PROOF. The first part is only a transcription of theorem 15.1 were we take corollary 15.3 into account. The second part can be brought back to the first part. If $\hat{F}(z) = F(1/z)$ and if we suppose that

$$F(z) = K z^k F_+(z)F_-(z),$$

according to our description of section 12.1, then

$$\hat{F}(z) = \hat{K} z^{\hat{k}} \hat{F}_+(z) \hat{F}_-(z) \qquad (15.15)$$

with $\hat{K} = K$, $\hat{k} = -\kappa$. $\hat{F}_+(z)$ has zeros $\hat{\zeta}_k$, $1 \leqslant k \leqslant \hat{Z}^+$ and poles $\hat{\pi}_k$, $1 \leqslant k \leqslant \hat{P}^+$ with $1/\rho < |\hat{\zeta}_1| \leqslant |\hat{\zeta}_2| \leqslant \cdots$ and $1/\rho < |\hat{\pi}_1| \leqslant |\hat{\pi}_2| \leqslant \cdots$. and $\hat{F}_-(z)$ has zeros $\hat{\zeta}_{-k}$, $0 \leqslant k \leqslant \hat{Z}^-$ and poles $\hat{\pi}_{-k}$, $0 \leqslant k \leqslant \hat{P}^-$, with $\cdots \leqslant |\hat{\zeta}_{-1}| \leqslant |\hat{\zeta}_0| < 1/\rho$ and $\cdots \leqslant |\hat{\pi}_{-1}| \leqslant |\hat{\pi}_0| < 1/\rho$, where $\hat{Z}^+ = Z^- + 1$, $\hat{Z}^- = Z^+ - 1$, $\hat{P}^+ = P^- + 1$, $\hat{P}^- = P^+ - 1$, and $\hat{\zeta}_k = 1/\zeta_{-k+1}$, $\hat{\pi}_k = 1/\pi_{-k+1}$. Part 1 of the theorem then says that we can define polynomials $P_n^{(-m,-m+h)}(z;\hat{F})$ of degree h by

$$P_n^{(-m,-m+k+1)}(z;\hat{F}) = P_n^{(-m,-m+k)}(z;\hat{F}) - za_{n+1}^{(-m+k+1)}(\hat{F})P_{n-1}^{(-m,-m+k)}(z;\hat{F});$$

$$P_n^{(-m,-m)}(z;\hat{F}) = 1$$

and if $|\hat{\zeta}_{-m-\hat{\kappa}}| < |\hat{\zeta}_{-m-\hat{\kappa}+1}|$ and $|\hat{\zeta}_{-m-\hat{\kappa}+h}| < |\hat{\zeta}_{-m-\hat{\kappa}+h+1}|$ and $0 \leqslant -m-\hat{\kappa} < -m-\hat{\kappa}+h \leqslant \hat{Z}^+$, then $P_n^{(-m,-m+h)}(z;\hat{F})$ converges to

$$(1 - z/\hat{\zeta}_{-m-\hat{\kappa}+1})(1 - z/\hat{\zeta}_{-m-\hat{\kappa}+2}) \cdots (1 - z/\hat{\zeta}_{-m-\hat{\kappa}+h}).$$

This can be reformulated as : If $|\zeta_{m-\kappa}| < |\zeta_{m-\kappa+1}|$ and $|\zeta_{m-\kappa-h}| < |\zeta_{m-\kappa-h+1}|$

and $0 \geqslant m - \kappa > m - \kappa - h \geqslant -Z^- - 1$, then $P_n^{(-m, -m+h)}(z; \hat{F})$ converges to

$$(1 - z\zeta_{m-\kappa})(1 - z\zeta_{m-\kappa-1}) \cdots (1 - z\zeta_{m-\kappa-h+1}).$$

If we recall from theorem 10.2 that $a_{n+1}^{(-m+k+1)}(\hat{F}) = \hat{a}_{n+1}^{(m-k-1)}(F)$ and rename $z^k P_n^{(-m, -m+k)}(1/z; \hat{F})$ as $\hat{P}_n^{(m, m-k)}(z; F)$ then the recursion for $P_n^{(-m, -m+k)}(z; \hat{F})$ becomes (15.11a) and the resulting polynomials will converge to (15.10a). The other relations are to be proved similarly.

$$\square$$

15.3 Convergence of parameters

The results given in corollary 14.4 were related to the column limits. We can now formulate the corresponding results for the row limits as a corollary of the previous theorem.

COROLLARY 15.5. *Let $F(z)$ be a meromorphic function as described in section 12.1. Associate with its Laurent series the SS parameters $\alpha_n^{(m)}$, $\hat{\alpha}_n^{(m)}$, the ab parameters, the FG parameters and the $\rho\sigma$ parameters whenever they exist as in theorem 9.2. Then we have the convergence results (1)–(6) below. (By $\lim$ we mean the limit for $n \to \infty$.)*

(1) If $|\zeta_m| < |\zeta_{m+1}|$, $-Z^- - 1 \leqslant m \leqslant Z^+$, then

$$\lim b_n^{(m+\kappa)} = \lim \hat{b}_n^{(m+\kappa)} = \lim \alpha_n^{(m+\kappa)} \hat{\alpha}_n^{(m+\kappa)}$$
$$= \lim \rho_n^{(m+\kappa)} = \lim \hat{\rho}_n^{(m+\kappa)} = 0. \tag{15.16}$$

(2) If $|\zeta_m| < |\zeta_{m+1}| < |\zeta_{m+2}|$, $-Z^- - 1 \leqslant m \leqslant Z^+ - 1$, then

$$\lim a_n^{(m+\kappa+1)} = \lim G_n^{(m+\kappa+1)} = -\lim F_n^{(m+\kappa+1)} = \lim \sigma_n^{(m+\kappa+1)}$$
$$= \lim \alpha_n^{(m+\kappa)} / \alpha_{n-1}^{(m+\kappa)} = 1 / \zeta_{m+1}, \tag{15.17a}$$

$$\lim \hat{a}_n^{(m+\kappa)} = \lim \hat{G}_n^{(m+\kappa)} = -\lim \hat{F}_n^{(m+\kappa)} = \lim \hat{\sigma}_n^{(m+\kappa)}$$
$$= \lim \alpha_{n-1}^{(m+\kappa)} / \alpha_n^{(m+\kappa)} = \zeta_{m+1}. \tag{15.17b}$$

(3) If $|\zeta_m| < |\zeta_{m+1}| \leqslant |\zeta_{m+2}| < |\zeta_{m+3}|$, $-Z^- - 1 \leqslant m \leqslant Z^+ - 2$, then

$$\lim (a_n^{(m+\kappa+1)} + a_n^{(m+\kappa+2)}) = \lim (G_n^{(m+\kappa+1)} + G_n^{(m+\kappa+2)})$$
$$= 1 / \zeta_{m+1} + 1 / \zeta_{m+2}, \tag{15.18a}$$

$$\lim a_n^{(m+\kappa+1)} a_{n+1}^{(m+\kappa+2)} = \lim G_n^{(m+\kappa+1)} G_n^{(m+\kappa+2)}$$
$$= 1 / (\zeta_{m+1} \zeta_{m+2}), \tag{15.18b}$$

$$\lim (\hat{a}_n^{(m+\kappa)} + \hat{a}_n^{(m+\kappa+1)}) = \lim (\hat{G}_n^{(m+\kappa)} + \hat{G}_n^{(m+\kappa+1)})$$
$$= \zeta_{m+1} + \zeta_{m+2}, \qquad (15.18c)$$

$$\lim \hat{a}_{n+1}^{(m+\kappa)} \hat{a}_n^{(m+\kappa+1)} = \lim \hat{G}_{n+1}^{(m+\kappa)} \hat{G}_n^{(m+\kappa+1)}$$
$$= \zeta_{m+1} \zeta_{m+2}. \qquad (15.18d)$$

PROOF. The proof of this is analogous to the proof for corollary 14.4. We now use the dual Rutishauser polynomials of theorem 15.4. The details are left to the reader.

$\square$

Chapter 16

Convergence in a row of the Laurent-Padé table

In chapter 13 we have studied the Montessus de Ballore theorem for Laurent-Padé approximants. It gave the convergence of LPAs when the numerator degree tends to infinity. In this chapter we shall study the convergence of LPAs when the denominator degree tends to infinity. The idea is to find $\lim_{n\to\infty} Q_n^{(m)}(z)$ first. This problem, or a variant thereof, has been studied in the literature. The vector $Q_n^{(m)}$ of coefficients of the polynomial $Q_n^{(m)}(z)$ is the solution of a $(n+1) \times (n+1)$ Toeplitz system of linear equations. If $n \to \infty$, the matrix $T_n^{(m)}$ of the system will become an infinite Toeplitz matrix. It is the representation in the natural basis $\{z^k\}_{-\infty}^{\infty}$ of a Toeplitz operator with symbol $z^{-m}F(z)$. Thus for $n = \infty$, the finite Toeplitz systems

$$T_n^{(m)}Q_n = E_{0,n} \quad , \quad n = 0,1,2, \cdots \tag{16.1}$$

with $T_n^{(m)} = (f_{m+i-j})_{i,j=0}^n \in \mathbb{C}^{(n+1)\times(n+1)}$, $E_{0,n} = [1\ 0 \cdots 0]^T \in \mathbb{C}^{n+1}$ and $Q_n \in \mathbb{C}^{n+1}$ will become

$$T_\infty^{(m)}Q_\infty = E_{0,\infty} \tag{16.2}$$

which is the representation in the natural basis of a Toeplitz operator equation

$$\Phi Q(z) = 1 \tag{16.3}$$

where Φ represents the Toeplitz operator with special symbol $z^{-m}F(z)$. The method of solving the operator equation (16.3) by successively solving the systems (16.1) for $n = 0,1,2, \cdots$ is called the projection method. This method and its convergence was studied by Gohberg and Feldman [GOF]. These authors studied the problem when $\{f_k\}_{-\infty}^{\infty}$ were the Fouriercoefficients of $F(z) \in L^1$ and for $Q(z) \in H^p$. Their result was that there can only be convergence of Q_n to Q_∞ (the Fourier coefficients of $Q(z)$) in L^p-norm for one specific value of m. We shall slightly adapt their development in section 16.1 and we shall use it to prove convergence of $Q_n^{(0)}(z)$ uniformly on compacts if the winding number κ of $F(z)$ is zero. This can be used to prove convergence of $(0,n)$ LPAs if $\kappa = 0$. (See section 16.2). Although, $m = 0$ is the only m-value for which convergence in L^p-norm can be obtained, it will be possible to prove convergence of some other $Q_n^{(m)}(z)$ uniformly on compacts, even when $m \neq 0$. This will allow us to prove also convergence for those (m,n) type LPAs.

16.1 Toeplitz operators and the projection method

Let us start with an adaption of the theory in [GOF] concerning Toeplitz operators and the projection method to solve operator equations. We shall need some notation and definitions first.

Define for $p = 1, 2, \cdots$ and $\rho > 0$

$$l_\rho^p := \{F = \{f_k\}_{-\infty}^\infty : \|f\|_{\rho,p} < \infty,\ f_k \in \mathbb{C}\}$$

where

$$\|f\|_{\rho,p} := \left(\sum_{k=-\infty}^\infty (|f_k|\rho^k)^p\right)^{1/p}$$

and

$$l_\rho^\infty := \{F = \{f_k\}_{-\infty}^\infty : \|f\|_{\rho,\infty} < \infty,\ f_k \in \mathbb{C}\}$$

where

$$\|f\|_{\rho,\infty} := \sup_{0 \leqslant k \leqslant \infty} |f_k|\rho^k.$$

Furthermore, define the subspaces

$$l_{\rho+}^p = \{f \in l_\rho^p : f_k = 0,\ k = -1, -2, ...\} \subset l_\rho^p$$

$$l_{\rho-}^p = \{f \in l_\rho^p : f_k = 0,\ k = 1, 2, ...\} \subset l_\rho^p.$$

Define a *shift operator* Λ on $l_{\rho+}^p$ by

$$\Lambda \{q_0\ q_1\ \cdots\} = \{0\ q_0\ q_1\ \cdots\}$$

and its *left inverse* $\Lambda^{(-1)}$ by

$$\Lambda^{(-1)} \{q_0\ q_1\ \cdots\} = \{q_1\ q_2\ \cdots\}.$$

Furthermore set

$$\begin{aligned}
\Lambda^{(k)} &:= I & \text{for } k = 0\\
&:= \Lambda^k & \text{for } k = 1, 2, ...\\
&:= (\Lambda^{(-1)})^k & \text{for } k = -1, -2, ... \ .
\end{aligned}$$

The norm of the operator Λ is

$$\|\Lambda\| := \sup_{q \in l_{\rho+}^p} \{\|\Lambda q\|_{\rho,p} : \|q\|_{\rho,p} = 1\}.$$

Clearly, $\|\Lambda q\|_{\rho,p} = \rho\|q\|_{\rho,p}$ so that $\|\Lambda\| = \rho$. You can similarly find that in general $\|\Lambda^{(k)}\| = \rho^k$, $k \in \mathbb{Z}$. Consider all complex linear combinations of $\Lambda^{(k)}$, $k \in \mathbb{Z}$. We denote the closure of this set by $\mathbb{T}$. Similarly $\mathbb{T}^+(\mathbb{T}^-)$ is the closed linear span of $\Lambda^{(k)}$, $k = 0, 1, 2, \cdots$ $(k = 0, -1, -2, \cdots)$. Thus if $\Phi \in \mathbb{T}$, then $\Phi = \sum_{-\infty}^\infty f_k \Lambda^{(k)}$ where $\sum_{-\infty}^\infty f_k z^k$ must converge absolutely for $|z| = \rho$. This means that $\{f_k\}_{-\infty}^{\infty} \in l_\rho^1$. If we define the function $F(z)$ by $F(z) = \sum_{-\infty}^{\infty} f_k z^k$ on $|z| = \rho$, then the relation between Φ and $F(z)$ is one to one. $F(z)$ is called the *symbol* of the operator Φ and we also denote Φ as $F(\Lambda)$.

Note that the uniqueness of the correspondence is through the coefficients f_k and these depend for a given function $F(z)$ on the value of ρ. In our context $F(z)$ will be a meromorphic function as described in section 12.1. Because $F(z)$ is supposed to have no poles (and no zeros) in $\mathbb{E} = \{z : r < |z| < R\}$ with $r < \rho < R$, $\sum f_k z^k$ will be a Laurent series for $F(z)$ which converges absolutely not only for $|z| = \rho$ but everywhere in $\mathbb{E}$.

The connection with Toeplitz systems is as follows. Let $Q = \{q_k\}_0^\infty$ and $R = \{r_k\}_0^\infty$ be in $l_{\rho+}^p$. The matrix representation of the equation $F(\Lambda)Q = R$ with respect to the natural basis in $l_{\rho+}^p$ (i.e. the columns of the identity matrix) is clearly the infinite dimensional Toeplitz system

$$\sum_{j=0}^\infty f_{k-j} q_j = r_k \quad , \quad k = 0,1,2,\dots .$$

In general, if F_1 and $F_2 \in l_\rho^1$ and $F(z) = F_1(z)F_2(z)$, we don't necessarily have $F(\Lambda) = F_1(\Lambda)F_2(\Lambda)$. However, it can be easily verified that we do have following classical factorization theorem.

THEOREM 16.1. *Let $F_-(\Lambda) \in \mathbb{T}^-$, $F_0(\Lambda) \in \mathbb{T}$ and $F_+(\Lambda) \in \mathbb{T}^+$ with respective symbols $F_-(z)$, $F_0(z)$ and $F_+(z)$. Define*

$$\Phi = F_-(\Lambda)F_0(\Lambda)F_+(\Lambda).$$

Then Φ has the symbol $F(z) := F_-(z)F_0(z)F_+(z)$, i.e. $\Phi = F(\Lambda)$.

PROOF. The reason for this partial multiplicativity of the correspondence is that $\Lambda^{(-1)}$ is only a left inverse for Λ. I.e. $\Lambda^{(-1)}\Lambda$ is the identity operator, but $\Lambda\Lambda^{(-1)}$ is not. Hence to maintain correspondence we can multiply $F_0(\Lambda)$ only from the right with positive powers of Λ and from the left with negative powers of Λ. $\square$

This theorem implies the invertibility of $F(\Lambda) \in \mathbb{T}^+$ and $F(\Lambda) \in \mathbb{T}^-$.

COROLLARY 16.2.

(1) *Let $F(z)$ be analytic and suppose it has no zeros in $|z| \leq R$. Hence the McLaurin coefficients around $z = 0$ are in l_ρ^1 if $\rho < R$. Then $F(\Lambda) \in \mathbb{T}^+$ and its inverse is $F^{-1}(\Lambda) \in \mathbb{T}^+$ where the symbol $F^{-1}(z)$ is the inverse of the symbol $F(\Lambda)$.*

(2) *Let $F(z)$ be analytic and suppose it has no zeros in $|z| \geq r$. Hence its McLaurin coefficients F around $z = \infty$ are in l_ρ^1, $\rho > r$. Then $F(\Lambda) \in \mathbb{T}^-$ and its inverse is $F^{-1}(\Lambda) \in \mathbb{T}^-$ where the symbol $F^{-1}(z) = 1/F(z)$ is the inverse of the symbol $F(\Lambda)$.*

PROOF.

(1) Since $F(z)$ has no zeros in $|z| \leqslant R$, its inverse $G(z) = 1/F(z)$ is analytic in $|z| \leqslant R$ and the McLaurin coefficients around $z = 0$ of $G(z)$ are in l_ρ^1 too. Therefore $F^{-1}(\Lambda) = G(\Lambda) \in \mathbb{T}^+$. Moreover since $F^{-1}(z)F(z) = F(z)F^{-1}(z) = 1$, we have by the previous theorem that also $F^{-1}(\Lambda)F(\Lambda) = F(\Lambda)F^{-1}(\Lambda)$ is the identity operator.

(2) The proof of (2) is analogous.

$\square$

Note that the infinite Toeplitz matrices representing these operators $F(\Lambda)$ in the natural basis are lower triangular in case (1) and upper triangular in case (2). From [GOF] we take the following slightly adapted theorem

THEOREM 16.3. *Suppose $F(z)$ is a meromorphic function, in $\{z : 0 < |z| < \infty\}$ with Laurent series $F(z) = \sum_{-\infty}^{\infty} f_k z^k$ which converges in a neighborhood of $|z| = \rho$. Suppose further that $F(z) \neq 0$ for $|z| = \rho$ and $\kappa = \text{ind } F = 0$. Then the system*

$$\sum_{k=0}^{n} f_{j-k} q_k = r_j \qquad j = 0,1,2,\ldots,n \qquad (16.4)$$

has a unique solution for n sufficiently large. Let $\{q_k^{(n)}\}_{k=0}^{n}$ be this solution. Then the vectors $\{q_0^{(n)}, q_1^{(n)}, \ldots, q_n^{(n)}, 0, 0, \cdots\}$ converge for $n \to \infty$ in l_ρ^p norm to the solution of the system

$$F(\Lambda)Q = R \quad , \text{ i.e. } \sum_{k=0}^{\infty} f_{j-k} q_k = r_j , \quad j = 0,1,2,\cdots \qquad (16.5)$$

for any vector $R \in l_{\rho+}^p$.

PROOF. Three different proofs of this theorem on discrete Wiener-Hopf equations were given in [GOF,p.75-77] for a more general version with $\rho = 1$.

$\square$

This method of solving the operator equation (16.5) by successively solving (16.4) for increasing values of n and taking the limit is called the *projection method*. Now we shall give the solution of the discrete Wiener-Hopf equation

$$F(\Lambda)Q = E_0$$

with $E_0 = [1,0,0,\cdots]$ and with $F(z)$ a meromorphic function as described in section 12.1.

THEOREM 16.4. *Let $F(z)$ be a meromorphic function as described in section 12.1 with $\kappa = 0$. This means that it can be factorized as $F(z) = G_\rho(F)F_+(z)F_-(z)$ such that $F_+(z)$ has no poles and no zeros in $|z| < R$, $F_-(z)$ has no poles and no zeros in $|z| > r$, $F_+(0) = F_-(\infty) = 1$ and $r < \rho < R$. Then $F(\Lambda)$ is well defined* *and the equation*

$$F(\Lambda) Q = E_0$$

with $E_0 = \{1,0,0,...\}$ has a solution in l_{p+}^p for $p \geq 1$ which is given by

$$\sum_{k=0}^{\infty} q_k z^k = [G_\rho(F)]^{-1}[F_+(z)]^{-1} , \quad |z| < R, \tag{16.6}$$

and, as a consequence of the previous theorem, the projection method will give solutions converging to (16.6) in l_ρ^p norm.

PROOF. Clearly $F(\Lambda) \in \mathbb{T}$ and the equation can be written as

$$[G_\rho(F)][F_-(\Lambda)][F_+(\Lambda)]Q = E_0.$$

Because of corollary 16.2, $[F_-(\Lambda)]^{-1} = [F_-^{-1}(\Lambda)]$. Since this is upper triangular and $F_-^{-1}(0) = 1$, we directly have $F_-^{-1}(\Lambda)E_0 = E_0$. Using Corollary 16.2 again we finally have

$$Q = [G_\rho(F)]^{-1}[F_+^{-1}(\Lambda)]E_0.$$

Since $F_+^{-1}(\Lambda)$ is lower triangular and the coefficients in its first column are $\{g_k^+\}_0^\infty$ with

$$F_+^{-1}(z) = \sum_{k=0}^{\infty} g_k^+ z^k , \quad |z| < |\zeta_1|,$$

we must have

$$Q = [G_\rho(F)]^{-1}\{g_0^+, g_1^+, g_2^+, \cdots\}.$$

Thus

$$\sum_{k=0}^{\infty} q_k z^k = [G_\rho(F) F_+(z)]^{-1} , \quad |z| < |\zeta_1|.$$

$|\zeta_1|$ is the zero of $F_+(z)$ with smallest modulus. Since $|\zeta_1| > R$, it lies outside $\{z : |z| < R\}$. All the conditions of theorem 16.3 are satisfied so that the projection method will converge in norm as claimed.

□

16.2 Convergence of the denominator

From the theory in previous section we can directly derive the convergence of the polynomials $Q_n^{(0)}(z)$ and $\hat{Q}_n^{(0)}(z)$ of the first kind for a meromorphic function with $\kappa = 0$. This is given in theorem 16.5 below. The convergence of the $(0,n)$ LPA (theorem 16.6) will then be immediate. The convergence of $Q_n^{(m)}(z)$ for general m will be somewhat more complicated. Our proof will be based on the convergence of the $Q_n^{(0)}(z)$ polynomials and the convergence of the dual Rutishauser polynomials $P_n^{(0,m)}(z)$. These Rutishauser polynomials appear here because $Q_n^{(m)}(z)$ can be expressed in terms of $P_n^{(0,m)}(z)$ and some $Q_{n-i}^{(0)}(z)$. (See lemma 16.7.) The convergence result for the $Q_n^{(m)}(z)$ polynomials is given as theorem 16.8. We start with the convergence of $Q_n^{(0)}(z)$ and $\hat{Q}_n^{(0)}(z)$.

THEOREM 16.5. *Let $F(z)$ be a meromorphic function as described in section 12.1 with $\kappa = 0$. I.e. $F(z) = G_\rho(F)F_+(z)F_-(z)$, with $F_+(z)$ analytic in $|z| < R$, $F_-(z)$ analytic in $|z| > r$, $F_+(z)$ having zeros ζ_k satisfying $\rho < R < |\zeta_1| \leqslant |\zeta_2| \leqslant \cdots$ and $F_-(z)$ having zeros ζ_{-k} satisfying $\rho > r > |\zeta_0| \geqslant |\zeta_{-1}| \geqslant \cdots$. Let $Q_n^{(0)}(z)$ and $\hat{Q}_n^{(0)}(z)$ be Q polynomials of the first kind associated with it. Then*

$$\lim_{n \to \infty} Q_n^{(0)}(z) = (F_+(z))^{-1} \qquad\qquad (16.7a)$$

uniformly on compact subsets of $|z| < R$ and

$$\lim_{n \to \infty} z^{-n} \hat{Q}_n^{(0)} = (F_-(z))^{-1} \qquad\qquad (16.7b)$$

uniformly on compact subsets of $|z| > r$.

PROOF. Using the projection method on the system

$$T_\infty^{(0)} Q_\infty^{(0)} = E_0, \qquad E_0 = [1\ 0\ 0\ \cdots]^T$$

we get as successive solutions $Q_n^{(0)}/v_n^{(0)}$. Indeed, $Q_n^{(0)}$ was a solution of $T_n^{(0)} Q_n^{(0)} = [v_n^{(0)}\ 0 \cdots 0]^T$.

Let $(F_+(z))^{-1}$ have the McLaurin series

$$(F_+(z))^{-1} = \sum_{k=0}^{\infty} g_k^+ z^k$$

around $z = 0$. This series exists and converges in $|z| < |\zeta_1|$ because $F_+(z)$ has no zeros in $|z| < |\zeta_1|$. Define $\tilde{Q}_\infty^{(0)}$ as the vector $[g_0^+\ g_1^+ \cdots]^T / G_\rho(F)$ and $\tilde{Q}_n^{(0)}$ as the vector $[(Q_n^{(0)})^T\ 0\ 0\ \cdots]^T / v_n^{(0)} = [q_0^{(n)}\ q_1^{(n)} \cdots q_n^{(n)}\ 0\ 0\ ...]^T / v_n^{(0)}$. Then we know that $\|\tilde{Q}_n^{(0)} - \tilde{Q}_\infty^{(0)}\|_{\rho,\rho}$ converges to zero. To obtain uniform convergence on compacts we have to look at

$$\tilde{Q}_n^{(0)}(z) := (\sum_{k=0}^{n} q_k^{(n)} z^k)/v_n^{(0)}$$

and

$$\tilde{Q}_\infty^{(0)}(z) := (F_+(z))^{-1}/G_\rho(F).$$

Now set $q_k^{(n)} := 0$ for $k > n$. Then

$$|\tilde{Q}_n^{(0)}(z) - \tilde{Q}_\infty^{(0)}(z)| = |\sum_{k=0}^{\infty} [q_k^{(n)}/v_n^{(0)} - g_k^+/G_\rho(F)]z^k|$$

$$\leqslant \sum_{k=0}^{\infty} |q_k^{(n)}/v_n^{(0)} - g_k^+/G_\rho(F)|\rho^k|z/\rho|^k.$$

Using Hölder's inequality we find that this is bounded by

$$\leqslant \|\tilde{Q}_n^{(0)} - \tilde{Q}_\infty^{(0)}\|_{\rho,p} (\sum_{k=0}^{\infty} |z/\rho|^{kq})^{1/q}$$

with $1/p + 1/q = 1$. Hence we have uniform convergence for $|z| < \rho$. Since ρ is arbitrary between r and R we may replace ρ by R. Using the determinant expression (9.3a) for $v_n^{(0)}$ and the asymptotics (12.12a) for Toeplitz determinants we get

$$v_n^{(0)} = T_n^{(0)}/T_{n-1}^{(0)} = G_\rho(F)\{1 + o(1)\},^{(\dagger)} \qquad (16.8)$$

and thus $v_n^{(0)}$ is bounded and nonzero for n sufficiently large. Also $\tilde{Q}_n^{(0)}(z)$ converges to $\tilde{Q}_\infty^{(0)}(z)$ which is uniformly bounded in compact subsets of $|z| < R$. We may conclude that $Q_n^{(0)}(z)$ is uniformly bounded in compact subsets of $|z| < R$ for n sufficiently large. Hence $Q_n^{(0)}(z)$ converges to $(F_+(z))^{-1}$ in the desired sense.

The proof of the second part is similar.

□

This result directly gives the convergence of the $(0/n)$ LPA for $n \to \infty$. We have

THEOREM 16.6. *Let $F(z)$ be as a meromorphic function described in section 12.1 with $\kappa = 0$. Then*

$$\lim_{n \to \infty} \frac{z^{-n}(B_n^{(0)}(z)\hat{Q}_n^{(0)}(z) - \hat{B}_n^{(0)}(z)Q_n^{(0)}(z))}{Q_n^{(0)}(z)z^{-n}\hat{Q}_n^{(0)}(z)} = F(z) \qquad (16.9)$$

uniformly on compact subsets of $r < |z| < R$.

PROOF. Recall that $B_n^{(0)}(z) = A_n^{(0)}(z)$ and $\hat{B}_n^{(0)}(z) = \hat{A}_n^{(0)}(z)$, so that by (4.5) the expression after the lim is equal to $v_n^{(0)}/[Q_n^{(0)}(z)z^{-n}\hat{Q}_n^{(0)}(z)]$. Because of the previous convergence results of $Q_n^{(0)}(z)$ and $z^{-n}\hat{Q}_n^{(0)}(z)$ and (16.8) which gives the convergence of $v_n^{(0)}$, we directly find that (16.9) is true.

□

$(\dagger)$ This is in fact a classical result which is called a Szego theorem. See theorem 2.2 in [GOF,p.77].

To treat the general case, we must consider $Q_n^{(m)}(z)$ and $z^{-n}\hat{Q}_n^{(-m)}(z)$ for $n \to \infty$. We shall reduce this to the case $m = 0$ with the polynomials defined in (15.3a) and (15.11a). The other dual Rutishauser polynomials defined in (15.3) and (15.11) could be used in a similar way. We start with a lemma, which gives dual results similar to relations (14.4a), (14.5a) which were given in chapter 14 for type 1 Rutishauser polynomials.

LEMMA 16.7. *Let $F(z) = \sum f_k z^k$ be a fls. Suppose that it is normal. Associate with it the Q polynomials of the first kind $Q_n^{(m)}(z)$ and $\hat{Q}_n^{(m)}(z)$, its P and R series $P_n^{(m)}(z)$, $\hat{P}_n^{(m)}(z)$, $R_n^{(m)}(z)$ and $\hat{R}_n^{(m)}(z)$ as well as the Laurent polynomials $B(p)_n^{(m)}(z)$ and $\hat{B}(p)_n^{(m)}(z)$. For $n \geqslant k$ we have the following two relations below :*
(1) Let the dual co-monic Rutishauser polynomial of type 1 for $F(z)$,

$$P_n^{(m-k,m)}(z) = \sum_{i=0}^{k} q_i z^i, \tag{16.10a}$$

be defined by (15.3a). Then

$$S_n^{(m)}(z) = \sum_{i=0}^{k} q_i z^i S_{n-i}^{(m-k)}(z), \tag{16.10b}$$

with S one of P, Q, R or $B(p)$.
(2) Similarly, if the dual monic Rutishauser polynomials of type 1 for $F(z)$,

$$\hat{P}_n^{(-m+k,-m)}(z) = \sum_{i=0}^{k} \hat{q}_i z^i, \tag{16.11a}$$

is defined by (15.11a), then

$$\hat{S}_n^{(-m)}(z) = \sum_{i=0}^{k} \hat{q}_{k-i} \hat{S}_{n-i}^{(-m+k)}(z) \tag{16.11b}$$

if S is one of P,Q,R or $B(p)$.

PROOF. The details of the proof are left to the reader. It can be most easily seen by constructing flow graphs for the defining recursions and the result follows from these just as in lemma 14.1.

□

In the rest of this section, we shall use the notations $P_n^{(m,k)}(z)$ and $\hat{P}_n^{(m,k)}(z)$ for the dual Ruthishauser polynomials as they are defined by the recursions (15.3a) and (15.11a). If these recusions are not defined due to singular blocks that may occur if $F(z)$ is not normal, we can eventually consider (16.10) and (16.11) as definitions, provided the $S_q^{(p)}(z)$ and $\hat{S}_q^{(p)}(z)$ used there do exist.
We are now ready to prove the convergence of the polynomials $Q_n^{(m)}(z)$ and $\hat{Q}_n^{(m)}(z)$.

THEOREM 16.8. *Let $F(z) = G_\rho(F)F_+(z)F_-(z)$ be a meromorphic function as described in section 12.1 with $\kappa=0$ and suppose that its zeros ζ_k satisfy*

$$|\zeta_m| < |\zeta_{m+1}| \text{ for some } m \geq 0.$$

Then its co-monic polynomials $Q_n^{(m)}(z)$ of the first kind satisfy

$$\lim_{n \to \infty} Q_n^{(m)}(z) = \prod_{k=1}^{m} (1 - z/\zeta_k)/F_+(z) \tag{16.12}$$

uniformly on compact subsets of $\mathbb{D}_m^+ = \{z : |z| < |\zeta_{m+1}|, z \neq \zeta_k, k = 1, 2, \ldots, m\}$. Similarly, if $|\zeta_{-m}| < |\zeta_{-m+1}|$ for some $m \geq 0$, then the monic polynomials $\hat{Q}_n^{(m)}(z)$ of the first kind satisfy

$$\lim_{n \to \infty} z^{-n} \hat{Q}_n^{(-m)}(z) = \prod_{k=1}^{-m+1} (1 - \zeta_k/z)/F_-(z), \tag{16.13}$$

uniformly on compact subsets of the pointed disc $\mathbb{D}_m^- = \{z : |z| > |\zeta_{-m}|, z \neq \zeta_{-k}, k = 0, 1, 2, \ldots, m-1\}$.

PROOF. By lemma 16.7 we have the following relation which relates $Q_{n-i}^{(0)}(z)$, $i = 0, 1, \ldots, m$ and $Q_n^{(m)}(z)$ through the coefficients of the dual Rutishauser polynomial $P_n^{(0,m)}(z)$:

$$Q_n^{(m)}(z) = \sum_{i=0}^{m} q_i z^i Q_{n-i}^{(0)}(z) \quad \text{if} \quad P_n^{(0,m)}(z) = \sum_{i=0}^{m} q_i z^i.$$

We know from theorem 15.4 that under the given conditions $P_n^{(0,m)}(z)$ exists for n sufficiently large and that it converges to $\prod_{k=1}^{m} (1 - z/\zeta_k)$ and $Q_n^{(0)}(z)$ converges to $(F_+(z))^{-1}$ by theorem 16.5. Hence (16.12) follows easily. (16.13) is shown analogously.

$\square$

16.3 Convergence of the numerator

In the previous section we have shown the convergence of $Q_n^{(m)}(z)$ and $\hat{Q}_n^{(m)}(z)$. These are the denominators in an (m/n) LPF for $F(z)$. We shall now have a look at the numerators $B_n^{(m)}(z)$ and $\hat{B}_n^{(-m)}(z)$. Compared with the denominators, the convergence of these will be easily established. Once this is found, we can give the convergence of an (m/n) LPF for $F(z)$.

THEOREM 16.9 *Let* $F(z) = G_\rho(F)F_+(z)F_-(z)$ *be a meromorphic function as in section 12.1 with* $\kappa = 0$. *If its Laurent series in the neighborhood of* $|z| = \rho$ *is* $\sum_{-\infty}^{\infty} f_k z^k$, *define as before* $Z(z) = Z^{(0)}(z) = \frac{1}{2}f_0 + \sum_1^{\infty} f_k z^k$ *and* $\hat{Z}(z) = \hat{Z}^{(0)}(z) = -\frac{1}{2}f_0 - \sum_1^{\infty} f_{-k}z^{-k}$. *Then we have uniform convergence of*

$$\lim_{n \to \infty} B_n^{(0)}(z) = Z(z)/F_+(z) \quad \text{in } |z| < R \text{ and}$$

$$\lim_{n \to \infty} z^{-n}\hat{B}_n^{(0)}(z) = \hat{Z}(z)/F_-(z) \quad \text{in } |z| > r.$$

PROOF. From the definition (11.3a)

$$B_n^{(0)}(z) = \Pi_{0:n}(Z(z)Q_n^{(0)}(z)).$$

Now $Z(z)Q_n^{(0)}(z)$ converges in norm in the function space $L_{\rho+}^1 = \{F(z) = \sum_0^{\infty} f_k z^k : \{f_k\}_0^{\infty} \in \ell_{\rho+}^1\}$ normed with $\|F\|_{\rho,1} = \sum_0^{\infty}|f_k|\rho^k$ and $\Pi_{0:n}$ converges strongly to the identity operator in this space, whence $B_n^{(0)}(z)$ converges in norm. The uniform convergence follows like in theorem 16.5. The second part can be proved similarly.

□

COROLLARY 16.10. *Under the conditions of theorem 16.8 we have uniform as* $n \to \infty$ *of*

$$S_n^{(m)}(z) = P_n^{(0,m)}(z)S_n^{(0)}(z) + o(1) , \qquad z \in \mathbb{D}_m^+$$

$$z^{-n}\hat{S}_n^{(-m)}(z) = z^{-m}\hat{P}_n^{(0,-m)}(z)z^{-n}\hat{S}_n^{(0)}(z) + o(1) , \ z \in \mathbb{D}_m^-$$

with S one of Q or B and $\mathbb{D}_m^+$ *and* $\mathbb{D}_m^-$ *as in theorem 16.8.*

PROOF. We shall only prove the first relation because the other follows by duality. By the remark preceding theorem 16.8 we know that $P_n^{(0,m)}(z)$ exists and by lemma 16.7 we know that if

$$P_n^{(0,m)}(z) = \sum_{i=0}^{m} q_i z^i,$$

$S_n^{(m)}(z)$ is given by

$$S_n^{(m)}(z) = \sum_{i=0}^{m} q_i z^i S_{n-i}^{(0)}(z).$$

Now for n sufficiently large $S_{n-i}^{(0)}(z) = S_n^{(0)}(z) + o(1)$ so that the result follows for $S_n^{(m)}(z)$ and $|z| < R$. Because the limit function has no singularities for $z = \zeta_1, \zeta_2, \ldots, \zeta_m$, the convergence is in the larger region $\mathbb{D}_m^+$.

□

We are now ready to prove the final convergence result.

THEOREM 16.11 *Let $F(z)$ be meromorphic function as described in section 12.1 with $\kappa = 0$ and suppose that its zeros satisfy for some $m \geq 0$: $|\zeta_{-m}| < |\zeta_{-m+1}| < \rho < |\zeta_m| < |\zeta_{m+1}|$. Then for $n \to \infty$*

$$(K_n^{(m)}(z)\begin{bmatrix}1\\1\end{bmatrix})^{-1} = \frac{Q_n^{(m)}(z)z^{-n}\hat{Q}_n^{(-m)}(z)}{L_n^{(m)}(z)}$$

with

$$L_n^{(m)}(z) = z^{-n}[B_n^{(m)}(z)\hat{Q}_n^{(-m)}(z) - \hat{B}_n^{(-m)}(z)Q_n^{(m)}(z)]$$

converges to $1/F(z)$ uniformly on compact subsets of

$$\mathbb{E}_m = \{z : |\zeta_{-m}| < |z| < |\zeta_{m+1}| \; ; \; z \neq \zeta_k \; , \; k = -m+1, \ldots, m\}$$

PROOF. By corollary 16.10 we may replace $L_n^{(m)}(z)$, for n sufficiently large, by

$$L_n^{(m)}(z) = z^{-m-n}P_n^{(0,m)}(z)\hat{P}_n^{(0,-m)}(z).$$

$$[B_n^{(0)}(z)\hat{Q}_n^{(0)}(z) - \hat{B}_n^{(0)}(z)Q_n^{(0)}(z)] + o(1)$$

$$= z^{-m}P_n^{(0,m)}(z)\hat{P}_n^{(0,-m)}(z)v_n^{(0)} + o(1).$$

The latter equality follows from the relation preceeding (4.5). (Recall that $B_n^{(0)}(z) = A_n^{(0)}(z)$.)
Similarly the numerator can be replaced by such expressions. This will give
$Q_n^{(m)}(z) \, z^{-n}\hat{Q}_n^{(m)}(z) = z^{-m}P_n^{(0,m)}(z) \, \hat{P}_n^{(0,-m)}(z) \, Q_n^{(0)}(z) \, z^{-n}\hat{Q}_n^{(0)}(z) + o(1)$. If we put this together, we find

$$(K_n^{(m)}(z)\begin{bmatrix}1\\1\end{bmatrix})^{-1} = (v_n^{(0)})^{-1}Q_n^{(0)}(z)z^{-n}\hat{Q}_n^{(0)}(z) + o(1), \quad n \to \infty,$$

uniformly in $\mathbb{E}_m$. By (16.8) and theorem 16.5, the result follows.

$\square$

Remark. In this chapter we have supposed that the winding number κ of $F(z)$ was zero. As we have mentioned many times before, this restriction is not essential. It was supposed to be zero for the simplicity of development and notation. If $\kappa \neq 0$ one should work with LPFs $K(\kappa)_n^{(m)}(z)$ as defined in chapter 4 rather than with $K_n^{(m)}(z) := K(0)_n^{(m)}(z)$.

Chapter 17

The positive definite case and applications

In this chapter we shall relate our results to some classical functional problems that were studied by Carathéodory and Schur and some related moment problems. A survey can be found in [AKH]. In this context $F(z)$ will have a Laurent series expansion $F(z) = \sum_{-\infty}^{\infty} f_k z^k$ in the neighborhood of $|z| = \rho = 1$ and $f_{-k} = \bar{f}_k$, $k \in \mathbb{Z}$. This means that our meromorphic function $F(z)$ will take real and positive values on the unit circle. The symmetry in the problem that is caused by $f_{-k} = \bar{f}_k$, $k \in \mathbb{Z}$ will essentially reduce the complexity of the problem to half the complexity for the general case. The quantities with and without hat will contain the same information, so that we can drop one of them. Many of the algorithms that we have seen before will reduce to well known classical algorithms.

In section 17.2 we shall give a connection with the linear prediction of stochastic processes. In this context, algorithm 1 of chapter 3 will reduce to an algorithm of Levinson for prediction.

In section 17.3 we relate these results to the problem of lossless inverse scattering. The physical meaning of the SS coefficients will be reflected part of a wave at the bounderies of successive layers of the medium through which the wave propagates. It explains why the SS coefficients are often called reflection coefficients.

17.1 Function classes

By H^p $(1 \leqslant p \leqslant \infty)$ we shall denote the Hardy spaces of functions analytic in the open unit disc and normed by

$$\|F\|_p = \lim_{r \uparrow 1} \{\frac{1}{2\pi} \int_{-\pi}^{\pi} |F(re^{i\theta})|^p d\theta\}^{1/p}, \quad 1 \leqslant p < \infty, F \in H^p$$

and

$$\|F\|_\infty = \lim_{r \uparrow 1} \sup_\theta |F(re^{i\theta})| , \quad F \in H^\infty.$$

H^p functions are known to have nontangential limits almost everywhere (a.e.) on $|z| = 1$ and the boundary functions belong to L^p.
L^p functions are defined on the unit circle only and are normed by

$$\|F\|_p = \{\frac{1}{2\pi} \int_{-\pi}^{\pi} |F(e^{i\theta})|^p d\theta\}^{1/p}, \quad 1 \leqslant p < \infty, \ F \in L^p$$

and

$$\|F\|_\infty = \operatorname*{ess.sup}_{-\pi \leqslant \theta < \pi} |F(e^{i\theta})| \ , \quad F \in L^\infty.$$

The norm of $F \in H^p$ equals the L^p norm of its boundary function.
A function V is called an *inner function of H^p* iff $V \in H^p$ and $|V(e^{i\theta})| = 1$ a.e. .
A *Blaschke product* which is defined by

$$B(z) = z^k \prod_{n=1}^{\infty} \frac{\alpha_n - z}{1 - \bar{\alpha}_n z} \frac{|\alpha_n|}{\alpha_n} \quad , \ |z| < 1 \ , \ |\alpha_n| < 1$$

with $\sum_1^\infty (1 - |\alpha_n|) < \infty$ is an example of an inner function in H^∞.
A function Q is called an *outer function of H^p* iff $Q \in H^p$ and

$$Q(z) = c \exp\{\frac{1}{2\pi} \int_{-\pi}^{\pi} \frac{e^{it} + z}{e^{it} - z} \log \sigma(e^{it}) dt\} \quad , \quad |z| < 1$$

with $c \in \mathbb{C}$, $|c| = 1$, σ positive measurable and $\log \sigma \in L^1$. Q will be in H^p iff $\sigma \in L^p$. In that case $\|Q\|_p = \|\sigma\|_p$ and

$$\lim_{r \uparrow 1} |Q(re^{i\theta})| = \sigma(e^{i\theta}) \quad \text{a.e. .}$$

If F as well as F^{-1} are in H^p then F and F^{-1} will be outer functions.
Let us set as before

$$F_*(z) := \overline{F(1/\bar{z})}.$$

We can then define Hardy spaces K^p for the complement of the unit disc by

$$K^p := \{F : F_* \in H^p\}.$$

There is also a classical Beurling factorization theorem [RUD,p.372] saying that every $F \in H^p$ which is not identically zero can be written as the product of an inner and an outer function. The outer factor is given by

$$Q(z) = \exp\{\frac{1}{2\pi} \int_{-\pi}^{\pi} \frac{e^{it} + z}{e^{it} - z} \log |F(e^{it})| dt\}. \tag{17.1}$$

We also have

$$\log |F(0)| \leqslant \frac{1}{2\pi} \int_{-\pi}^{\pi} \log |F(e^{it})| dt \tag{17.2}$$

where equality holds iff F is outer.
We shall say that $F_- \in K^2$ has a *pseudo meromorphic extension* [DED] inside the unit disc if $F_-(z)/F_{-*}(z)$ is equal to the ratio of two inner functions a.e. on the

unit circle $|z| = 1$. Thus, if we denote these inner functions as U and V, then

$$F_-(z)/F_{-*}(z) = U(z)/V(z) \quad \text{a.e. on } |z| = 1,$$

or

$$F_-(z) = [V(z)]^{-1}G(z) \quad \text{a.e. on } |z| = 1,$$

with $V \in H^2$ inner and $G = UF_{-*} \in H^2$ having no common inner factor. Now, since $F_- \in K^2$ has an analytic extension outside the unit disc, it is defined for every $|z| \geqslant 1$. On the other hand, $V \in H^2$ and $G \in H^2$ have analytic extensions inside the unit disc. They are defined for every $|z| \leqslant 1$. By setting

$$F_-(z) = [V(z)]^{-1}G(z) \quad \text{for } |z| \leqslant 1,$$

we may presume a function $F_-(z)$ with a pseudomeromorphic extension to be defined in the whole complex plane.

We shall now introduce the function class $\mathbb{F}$ of L^1 functions with some special properties.

Let $F \in L^1$ be a nonnegative function on the unit circle. Then its Fourier coefficients

$$f_k := \frac{1}{2\pi} \int_{-\pi}^{\pi} e^{-ik\theta} F(e^{i\theta})d\theta$$

satisfy $f_{-k} = \bar{f}_k$. This means e.g. that f_0 is real and since $F(e^{i\theta})$ is nonnegative we shall have $f_0 > 0$. Suppose also that $\log F \in L^1$. Then the function

$$F_+(z) := c \exp \left\{ \frac{1}{4\pi} \int_{-\pi}^{\pi} \frac{e^{it}+z}{e^{it}-z} \log F(e^{it})dt \right\} \quad , \quad |z| < 1 \tag{17.3}$$

with $c \in \mathbb{C}$, $|c| = 1$ will be an outer function of H^2 and

$$F(e^{i\theta}) = |F_+(e^{i\theta})|^2 = F_+(e^{i\theta})F_{+*}(e^{i\theta}).$$

where

$$F_+(e^{i\theta}) := \lim_{r \uparrow 1} F_+(re^{i\theta}).$$

The constant c can be chosen such that $F_+(y) > 0$ for some y, $|y| < 1$. Suppose that $F_{+*}(z)$ has a pseudo meromorphic extension in $|z| > 1$. Then $F_{+*}(z)$ may be considered to be defined in the whole complex plane and so will be $F_+(z)$. Hence we can write the relation (17.4a) below, defining $F(z)$, $\forall z \in \mathbb{C}$

$$F(z) = F_+(z)F_{+*}(z) \quad , \quad \forall z \in \mathbb{C}. \tag{17.4a}$$

A similar construct also gives

$$F(z) = F_{-*}(z)F_-(z) \quad , \quad \forall z \in \mathbb{C} \tag{17.4b}$$

with F_- outer in K^2. With the notation used above, F_- and F_+ are related by

$F_+ = G = UF_{-*}.$

The factorizations (17.4) for F meromorphic correspond to the factorization considered in section 12.1 where the constant

$$G_\rho(F) = |F_+(0)|^2 \tag{17.5}$$

is distributed over the factors.

The set of functions F having the properties described above will be denoted by IF. This means that for $F \in$ IF we have

1. $F \in L^1$
2. $\log F \in L^1$
3. $F(e^{i\theta}) \geqslant 0, \ -\pi \leqslant \theta < \pi$
4. F_+ as in (17.3) is such that F_{+*} has a pseudo meromorphic extension
5. $F(z)$ and $F_+(z)$ can be presumed to be defined $\forall z \in \mathbb{C}$.

        With a function of class IF we can associate a function of the class IP which is the class of Carathéodory functions or positive real functions and a function of the class $ which is the class of Schur functions or the contractions of the unit disc.

        The *Carathéodory class* or the class of *positive real functions* is defined by

IP $:= \{Z(z) : Z(z)$ is analytic in $|z| < 1$ and maps the open
        unit disk $|z| < 1$ into the right half plane : Re $Z(z) \geqslant 0\}.$

A function in IP has the so called *Riesz-Herglotz representation* [AKH,p.179]. I.e.

$$Z(z) = ic + \frac{1}{2\pi} \int_{-\pi}^{\pi} \frac{e^{i\theta}+z}{e^{i\theta}-z} \, d\sigma(\theta)$$

where $c = $ Im $Z(0)$ and $\sigma(\theta)$ is a non–decreasing function of bounded variation which is essentially uniquely defined by $Z(z)$.

        The *Schur class of functions* or the *class of contractions* is defined by

$ $:= \{\Gamma(z) : \Gamma(z)$ is analytic in $|z| < 1$ and maps the open
        unit disc $|z| < 1$ into the closed unit disc : $|\Gamma(z)| \leqslant 1\}$.

        Let $F \in$ IF have the Fourier series $F(e^{i\theta}) = \sum_{-\infty}^{\infty} f_k e^{ik\theta}$. Consider the function

$$Z(z) = \tfrac{1}{2} f_0 + \sum_{k=1}^{\infty} f_k z^k + ic \tag{17.6}$$

with c a real constant. In our further discussion we shall suppose that $c = 0$. $Z(z)$ is clearly analytic in $|z| \leqslant 1$ and

$$2\text{Re } Z(z) = Z(z) + \overline{Z(z)} = \frac{1}{2\pi} \int_{-\pi}^{\pi} \frac{1-|z|^2}{|z-e^{i\theta}|^2} F(e^{i\theta})d\theta \geqslant 0 \tag{17.7}$$

for $|z| < 1$ (recall that $F(e^{i\theta})$ is nonnegative). This means that $Z \in \mathbb{P}$. Clearly

$$F(e^{i\theta}) = 2\text{Re } Z(e^{i\theta}) + Z_*(e^{i\theta})$$

where $Z(e^{i\theta})$ is the radial limit of $Z(z)$ for $|z| \uparrow 1$. Although $Z(z)$ was only defined for $|z| \leqslant 1$ we can define it for $|z| > 1$ by

$$Z(z) = F(z) - Z_*(z).$$

This makes sense since $F(z)$ is defined $\forall z \in \mathbb{C}$ and $Z_*(z)$ is defined for $|z| \geqslant 1$. These extensions give us the relations

$$F(z) = F_+(z)F_{+*}(z) = Z(z) + Z_*(z) \;, \quad \forall z \in \mathbb{C} \tag{17.8}$$

if $F \in \mathbb{IF}$. Functions in the Schur class and in the Carathéodory class are related by some Moebius transforms. Also, some Moebius transforms will generate Schur functions from Schur functions. These are given in lemma 17.1 below.

LEMMA 17.1. *Let $\$$ and $\mathbb{P}$ denote the Schur and Carathéodory classes. Then we have (1) - (4) below.*

(1)   If $F \in \$$, then $t(F) \in \$$ with $t(w) = (w-\rho)/(1-\bar{\rho}w)$, $|\rho| < 1$.
If moreover $\rho = F(z_0)$ with $|z_0| < 1$ then also $t(F(z))/\zeta(z) \in \$$ with $\zeta(z) = (z-z_0)/(1-\bar{z}_0z)$.
(2)   If $F, G \in \$$, then $F(z)G(z) \in \$$.
(3)   If $Z \in \mathbb{P}$, then $c(Z) \in \$$ where $c(w) = (w-\gamma)/(w+\bar{\gamma})$ and Re $\gamma > 0$.
If moreover $\gamma = Z(z_0)$, $|z_0| < 1$, then $c(Z(z))/\zeta(z) \in \$$ with $\zeta(z) = (z-z_0)/(1-\bar{z}_0z)$.
(4)   If $\sigma \in \$$, then $c'(\sigma) \in \mathbb{P}$ where $c'(w) = \gamma(1-w)/(1+w)$ and $\gamma > 0$.

PROOF. All these are trivial to verify. See also [AKH p. 92 and 102].

□

Let F be in the class $\mathbb{IF}$. We have associated with F the $\mathbb{P}$ function Z. Now, we can associate with this $Z \in \mathbb{P}$ some function Γ_0 by

$$\Gamma_0(z) = \frac{1}{z} \frac{Z(z) - \tfrac{1}{2}f_0}{Z(z) + \tfrac{1}{2}f_0} \cdot \tag{17.9a}$$

I.e.

$$\Gamma_0(z) = \frac{f_1+f_2z+\cdots}{f_0+f_1z+f_2z^2+\cdots} \cdot \tag{17.9b}$$

Using (3) of lemma 17.1 and the fact that $f_0 > 0$, we may conclude that $\Gamma_0 \in \$$.

We recapitulate the constructs of this section. With some function $F \in \mathbb{F}$, being nonnegative on the unit circle and with $\log F \in L^1$, we have associated the factorization (17.4), i.e.

$$F(z) = F_+(z)F_{+*}(z) = F_{-*}(z)F_-(z), \quad \forall z \in \mathbb{C}$$

where F_+ is some outer function of H^2 defined by (17.3) which has a pseudo meromorphic extension outside the unit disc and F_- outer in K^2. Both are defined up to a multiplicative constant of modulus 1. We also had an additive splitting (17.8), i.e.

$$F(z) = Z(z) + Z_*(z) \quad , \quad \forall z \in \mathbb{C}$$

where Z is a Carathéodory function ($Z \in \mathbb{P}$) defined by (17.6) for $|z| \leqslant 1$ and which can be extended to all of $\mathbb{C}$. It is defined up to an additive imaginary constant (which we have chosen to be zero). Finally with this $Z \in \mathbb{P}$, we associated a Schur function $\Gamma_0 \in \$$ by (17.9) which is defined by this relation for all $z \in \mathbb{C}$. If F is as described in section 12.1 with $\rho = 1$, $\kappa = 0$ and positive on the unit circle (whence $F(z) = F_*(z)$), then it will be in $\mathbb{F}$.

17.2 Connection with the previous results

The notation used in previous section is deliberately chosen to match the notation of earlier chapters. $F(z)$ will play the role of the formal Laurent series $F(z)$. This series has the special property that $f_k = \bar{f}_{-k}$. Thus $F_*(z) = F(z)$, and $\hat{F}(z) = F(1/z) = \bar{F}(z)$.

These symmetry properties of $F(z)$ will simplify the symmetry relations we derived in section 10.1. These simplified relations are given in the theorem below. Recall the notation we have introduced in chapter 8

$$p^*(z) = z^n p_*(z)$$

for any polynomial p of degree n.

THEOREM 17.2. *Let $F(z) = \sum f_k z^k$ be a normal fls satisfying $F_*(z) = F(z)$, i.e. $f_k = \bar{f}_{-k}$. Then we have the symmetry relations below for $m \in \mathbb{Z}$ and $n \in \mathbb{N}$.*

(1)   If $T_n^{(m)}$ are the Toeplitz determinants $\det [f_{m+i-j}]_{i,j=0}^n$, then

$$T_{-n}^{(-m)} = T_n^{(-m)} = \overline{T_n^{(m)}}$$

(2)   For the uv parameters, the SS parameters, the ab parameters, the FG parameters and the $\rho\sigma$ parameters that can be associated with $F(z)$, we have

$$s_n^{(-m)} = \overline{\hat{s}_n^{(m)}}$$

with s one of u,v,α,a,b,F,G,ρ or σ.

(3) If $Q_n^{(m)}(z)$ and $\hat{Q}_n^{(m)}(z)$ are the polynomials of the first kind $P_n^{(m)}(z)$, $\hat{P}_n^{(m)}(z)$ the P-series and $R_n^{(m)}(z)$, $\hat{R}_n^{(m)}(z)$ the R-series of $F(z)$ then we have

$$Q_n^{(m)}(z) = z^n \hat{Q}_{n*}^{(-m)}(z) = \hat{Q}_n^{(-m)*}(z),$$

$$P_n^{(m)}(z) = z^n \hat{R}_{n*}^{(-m)}(z)$$

and

$$R_n^{(m)}(z) = z^n \hat{P}_{n*}^{(-m)}(z).$$

(4) If $A_n^{(m)}(z)$, $\hat{A}_n^{(m)}(z)$ are the polynomials of the second kind, $B_n^{(m)}(z)$, $\hat{B}_n^{(m)}(z)$ the Laurent polynomials as defined in (4.7) with $p = 0$ for $F(z)$, then

$$A_n^{(m)}(z) = -z^n \hat{A}_{n*}^{(-m)}(z) = -\hat{A}_n^{(-m)*}(z)$$

and

$$B_n^{(m)}(z) = -z^n \hat{B}_{n*}^{(-m)}(z)$$

(5) If $K_n^{(m)}(z)$ and $\hat{K}_n^{(m)}(z)$ represent the (n/m) LPAs of $F(z)$ for $p = 0$ and $L_n^{(m)}(z)$ and $\hat{L}_n^{(m)}(z)$ are their numerators as defined in (4.10) for $p = 0$, then

$$K_n^{(m)}(z) = -\hat{K}_{n*}^{(-m)}(z) \quad and \quad L_n^{(m)}(z) = -\hat{L}_{n*}^{(-m)}(z).$$

(6) If $\theta_n^{(m)}(z)$ are the θ-matrices associated with the SS parameters as in (6.1) then

$$\theta_n^{(m)}(z) = z\, \mathbf{K}_1\, \theta_{n*}^{(-m)}(z)\, \mathbf{K}_1 \quad with \quad \mathbf{K}_1 := \begin{vmatrix} 0 & 1 \\ 1 & 0 \end{vmatrix}$$

and if $t_n^{(m)}(\cdot)$ and $\hat{t}_n^{(m)}(\cdot)$ are the Moebius transforms as in (6.4), then

$$t_n^{(m)}(\cdot) = \overline{\hat{t}_n^{(-m)}(\cdot)}.$$

(7) For the Π, Γ, Σ and Ω-series associated with $F(z)$ by (6.6), (6.13) and corollary 6.4, be have

$$\Pi_n^{(m)}(z) = \hat{\Pi}_{n*}^{(-m)}(z), \quad \Gamma_n^{(m)}(z) = \hat{\Gamma}_{n*}^{(-m)}(z), \quad \Sigma_n^{(m)}(z) = \hat{\Sigma}_{n*}^{(-m)}(z)$$

and

$$\Omega_n^{(m)}(z) = -\hat{\Omega}_{n*}^{(-m)}(z).$$

(8) If for $k = 0,1,\dots,n$, the polynomials $U_{k,n}^{(m)}(z)$ and $V_{k,n}^{(m)}(z)$ are defined by (6.15), the Rutishauser polynomials $Q_{k,n}^{(m)}(z)$ by (9.11) and the $\Pi_{k,n}^{(m)}(z)$ series

by (6.16), then

$$Q_{k,n}^{(m)}(z) = z^{n-k} \hat{Q}_{k,n*}^{(-m)}(z) = \hat{Q}_{k,n}^{(-m)*}(z),$$

$$U_{k,n}^{(m)}(z) = z^{n-k} \hat{V}_{k,n*}^{(-m)}(z) = \hat{V}_{k,n}^{(-m)*}(z),$$

$$V_{k,n}^{(m)}(z) = z^{n-k} \hat{U}_{k,n*}^{(-m)}(z) = \hat{U}_{k,n}^{(-m)*}(z)$$

and

$$\Pi_{k,n}^{(m)} = \hat{\Pi}_{k,n*}^{(-m)}(z).$$

PROOF. This immediately follows from theorem 10.3.

$\square$

From now on we shall be mainly interested in the case $m = 0$. To simplify the notation we shall drop the superscript m whenever it is zero. E.g. $T_n = T_n^{(0)}$ and it follows from (1) in the previous theorem that $T_n = \overline{T_n}$ so that it is real. Some other relations we find as a special case of the previous theorem are :

$$\hat{\alpha}_n = \overline{\alpha}_n \quad , \quad Q_n(z) = \hat{Q}_n^*(z),$$

$$A_n(z) = B_n(z) = -\hat{B}_n^*(z) = -\hat{A}_n^*(z),$$

$$U_{k,n}(z) = \hat{V}_{k,n}^*(z) \quad , \quad V_{k,n}(z) = \hat{U}_{k,n}^*(z) \quad , \quad Q_{k,n}(z) = \hat{Q}_{k,n}^*(z).$$

Now if $\sum_{-\infty}^{\infty} f_k z^k$ is not just a formal series but if it is the Fourier series of some function in $\mathbb{F}$, then our notation is chosen such that $\Gamma_0(z)$ of (17.9) is the same as $\Gamma_0^{(0)}(z)$ of theorem 6.1. Thus, $\Gamma_0(z) = \Gamma_0^{(0)}(z)$ will be in the Schur class \$. By (6.7), the SS parameter $\alpha_1 := \alpha_1^{(0)}$ can be found as $\Gamma_0(0)$ and since Γ_0 maps the unit disc into itself, we shall have $|\alpha_1| \leqslant 1$. If $|\alpha_1| < 1$, then

$$\Gamma_1(z) := z^{-1}(\Gamma_0(z) - \alpha_1)/(1 - \overline{\alpha}_1 \Gamma_0(z))$$

will be a Schur function too (lemma 17.1 (1)) and the process can be repeated. If $|\alpha_1| = 1$, then $|\Gamma_0(z)|$ reaches its maximum in the interior of $|z| < 1$ whence it is a constant by the maximum modulus principle : $\Gamma_0(z) = \alpha_1$. Taking all the symmetry into account, it can be seen that we are applying here algoritm 2a of figure 6.3 which simplifies to the algorithm given in fig. 17.1 where we used that $t_n(w) = (w - \alpha_n)/(1 - \overline{\alpha}_n w)$. In general, Schur used this algorithm to check whether a function $\Gamma_0(z)$ is in \$ or not. His result is given in the next theorem.

THEOREM 17.3. *Starting from a given function $\Gamma_0(z)$, we generate numbers α_k and functions $\Gamma_k(z)$ by the Schur algorithm of fig. 17.1. Then $\Gamma_0(z) \in$ \$ iff*

$\Gamma_0(z)$ is some given function

for $n = 0,1,2, \cdots$

$\alpha_{n+1} = \Gamma_n(0)$

$\Gamma_{n+1}(z) = z^{-1}(\Gamma_n(z)-\alpha_{n+1})/(1-\bar{\alpha}_{n+1}\Gamma_n(z))$

Figure 17.1: Schur algorithm

(1) $|\alpha_k| < 1$, $k = 1,2,3, \cdots$ *or*
(2) $|\alpha_k| < 1$, $k = 1,2,\ldots,n$ *and* $|\alpha_{n+1}| = 1$. *In this case* $\Gamma_0(z)$ *is a finite Blaschke product of degree n,* $\Gamma_n(z) = \alpha_{n+1}$ *and* $\Gamma_k(z) = \alpha_{k+1} = 0$ *for all* $k > n+1$.

PROOF. See [SCH].

□

Because of this connection with the theory of Schur functions, the algorithm of fig. 17.1 is called Schur's algorithm. Its generalization, algorithm 2a of fig. 6.3, and the homogeneous form, algorithm 2 of fig. 3.2, are therefore often referred to as Schur algorithms. The coefficients α_k are the Schur parameters, and this justifies the name Schur in reference to the parameters $\alpha_n^{(m)}$ and $\hat{\alpha}_n^{(m)}$ which are their direct generalizations.

The functions $\Gamma_k^{(m)}$ emanated from the general recursion in (6.4) for the choice $S = R$. Other choices for S were possible. Take e.g. relation (6.5b) for $m = 0$ and $S = Q$. If we take the symmetry of $F(z)$ into account, then it reduces to

$$\frac{Q_n^*(z)}{Q_n(z)} = \hat{t}_n \left| \frac{zQ_{n-1}^*(z)}{Q_{n-1}(z)} \right|$$

where

$$\hat{t}_n(w) := \frac{w-\bar{\alpha}_n}{1-\alpha_n w}$$

and $Q_n(z) := Q_n^{(0)}(z)$ are polynomials of the first kind for $m = 0$.
Note that, since we are dealing with functions, me don't need the notation L_+ or L_- anymore. The Moebius transformations are now transformations for functions.
If we define as in theorem 6.1 the functions $\hat{\Pi}_n(z)$ by

$$\hat{\Pi}_n(z) := \frac{Q_n^*(z)}{Q_n(z)},$$

then these are finite Blaschke products. As it was stated in that theorem, they will satisfy the recursion

$$\hat{\Pi}_{n-1}(z) = z^{-1}\hat{t}_n^{-1}(\hat{\Pi}_n(z)) = z^{-1}(\hat{\Pi}_n(z)+\bar{\alpha}_n)/(1+\alpha_n\hat{\Pi}_n(z)).$$

The numbers α_k, $k = 1,2,\ldots,n$ can be recovered from $\hat{\Pi}_n(z)$ by algorithm inverse 1a of fig. 6.4. It simplifies now to the algorithm given in fig. 17.2.

$$\hat{\Pi}_n(z) = Q_n^*/Q_n(z)$$

for $k = n,n-1,\ldots,1$

$$\bar{\alpha}_k = -\hat{\Pi}_k(0)$$

$$\hat{\Pi}_{k-1}(z) = z^{-1}(\hat{\Pi}_k(z)+\bar{\alpha}_k)/(1+\alpha_k\hat{\Pi}_k(z))$$

Figure 17.2: Schur–Cohn algorithm

This is clearly similar to the Schur recusion for $\Gamma_n(z)$. Since we know that all $|\alpha_k| < 1$ for $k=1,2,\ldots,n$ and $\alpha_0 = -\hat{\Pi}_0(0) = -1$, we may conclude from the above theorem of Schur that $\hat{\Pi}_n(z)$ is a Blaschke product, which we already knew, but that it is also a Schur function. I.e. $\hat{\Pi}_n(z)$ is analytic in $|z| < 1$. Hence $Q_n(z)$ can have no zeros in the unit disc $|z| < 1$. This result may not be surprising because the presented algorithm is nothing but the Schur-Cohn test to see if a polynomial $Q_n(z)$ has all its zeros outside the unit disc.

Another set of functions was obtained by a Schur recursion in chapter 6. It is called algorithm inverse 1b in fig. 6.5. It gives a recurrence for the functions $\Pi_{0,n}(z) = \Sigma_n(z) = U_n(z)/V_n(z)$ ($m=0$). The polynomials $U_n(z)$ and $V_n(z)$ were defined by (4.13) with $m=0$, i.e.

$$V_n(z) = (\tfrac{1}{2}f_0\, Q_{n+1}(z) + A_{n+1}(z))/f_0 \qquad (17.10)$$

and

$$U_n(z) = z^{-1}(\tfrac{1}{2}f_0\, Q_{n+1}(z) - A_{n+1}(z))/f_0 \qquad (17.11)$$

where $Q_n(z)$ and $A_n(z)$ are polynomials of the first, respectively second kind for $F(z)$. Algorithm inverse 1b then defines recursively

$$\Pi_{k+1,n}(z) = \frac{1}{z} \frac{\Pi_{k,n}(z) + \alpha_{k+1}}{1 + \bar{\alpha}_{k+1} \Pi_{k,n}(z)}$$

with $\Pi_{k,n}(0) = -\alpha_{k+1}$. The recursion ends because $\Pi_{k,n}(z) = 0$ for $k > n$. Again we may conclude from Schur's theorem that $\Pi_{0,n}(z) \in \$$ and hence $V_n(z)$ has no zeros in $|z| < 1$. Thus we have almost shown (1) and (2) of the next theorem.

THEOREM 17.4. *Let $F \in \mathbb{IF}$ and associate with it for $m=0$, the SS parameters α_k, $k = 1,2,\ldots,n$. If $|\alpha_k| < 1$, $k = 0,1,\ldots,n$, then*

(1) $Q_k(z)$ and $V_k(z)$ can have no zeros in $|z| \leqslant 1$ for $k = 0,1,\ldots,n$ where $Q_k(z) = Q_k^{(0)}(z)$, $k = 0,1,\ldots,n$ are polynomials of the first kind for $F(z)$ and $V_k(z)$ are defined by (17.10),

(2) $z\Gamma_k(z) := z^{-1} R_k(z)/P_{k*}(z)$ and $\Sigma_k(z) := U_k(z)/V_k(z)$ are in $\$$ for $k = 0,1,\ldots,n$ where $P_k(z) = P_k^{(0)}(z)$ and $R_k(z) = R_k^{(0)}(z)$ are the P and R series for $F(z)$ and $V_n(z)$ and $U_n(z)$ are as defined in (17.10) and (17.11),

(3) $\Omega_k(z) := A_k(z)/Q_k(z) \in \mathbb{P}$ for $k = 0,1,\ldots,n$, where $A_k(z) = A_k^{(0)}(z)$ are polynomials of the second kind for $F(z)$ and $Q_k(z) = Q_k^{(0)}(z)$ are polynomials of the first kind.

PROOF. For (1) it only remains to show that the zeros are not on $|z| = 1$. Suppose ζ is a zero of $Q_n(z)$ and $|\zeta| = 1$. Then we have from the recursion (3.6) for $\hat{Q}_n(z) = Q_n^*(z)$:

$$\left| \frac{Q_n^*(z) - Q_{n-1}^*(z)}{Q_{n-1}(z)} \right| = |z\alpha_n|$$

and for $z = \zeta$:

$$\left| \frac{Q_{n-1}^*(\zeta)}{Q_{n-1}(\zeta)} \right| = 1 = |\alpha_n|,$$

which contradicts the hypothesis. The proof is similar for $V_n(z)$. (2) is trivial to prove.

It remains to prove (3). Because (see corollary 6.4)

$$\Omega_n(z) = -\frac{2}{f_0} \frac{z\Sigma_{n-1}(z)-1}{z\Sigma_{n-1}(z)+1}, \quad \text{with } \Sigma_{n-1} \in \$,$$

(2) and (4) of lemma 17.1 and the fact that $f_0 > 0$ give the result.

$\square$

Theorem 17.3 has another classical corollary given below.

COROLLARY 17.5. *Under the conditions of theorem 17.3, $\Gamma_0(z) \in \$$ iff*
(1) $T_k > 0$ for $k = 1, 2, \ldots$, i.e. $\mathbf{T}_k$ is positive definite for $k = 0, 1, 2, \ldots$ or
(2) $T_k > 0$ for $k = 1, 2, \ldots, n$ and $T_{n+1} = 0$, i.e. $\mathbf{T}_k$ is positive definite for $k = 0, 1, \ldots, n$ and $\mathbf{T}_{n+1}$ is singular.
T_k *denote the Toeplitz matrices* $(f_{i-j})_{i,j=0}^k$ *and* $T_k = \det \mathbf{T}_k$. *The* f_k *are the Fourier coefficients of* $F \in$ IF *that is related to* $\Gamma_0(z) \in \$$.

PROOF. Use the fact that $T_n = v_n v_{n-1} \cdots v_0 = \prod_{k=1}^{n} (1-|\alpha_k|^2) f_0$ which follows from (9.24) and (3.2c) and theorem 17.3 to find that all T_k are positive as stated. This is necessary and sufficient for the $\mathbf{T}_k$ to be positive definite.

□

THEOREM 17.6. *The polynomials* $\hat{Q}_n(z) = Q_n^*(z) = \hat{Q}_n^{(0)}(z)$ *of the first kind, associated with* $F \in$ IF *are orthogonal with respect to the inner product*

$$(P,Q) = \frac{1}{2\pi} \int_{|z|=1} P(z)\, F(z)\, Q_*(z)\, \frac{dz}{z}. \tag{17.12}$$

Their norm is given by

$$\|\hat{Q}_n\|^2 = \hat{v}_n = v_n = f_0 \prod_{k=1}^{n} (1-|\alpha_k|^2).$$

where $v_n = v_n^{(0)}$ *are* v *parameters of* F *and* $\alpha_k = \alpha_k^{(0)}$ *its SS parameters.*

PROOF. The Gram matrix of the finite dimensional Hilbert space of polynomials of degree n is given by the Toeplitz matrix $\mathbf{T}_n$. I.e., $\mathbf{T}_n = [(z^p, z^q)]_{p,q=0}^n$. The inner product can therefore be written as

$$(P,Q) = \sum_{l=0}^{n} \sum_{k=0}^{n} p_k\, (z^l, z^k)\, \bar{q}_l = \sum_{l=0}^{n} \sum_{k=0}^{n} p_k\, f_{k-l}\, \bar{q}_l$$

with

$$P(z) = \sum_{k=0}^{n} p_k z^k \quad \text{and} \quad Q(z) = \sum_{k=0}^{n} q_k z^k.$$

Because $\mathbf{T}_n \hat{Q}_n = [0 \cdots 0\, \hat{v}_n]^T$ the result follows directly.

□

The orthonormal polynomials $(v_n)^{-1/2} Q_n^*(z)$ are called the *Szegő polynomials*. They are orthonormal on the unit circle with respect to the weight function $F(z)$. It is seen that (17.12) is a special case of the bilinear form $<\cdot,\cdot>^{(m)}$ of chapter 8 with $m = 0$. All the results given there reduce in this special case to classical relations that have been extensively studied in the literature. [AKH], [SZE], [SCH], [GER]. We do not repeat them here.

For the block structure, studied in chapter 11 we have, because of the symmetry of F, that $\mathbb{B}_n^{(m)} = \hat{\mathbb{B}}_n^{(m)} = \mathbb{D}_n^{(m)}$. $\mathbb{B}_n^{(m)}$ was defined in (11.19), $\hat{\mathbb{B}}_n^{(m)} = \mathbb{B}_n^{(m)}(\hat{F})$ was defined in (11.26) or (11.27) and $\mathbb{D}_n^{(m)} = \mathbb{B}_n^{(m)} \cap \hat{\mathbb{B}}_n^{(m)}$. This means that there is complete symmetry in fig. 11.3 with respect to the row $m=-\frac{1}{2}$. The blocks in the table with LPFs $K_n^{(m)}(z)$ are square. The LPFs are called in the case where $f_k = f_{-k}$ Fourier-Padé forms and in the case of real f_k they are called Chebyshev-Padé forms (theorem 11.8) [GRJ], [GR1].

Now we come to the meromorphic case. Suppose $F \in \mathbb{F}$ is meromorphic with $\kappa = 0$, $\rho = 1$ and with poles and zeros as described in section 12.1. The outer factor F_+ of F will have the poles and zeros of F which are in $|z| > 1$. It will be meromorphic too. It is simple to verify that $F_+(z)$ allows for a pseudomeromorphic extension in $|z| > 1$. Since

$$F(z) = F_+(z) F_{+*}(z),$$

we must have in the notation of section 12.1 that

$$\zeta_{-k} = 1/\bar{\zeta}_{k+1} \quad , k = 0,1,2,\ldots, \quad Z^+ = Z^- + 1$$
$$\pi_{-k} = 1/\bar{\pi}_{k+1} \quad , k = 0,1,2,\ldots, \quad P^+ = P^- + 1$$

It was shown in corollarly 15.5 that we have e.g.

THEOREM 17.7. Let $F(z)$ be as above and suppose $|\zeta_1| < |\zeta_2|$. Then

$$\lim_{n\to\infty} |\alpha_n| = 0 \quad and \quad \lim_{n\to\infty} \alpha_{n-1}/\alpha_n = \zeta_1$$

if α_k represent the SS parameters of F for $m = 0$.

$\square$

17.3 Stochastic processes and systems

What we have seen in the previous section can be given an interpretation for stochastic processes.

A *discrete-time stochastic proces* is a sequence of random variables $\{x_k\}_{k\in\mathbb{Z}}$. If this process is *wide-sense stationary*, then the autocorrelation function

$$f_n = E[x_k \bar{x}_{k-n}]$$

where E is the expectation operator, will be independent of k. Note that $f_{-n} = \bar{f}_n$. The discrete Fourier transform

$$F(e^{i\theta}) = \sum_{k=-\infty}^{\infty} f_k e^{ik\theta}$$

is called the *spectral density* of the stochastic process.
The *Wiener-Kinchin theorem* says that the spectral density of a stochastic process

is nonnegative.

If we interpret the index as a time variable, then a linear combination of the form

$$x_{k|\infty} = -\sum_{j=1}^{\infty} q_j x_{k-j}$$

can be seen as an *estimate* or *prediction* for x_k, given its past. The coefficients q_k could be found by minimizing the prediction error in least squares sense. I.e. we minimize with respect to q_k, $k = 1, 2, \ldots$ the expression

$$E[|e_k|^2]$$

where

$$e_k := x_k - x_{k|\infty}$$

is the *forward prediction error*. e_k forms a stochastic process which is called the process of *forward innovations*.

Rather than solving the minimization problem for the complete past, we can solve the problem for a finite past : $x_{k-1}, \ldots, x_{k-n}$. I.e. minimize

$$\nu_n = E[|e_{k|n}|^2]$$

with

$$e_{k|n} = x_k - x_{k|n} = x_k + \sum_{j=1}^{n} q_{j,n} x_{k-j}.$$

The well known *orthogonality principle* says that this error is minimized if

$$e_{k|n} \perp x_{k-j}, \quad \text{i.e.} \quad E[e_{k|n} \bar{x}_{k-j}] = 0, \quad j = 1, 2, \ldots, n.$$

This is expressed by the *Yule-Walker equations*

$$\mathbf{T}_n Q_n = [\nu_n \ 0 \cdots 0]^T$$

where

$$\mathbf{T}_n = [f_{i-j}]_{i,j=0}^{n} \quad \text{and} \quad Q_n = [1 \ q_{1,n} \cdots q_{n,n}]^T.$$

This is exactly the system considered in (3.1) for $m = 0$. The other system, i.e.

$$\mathbf{T}_n \hat{Q}_n = [0 \cdots 0 \ \hat{\nu}_n]^T$$

will solve the *backward prediction problem*, i.e. it finds coefficients $\hat{Q}_n = [\hat{q}_{0n} \cdots \hat{q}_{n-1,n} \ 1]$ such that

$$\hat{e}_{k|n} = x_k - \hat{x}_{k|n} = x_k + \sum_{j=1}^{n} \hat{q}_{n-j,n} x_{k-j}$$

is a *backward innovation process*, i.e. such that

$$\hat{v}_n = E\left[|\hat{e}_{k|n}|^2\right]$$

is minimized.

Since we have the same symmetry properties for F as in the previous section, the SS parameters α_k will satisfy $\hat{\alpha}_k = \alpha_k$ while $Q_n(z) = Q_n^*(z)$ etc. The SS parameters are called in this context *partial correlation coefficients*. Algorithm 1 of fig. 3.1 will simplify to the algorithm given in fig. 17.3.

$$Q_0 = 1$$

$$v_0 = f_0$$

for $n = 0, 1, 2, \cdots$

$$u_n = \Pi_{0:0}\left(z^{-n-1}F(z)Q_n(z)\right)$$

$$\alpha_{n+1} = u_n/v_n$$

$$Q_{n+1}(z) = Q_n(z) - z\alpha_{n+1}Q_n^*(z)$$

Figure 17.3: The Levinson algorithm

It is called the Levinson algorithm [LEV]. Therefore, algorithm 1 is a generalized Levinson algorithm. We know from previous section that $|\alpha_k| < 1$ for $k = 1, 2, \cdots$ or $|\alpha_k| < 1$ for $k = 1, 2, \ldots, N$ and $|\alpha_N| = 1$, in which case the prediction error $v_n = 0$. The stochastic process is then *predictable*. The *predictor* $Q_n(z)$ is a polynomial of degree n which satisfies the orthogonality relation

$$\frac{1}{2\pi}\int_{-\pi}^{\pi} Q_k(e^{i\theta})\,\overline{Q_l(e^{i\theta})}\,F(e^{i\theta})d\theta = \delta_{kl}v_k.$$

Hence the set $\{Q_k(z)\}$ of polynomials forms a set of othogonal polynomials on the unit circle with respect to the weight function $F(z)$. They were studied by Szegö [SZE]. The recurrence (3.3) is for this case the recurrence of Szegö and the parameters α_k are therefore given the name of Szegö parameters.

If $\{x_k\}_{k \in \mathbb{Z}}$ is a stochastic process as before, then

$$y_n = \sum_{k=-\infty}^{\infty} h_k x_{n-k}$$

specifies a linear time-invariant system with *input* $\{x_n\}$ and *output* $\{y_n\}$. The sequence $\{h_k\}$ is called its *impulse response* and its z-transform

$$H(z) = \sum_{n=-\infty}^{\infty} h_n z^n$$

is the *system function*. If the region of analyticity of $H(z)$ includes the unit circle $|z| = 1$, then the system is called *stable* and if $h_n = 0$ for $n < 0$, it is called *causal*. In that case $H(z)$ is analytic in $|z| \leqslant 1$. Since

$$x_{k|n} = - \sum_{j=1}^{n} q_{j,n} x_{k-j},$$

$x_{k|n}$ is the output of the system

$$\tilde{Q}_n(z) = - \sum_{j=1}^{n} q_{jn} z^j.$$

It is called the *forward prediction filter* of $\{x_k\}$ and

$$Q_n(z) = 1 - \tilde{Q}_n(z)$$

is the *forward error filter*. As we may conclude from theorem 17.4, it will be stable and causal. The *backward error filter* is $\hat{Q}_n(z)/z^n = Q_{n*}(z)$.

If $\alpha_k = 0$ for all $k > n$, the Levinson algorithm will end at step n. The prediction error $\{e_{n|n}\}$ will then be a *white noise* process because its spectral density equals v_n which is a constant. The process $\{x_k\}$ is then called *autoregressive* (AR). The forward error filter $Q_n(z)$ will generate white noise from the input $\{x_k\}$. It is therefore called a *whitening filter*, while the inverse filter, which generates $\{x_k\}$ from a white noise input has system function $1/Q_n(z)$ and is called *modelling filter*.

In the limit as $n \to \infty$, we will obtain a *Wiener filter*. If the process is unpredictable, i.e. if $\lim_{n \to \infty} v_n > 0$, the Levinson algorithm does not break down.

Suppose moreover that the process is *regular*, i.e. that its spectral density can be factorized as

$$F(z) = F_+(z)F_{+*}(z)$$

with $F_+(z)$ outer. Such an outer function F_+ is called a *minimal phase* filter. As we have seen, the filter $1/F_+(z)$, which will be approximated by $Q_k(z)$, $k = 1,2, \cdots$, will give the orthogonal process of innovations $\{e_k\}$ when we take $\{x_k\}$ for its input.

A whitening filter can be realized by a tapped delay line as e.g. in fig. 17.4, where z denotes the delay operator : $zx_n = x_{n-1}$. However we can also realize it without using the predictor coefficients $q_{k,N}$ but by using the *SS* parameters α_k as in fig. 17.5. This is in fact the flow graph of fig. 6.1. The modelling filter is given in fig. 17.6. It is a realization of (6.6b) with a flow graph which is much like in fig. 6.2. The proof is simple. The transfer from node n_k to node m_k is $\hat{Q}_n(z)/Q_n(z)$ (see (6.6b)). Hence the node value m_N satisfies :

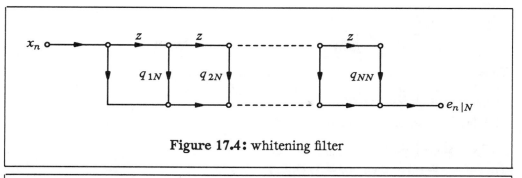

Figure 17.4: whitening filter

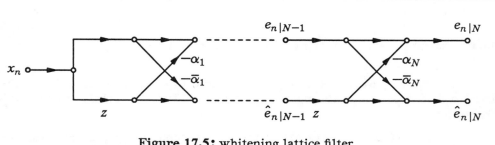

Figure 17.5: whitening lattice filter

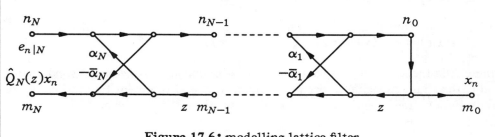

Figure 17.6: modelling lattice filter

$$n_N = Q_N(z)/\hat{Q}_N(z)\, m_N.$$

But

$$m_N = z\, m_{N-1} - \bar{\alpha}_N n_{N-1} = z\, m_{N-1} - \bar{\alpha}_N \frac{Q_{N-1}(z)}{\hat{Q}_{N-1}(z)}\, m_{N-1}$$

$$= \frac{1}{\hat{Q}_{N-1}(z)}\, (z\, \hat{Q}_{N-1}(z) - \bar{\alpha}_N Q_{N-1}(z))\, m_{N-1}$$

$$= \frac{\hat{Q}_N(z)}{\hat{Q}_{N-1}(z)} \, m_{N-1}.$$

Thus

$$n_N = Q_N(z)/\hat{Q}_{N-1}(z) m_{N-1}.$$

This process can be repeated until we find

$$n_N = Q_N(z) \, m_0.$$

Thus if $n_N = e_{n|N}$, then $m_0 = 1/Q_N(z) \, e_{n|N} = x_n$.

17.4 Lossless inverse scattering and transmission lines

The SS parameters α_k are often referred to as *reflection coefficients*. this term comes from a scattering interpretation. We shall briefly outline this connection.

Let $v(t,x)$ and $i(x,t)$ be the voltage and current in an electrical transmission line. Their interaction is described by the telegrapher's equations :

$$\frac{\partial}{\partial x} v(x,t) = - R(x) \, i(x,t) - L(x) \, \frac{\partial}{\partial t} \, i(x,t)$$

$$\frac{\partial}{\partial x} i(x,t) = - G(x) \, v(x,t) - C(x) \, \frac{\partial}{\partial t} \, v(x,t)$$

$$(17.13)$$

where R is the series resistance, L the series inductance, G the shunt conductance and C the shunt capacitance per unit length. R and G represent loss terms. If the transmission line is supposed to be lossless, then the corresponding terms are neglected. Thus

$$\frac{\partial v}{\partial x} = - L \, \frac{\partial i}{\partial t}$$

$$\frac{\partial i}{\partial x} = - C \, \frac{\partial v}{\partial t}.$$

Suppose that L and C are constant, then we find the wave equations

$$\frac{\partial^2 v}{\partial x^2} = LC \, \frac{\partial^2 v}{\partial t^2} \quad \text{and} \quad \frac{\partial^2 t}{\partial x^2} = LC \, \frac{\partial^2 i}{\partial t^2}.$$

$c = (LC)^{-\frac{1}{2}}$ is the propagation velocity of the wave. $Z = (LC)^{\frac{1}{2}}$ is the characteristic impedance.

With a change of variables : $\xi := x - ct$ and $\eta := x + ct$, it can be derived from the wave equations that

$$\frac{\partial^2 v}{\partial \xi \partial \eta} = \frac{\partial^2 i}{\partial \xi \partial \eta} = 0.$$

Hence there must exist waves v_i and v_o such that

$$v(x,t) = v_i(x-ct) + v_o(x+ct).$$

Similarly

$$i(x,t) = i_i(x-ct) + i_o(x+ct).$$

The waves v_i and i_i propagate in the $+x$ direction, the waves v_o and i_o propagate in the $-x$ direction. It follows from the telegrapher's equations that

$$v_i = Z\, i_i \quad \text{and} \quad v_o = -Z\, i_o$$

so that only two independent solutions describe the whole problem, which we take to be

$$\hat{w} := i_i \sqrt{Z} \quad \text{and} \quad w := i_o \sqrt{Z}.$$

$\hat{w}$ is called the *incoming wave* and w is the *outgoing wave*.
Hence the normalized voltage $V := v/\sqrt{Z}$ and the normalized current $I := i\sqrt{Z}$ satisfy :

$$\begin{vmatrix} V \\ I \end{vmatrix} = \begin{vmatrix} -1 & 1 \\ 1 & 1 \end{vmatrix} \begin{vmatrix} w \\ \hat{w} \end{vmatrix} \quad \text{and} \quad \begin{vmatrix} w \\ \hat{w} \end{vmatrix} = \frac{1}{2} \begin{vmatrix} Z^{-\frac12} & -Z^{\frac12} \\ Z^{-\frac12} & Z^{\frac12} \end{vmatrix} \begin{vmatrix} v \\ i \end{vmatrix}. \tag{17.14}$$

Now we shall study the scattering of these waves in the transmission line. Therefore, we subdivide this line in several layers where we suppose that Z is constant. Suppose Z_n is the value of Z in the n-th layer : $Z_n = Z(x)$, $x_n \leqslant x \leqslant x_{n+1}$. The thickness of the layers is chosen such that the waves propagate through a layer in ½ time unit. $x = x_n$ is the boundary between layer n and layer $n+1$. The value of a wave $w(x,t)$ immediately after position x_n is denoted by $w_n(t) := w(x_n+0,t)$ and the value just in front of x_n is denoted as $w'_n := w(x_n-0,t)$. Since Z_n is constant, and since the layer is traversed in ½ time unit, it is clear that

$$\begin{vmatrix} w'_n(t) \\ \hat{w}'_n(t) \end{vmatrix} = \begin{vmatrix} w_{n-1}(t+\frac12) \\ \hat{w}_{n-1}(t-\frac12) \end{vmatrix}. \tag{17.15}$$

At the boundary x_n, we use the continuity of voltage and current :

$$[v_n(t)\ \ i_n(t)] = [v'_n(t)\ \ i'_n(t)].$$

Thus we get from (17.14)

$$\begin{bmatrix} w_n(t) \\ \hat{w}_n(t) \end{bmatrix} = \frac{1}{2} \begin{bmatrix} Z_n^{-\frac{1}{2}} & -Z_n^{\frac{1}{2}} \\ Z_n^{-\frac{1}{2}} & Z_n^{\frac{1}{2}} \end{bmatrix} \begin{bmatrix} v_n(t) \\ i_n(t) \end{bmatrix}$$

and

$$\begin{bmatrix} w_n'(t) \\ \hat{w}_n'(t) \end{bmatrix} = \frac{1}{2} \begin{bmatrix} Z_{n-1}^{-\frac{1}{2}} & -Z_{n-1}^{\frac{1}{2}} \\ Z_{n-1}^{-\frac{1}{2}} & Z_{n-1}^{\frac{1}{2}} \end{bmatrix} \begin{bmatrix} v_n'(t) \\ i_n'(t) \end{bmatrix} .$$

Thus at the boundary x_n we have

$$\begin{bmatrix} w_n(t) \\ \hat{w}_n(t) \end{bmatrix} = \theta_n \begin{bmatrix} w_n'(t) \\ \hat{w}_n'(t) \end{bmatrix} = \theta_n \begin{bmatrix} z^{-\frac{1}{2}} & 0 \\ 0 & z^{\frac{1}{2}} \end{bmatrix} \begin{bmatrix} w_{n-1}(t) \\ \hat{w}_{n-1}(t) \end{bmatrix} \tag{17.16}$$

with

$$\theta_n = \tau_n^{-1} \begin{vmatrix} 1 & -\alpha_n \\ -\alpha_n & 1 \end{vmatrix} ,$$

$$\alpha_n = \frac{Z_n - Z_{n-1}}{Z_n + Z_{n-1}} \ , \quad \tau_n = \frac{2(Z_n Z_{n-1})^{\frac{1}{2}}}{Z_n + Z_{n-1}} = (1 - \alpha_n^2)^{\frac{1}{2}}$$

and z is the delay operator : $zf(t) = f(t-1)$.

Because $Z_k > 0$, all α_k will be bounded by 1 in modulus. The losslessness is expressed by the relation $\alpha_k^2 + \tau_k^2 = 1$. Because $\hat{w}_n$ is propragating in the opposite direction of w_n, it may seem more natural to express the emerging waves at $x = x_n$ in terms of the incident waves (see fig. 17.7).

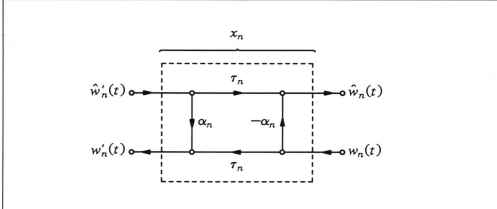

Figure 17.7: reflection/transmission at boundary n

(17.16) may be rewritten as

$$\begin{bmatrix} w_n'(t) \\ \hat{w}_n(t) \end{bmatrix} = s_n \begin{bmatrix} w_n(t) \\ \hat{w}_n'(t) \end{bmatrix}$$

with s_n the scattering matrix

$$s_n := \begin{bmatrix} \tau_n & \alpha_n \\ -\alpha_n & \tau_n \end{bmatrix}.$$

As you can see, when the incident wave $\hat{w}_n'(t)$ hits the boundary at x_n, it is partially reflected into layer n ($\alpha_n \hat{w}_n'(t)$) and partially transmitted to the next layer ($\tau_n \hat{w}_n'(t)$). Similarly for the other incident wave $w_n(t)$. The wave $w_n'(t)$ emerging from the boundary in the $-x$ direction is composed by the reflection of $\hat{w}_n'(t)$ and the transmission of $w_n(t)$ and similarly for $\hat{w}_n(t)$. This justifies the name *reflection coefficient* for α_n and *transmission coefficient* for τ_n. Although the matrix s_n has a physical meaning, it is computationally more interesting to work with the *chain scattering matrix* θ_n. Indeed the chain scattering matrix for a medium consisting of several layers is given by the product of the chain scattering matrices for each layer. Suppose now that we apply a pulse train with unit time interval at time $t = 0$ just after the boundary $x = x_0$. Then the responses at $x = x_n$ will be pulse trains with unit time interval as you can see in the x,t diagrams of fig. 17.8.

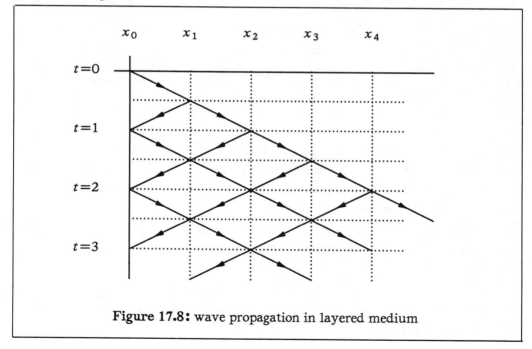

Figure 17.8: wave propagation in layered medium

The z-transforms, taking into account a time delay of $n/2$ for boundary x_n are defined by

$$W_n(z) := \sum_{t=0}^{\infty} w_n(t)z^t \quad \text{and} \quad \hat{W}_n(z) := \sum_{t=1}^{\infty} \hat{w}_n(t)z^t.$$

The others ($W'_n(z)$ and $\hat{W}'_n(z)$) are similarly defined. Finally we set

$$W_0(z) := W'_1(z) \quad \text{and} \quad \hat{W}_0 := \hat{W}'_1(z).$$

Thus we get

$$\begin{vmatrix} W_{n+1}(z) \\ \hat{W}_{n+1}(z) \end{vmatrix} = \theta_{n+1} \begin{vmatrix} 1 & 0 \\ 0 & z \end{vmatrix} \theta_n \cdots \theta_1 \begin{vmatrix} 1 & 0 \\ 0 & z \end{vmatrix} \begin{vmatrix} W_0(z) \\ \hat{W}_0(z) \end{vmatrix}. \tag{17.17}$$

Taking the transpose, we can write this as

$$[W_{n+1}(z) \ \hat{W}_{n+1}(z)] = [W_0(z) \ \hat{W}_0(z)] \Theta_{n+1}(z)$$

where

$$\Theta_{n+1}(z) = \theta_1(z)\theta_2(z) \cdots \theta_{n+1}(z); \quad \theta_k(z) = \begin{vmatrix} 1 & 0 \\ 0 & z \end{vmatrix} \theta_k, \quad k = 1,2,\ldots$$

Except for the normalisation by τ_k^{-1}, these are the θ-matrices as we have used them before.

If one stands at the boundary x_0 and measures the reflection $W_0(z)$ generated by an input $\hat{W}_0(z)$, then we can compute the transfer $W_0(z)/\hat{W}_0(z)$ which is called the *scattering function* of the medium. In the *inverse scattering problem* one tries to find a model for the scattering medium, given the scattering function. E.g. we could compute the reflection coefficients at the boundaries of the layers of the medium. This can be done as follows : The first response will arrive at $t = 1$ and it is the reflection of $\hat{W}_0(0)$ at the boundary $x = x_1$. Hence $W_0(z)/z|_{z=0} = \alpha_1 \hat{W}_0(0)$. In other words, $\alpha_1 = \Gamma_0(0)$ with $\Gamma_0(z) := z^{-1}W_0(z)/\hat{W}_0(z)$. Now the scattering function at $x = x_1$ which is given by $z^{-1}\Gamma_1(z) := W_1(z)/\hat{W}_1(z)$ is related to $\Gamma_0(z)$ by

$$\Gamma_1(z) = z^{-1} (\Gamma_0(z)-\alpha_1)/(1-\alpha_1\Gamma_0(z)),$$

as can be easily derived from (17.17). This is exactly the relation as given in the Schur algorithm of fig. 17.1. Since all reflection coefficients must satisfy $|\alpha_k| < 1$ for physical reasons, all $\Gamma_k(z)$ will be Schur functions. The reflection coefficients turn out to be the Schur parameters of $\Gamma_0(z)$.

In a more general situation, the effect of a scattering medium can be described by (see fig. 17.7)

$$\begin{vmatrix} W'(z) \\ \hat{W}(z) \end{vmatrix} = S(z) \begin{vmatrix} W(z) \\ \hat{W}'(z) \end{vmatrix} \; ; \; S(z) := \begin{vmatrix} S(z) & S_c(z) \\ T(z) & T_c(z) \end{vmatrix} .$$

$S(z)$ is called the scattering function and $T(z)$ is the transmission function. $S_c(z)$ is a complementary scattering function and $T_c(z)$ a complementary transmission function. $S(z)$ is the *scattering matrix*. The chain scattering matrix $\Theta(z)$ can be derived from $S(z)$ by

$$\Theta(z) = \begin{vmatrix} S - TT_c^{-1}S_c & S_cT_c^{-1} \\ -T_c^{-1}T & T_c^{-1} \end{vmatrix} .$$

Losslessness is expressed by

$$\begin{vmatrix} 1 & 0 \\ 0 & -1 \end{vmatrix} - \Theta(z) \begin{vmatrix} 1 & 0 \\ 0 & -1 \end{vmatrix} \Theta_*(z) = 0$$

with $\Theta_*(z) = [\Theta(1/\bar{z})]^H$.
$S(z)$ will be a Schur function and hence

$$Z(z) := \tfrac{1}{2} f_0 \frac{1+S(z)}{1-S(z)} \in \mathbb{P} \quad \text{for some } f_0 > 0$$

and

$$F(z) := Z(z) + Z_*(z) \in \mathbb{F}.$$

The factorization of $F(z)$ can be obtained as

$$F(z) = F_+(z)F_{+*}(z)$$

with

$$F_+(z) = T_c(z)/(1-S(z)).$$

This factor will be outer if $T_c(z)$ is outer.

This relates the theory to what was given in section 17.1. More on scattering theory can be found e.g. in [ROB,DED,PRAB]. We only mention that the factorization of the chain scattering matrix $\Theta(z)$ in elementary (degree 1) matrices $\theta_k(z)$ as described above, is only one of the possibilities. Such an elementary section described by $\theta_k(z)$ is called a Schur section for obvious reasons. There exist more general elementary sections which are essentially obtained by replacing z in $\theta_k(z)$ by $(z-\zeta_k)/(1-\bar{\zeta}_k z)$. The ζ_k are called transmission zeros (they are zeros of the transmission function). The algorithm of Schur can be generalized for this case (see [DED,PRAB]) in which case it becomes the Pick–Nevanlinna algorithm [AKH]. Instead of rational approximants in a Padé sense, we shall obtain rational approximants interpolating in the transmission zeros.

17.5 Laurent-Padé approximation and ARMA-filtering

We have seen before that

$$K_n(z) = \frac{\nu_n}{Q_n(z)Q_{n*}(z)}$$

was a $(0/n)$ LPA for $F(z)$ and that $Q_n(z)$ had no zeros inside the unit disc. Thus the factorization of the spectral density :

$$F(z) = F_+(z)F_{+*}(z)$$

with $F_+(z)$ outer, is approximated by

$$K_n(z) = F_{n+}(z)F_{n+*}(z) \tag{17.18}$$

with $F_{n+}(z) := \nu_n^{\frac{1}{2}}/Q_n(z)$ outer. The relation (17.18) gives a $(0/n)$ LPA for $F(z)$. Consequently, the modelling filter $F_{n+}(z)$ is of autoregressive (AR) type, i.e. it is a rational function with constant numerator. One could ask whether a more general (m/n) LPA can give an autoregressive-moving average (ARMA) filter i.e. with a non constant numerator. Thus consider the (m/n) LPA of $F(z)$:

$$K_n^{(m)}(z) = \frac{L_n^{(m)}(z)}{Q_n^{(m)}(z)\hat{Q}_n^{(-m)}(z)z^{-n}}$$

with

$$L_n^{(m)}(z) = z^{-n}[B_n^{(m)}(z)\hat{Q}_n^{(-m)}(z) - \hat{B}_n^{(-m)}(z)Q_n^{(m)}(z)].$$

It becomes with the symmetry we have for $F(z)$ (see Theorem 17.2)

$$K_n^{(m)}(z) = \frac{L_n^{(m)}(z)}{Q_n^{(m)}(z)Q_{n*}^{(m)}(z)}$$

where

$$L_n^{(m)}(z) = B_n^{(m)}(z)Q_{n*}^{(m)}(z) + B_{n*}^{(m)}(z)Q_n^{(m)}(z) = L_{n*}^{(m)}(z).$$

This relation shows that $L_n^{(m)}(z)$ must be real on the unit circle $|z| = 1$. However to obtain an approximation $F_{n+}^{(m)}(z)$ for $F_+(z)$, we should be able to factorize $K_n^{(m)}(z)$ as

$$K_n^{(m)}(z) = F_{n+}^{(m)}(z)F_{n+*}^{(m)}(z).$$

But this means that on the unit circle we should have

$$K_n^{(m)}(z) = |F_{n+}^{(m)}(z)|^2 > 0 \ , \quad |z| = 1.$$

Thus such a factorization is only possible if $L_n^{(m)}(e^{i\theta}) > 0$ (The denominator satisfies $Q_n^{(m)}(z)Q_{n*}^{(m)}(z)|_{z=e^{i\theta}} = |Q_n^{(m)}(e^{i\theta})|^2 > 0$.) The positivity of $L_n^{(m)}(e^{i\theta})$ can not be guaranteed in general. If $L_n^{(m)}(z)$ has a zero on the unit circle of odd multiplicity, the factorization cannot be done. However, if $F_+(z)$ has the zeros $1 < |\zeta_1| \leqslant |\zeta_2| \leqslant \cdots$, and if $|\zeta_m| < |\zeta_{m+1}|$, then we have seen in chapter 16 that $L_n^{(m)}(z)$ will approximate

$$\prod_{k=1}^{m} (1-z/\zeta_k)(1-1/(z\bar{\zeta}_k)) \cdot |F_+(0)|^2$$

if n is large enough. Thus, if the zeros $F_+(z)$ are bounded away from the unit circle $|z| = 1$, then $L_n^{(m)}(z)$ will have no zeros on the unit circle if n is large, whence it will be possible to get a spectral factorization for it. The outer spectral factor will then give an ARMA approximation for $F_+(z)$ which will be stable and of minimal phase. If $1 < |\tilde{\zeta}_1| \leqslant |\tilde{\zeta}_2| \leqslant \cdots \leqslant |\tilde{\zeta}_m|$ are the zeros of this approximate ARMA filter, then the same result could be obtained with the Pick-Nevanlinna algorithm which interpolates at $\tilde{\zeta}_1, \ldots, \tilde{\zeta}_m$ and $n-m$ times in $\zeta = \infty$.

17.6 Concluding remarks

The applications considered in this chapter inspired us to generalise the results obtained here to the complete Laurent-Padé table. This is the reason why the algorithms 1 (Levinson type) and 2 (Schur type) considered in chapter 3 are central in our development.

Also the use of flow graphs to represent the recursive relations which is common in digital filtering literature and network theory is introduced because in our opinion it gives a clear representation of the building blocks for the algorithms.

In Padé literature the algorithms of type 1 (recursions between the denominators of Padé approximants) and of type 2 (division algorithms to obtain a continued fraction expansion) were well known. Their application in a situation of Laurent-Padé approximation is straightforward. In the engineering applications these two type of algorithms are frequently used as methods for the computation of reflection coefficients. They are known there as Levinson or Schur-type algorithms. In a scattering terminology, this duality could be described as "layer-adjoining" and "layer-peeling". The first type of methods propagate the original scattering data through the portion of the medium already determined, thus obtaining the information for continuing the identification process. The second type of methods replaces at each step the original scattering data with some synthetic data which correspond to the portion of the medium not yet identified. Although both types are closely related, the layer-peeling methods do not need inner products, while layer-adjoining methods do. This makes the layer-peeling methods more suitable for parallel computation, a property which can not be underestimated these days.

The third type of algorithm, i.e. the rhombus rules of the qd- and related algorithms is even more natural in its extension to the Laurent-Padé case, since we only have to extend the half infinite table of numbers for a Padé case to a bi-infinite one without problems in crossing the border. To our knowledge, there is not such an algorithm for computing the reflection coefficients of a predictive filter. It has led us to the interesting result that the zero of a meromorphic function can be computed from its Laurent series coefficients. This is translated in a digital filtering situation into the result that under certain conditions, the limit of the ratio of two successive reflection coefficients converges to the transmission zero which is closest to the unit circle of the complex plane.

The orthogonal polynomials introduced in chapter 8 can be related to interpolatory quadrature formulas for integration over the unit circle in analogy with quadrature results for the classical Padé theory which are related to integration over a line. The bi-orthogonal polynomials generalize the Szegö orthogonal polynomials which are known in an engineering context to give the prediction coefficients of a predictive filter.

Chapter 18

Examples

In this chapter we shall give some simple examples to illustrate the meaning of the theorems and the computations performed by the algoritms. The reader should be warned for the poor numerical performance of these algorithms when implemented in finite arithmetic. Only for the positive definite case considered in previous chapter, the Levinson and Schur algorithm can be considered to be numerically stable [CYB,BU10]. To avoid numerical difficulties, we shall give examples that are computable in exact arithmetic.

18.1 Example 1

The first example is based on the formal Laurent series $\sum f_k z^k$

$$f_k = k+1 \quad \text{for } k \geqslant 0$$
$$= k-1 \text{ for } k < 0.$$

As we shall see later on, this is not a normal series. There are two infinite blocks: in the right lower corner and in the right upper corner of the T-table. As long as we do not enter these blocks, everything that was derived in the first 10 chapters under the assumption that the fls was normal remains valid.

We start with algorithm 1 of fig 3.1, which we apply for $m = 0$. It gives the following results that can easily be traced.

$$[\varrho_0^{(0)} \quad \hat{\varrho}_0^{(0)}] = [1 \quad 1]$$

$$v_0^{(0)} = \hat{v}_0^{(0)} = 1$$

$$u_0^{(0)} = 2 \, , \, \hat{u}_0^{(0)} = -2$$

$$\alpha_1^{(0)} = 2 \, , \, \hat{\alpha}_1^{(0)} = -2$$

$$[\varrho_1^{(0)}(z) \quad \hat{\varrho}_1^{(0)}(z)] = [1-2z \quad 2+z]$$

$$v_1^{(0)} = \hat{v}_1^{(0)} = 5$$

$$u_1^{(0)} = -1 \, , \, \hat{u}_1^{(0)} = -7$$

$$\alpha_2^{(0)} = -\frac{1}{5} \, , \, \hat{\alpha}_2^{(0)} = -\frac{7}{5}$$

$$[Q_2^{(0)}(z) \ \hat{Q}_2^{(0)}(z)] = [1 - \frac{8}{5}z + \frac{1}{5}z^2 \quad \frac{7}{5} - \frac{4}{5}z + z^2]$$

etc.

A similar computation for $m = -1$ gives :

$$[Q_0^{(-1)} \ \hat{Q}_0^{(-1)}] = [1 \ 1]$$

$$v_0^{(-1)} = \hat{v}_0^{(-1)} = -2$$

$$u_0^{(-1)} = 1 \ , \ \hat{u}_0^{(-1)} = -3$$

$$\alpha_1^{(-1)} = -\frac{1}{2} \ , \ \hat{\alpha}_1^{(-1)} = \frac{3}{2}$$

$$[Q_1^{(-1)}(z) \ \hat{Q}_1^{(-1)}(z)] = [1 + \frac{1}{2}z \quad -\frac{3}{2} + z]$$

$$v_1^{(-1)} = \hat{v}_1^{(-1)} = -\frac{7}{2}$$

$$u_1^{(-1)} = \frac{5}{2} \ , \ \hat{u}_1^{(-1)} = \frac{1}{2}$$

$$\alpha_2^{(-1)} = -\frac{5}{7} \ , \ \hat{\alpha}_2^{(-1)} = -\frac{1}{7}$$

$$[Q_2^{(-1)}(z) \ \hat{Q}_2^{(-1)}(z)] = [1 - \frac{4}{7}z + \frac{5}{7}z^2 \quad \frac{1}{7} - \frac{10}{7}z + z^2]$$

etc.

As you can see $\hat{Q}_k^{(0)} = Q_k^{(-1)}(z)/(-\alpha_k^{(-1)})$.

Algorithm 2 of fig 3.2 gives for $m = 0$:

$$P_0^{(0)}(z) = 1 - 2z^{-1} - 3z^{-2} - 4z^{-3} - \cdots$$

$$\hat{P}_0^{(0)}(z) = -2z^{-1} - 3z^{-2} - 4z^{-3} - \cdots$$

$$R_0^{(0)}(z) = 2z + 3z^2 + 4z^3 + \cdots$$

$$\hat{R}_0^{(0)}(z) = 1 + 2z + 3z^2 + 4z^3 + \cdots$$

$$u_0^{(0)} = 2 \ , \ \hat{u}_0^{(0)} = -2 \ , \ v_0^{(0)} = \hat{v}_0^{(0)} = 1$$

$$\alpha_1^{(0)} = 2 \ , \ \hat{\alpha}_1^{(0)} = -2$$

$$P_1^{(0)}(z) = 5 + 4z^{-1} + 5z^{-2} + 6z^{-3} + \cdots$$

$$\hat{P}_1^{(0)}(z) = -7z^{-1} - 10z^{-2} - 13z^{-3} - \cdots$$

$$R_1^{(0)}(z) = -z^2 - 2z^3 - 3z^3 - \cdots$$

$$\hat{R}_1^{(0)}(z) = 5z + 8z^2 + 11z^3 + \cdots$$

$$u_1^{(0)} = -1 \,,\ \hat{u}_1^{(0)} = -7 \,,\ v_1^{(0)} = \hat{v}_1^{(0)} = 5$$

$$\alpha_2^{(0)} = -\frac{1}{5} \,,\ \hat{\alpha}_2^{(0)} = -\frac{7}{5}$$

$$P_2^{(0)}(z) = \frac{18}{5} + 2z^{-1} + \frac{12}{5}z^{-2} + \cdots$$

$$\hat{P}_2^{(0)}(z) = -\frac{22}{5}z^{-1} - 5z^{-2} + \cdots$$

$$R_2^{(0)}(z) = -\frac{2}{5}z^3 - \frac{4}{5}z^4 + \cdots$$

$$\hat{R}_2^{(0)}(z) = \frac{18}{5}z^2 + \frac{26}{5}z^3 + \cdots$$

$$u_2^{(0)} = -\frac{2}{5} \,,\ \hat{u}_2^{(0)} = -\frac{22}{5} \,,\ v_2^{(0)} = \hat{v}_2^{(0)} = \frac{18}{5}$$

etc.

The polynomials of the second kind can be found from their definitions (4.3a,b) or from the recursion (3.6) with $S = A$. This results in the following polynomials :

$$\begin{vmatrix} A_0^{(0)}(z) & \hat{A}_0^{(0)}(z) \\ A_1^{(0)}(z) & \hat{A}_1^{(0)}(z) \\ A_2^{(0)}(z) & \hat{A}_2^{(0)}(z) \end{vmatrix} = \begin{vmatrix} \frac{1}{2} & -\frac{1}{2} \\ \frac{1}{2} + z & 1 - \frac{1}{2}z \\ \frac{1}{2} + \frac{6}{5}z - \frac{1}{10}z^2 & \frac{7}{10} + \frac{12}{5}z - \frac{1}{2}z^2 \end{vmatrix}.$$

Some algebra yields

$$A_2^{(0)}(z)\hat{Q}_2^{(0)}(z) - \hat{A}_2^{(0)}(z)Q_2^{(0)}(z) = \frac{18}{5}z^2 = v_2^{(0)}z^2$$

as predicted by the determinant relation (see (4.5)). The expansions

$$L_+\left(\frac{A_2^{(0)}(z)}{Q_2^{(0)}(z)}\right) = \frac{1}{2} + 2z + 3z^2 + \frac{22}{5}z^3 + \cdots$$

and

$$L_-\left(\frac{z^{-2}\hat{A}_2^{(0)}(z)}{z^{-2}\hat{Q}_2^{(0)}(z)}\right) = -\frac{1}{2} + 2z^{-1} + 3z^{-2} - \frac{2}{5}z^{-3} + \cdots$$

are easily verified. They show that

$$\left(\frac{A_2^{(0)}(z)}{Q_2^{(0)}(z)} , -\frac{z^{-2}\hat{A}_2^{(0)}(z)}{z^{-2}\hat{Q}_2^{(0)}(z)} \right)$$

is a $(0/2)$ LPA for $F(z)$. (See Theorem 4.2.)

We now compute the polynomials $B(p)_n^{(m)}(z)$ and $\hat{B}(p)_n^{(m)}(z)$ defined by (4.7). Since

$$Z^{(1)}(z) = z + 3z^2 + 4z^3 + 5z^4 + \cdots$$

and

$$\hat{Z}^{(1)}(z) = -z - 1 + 2z^{-1} + 3z^{-2} + \cdots .$$

We get with $Q_k^{(0)}(z)$, $\hat{Q}_k^{(0)}(z)$, $R_k^{(0)}(z)$ and $\hat{R}_k^{(0)}(z)$ as given before that

$$\begin{vmatrix} B(1)_0^{(0)}(z) & \hat{B}(1)_0^{(0)}(z) \\ B(1)_0^{(1)}(z) & \hat{B}(1)_0^{(1)}(z) \\ B(1)_0^{(2)}(z) & \hat{B}(1)_0^{(2)}(z) \end{vmatrix} = \begin{vmatrix} -z & -1-z \\ z+2z^2 & -3z-z^2 \\ z-\frac{7}{5}z^2-\frac{1}{5}z^3 & \frac{7}{5}z-\frac{1}{5}z^2-z^3 \end{vmatrix}.$$

These can also be obtained with the appropriate initial conditions (4.8) and recursion (3.6) with $S = B(1)$. With these polynomials we can find the LPAs defined in (4.9). It can be verified that

$$K(1)_0^{(1)}(z) = \left(\frac{z^{-1}B(1)_0^{(2)}(z)}{Q_0^{(2)}(z)} , -\frac{z^{-1}\hat{B}(1)_0^{(0)}(z)}{\hat{Q}_0^{(0)}(z)} \right) = (1+3z , 1+z^{-1}).$$

As you can see, this gives a $(1/0)$ LPA for

$$z^{-1}F(z) = \cdots - 4z^{-3} - 2z^{-2} + z^{-1} + 2 + 3z + 4z^2 + \frac{16}{3}z^3 + \cdots$$

On the other hand

$$\hat{K}(1)_0^{(1)}(z) = \left(\frac{z^{-1}\hat{B}(1)_0^{(2)}(z)}{\hat{Q}_0^{(2)}(z)} , -\frac{z^{-1}B(1)_0^{(0)}(z)}{Q_0^{(0)}(z)} \right) = (1 , 1)$$

is a $(0/0)$ LPA for the same series.
A less trivial example of an LPA is :

$$K(1)_1^{(1)}(z) = \left(\frac{1+\dfrac{5}{3}z}{1-\dfrac{4}{3}z} , \frac{1+3z^{-1}}{1+2z^{-1}} \right)$$

$$= (1 + 3z + 4z^2 + \frac{16}{3}z^3 + \cdots, \ 1+z^{-1} - 2z^{-2} + 4z^{-3} + \cdots)$$

which is a $(1/1)$ LPA for $z^{-1}F(z)$ and

$$\hat{K}(1)\{_1^{(1)}\}(z) = (\frac{-\dfrac{2}{3} - z}{-\dfrac{2}{3} + z}, \ \frac{2+z^{-1}}{2-z^{-1}})$$

$$= (1 + 3z + \frac{9}{2}z^2 + \cdots, \ 1 + z^{-1} + \frac{1}{2}z^{-2} + ...)$$

is a $(0/1)$ LPA for the same series. (See theorem 4.3.)

The two-point Padé approximation property of theorem 4.6 can be verified too. Indeed, the expansions

$$L_+(\frac{A_2^{(0)}(z)}{Q_2^{(0)}(z)}) = \frac{1}{2} + 2z + 3z^2 + \frac{22}{5}z^3 + \cdots$$

$$L_-(\frac{A_2^{(0)}(z)}{Q_2^{(0)}(z)}) = -\frac{1}{2} + 2z^{-1} + 21z^{-2} + \cdots$$

$$L_-(\frac{\hat{A}_2^{(0)}(z)}{\hat{Q}_2^{(0)}(z)}) = -\frac{1}{2} + 2z^{-1} + 3z^{-2} - \frac{2}{5}z^{-3} + \cdots$$

$$L_+(\frac{\hat{A}_2^{(0)}(z)}{\hat{Q}_2^{(0)}(z)}) = \frac{1}{2} + 2z + \frac{3}{7}z^2 + \cdots$$

have to be compared with the series

$$Z^{(0)}(z) = \frac{1}{2} + 2z + 3z^2 + 4z^3 + \cdots$$

and

$$\hat{Z}^{(0)}(z) = -\frac{1}{2} + 2z^{-1} + 3z^{-2} + 4z^{-3} + \cdots,$$

showing that $A_2^{(0)}(z)/Q_2^{(0)}(z)$ is a two-point PA of type $(2,2)$ and $\hat{A}_2^{(0)}(z)/\hat{Q}_2^{(0)}(z)$ is a two-point PA of type $(1,2)$ for the pair $(Z^{(0)}(z), \hat{Z}^{(0)}(z))$.

From the above polynomials, we can find the U and V polynomials by (4.13) giving

$$\begin{vmatrix} V_1^{(0)}(z) & \hat{V}_1^{(0)}(z) \\ U_1^{(0)}(z) & \hat{U}_1^{(0)}(z) \end{vmatrix} = \begin{vmatrix} 1 + \dfrac{2}{5}z & \dfrac{7}{5} + 2z \\ -2 + \dfrac{1}{5}z & -\dfrac{14}{5} + z \end{vmatrix}.$$

The evaluations

$$L_+\left(\frac{U_1^{(0)}(z)}{V_1^{(0)}(z)}\right) = -2 + z - \frac{2}{5}z^2 + \cdots$$

$$L_-\left(\frac{U_1^{(0)}(z)}{V_1^{(0)}(z)}\right) = \frac{1}{2} - \frac{25}{4}z^{-1} + \cdots$$

$$L_+\left(\frac{\hat{U}_1^{(0)}(z)}{\hat{V}_1^{(0)}(z)}\right) = -2 + \frac{25}{7}z + \cdots$$

$$L_-\left(\frac{\hat{U}_1^{(0)}(z)}{\hat{V}_1^{(0)}(z)}\right) = \frac{1}{2} - \frac{7}{4}z^{-1} + \frac{6}{5}z^{-2} + \cdots$$

are to be compared with

$$-\frac{R_0^{(0)}(z)}{z\hat{R}_0^{(0)}(z)} = -2 + z - 4z^2 + \cdots$$

and

$$-\frac{P_0^{(0)}(z)}{z\hat{P}_0^{(0)}(z)} = \frac{1}{2} - \frac{7}{4}z^{-1} - \frac{1}{8}z^{-2} + \cdots.$$

They reveal that $U_1^{(0)}(z)/V_1^{(0)}(z)$ is a (1,1) two–point PA for $\left(-\dfrac{R_0^{(0)}(z)}{z\hat{R}_0^{(0)}(z)}, -\dfrac{P_0^{(0)}(z)}{z\hat{P}_0^{(0)}(z)}\right)$ and $\dfrac{\hat{U}_1^{(0)}(z)}{\hat{V}_1^{(0)}(z)}$ is a (0,1) two–point PA for the same pair. (See theorem 4.7.)

The computations of algorithm 2a in fig. 6.3 repeat more or less the computations of algorithm 2. They go as follows:

$$\Gamma_0^{(0)}(z) = \frac{2 + 3z + 4z^2 + \cdots}{1 + 2z + 3z^2 + 4z^3 + \cdots} \qquad \rightarrow \alpha_1^{(0)} = 2$$

$$\hat{\Gamma}_0^{(0)}(z) = \frac{2 + 3z^{-1} + 4z^{-2} + \cdots}{-1 + 2z^{-1} + 3z^{-2} + 4z^{-3} + \cdots} \qquad \rightarrow \hat{\alpha}_1^{(0)} = -2$$

$$\Gamma_1^{(0)}(z) = \frac{1}{z} \frac{\Gamma_0^{(0)}(z) - 2}{1 + 2\Gamma_0^{(0)}(z)} = \frac{-1 - 2z - 3z^2 - \cdots}{5 + 8z + 11z^2 + 14z^3 + \cdots}$$

$$\rightarrow \alpha_2^{(0)} = -\frac{1}{5}$$

$$\hat{\Gamma}_1^{(0)}(z) = z \frac{\hat{\Gamma}_0^{(0)}(z) + 2}{1 - 2\hat{\Gamma}_1^{(0)}(z)} = \frac{7 + 10z^{-1} + 13z^{-2} + \cdots}{-5 - 4z^{-1} - 5z^{-2} + \cdots}$$

$$\rightarrow \hat{\alpha}_2^{(0)} = -\frac{7}{5}$$

$$\Gamma_2^{(0)}(z) = \frac{1}{z} \frac{\Gamma_1^{(0)}(z) + \dfrac{1}{5}}{1 + \dfrac{7}{5}\Gamma_1^{(0)}(z)} = \frac{-1 - 2z + \cdots}{9 + 13z + 17\,z^2 + \cdots}$$

$$\rightarrow \alpha_3^{(0)} = -\frac{1}{9}$$

$$\hat{\Gamma}_2^{(0)}(z) = z \frac{\hat{\Gamma}_1^{(0)}(z) + \dfrac{7}{5}}{1 + \dfrac{1}{5}\hat{\Gamma}_1^{(0)}(z)} = \frac{2z + 25z^{-1} + \cdots}{-18 - 10z^{-1} - 12z^{-2} + \cdots}$$

$$\rightarrow \hat{\alpha}_3^{(0)} = -\frac{11}{9}.$$

To recapture the $\alpha_k^{(m)}$ and $\hat{\alpha}_k^{(m)}$, $k = 1, 2, ..., n$ from $Q_n^{(m)}(z)$ and $\hat{Q}_n^{(m)}(z)$ we can use algorithm inverse 1a of fig. 6.4. The computations for our example will go as follows:

$$\Pi_2^{(0)}(z) = L_-\left(\frac{1 - \dfrac{8}{5}z + \dfrac{1}{5}z^2}{\dfrac{7}{5} - \dfrac{4}{5}z + z^2}\right) = L_-\left(\frac{Q_2^{(0)}(z)}{\hat{Q}_2^{(0)}(z)}\right) \quad \rightarrow \alpha_2^{(0)} = -\frac{1}{5}$$

$$\hat{\Pi}_2^{(0)}(z) = L_+\left(\frac{\dfrac{7}{5} - \dfrac{4}{5}z + z^2}{1 - \dfrac{8}{5}z + \dfrac{1}{5}z^2}\right) = L_+\left(\frac{\hat{Q}_2^{(0)}(z)}{Q_2^{(0)}(z)}\right) \quad \rightarrow \hat{\alpha}_2^{(0)} = -\frac{7}{5}$$

$$\Pi_1^{(0)}(z) = z\, L_-\left(\frac{\Pi_2^{(0)}(z) - \frac{1}{5}}{1 - \frac{7}{5}\Pi_2^{(0)}(z)}\right)$$

$$= L_-\left(\frac{1 - 2z}{2 + z}\right) = L_-\left(\frac{Q_1^{(0)}(z)}{\hat{Q}_1^{(0)}(z)}\right) \rightarrow \alpha_1^{(0)} = 2$$

$$\hat{\Pi}_1^{(0)}(z) = \frac{1}{z}\, L_+\left(\frac{\hat{\Pi}_2^{(0)}(z) - \frac{7}{5}}{1 - \frac{1}{5}\hat{\Pi}_2^{(0)}(z)}\right)$$

$$= L_+\left(\frac{2 + z}{1 - 2z}\right) = L_+\left(\frac{\hat{Q}_1^{(0)}(z)}{Q_1^{(0)}(z)}\right) \rightarrow \hat{\alpha}_1^{(0)} = -2.$$

As you can see from this example, it is not necessary to compute both the recursions on $\Pi_k^{(m)}(z)$ and $\hat{\Pi}_k^{(m)}(z)$. Both coefficients $\alpha_k^{(m)}$ and $\hat{\alpha}_k^{(m)}$ can be read off from the expression for $\Pi_k^{(m)}(z)$ or $\hat{\Pi}_k^{(m)}(z)$. This is not true for algorithm inverse 1b of fig. 6.5. The computations for this algorithm are:

$$\Pi_{0,2}^{(0)}(z) = \Sigma_2^{(0)}(z) = L_+\left(\frac{U_2^{(0)}(z)}{V_2^{(0)}(z)}\right) = L_+\left(\frac{-2 - \frac{1}{9}z + \frac{1}{9}z^2}{1 + \frac{5}{9}z + \frac{2}{9}z^2}\right) \rightarrow \alpha_1^{(0)} = 2$$

$$\hat{\Pi}_{0,2}^{(0)}(z) = \hat{\Sigma}_2^{(0)}(z) = L_-\left(\frac{\hat{V}_2^{(0)}(z)}{\hat{U}_2^{(0)}(z)}\right) = L_-\left(\frac{\frac{11}{9} + \frac{17}{9} + 2z^2}{-\frac{22}{9} - \frac{23}{9} + z^2}\right) \rightarrow \hat{\alpha}_1^{(0)} = -2$$

$$z^{-1}\hat{\Pi}_{1,2}^{(0)}(z) = \frac{\Pi_{0,2}^{(0)}(z) + 2}{1 - 2\Pi_{0,2}^{(0)}(z)} \rightarrow \Pi_{1,2}^{(0)}(z) = L_+\left(\frac{1 + \frac{5}{9}z}{5 + \frac{7}{9}z}\right) \rightarrow \alpha_2^{(0)} = -\frac{1}{5}$$

$$z^{-1}\hat{\Pi}_{1,2}^{(0)}(z) = \frac{\hat{\Pi}_{0,2}^{(0)}(z) - 2}{1 + 2\hat{\Pi}_{0,2}^{(0)}(z)} \rightarrow \hat{\Pi}_{1,2}^{(0)}(z) = L_-\left(\frac{\frac{55}{9} + 7z}{\frac{11}{9} + 5z}\right) \rightarrow \hat{\alpha}_2^{(0)} = -\frac{7}{5}$$

$$z\Pi^{(0)}_{2,2}(z) = \frac{\Pi^{(0)}_{1,2}(z) - \frac{1}{5}}{1 - \frac{7}{5}\Pi^{(0)}_{1,2}(z)} \rightarrow \Pi^{(0)}_{2,2}(z) = \frac{1}{9} \rightarrow \alpha^{(0)}_3 = -\frac{1}{9}$$

$$z^{-1}\hat{\Pi}^{(0)}_{2,2}(z) = \frac{\hat{\Pi}^{(0)}_{1,2}(z) - \frac{7}{5}}{1 - \frac{1}{5}\hat{\Pi}^{(0)}_{1,2}(z)} \rightarrow \hat{\Pi}^{(0)}_{2,2} = \frac{11}{9} \rightarrow \hat{\alpha}^{(0)}_3 = -\frac{11}{9}.$$

With algorithm 3a of fig. 7.2 we can produce a table as in fig 7.1. The result is given in figs. 18.1.

	$a^{(m)}_1$	$b^{(m)}_1$	$a^{(m)}_2$	$b^{(m)}_2$	$a^{(m)}_3$	$b^{(m)}_3$
$a^{(-2)}_n$	0					
$b^{(-2)}_n$		2/3				
$a^{(-1)}_n$	0		-7/6			
$b^{(-1)}_n$		-1/2		15/14		
$a^{(0)}_n$	0		5/2		36/14	
$b^{(0)}_n$		2		-2/5		-7/45
$a^{(1)}_n$	0		-1/2		2/5	
$b^{(1)}_n$		3/2		1/2		
$a^{(2)}_n$	0		-1/6			
$b^{(2)}_n$		4/3				

Figure 18.1a: ab table

With these numbers, the validity of the relations (7.10) can be checked for our example.

Algorithm 4 of fig. 7.7 computes a descending staircase. For our example, with $m = -1$, it gives the following results:

$$S_{-1} = S_0 = 1$$
$$u_{-1} = f_0 = 1$$
$$u_0 \equiv u^{(0)}_0 = 2$$
$$c_0 \equiv b^{(0)}_1 = 2$$

	$\rho_1^{(m)}$	$\sigma_1^{(m)}$	$\rho_2^{(m)}$	$\sigma_2^{(m)}$	$\rho_3^{(m)}$	$\sigma_3^{(m)}$
$\rho_n^{(-2)}, \sigma_n^{(-2)}$	0	2/3				
$\rho_n^{(-1)}, \sigma_n^{(-1)}$	0	-1/2	-5/4	-1/8		
$\rho_n^{(0)}, \sigma_n^{(0)}$	0	2	-1	21/10	-4/25	55/63
$\rho_n^{(1)}, \sigma_n^{(1)}$	0	3/2	-1/4	0		
$\rho_n^{(2)}, \sigma_n^{(2)}$	0	4/3				

Figure 18.1b: $\rho\sigma$ values

$$S_1(z) \equiv Q_1^{(0)}(z) = S_0(z) - 2zS_{-1}(z) = 1 - 2z$$

$$u_1 \equiv u_1^{(0)} = -1$$

$$c_1 \equiv a_1^{(1)} = -\frac{1}{2}$$

$$S_2(z) \equiv Q_1^{(1)}(z) = S_1(z) + \frac{1}{2}zS_0(z) = 1 - \frac{3}{2}z$$

$$u_2 \equiv u_1^{(1)} = -\frac{1}{2}$$

$$c_2 \equiv b_2^{(1)} = \frac{1}{2}$$

$$S_3(z) \equiv Q_2^{(1)}(z) = S_2(z) - \frac{1}{2}zS_1(z) = 1 - 2z + z^3$$

etc.

Algorithm 5 of fig. 7.8 produces similar results as you can see below.

$$S_{-1}(z) = 1 + 2z + 3z^2 + 4z^3 + \cdots$$

$$S_0(z) = 2z + 3z^2 + 4z^3 + \cdots$$

$$u_{-1} = f_0 = 1$$

$$u_0 \equiv u_0^{(0)} = 2$$

$$c_0 \equiv b_1^{(0)} = 2$$

$$S_1(z) \equiv R_1^{(0)}(z) = S_0(z) - 2zS_{-1}(z) = -z^2 - 2z^3 - 3z^4 - \cdots$$

$$u_1 \equiv u_1^{(0)} = -1$$

$$c_1 \equiv a_2^{(1)} = -\frac{1}{2}$$

$$S_2(z) \equiv R_1^{(1)}(z) = S_1(z) + \frac{1}{2}S_0(z) = -\frac{1}{2}z^3 - z^4 - \frac{3}{2}z^5 + \cdots$$

$$u_2 \equiv u_1^{(1)} = -\frac{1}{2}$$

$$c_2 \equiv b_2^{(1)} = \frac{1}{2}$$

$$S_3(z) \equiv R_2^{(1)}(z) = S_2(z) - \frac{1}{2}zS_1(z) = 0$$

etc.

The last result, viz. $R_2^{(1)}(z) = 0$ means that we hit here a singular block where the approximation $B_2^{(1)}(z)/Q_2^{(1)}(z)$ for $Z^{(0)}(z)$ is exact. Indeed:

$$Z^{(0)}(z) = \frac{1}{2} + 2z + 3z^2 + 4z^3 + \cdots = L_+(\frac{1 + 2z - z^2}{2(1 - 2z + z^2)})$$

The testing of algorithm 3b and related recursions is left as an exercise. We immediately switch to chapter 8 and check some of the biorthogonality relations (8.3). E.g.

$$<\hat{Q}_2^{(0)}(z), Q_1^{(0)*}(z)>^{(0)} = [\frac{7}{5} \ -\frac{4}{5} \ 1]\begin{vmatrix} 1 & 2 & 3 \\ -2 & 1 & 2 \\ -3 & -2 & 1 \end{vmatrix}\begin{vmatrix} -2 \\ 1 \\ 0 \end{vmatrix} = 0$$

$$<\hat{Q}_2^{(0)}(z), Q_2^{(0)*}(z)>^{(0)} = [\frac{7}{5} \ -\frac{4}{5} \ 1]\begin{vmatrix} 1 & 2 & 3 \\ -2 & 1 & 2 \\ -3 & -2 & 1 \end{vmatrix}\begin{vmatrix} 1/5 \\ -8/5 \\ 1 \end{vmatrix} = \frac{18}{5} = v_2^{(0)}$$

and for relation (8.4)

$$<z\hat{Q}_2^{(0)}(z), Q_2^{(0)}(z)>^{(0)} = [0 \ \frac{7}{5} \ -\frac{4}{5} \ 1]\begin{vmatrix} 1 & 2 & 3 & 4 \\ -2 & 1 & 2 & 3 \\ -3 & -2 & 1 & 2 \\ -4 & -3 & -2 & 1 \end{vmatrix}\begin{vmatrix} 1 \\ -8/5 \\ 1/5 \\ 0 \end{vmatrix}$$

$$= -\frac{22}{5} = \hat{u}_2^{(0)}$$

$$<Q_2^{(0)}(z), z\hat{Q}_2^{(0)}(z)>^{(0)} = [1 \ -\frac{8}{5} \ \frac{1}{5} \ 0]\begin{vmatrix} 1 & 2 & 3 & 4 \\ -2 & 1 & 2 & 3 \\ -3 & -2 & 1 & 2 \\ -4 & -3 & -2 & 1 \end{vmatrix}\begin{vmatrix} 0 \\ 7/5 \\ -4/5 \\ 1 \end{vmatrix}$$

$$= -\frac{2}{5} = u_2^{(0)}.$$

To check theorem 8.7 for $p = 1$, $P(z) = z^3 + 1$, $n = 1$ and $m = -1$, we have to compute the zeros of $\hat{Q}_2^{(-1)}(z) = \frac{1}{7} - \frac{10}{7}z + z^2$. They are $z_0 = (5 - 3\sqrt{2})/7$

and $z_1 = (5 + 3\sqrt{2})/7$. Thus

$$l_0(z) = \frac{7z - 5 - 3\sqrt{2}}{-6\sqrt{2}} \quad \text{and} \quad l_1(z) = \frac{7z - 5 + 3\sqrt{2}}{6\sqrt{2}}.$$

Furthermore

$$w_0 = \lambda^{(0)}(l_0) = \frac{13 - 9\sqrt{2}}{6\sqrt{2}} \quad \text{and} \quad w_1 = \lambda^{(0)}(l_1) = \frac{-13 - 9\sqrt{2}}{6\sqrt{2}},$$

$$\lambda^{(-1)}(z^{-1}P(z)) = \lambda^{(-1)}(z^2 + z^{-1}) = -3$$

which is exactly the same as $w_0 P(z_0) + w_1 P(z_1) = -3$.
We now give a similar computation for theorem 8.8. We take $\tau = -1$, $n = 1$, $m = -1$, $p = 1$ and $P(z) = z^2 + 1$.

$$\psi(z) = \hat{Q}_2^{(-1)}(z) + \tau Q_2^{(-1)}(z) = \frac{1}{7}(-6 - 6z + 2z^2).$$

Its zeros are $z_0 = \dfrac{3 - \sqrt{21}}{2}$ and $z_1 = \dfrac{3 + \sqrt{21}}{2}$. Therefore

$$l_0(z) = \frac{2z - 3 - \sqrt{21}}{-2\sqrt{21}} \quad \text{and} \quad l_1(z) = \frac{2z - 3 + \sqrt{21}}{2\sqrt{21}}$$

$$w_0 = \lambda^{(0)}(l_0) = \frac{7 + \sqrt{21}}{2\sqrt{21}}, \quad w_1 = \lambda^{(0)}(l_1) = \frac{-7 + \sqrt{21}}{2\sqrt{21}}$$

$$w_0 P(z_0) + w_1 P(z_1) = -2 = \lambda^{(-1)}(z^{-1}P(z)) = \lambda^{(-1)}(z + z^{-1})$$

which was predicted by theorem 8.8.

The reproducing kernel $k_1^{(0)}(x,y)$ of (8.8) equals

$$k_1^{(0)}(x,y) = \frac{1}{5}(1 - 2y + 2\bar{x} + \bar{x}y).$$

For which the Christoffel-Darboux relations of theorem 8.10 can be verified. As predicted by corollary 8.11, we have

$$k_1^{(0)}(0,y) = \frac{1}{5}(1 - 2y) = Q_1^{(0)}(y)/v_1^{(0)}$$

$$k_1^{(0)}(x,0) = \frac{1}{5}(1 + 2\bar{x}) = \hat{Q}_1^{(0)*}(x)/v_1^{(0)}$$

$$k_1^{(0)}(0,0) = 1/5 = 1/v_1^{(0)}.$$

Checking the other orthogonality relations of section 8.4 is left as an exercise.

The determinant expressions (9.9) are verified as follows.

$$Q_2^{(0)}(z) = \det \begin{vmatrix} 1 & z & z^2 \\ 2 & 1 & -2 \\ -3 & 2 & 1 \end{vmatrix} /5 = 1 - \frac{8}{5}z + \frac{1}{5}z^2$$

$$\hat{Q}_2^{(0)}(z) = \det \begin{vmatrix} 1 & -2 & -3 \\ 2 & 1 & -2 \\ 1 & z & z^2 \end{vmatrix} /5 = \frac{7}{5} - \frac{4}{5}z + z^2$$

$$z^2 Q_2^{(0)}(z) = Q_2^{(0)\times}(z) = \det \begin{vmatrix} -2 & 1 & 2 \\ 1 & 2 & 3 \\ 1 & z & z^2 \end{vmatrix} /(-5) = \frac{1}{5} - \frac{8}{5} + z^2$$

$$\hat{Q}_2^{(0)}(z) = \det \begin{vmatrix} 1 & z & z^2 \\ 2 & 1 & -2 \\ 1 & -2 & -3 \end{vmatrix} /(-5) = \frac{7}{5} - \frac{4}{5}z + z^2$$

and (9.10) gives

$$Q_2^{(0)}(z) = \det \begin{vmatrix} 1 - z\sigma_2^{(0)} & -z\rho_2^{(-1)} \\ -1 & 1 - z\sigma_1^{(-1)} \end{vmatrix} = \det \begin{vmatrix} 1 - \frac{21}{10}z & \frac{5}{4}z \\ -z & 1 + \frac{1}{2}z \end{vmatrix}$$

$$= 1 - \frac{8}{5}z + \frac{1}{5}z^2$$

and

$$\hat{Q}_2^{(0)}(z) = \det \begin{vmatrix} z - \hat{\sigma}_2^{(0)} & -\hat{\rho}_2^{(1)} \\ -1 & z - \hat{\sigma}_1^{(-1)} \end{vmatrix} = \det \begin{vmatrix} z - \frac{3}{10} & \frac{5}{4} \\ -1 & z - \frac{1}{2} \end{vmatrix}$$

$$= \frac{7}{5} - \frac{4}{5}z + z^2 .$$

The factorization of a Toeplitz matrix (9.19) and its inverse (9.22–23) are checked for $m = 0$ and $n = 2$ to give (unmentioned elements are zero)

$$\begin{vmatrix} 1 & & \\ -2 & 1 & \\ 1/5 & -8/5 & 1 \end{vmatrix} \begin{vmatrix} 1 & -2 & -3 \\ 2 & 1 & -2 \\ 3 & 2 & 1 \end{vmatrix} \begin{vmatrix} 1 & 2 & 7/5 \\ & 1 & -4/5 \\ & & 1 \end{vmatrix} = \begin{vmatrix} 1 & & \\ & 5 & \\ & & 18/5 \end{vmatrix}$$

and

$$\begin{vmatrix} 1 & -2 & -3 \\ 2 & 1 & -2 \\ 3 & 2 & 1 \end{vmatrix}^{-1} = \begin{vmatrix} 5/18 & -2/9 & 7/18 \\ -4/9 & 5/9 & -2/9 \\ 1/18 & -4/9 & 5/18 \end{vmatrix}$$

$$= \begin{bmatrix} 1 & 2 & 7/5 \\ & 1 & -4/5 \\ & & 1 \end{bmatrix} \begin{bmatrix} 1 & & \\ & 1/5 & \\ & & 5/18 \end{bmatrix} \begin{bmatrix} 1 & & \\ -2 & 1 & \\ 1/5 & -8/5 & 1 \end{bmatrix}$$

$$= \begin{bmatrix} 1 & & \\ -8/5 & 1 & \\ 1/5 & -2 & 1 \end{bmatrix} \begin{bmatrix} 5/18 & & \\ & 1/5 & \\ & & 1 \end{bmatrix} \begin{bmatrix} 1 & -4/5 & 7/5 \\ & 1 & 2 \\ & & 1 \end{bmatrix}$$

while corollary 9.9 gives

$$\hat{R}_2^{(0)}[D_2^{(0)}]^{-1} = \begin{vmatrix} 1 & & \\ 2 & 5 & \\ 3 & 8 & 18/5 \end{vmatrix} \begin{vmatrix} 1 & & \\ & 1/5 & \\ & & 5/18 \end{vmatrix} = \begin{vmatrix} 1 & & \\ 2 & 1 & \\ 3 & 8/5 & 1 \end{vmatrix}$$

$$= \begin{vmatrix} 1 & & \\ -2 & 1 & \\ 1/5 & -8/5 & 1 \end{vmatrix}^{-1} = [Q_2^{(0)}]^{-T}$$

and

$$[D_2^{(0)}]^{-1}[P_2^{(0)}]^T = \begin{vmatrix} 1 & & \\ & 1/5 & \\ & & 5/18 \end{vmatrix} \begin{vmatrix} 1 & -2 & -3 \\ & 5 & 4 \\ & & 18/5 \end{vmatrix} = \begin{vmatrix} 1 & -2 & -3 \\ & 1 & 4/5 \\ & & 1 \end{vmatrix}$$

$$= \begin{vmatrix} 1 & 2 & 7/5 \\ & 1 & -4/5 \\ & & 1 \end{vmatrix}^{-1} = [\hat{Q}_2^{(0)}]^{-1}$$

and the corresponding factorization (9.24) is

$$\begin{vmatrix} 1 & -2 & -3 \\ 2 & 1 & -2 \\ 3 & 2 & 1 \end{vmatrix} = \begin{vmatrix} 1 & & \\ 2 & 1 & \\ 3 & 8/5 & 1 \end{vmatrix} \begin{vmatrix} 1 & & \\ & 5 & \\ & & 18/5 \end{vmatrix} \begin{vmatrix} 1 & -2 & -3 \\ & 1 & 4/5 \\ & & 1 \end{vmatrix}.$$

The factorizations for Hankel matrices are left to the reader.

We shall give an example of how the inversion formulas (9.40) work for the inversion of $T_1^{(0)} = \begin{bmatrix} 1 & 2 \\ -2 & 1 \end{bmatrix}$. Since this matrix depends only on $f_0 = 1$, $f_{-1} = -2$ and $f_1 = 2$, any other coefficient appearing in the inversion formulas must be a parameter. Its result must be independent of it. To illustrate this, we set $f_2 = b$ and $f_{-2} = a$. We obtain for these data the following results. The matrices of (9.39) are given by

$$X_1^{(0)} = \begin{bmatrix} 1 & \\ -2 & 1 \end{bmatrix}, \ Y_1^{(0)} = \begin{bmatrix} 1 & \\ 2 & 1 \end{bmatrix}, \ \hat{X}_1^{(0)} = \begin{bmatrix} 0 & \\ -2 & 0 \end{bmatrix}, \ \hat{Y}_1^{(0)} = \begin{bmatrix} 0 & \\ 2 & 2 \end{bmatrix},$$

$$\mathbf{V}_1^{(0)} = \begin{vmatrix} 1 & \\ -\frac{2}{5}(b+1) & 1 \end{vmatrix}, \quad \mathbf{W}_1^{(0)} = \begin{vmatrix} 1 & \\ \frac{2}{5}(a+1) & 1 \end{vmatrix},$$

$$\hat{\mathbf{V}}_1^{(0)} = \begin{vmatrix} -\frac{1}{5}(b-4) & \\ -\frac{2}{5}(b+1) & -\frac{1}{5}(b-4) \end{vmatrix}, \quad \hat{\mathbf{W}}_1^{(0)} = \begin{vmatrix} -\frac{1}{5}(a-4) & \\ \frac{2}{5}(a+1) & -\frac{1}{5}(a-4) \end{vmatrix}$$

$$v_1^{(0)} = 5 \ , \quad v_2^{(0)} = (9 + 4a + 4b - ab)/25$$

which gives by (9.40a)

$$\begin{vmatrix} 1 & -2 \\ 2 & 1 \end{vmatrix}^{-1} = (v_1^{(0)})^{-1}\{(\mathbf{X}_1^{(0)})(\mathbf{Y}_1^{(0)})^T - (\hat{\mathbf{Y}}_1^{(0)})(\hat{\mathbf{X}}_1^{(0)})^T\} =$$

$$= \frac{1}{5} \ \{\begin{vmatrix} 1 & 2 \\ -2 & -3 \end{vmatrix} - \begin{vmatrix} 0 & 0 \\ 0 & -4 \end{vmatrix}\} = \frac{1}{5}\begin{vmatrix} 1 & 2 \\ -2 & 1 \end{vmatrix}$$

$$= (v_2^{(0)})^{-1}\{(\mathbf{V}_1^{(0)})(\mathbf{W}_1^{(0)})^T - (\hat{\mathbf{W}}_1^{(0)})(\hat{\mathbf{V}}_1^{(0)})^T\}$$

$$= \frac{25}{9+4a+4b-ab} \ \{\frac{1}{25}\begin{vmatrix} 25 & 10(a+1) \\ -10(b+1) & 21-4a-4b-4ab \end{vmatrix}$$

$$- \frac{1}{25}\begin{vmatrix} (4-a)(4-b) & -2(4-a)(b+1) \\ 2(a+1)(4-b) & 12-8a-8b-3ab \end{vmatrix}\} \ .$$

The matrices for formulas (9.52a,b) are

$$\mathbf{X}_1^{(-2)} = \begin{vmatrix} \frac{1}{2} & \\ 1 & \frac{1}{2} \end{vmatrix}, \quad \mathbf{Y}_1^{(-2)} = \begin{vmatrix} -\frac{2}{5}(b+1) & 1 \\ & 1 \end{vmatrix}$$

$$\mathbf{W}_1^{(-2)} = \begin{vmatrix} 1 & 0 \\ 0 & \end{vmatrix}, \quad \mathbf{V}_1^{(-2)} = \begin{vmatrix} -\frac{1}{5}(b-4) & \\ -\frac{2}{5}(b+1) & -(b-4)/5 \end{vmatrix}$$

$$u_1^{(-1)} = \frac{5}{2}$$

giving

$$\begin{vmatrix} 1 & -2 \\ 2 & 1 \end{vmatrix}^{-1} = (u_1^{(-1)})^{-1}\{(K_1 X_1^{(-2)})(Y_1^{(-2)}) - (K_1 V_1^{(-2)})(W_1^{(-2)})\}$$

$$= \frac{2}{5}\left\{ \begin{vmatrix} -\dfrac{1}{10}(4b-1) & 1 \\ -\dfrac{1}{5}(b+1) & \dfrac{1}{2} \end{vmatrix} - \begin{vmatrix} -\dfrac{2}{5}(b+1) & 0 \\ -\dfrac{1}{5}(b-4) & 0 \end{vmatrix} \right\} = \frac{2}{5}\begin{vmatrix} \dfrac{1}{2} & 1 \\ -1 & \dfrac{1}{2} \end{vmatrix}.$$

For (9.52c) and (9.52d) the result is similar.

The block structure of this example is very simple as we said in the beginning. It can be verified that

$$Z^{(0)}(z) = L_+\left(\frac{1 + 2z - z^2}{2(1 - z)^2}\right)$$

and it converges for $|z| < 1$. On the other hand,

$$\hat{Z}^{(0)}(z) = L_-\left(\frac{-1 + 6z^{-1} - 3z^{-2}}{2(1 - z^{-1})^2}\right)$$

and it converges for $|z| > 1$.

The sum $Z^{(0)}(z) - \hat{Z}^{(0)}(z)$ is not the Laurent series of a rational function since the convergence regions of $Z^{(0)}(z)$ and $\hat{Z}^{(0)}(z)$ do not overlap. The T-table gives nonzero determinants except for the two blocks $\{(m,n): m \geqslant 2, n \geqslant 2\}$ and $\{(m,n): m \leqslant -3, n \geqslant 2\}$ where they are zero. We shall give a more complicated block structure for another example in the next subsection.

18.2 Example 2

For our second example we consider the Laurent series $F(z) = Z^{(0)}(z) - \hat{Z}^{(0)}(z)$ with

$$Z^{(0)}(z) = \frac{1}{2}z^2 + \frac{1}{4}z^3 + \frac{1}{8}z^4 + \frac{5}{16}z^5 + \frac{9}{32}z^6 + \cdots = L_+\left(\frac{z^2/2}{1 - z/2 - z^3/2}\right),$$

which converges for $|z| < 1$ and

$$\hat{Z}^{(0)}(z) = -z^{-1} + \frac{1}{2}z^{-3} - \frac{1}{4}z^{-5} - \cdots = L_-\left(\frac{-z^{-1}}{1 + \frac{1}{2}z^{-2}}\right),$$

which converges for $|z| > \sqrt{2}/2$, so that $F(z)$ is the Laurent series of $F(z)$ in the annulus $\{z: \sqrt{2}/2 < |z| < 1\}$.

It can be verified that its T-table has the structure of fig. 18.2 where a cross means a nonzero entry. The infinite blocks are predicted by theorem 12.4 since $F(z) =$

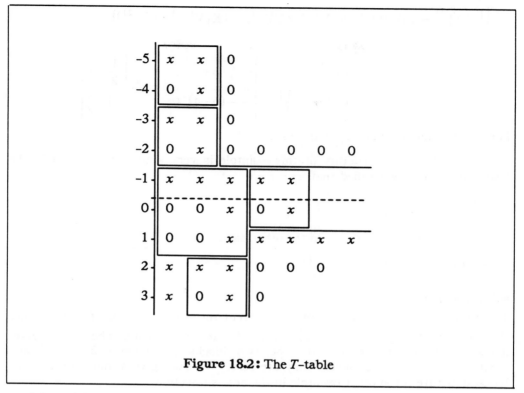

Figure 18.2: The T-table

$F_+(z) F_-(z) z^\kappa$ with

$$F_+(z) = \frac{1 - \frac{1}{4}z}{1 - \frac{1}{2}z - \frac{1}{2}z^3} \quad , \quad Z^+ = 1 \ , \quad P^+ = 3$$

$$F_-(z) = \frac{1}{1 + \frac{1}{2}z^{-2}} \quad , \quad Z^- = -1 \ , \quad P^- = 1$$

$\kappa = -1$

$G_\rho(\tilde{F}) = 1$

The poles of $F_+(z)$ are $\pi_1 = 1$, $\pi_2 = (-1+\sqrt{-7})/2$ and $\pi_3 = (-1-\sqrt{-7})/2$. It has only one finite pole : $\zeta_1 = 4$. The poles of $F_-(z)$ are $\pi_0 = 1/\sqrt{-2}$ and $\pi_{-1} = -1/\sqrt{-2}$. There are no zeros different from 0. As explained in fig 11.3 we can derive from fig 18.2 the blocks $\mathbb{D}_n^{(m)}$ for the LPF table containing $K_n^{(m)}(z)$ for $m,n \geqslant 0$. It is like in fig 18.3 where a cross now means an entry that is not only an LPF but also an LPA. The validity of this can be verified by computing these

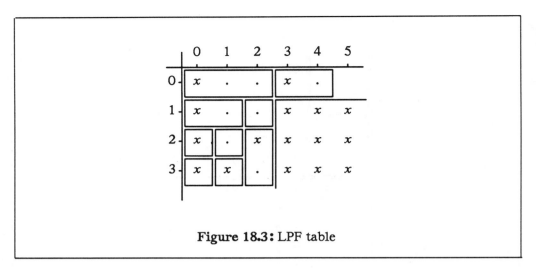

Figure 18.3: LPF table

LPFs. They are given by

$$K_0^{(0)} = K_1^{(0)} = K_2^{(0)} = (0,0),$$

$$K_0^{(1)} = K_1^{(1)} = (0, z^{-1}) \ , \ K_2^{(1)} = (0 \ , \ \frac{z^{-1}}{1 + \frac{1}{2}z^{-2}}),$$

$$K_0^{(2)} = (\frac{1}{2}z^2, \ z^{-1}) \ , \ K_1^{(2)} = (\frac{\frac{1}{2}z^2}{1 - \frac{1}{2}z} \ , \ \frac{z^{-2}}{z^{-1}}),$$

$$K_2^{(2)} = K_2^{(3)} = (\frac{\frac{1}{2}z^2}{1 - \frac{1}{2}z} \ , \ \frac{z^{-1}}{1 + \frac{1}{2}z^{-2}}),$$

$$K_0^{(3)} = (\frac{1}{2}z^2 + \frac{1}{4}z^3 \ , \ z^{-1} - \frac{1}{2}z^{-3}) \ ,$$

$$K_3^{(0)} = K_4^{(0)} = (\frac{\frac{1}{2}z^2}{1 - \frac{1}{2}z - \frac{1}{2}z^3} \ , \ \frac{z^{-1}}{1 + \frac{1}{2}z^{-2} - 2z^{-3}}),$$

$$K_1^{(3)} = (\frac{\frac{1}{2}z^2}{1 - \frac{1}{2}z} \ , \ z^{-1} - \frac{1}{2}z^{-3})$$

and

$$K_n^{(m)} = (\frac{\frac{1}{2}z^2}{1 - \frac{1}{2}z - \frac{1}{2}z^3}, \frac{z^{-1}}{1 + \frac{1}{2}z^{-2}}) \text{ for } m \geq 1 \text{ and } n \geq 3.$$

Now we shall look at the limit of

$$b_1^{(k)} = \frac{T_0^{(k+1)}T_{-1}^{(k-1)}}{T_0^{(k)}T_{-1}^{(k)}} = \frac{T_0^{(k+1)}}{T_0^{(k)}} = \alpha_1^{(k)} = \frac{1}{\hat{\alpha}_1^{(k+1)}} = \sigma_1^{(k)} = -G_1^{(k+1)}$$

and

$$\hat{b}_1^{(k)} = \frac{T_0^{(k-1)}T_{-1}^{(k+1)}}{T_0^{(k)}T_{-1}^{(k)}} = \frac{T_0^{(k-1)}}{T_0^{(k)}} = \hat{\alpha}_1^{(k)} = \frac{1}{\alpha_1^{(k-1)}} = \hat{\sigma}_1^{(k)} = -\hat{G}_1^{(k-1)}$$

as k goes to ∞. thus we have to find $\lim_{k \to \infty} f_{k+1}/f_k$ because $b_1^{(k)} = f_{k+1}/f_k$.
The coefficients f_k for $k \geq 0$ are rational numbers of the form

$$f_k = \frac{n_k}{d_k}$$

where $d_k = 2^{k-1}$ and n_k satisfies the difference equation $n_{k+3} = n_{k+2} + 4n_k$ for $k \geq 3$ with $n_0 = n_1 = 0$ and $n_2 = 1$. The solution of this difference equation for the numerator has basic solutions 2^k, $2^{k/2} \cos k\theta$ and $2^{k/2} \sin k\theta$ where $\mathrm{tg}\,\theta = \sqrt{7}$ Thus there exist some numbers a, b, c such that

$$f_k = a + b(\frac{\sqrt{2}}{2})^k \cos k\theta + c(\frac{\sqrt{2}}{2})^k \sin k\theta \quad , \mathrm{tg}\,\theta = \sqrt{7}, \quad k \geq 3.$$

Hence it follows that

$$\lim_{k \to \infty} \frac{f_{k+1}}{f_k} = 1$$

since $2^{-k/2} \cos k\theta$ and $2^{-k/2} \sin k\theta$ converge to zero as $n \to \infty$. Now the pole of $F(z)$ which is at the outer boundary of the annulus of convergence is $\pi_1 = 1$ and its modulus is isolated from the moduli of the other poles. Thus, since $b_1^{(k)}$, $\alpha_1^{(k)}$, $1/\hat{\alpha}_1^{(k)}$, $\sigma_1^{(k)}$ and $-G_1^{(k+1)}$ all converge to $1 = 1/\pi_1$, the convergence results (14.19a) of corollary 14.4 are confirmed. Similarly, the convergence of $\hat{b}_1^{(k)}$, $\hat{\alpha}_1^{(k)}$, $\hat{\sigma}_1^{(k)}$ and $-\hat{G}_1^{(k-1)}$ to $1 = \pi_1$ verifies (14.19b) of the same corollary. To check the results (14.11) for $n = 1$ and $h = 2$ in our example, we have to compute the Rutishauser polynomials $Q_{1,3}^{(m)}(z)$. The computation of these polynomials with their recurrence relation would take some time. It is much easier to observe that $Q_{0,1}^{(m)}(z) = 1 - b_1^{(m)}z$ by definition and that for $m \geq 1$ we must have $Q_{0,3}^{(m)}(z) = 1 - \frac{1}{2}z - \frac{1}{2}z^3$, the exact denominator. If we set $Q_{1,3}^{(m)}(z) = q_0 + q_1 z + q_2 z^2$, then it follows from lemma 14.1 that

$$Q_{0,3}^{(m)}(z) = q_0\, Q_{0,1}^{(m)}(z) + q_1\, z Q_{0,1}^{(m-1)}(z) + q_2\, z^2 Q_{0,1}^{(m-2)}(z).$$

From this we get $q_0 = 1$, $q_1 = -\dfrac{1}{2} + b_1^{(m)}$ and $q_2 = (2b_1^{(m-2)})^{-1}$. Because we know the limit of $b_1^{(k)}$ it follows that $Q_{1,3}^{(m)}(z)$ converges to

$$Q_{1,3}(z) = 1 + \frac{1}{2}z + \frac{1}{2}z^2$$

which gives the other two poles $\pi_{1,2} = \dfrac{1 \pm \sqrt{-7}}{2}$. This is the content of theorem 14.3 for the polynomials defined in (14.13a). For the other polynomials in theorem 14.3, this result can also be verified in a similar way.

For the upward limit, the situation is rather simple. $\hat{Q}_{0,2}^{(-m)}(z) = z^2 + \dfrac{1}{2}$ for all $m \geqslant 2$. Thus it equals its limit for $m \to \infty$, which is the polynomial $\hat{Q}_{0,2}(z)$ with two zeros of equal modulus $\pi_0 = -\pi_{-1} = 1/\sqrt{-2}$. To pick a simple example for the illustration of corollary 14.4(3), we should have by (14.21c) that $\alpha_2^{(-m)} = -T_1^{(-m+1)}/T_1^{(-m)}$ converges to $-\pi_0\pi_{-1} = -1/2$. Now, $f_{-(2k+1)} = (-1)^{k+1}2^{-k}$ and $f_{-2k} = 0$, so that $T_1^{(-m)} = 2^{-m+1}$ and thus $\alpha_2^{(-m)} = -1/2$.

For the horizontal limits, consider $m = 0$. By (15.17a), we should have e.g. that $\lim a_n^{(0)} = 1/\zeta_1 = 1/4$. As it was shown in chapter 7 or, as we can derive from the determinant expressions in chapter 9, we know that $a_{n+1}^{(0)} = u_n^{(-1)}/u_{n-1}^{(-1)}$. Computation of the $u_n^{(-1)}$, e.g. by algorithm 2 in fig. 3.2, gives for these numbers

$$v_0^{(-1)} = 1\,,\ u_0^{(-1)} = 0\,,\ \alpha_1^{(-1)} = \hat{\alpha}_1^{(-1)} = 0,$$

$$v_1^{(-1)} = 1\,,\ u_1^{(-1)} = 0\,,\ \hat{u}_1^{(-1)} = -1/2\,,\ \alpha_2^{(-1)} = 0\,,\ \hat{\alpha}_2^{(-1)} = -1/2,$$

and from then on

$$v_k^{(-1)} = 1\,,\ u_k^{(-1)} = \alpha_{k+1}^{(-1)} = 2^{-2k+3}\,,\ \hat{u}_k^{(-1)} = \hat{\alpha}_{k+1}^{(-1)} = 0\,,\ k \geqslant 2,$$

so that we have indeed that $a_{n+1}^{(0)} = 1/4$ for $n \geqslant 3$.

With the $\alpha_k^{(-1)}$ and $\hat{\alpha}_k^{(-1)}$ that we just found, we can apply recursion (3.6) with $S = Q$ to find

$$[Q_0^{(-1)}\ \ \hat{Q}_0^{(-1)}] = [1\ \ 1],$$

$$[Q_1^{(-1)}(z)\ \ \hat{Q}_1^{(-1)}(z)] = [1\ \ z],$$

$$[Q_2^{(-1)}(z)\ \ \hat{Q}_2^{(-1)}(z)] = [1\ \ \tfrac{1}{2}+z^2],$$

and from there on

$$\hat{Q}_n^{(-1)}(z) = z^{n-2}(\frac{1}{2} + z^2)$$

while

$$Q_3^{(-1)}(z) = 1 - \frac{1}{4}z - \frac{1}{2}z^2,$$

$$Q_4^{(-1)}(z) = 1 - \frac{1}{4}z - \frac{1}{16}z^2 - \frac{1}{2}z^3 - \frac{1}{8}z^4,$$

$$Q_5^{(-1)}(z) = 1 - \frac{1}{4}z - \frac{1}{16}z^2 - \frac{33}{64}z^3 - \frac{1}{8}z^4 - \frac{1}{32}z^5,$$

$$Q_6^{(-1)}(z) = 1 - \frac{1}{4}z - \frac{1}{16}z^2 - \frac{33}{64}z^3 - \frac{33}{256}z^4 - \frac{1}{32}z^5 - \frac{1}{128}z^6$$

etc., which shows clearly that

$$z^{-n}\hat{Q}_n^{(-1)}(z) = (F_-(z))^{-1} = 1 + \frac{1}{2}z^{-2} \quad \text{for } n \geqslant 2$$

and $Q_n^{(-1)}(z)$ converges to

$$(F_+(z))^{-1} = 1 - \frac{1}{4}z - \frac{1}{16}z^2 - \frac{33}{64}z^3 - \frac{33}{256}z^4 - \frac{33}{1024}z^5 - \cdots .$$

This confirms the result of theorem 16.5 since $\kappa = -1$ in our example.

Similarly, by (16.12) we should have that

$$\lim_{n\to\infty} Q_n^{(0)}(z) = \frac{(1 - \frac{1}{4}z)}{F_+(z)} = 1 - \frac{1}{2}z - \frac{1}{2}z^3.$$

(We took care of the shift over $\kappa = -1$.) Now, it can be verified that

$$Q_n^{(0)}(z) = 1 - \frac{1}{2}z - \frac{1}{2}z^3 \quad , \quad \forall n \geqslant 3.$$

This shows that (16.12) works for our example.

18.3 Example 3

We give one last example to illustrate how equimodular zeros can be found.
We take

$$F(z) = 1 + \frac{2}{5}(z^2 + z^{-2}).$$

This is an example of a function which is positive on the unit circle. It can be factorized as

$$F(z) = \frac{4}{5} F_+(z) F_-(z)$$

with

$$F_+(z) = 1 + \frac{1}{2}z^2 \quad \text{and} \quad F_-(z) = F_{+*}(z) = 1 + \frac{1}{2}z^{-2}.$$

The zeros of $F_+(z)$ are $\zeta_1 = \sqrt{-2}$ and $\zeta_2 = -\sqrt{-2}$. For the T-table we can derive the following structure :

$$T_n^{(-m)} = T_n^{(m)},$$

$$T_n^{(m)} = 0 \quad \text{for} \quad m \geqslant 3,$$

$$T_n^{(2)} = (2/5)^{n+1} \quad \text{and} \quad T_n^{(0)} \neq 0 \quad \forall n \in \mathbb{N},$$

$$T_{2n}^{(1)} = 0, \quad \text{and} \quad T_{2n+1}^{(1)} \neq 0 \quad \forall n \in \mathbb{N}.$$

From the expressions (9.3d) we find that then

$$\alpha_{2n+1}^{(0)} = T_{2n}^{(1)}/T_{2n}^{(0)} = 0 = \hat{\alpha}_{2n+1}^{(0)} = 1/\hat{\alpha}_{2n+1}^{(1)}$$

and

$$\alpha_{2n+1}^{(1)} = T_{2n}^{(2)}/T_{2n}^{(1)} = \infty.$$

Furthermore, we get from Jacobi's identity (9.4) that

$$T_{2n-1}^{(2)} \, T_{2n-1}^{(0)} = T_{2n-1}^{(1)} \, T_{2n-1}^{(1)}$$

so that

$$\alpha_{2n}^{(1)} = -T_{2n-1}^{(2)}/T_{2n-1}^{(1)} = -T_{2n-1}^{(1)}/T_{2n-1}^{(0)} = \alpha_{2n}^{(0)} = \hat{\alpha}_{2n}^{(0)} = 1/\hat{\alpha}_{2n}^{(1)}.$$

Szegö's classical limit theorem, which applies to our example states that

$$\lim_{n \to \infty} T_{n+1}^{(0)}/T_n^{(0)} = G_1(F) = 4/5.$$

Because $|\zeta_0| = |1/\sqrt{-2}| < \rho = 1 < |\zeta_1| = |\sqrt{-2}|$, corollary 15.5 states that in that case $\alpha_n^{(0)} \hat{\alpha}_n^{(0)} \to 0$. To prove this for our example, note that $\alpha_{2n+1}^{(0)} \hat{\alpha}_{2n+1}^{(0)} = 0$ because both factors are zero. Now, it can be shown with some algebra that

$$\alpha_{2n}^{(0)} \hat{\alpha}_{2n}^{(0)} = \frac{T_{2n-1}^{(2)}}{T_{2n-1}^{(0)}} = 1 - \frac{T_{2n+1}^{(0)}/T_{2n}^{(0)}}{T_{2n-1}^{(0)}/T_{2n-2}^{(0)}}.$$

Since the numerator and the denominator in the right hand side both converge to the same limit, the right hand side will converge to zero. Because $|\zeta_1| = |\zeta_2| = 4\sqrt{2}$, $\alpha_n^{(1)} \hat{\alpha}_n^{(1)}$ need not converge, and you can indeed verify that

$$\alpha_{2n}^{(1)}\hat{\alpha}_{2n}^{(1)} = 1$$

and

$$\alpha_{2n+1}^{(1)}\hat{\alpha}_{2n+1}^{(1)} = \infty.$$

But (15.18c) of corollary 15.5 states that

$$\lim_{n\to\infty}(\hat{a}_n^{(0)} + \hat{a}_n^{(1)}) = \zeta_1 + \zeta_2 = 0$$

and

$$\lim_{n\to\infty}\hat{a}_{n+1}^{(0)}\hat{a}_n^{(1)} = \zeta_1\zeta_2 = 2.$$

It should be emphasized that the sum and the product of the $\hat{a}$ parameters converge as indicated above, but the $\hat{a}$ parameters themselves don't converge. E.g.

$$\hat{a}_{n+1}^{(0)} = -\frac{T_{n-2}^{(1)}T_n^{(0)}}{T_{n-1}^{(1)}T_{n-1}^{(0)}} \quad\text{and}\quad \hat{a}_{n+1}^{(1)} = -\frac{T_{n-2}^{(2)}T_n^{(1)}}{T_{n-1}^{(2)}T_{n-1}^{(1)}}$$

are alternatingly zero and infinite. However

$$\hat{a}_{n+1}^{(0)}\hat{a}_{n+2}^{(1)} = \frac{T_{n-2}^{(2)}T_{n+1}^{(0)}}{T_{n-1}^{(2)}T_n^{(0)}} \underset{n\to\infty}{=} \frac{5}{2}\frac{4}{5} = 2.$$

The expression for the sum $\hat{a}_n^{(0)} + \hat{a}_n^{(1)}$, which is

$$\hat{a}_{n+1}^{(0)} + \hat{a}_{n+1}^{(1)} = -\frac{T_{n-2}^{(1)}T_n^{(0)}T_{n-1}^{(2)} + T_{n-2}^{(2)}T_n^{(1)}T_{n-1}^{(0)}}{T_{n-1}^{(0)}T_{n-1}^{(1)}T_{n-1}^{(2)}}$$

is zero for n even, since the numerator is zero while the denominator is not zero. For n odd, the result is zero over zero. However, in this case we can rework this expression, using Jacobi's identity, to find that

$$\hat{a}_{2n}^{(0)} + \hat{a}_{2n}^{(1)} = -\frac{N}{T_{2n-1}^{(0)}T_{2n-1}^{(0)}T_{2n-2}^{(2)}}.$$

with

$$N = T_{2n-1}^{(0)}T_{2n-3}^{(1)}T_{2n-2}^{(1)} + T_{2n-1}^{(1)}T_{2n-3}^{(2)}T_{2n-2}^{(1)} - T_{2n-4}^{(1)}T_{2n-1}^{(0)}t_{2n-1}^{(1)}$$

Now, the numerator N is zero because $T_{2n-2}^{(1)} = T_{2n-1}^{(1)} = 0$, while the denominator is not zero. Thus $\hat{a}_{2n}^{(1)} + \hat{a}_{2n}^{(1)}$ converges to zero as stated. The dual Rutishauser polynomial $\hat{P}_n^{(0,2)}(z)$ as defined by (15.11a) is

$$\hat{P}_n^{(0,2)}(z) = z^2 - z(\hat{a}_{n+1}^{(0)} + \hat{a}_{n+1}^{(1)}) + \hat{a}_{n+1}^{(1)}\hat{a}_{n+2}^{(0)}$$

and we have shown that for our example it converges to $z^2 + 2$ and of course, its zeros are $\zeta_{1,2} = \pm\sqrt{-2}$, as stated in theorem 15.4.

For other numerical examples see also [BU2] and for the positive definite case see [BU3] and [BU4].

REFERENCES

[AKH] N.I.AKHIEZER : *The classical moment problem*, Oliver and Boyd, Edinburgh, 1965.

[ARO] N.ARONSZAJN : Theory of reproducing kernels, Trans. Amer. Math. Soc., **68** , 1950, 337–404.

[BGM] G.A.BAKER JR., P.GRAVES-MORRIS : *Padé approximants*, Addison-Wesley Publ. Comp., Reading, Massachusetts, 1981.

[BOG] J. BOGNAR : *Indefinite inner product spaces* Springer verlag, Berlin, 1874.

[BOT1] A.BÖTTCHER, B.SILVERMANN : The asymptotic behavior of Toeplitz determinants for generating functions with zeros of integral orders, Math. Nachr., **102** , 1981,79–105.

[BOT2] A.BÖTTCHER, B.SILVERMANN : *Invertibility and asymptotics of Toeplitz matrices*, Akademie Verlag, Berlin, 1983.

[BGY] R.P.BRENT, F.G.GUSTAVSON, D.Y.Y.YUN : Fast solution of Toeplitz systems of equations and computation of Padé approximants, Journal of Algorithms, **1** , 1980, 259–295.

[BRE] C.BREZINSKI : *Padé type approximations and general orthogonal polynomials*, Birkhäuser Verlag, Basel, 1980.

[BU1] A.BULTHEEL : The asymptotic behavior of Toeplitz determinants generated by the Laurent series of a meromorphic function, SIAM J. Algebraic and Discrete Math., **6** (4), 1985, 624–629.

[BU2] A.BULTHEEL : Zeros of a rational function defined by its Laurent series. in *Padé approximation and its applications, Bad Honnef 1983* , H.Werner, H.J. Bünger (eds.), Lect. Notes Math. 1071, Springer Verlag, Berlin, 1984, 34–48.

[BU3] A.BULTHEEL : Algorithms to compute the reflection coefficients of digital filters. in *Numerische Methoden der Approximationstheorie* 7 L. Collatz, G. Meinardus, H. Werner (eds.), ISNM 67, Birkhäuser Verlag, 1984, 33–50.

[BU4]   A.BULTHEEL : Quotient-difference relations in connection with AR filtering. in *Proc. ECCTD'83*, Stuttgart, VDE Verlag, Berlin, 1983, 395-399.

[BU5]   A.BULTHEEL : Recursive relations for block Hankel and Toeplitz systems.
         Part I : Direct recursions. Journ. Comp. Appl. Math., **10** , 1984, 301-328.
         Part II : Dual recursions. Journ. Comp. Appl. Math., **10** , 1984, 329-328.

[BU6]   A.BULTHEEL : Division algorithms for continued fractions and the Padé table. Journ. Comp. Appl. Math., **6** (4), 1980, 259-266.

[BU7]   A.BULTHEEL : Recursive algorithms for the matrix Padé problem. Math. of Comp., **35** (151), 1980, 875-892.

[BU8]   A.BULTHEEL, M. VAN BAREL : Padé techniques for model reduction in linear system theory: A survey., J. Comp. Appl. Math., **14** , 1985, 401-438.

[BU9]   A.BULTHEEL : Triangular decomposition of Toeplitz and related matrices: a guided tour in the algorithmic aspects. Tijdschrift Belgisch Wiskundig Genootschap, Series A, **36** (3), 1986.

[BU10]   A.BULTHEEL : Error analysis of incoming and outgoing schemes for the trigonometric momemt problem. in *Pade' approximation and its applications, Amsterdam 1980*, M.G.de Bruin, H. van Rossum (eds.), Lecture Notes in Math. 888, Springer Verlag, Berlin, 1981, 100-109.

[CYB]   G.CYBENKO : The numerical stability of the Levinson-Durbin algorithm for Toeplitz systems of equations. SIAM J. Scient. Stat. Comp. **1** , 1980, 303-319.

[DAY]   K.M.DAY : Toeplitz matrices generated by Laurent series expansion of an arbitrary rational function, Trans. Amer. Math. Soc., **206** , 1975, 224-245.

[DED]   P.DEWILDE, H.DYM : Schur recursions, error formulas and convergence of rational estimators for stationary stochastic sequences, IEEE trans. on Information Theory, **IT-27** , 1981, 446-461.

[DRA]   A.DRAUX : *Polynômes orthogonaux formels - applications.*, Springer Verlag, Berlin, 1983.

[GED]   K.O.GEDDES : Block structure in the Chebyshev-Padé table, SIAM J. Numer. Anal., **18** , 1981, 844-861.

[GER]   L.Y.GERONIMUS : *Orthogonal polynomials*, Consultants Bureau, New york, 1961.

[GOF] I.Z.GOHBERG, I.A.FELDMAN : *Convolution equations and projection methods for their solution.* Translations of mathematical monographs **41** ,AMS, Rhode Island, 1974.

[GR1] W.B.GRAGG : Laurent, Fourier and Chebyshev-Padé tables, in *Padé and rational approximation, Theory and Applications,* E.B.Saff, R.S.Varga (eds.), Acad. Press, New York, 1977, 61-72.

[GR2] W.B.GRAGG : The Padé table and its relation to certain algorithms in numerical analysis, SIAM Review, **14** , 1972, 1-69.

[GR3] W.B.GRAGG : Matrix interpretation and applications of the continued fraction algorithm. Rocky Mountain J. Math., **4** , 1974, 491-500.

[GRL] W.B.GRAGG, A.lINDQUIST : On the partial realization problem. Lin. Alg. Appl., **50** , 1983, 277-319.

[GRJ] W.B.GRAGG, G.D.JOHNSON : The Laurent-Padé table, In *Information Processing 74,* North Holland, Amsterdam, 1974, 632-637.

[GRE] U.GRENANDER, G.SZEGÖ : *Toeplitz forms and their applications* ,John Wiley & Sons, 1968.

[HAM] G.HAMEL : Eine charakteristische Eigenschaft beschränter analytische Funktionen, Math. Annal., **78** , 1918, 257-269.

[HER] G. HEINIG, K.ROST : *Algebraic methods for Toeplitz-like matrices and operators,* Akademie-Verlag, Berlin, and Birkhäuser Verlag, Basel, 1984.

[HEN] P.HENRICI : *Applied and Computational complex analysis,* John Wiley & sons, 1977.

[JOM] W.B.JONES, A.MAGNUS : Computation of poles of two-point Padé approximants and their limits, J.Comput. Appl. Math., **6** , 1980, 105-119.

[JOT] W.B.JONES, W.J.THRON : *Continued fractions: Analytic theory and applications,* Addison Wesley Publ. Comp., Reading, Massachusetts, 1980.

[KAI] T.KAILATH, S.-Y.KUNG, M.MORF : Displacement ranks of matrices and linear equations, J. Math. Anal. Appl., **68** ,1979, 395-407.

[KVM] T.KAILATH, A.VIERA, M.MORF : Inverses of Toeplitz operators, innovations and orthogonal polynomials, SIAM review, **20** ,1978, 106-119.

[LAN] I.P.LANDAU : *Outils et modèles mathématiques pour l'automatique,l'analyse de systèmes et le traitement du signal,* Ed. du centre de la recherche scientifique, Paris, 1982.

[LEV] N.LEVINSON : The Wiener RMS (root mean square) error criterion in filter design and prediction, J.Math. Phys:, **25** , 1947, 261-278.

[MAR]   J.D.MARKEL, A.H.GRAY Jr. : *Linear prediction of speech*, Springer Verlag, Berlin, 1976.

[MCM]   J.MCCABE, J.A.MURPHY : Continued fractions which correspond to power series expansions in two points, J. Inst. Math. Applics., **17** , 1976, 233-247.

[MC1]   J.MCCABE : A formal extension of the Padé table to include two-point Padé quotients, J. Inst. Math. Applics., **15** , 1975, 363-372.

[MC2]   J.MCCABE : The quotient-difference algorithm and the Padé table: an alternative form and a general continued fraction, Math. Comp. **41** , 1983, 183-197.

[MES]   H.MESCHKOWSKI : *Hilbertsche Räume mit Kernfunktion*, Springer Verlag, Berlin, 1962.

[MUS]   B.R.MUSICUS : Levinson and fast Cholesky algorithms for Toeplitz and almost Toeplitz matrices. Manuscript MIT, 1984.

[NEV]   R.NEVANLINNA : Ueber beschränkte Funktionen die in gegeben Punkten vorgeschriebene Werte annehmen, Ann. Acad. Sci. Fenn. Ser A, **13** , 1919.

[OPS]   A.V.OPPENHEIM, R.W.SCHAFER : *Digital signal processing*, Prentice-Hall, Englewood Cliffs, 1975.

[PRAB] C.V.K.PRABHAKARA RAO : *A system approach to the multiport inverse scattering problem*, Ph. D. Thesis, T.H. Delft, The Netherlands, 1985.

[PIC]   G.PICK : Ueber beschränkte Funktionen mit vorgegebenen Wertzuordnung, Ann. Acad. Sci. Fenn. Ser A, **15** , 1920.

[RED]   R.REDHEFFER : On the relation of transmission-line theory to scattering and transfer. J. Math. Phys., **41** , 1962, 1-41.

[ROB]   E.A.ROBINSON : Waves propagationg in random media as statistical time series. in *Applied time series analysis*, D.F.Findley (ed.), Ac.Press, New York, 1978, 287-323.

[RUD]   W.RUDIN : *Real and Complex analysis*, 2nd edition, McGraw Hill, New York, 1974.

[RUT]   H.RUTISHAUSER : *Der Quotienten-differenzen Algorithmus*, Mittlg. Inst. f. Angew. Math., ETH nr 7, Birkhäuser Verlag, 1957.

[SCH]   J.SCHUR : Ueber Potenzreihen die im Innern des Einheitskreises beschränkt sind, Z. Reine Angew. Math., **147** , 1917, 205-232, **148** , 1918, 122-145.

[SEE]   W.SEEWALD : Quotienten- Differenzen- Algorithmus: Beweis der Regeln von Rutishauser, Numer. Math., **40** , 1982, 93-98.

[SWE]   D.R.SWEET : *Numerical methods for Toeplitz matrices.* Ph.D. Thesis, Dept. of computer Science, Univ. of Adelaide, 1982.

[SZE]   G.SZEGÖ : *Orthogonal polynomials,* AMS Colloquium Publ., XXIII, AMS, Providence, 1939.

[TRE1] W.F.TRENCH : An algorithm for the inversion of finite Toeplitz matrices, SIAM J. Appl. Math., **12** , 1964, 515-522.

[TRE2] W.F.TRENCH : An algorithm for the inversion of finite Hankel matrices, SIAM J. Appl. Math., **13** , 1965, 1102-1107.

[ZOH1] S.ZOHAR : Toeplitz matrix inversion, the algorithm of W.F.Trench, J. Assoc. Comput. Mach., **16** , 1969, 592-601.

[ZOH2] S.ZOHAR : The solution of a Toeplitz set of linear equations, J. Assoc. Comp. Mach., **21** , 1975, 272-276.

LIST OF SYMBOLS

The most important symbols used are given. The number following the short description of the symbol indicates the page on which the symbol is first introduced.

$\square$	end of a proof, 12
$\dfrac{a_0}{b_0} + \Sigma \dfrac{a_k\mid}{\mid b_k}$	continued fraction, 18
$\bar{z}$	bar means complex conjugation, 83
$\circ$	composition of transformations, 13
$<\cdot,\cdot>^{(m)}$	bilinear form, 84
$[\cdot,\cdot]^{(m)}$	bilinear form, 98
$\{\cdot,\cdot\}^{(m)}$	bilinear form, 101
$(\cdot/\cdot)$	couple of elements, 11
$\|\cdot\|$	operator norm, 196
$\|\cdot\|_p$	L^p or H^p norm, 207
$\|\cdot\|_{\rho,p}$	l^p_ρ norm, 196
a_k	a-parameter of Moebius transform t_k, 12
$a_n^{(m)}$	a-parameter for a Laurent series, 67
b_k	b-parameter of Moebius transform t_k, 12
$b_n^{(m)}$	b-parameter for a Laurent series, 67
$\hat{a}_n^{(m)}$	$\hat{a}$-parameter for a Laurent series, 78
$\hat{b}_n^{(m)}$	$\hat{b}$-parameter for a Laurent series, 78
$\mathrm{lb}_n^{(m)}$	square block grid, 148
c_k	c-parameter of Moebius transform t_k, 12
d_k	d-parameter of Moebius transform t_k, 12

$\det(M)$	determinant of M, 104
$e_k, \hat{e}_k$	forward and backward prediction error, 220
$e_{k\mid n}, \hat{e}_{k\mid n}$	forward and backward innovations, 220
f_k	coefficients of fls, 22
f'_m	$\frac{1}{2} f_m$, 38
fls	formal Laurent series, 22
fps	formal power series, 23
$\mathrm{ind}(\cdot)$	winding number or index, 156
$k_n^{(m)}(z)$	reproducing kernel for $\langle \cdot, \cdot \rangle^{(m)}$, 94
$l_n^{(m)}(z)$	reproducing kernel for $[\cdot, \cdot]^{(m)}$, 100
$\hat{l}_n^{(m)}(z)$	reproducing kernel for $\{\cdot, \cdot\}^{(m)}$, 100
$l_\rho^p, l_{\rho+}^p, l_{\rho-}^p$	Banach spaces, 196
$m_n^{(m)}, n_n^{(m)}$	coefficients of a CF, 48
$o(\cdot)$	Landau symbol small oh, 160
$\mathrm{ord}_+, \mathrm{ord}_-$	$+$ and $-$ order, 23
$p^*(z)$	parahermitean conjugate of a polynomial, 83
$p^\times(z)$	$\times$ operation on a polynomial, 98
$t(\cdot), t_n(\cdot), t_n^{(m)}(\cdot)$	Moebius transforms, 11,12,56
$\hat{t}(\cdot), \hat{t}_n(\cdot)$	dual Moebius transforms, 13
$\mathrm{t}_n(\cdot)$	composite Moebius transform, 12
$\hat{\mathrm{t}}_n(\cdot)$	dual composite Moebius transform, 13
$u_n^{(m)}, \hat{u}_n^{(m)}$	u and $\hat{u}$ parameters of a fls, 30
v_n	square norm of prediction error, 220
$v_n^{(m)}, \hat{v}_n^{(m)}$	v and $\hat{v}$ parameters of a fls, 30
x_n	stochastic proces, 219
$x_{k\mid n}, \hat{x}_{k\mid n}$	forward and backward predictor, 220
A_k	A-parameter of composite Moebius transform t_k, 12
$A_n^{(m)}(z), \hat{A}_n^{(m)}(z)$	A and $\hat{A}$ polynomials of the second kind, 38

$A_n(z) = A_n^{(0)}(x)$	A polynomial, 214
$\mathbf{A}_n^{(m)}, \hat{\mathbf{A}}_n^{(m)}$	bi–diagonal matrices, 127
B_k	B-parameter of composite Moebius transform t_k, 12
$B(p)_n^{(m)}(z), \hat{B}(p)_n^{(m)}(z)$	B and $\hat{B}$ Laurent polynomials, 40
$B_n^{(m)}(z), \hat{B}_n^{(m)}(z)$	B and $\hat{B}$ Laurent polynomials for $p = 0$, 142
$B_n(z) = B_n^{(0)}(z)$	B polynomial, 214
$\mathbf{B}_n^{(m)}, \hat{\mathbf{B}}_n^{(m)}$	bi–diagonal matrices, 128
$\mathbb{B}_n^{(m)}, \hat{\mathbb{B}}_n^{(m)}$	square block grids, 148,151
C_k	C-parameter of composite Moebius transform t_k, 12
CF	continued fraction, 18
$\mathbb{C}$	complex plane, 181
D_k	D-parameter of composite Moebius transform t_k, 12
$\mathbf{D}_n^{(m)}$	diagonal matrix, 114,122
$\mathbb{D}_n^{(m)}$	intersection of square block grids, 151
$\mathbb{D}$	complex plane without 0 and ∞, 155
$\mathbb{D}_n, \hat{\mathbb{D}}_n$	regions in the complex plane, 169
$\mathbb{D}_n^+, \mathbb{D}_n^-$	pointed discs, 203
E	Expectation operator, 219
$\mathbb{E}$	annular region, 156
$\mathbb{E}_n$	annular region, 170
$F(z)$	formal Laurent series, 22
$F_+(z), F_-(z)$	analytic and coanalytic factors, 156
$\hat{F}(z)$	the formal Laurent series $F(1/z)$, 131
$F_n^{(m)}$	F-parameter for a Laurent series, 72
$\hat{F}_n^{(m)}$	$\hat{F}$-parameter for a Laurent series, 79
$\mathbb{F}$	function class, 209
$G_n^{(m)}$	G-parameter for a Laurent series, 72
$\hat{G}_n^{(m)}$	$\hat{G}$-parameter for a Laurent series, 79
$G_\rho(\cdot)$	geometric mean,coefficient in factorization, 156

$H(z)$	system function, 222
$H_n^{(m)}$	Hankel determinant, 104
H^p	Hardy space of the unit disc, 207
$\mathbf{H}_n^{(m)}$	Hankel matrix, 104
$\mathbf{I}_n$	unit matrix, 110
$\mathbf{J}_n^{(m)}, \hat{\mathbf{J}}_n^{(m)}$	Jacobi matrices, 110
K^p	Hardy space for the complement of the unit disc, 208
$K(p)_n^{(m)}(z), \hat{K}(p)_n^{(m)}(z)$	Laurent-Padé approximants, 41
$K_n^{(m)}(z), \hat{K}_n^{(m)}(z)$	Laurent-Padé approximants for $p = 0$, 142
$K_n(z) = K_n^{(0)}(z)$	Laurent-Padé approximant, 230
$\mathbf{K}_n$	anti-unit matrix, 104
$\mathbb{K}$	compact subset of $\mathbb{C}$, 181
LPA	Laurent-Padé approximant, 26
LPF	Laurent-Padé form, 27
L^p	Hilbert space, 208
L_+, L_-	+ and − expansion operators, 24
$L(p)_n^{(m)}(z), \hat{L}(p)_n^{(m)}(z)$	numerator of Laurent-Padé approximants, 41
$\mathbb{L}_n^{(m)}, \tilde{\mathbb{L}}_n^{(m)}, \hat{\tilde{\mathbb{L}}}_n^{(m)}$	triangular grids, 148,150,153
$\mathbb{L}(Y)$	lower triangular Toeplitz matrix, 120
$\mathbb{N}$	the set of nonnegative integers, 39
$O(\cdot)$	Landau symbol big oh, 157
$O_+(z^m), O_-(z^n)$	set of semi infinite Laurent series, 23
PA	Padé approximant, 24
PF	Padé form, 26
P^+, P^-	index boundaries for poles, 155
$P_n^{(m)}(z), \hat{P}_n^{(m)}(z)$	P and $\hat{P}$ (numerator) series for a fls, 32
$P_n(z) = P_n^{(0)}(z)$	P series, 217
$P_n^{(m,m+h)}(z), \hat{P}_n^{(m,m+h)}(z)$	dual Rutishauser polynomials, 188
$P^{(m,m+h)}(z), \hat{P}^{(m,m+h)}(z)$	polynomials, 187,188
$\mathbf{P}_n^{(m)}, \hat{\mathbf{P}}_n^{(m)}$	triangular matrices, 113,116

$\mathbb{P}$	Carathéodory class or positive real functions, 210
$Q_n^{(m)}(z), Q_n^{(m)}$	Q polynomials of the first kind and the coef. vector, 30
$Q_n(z) = Q_n^{(0)}(z)$	Q polynomial, 214
$Q_{n,n+k}^{(m)}(z), \hat{Q}_{n,n+k}^{(m)}(z)$	Rutishauser polynomials, 173,174,179
$Q_{k,n}(z) = Q_{k,n}^{(0)}(z)$	Rutishauser polynomials, 214
$Q_{n,n+h}(z), \hat{Q}_{n,n+h}(z)$	polynomials, 177,181
$\mathbf{Q}_n^{(m)}, \hat{\mathbf{Q}}_n^{(m)}$	triangular matrices, 113,122
$R_n^{(m)}(z), \hat{R}_n^{(m)}(z)$	R and $\hat{R}$ (residual) series for a fls, 32
$R_n(z) = R_n^{(0)}(z)$	R series, 217
$\mathbf{R}_n^{(m)}, \hat{\mathbf{R}}_n^{(m)}$	triangular matrices, 116,114,122
SS	Schur-Szegő , 32
$S_*(z)$	lower star operation on fls, 83
$	Schur class of contractions, 210
$T_n^{(m)}$	Toeplitz determinant, 104
$T_n = T_n^{(0)}$	Toeplitz determinant, 214
$\mathbf{T}_n^{(m)}$	Toeplitz matrix, 24
$\mathbf{T}_n = \mathbf{T}_n^{(0)}$	Toeplitz matrix, 218
$\mathbb{T}, \mathbb{T}^+, \mathbb{T}^-$	operator spaces, 196
$U_n^{(m)}(z), \hat{U}_n^{(m)}(z)$	U and $\hat{U}$ polynomials for a fls, 44
$U_n(z) = U_n^{(m)}(z)$	U polunomial, 216
$U_{k,n}^{(m)}(z), \hat{U}_{k,n}^{(m)}(z)$	partial U and $\hat{U}$ polynomials for a fls, 62
$U_{k,n}(z) = U_{k,n}^{(0)}(z)$	partial U polynomial, 214
$\mathbf{U}_n^{(m)}, \hat{\mathbf{U}}_n^{(m)}$	triangular matrices, 116
$V_n^{(m)}(z), \hat{V}_n^{(m)}(z)$	V and $\hat{V}$ polynomials for a fls, 44
$V_n(z) = V_n^{(m)}(z)$	V polunomial, 216
$V_{k,n}^{(m)}(z), \hat{V}_{k,n}^{(m)}(z)$	partial V and $\hat{V}$ polynomials for a fls, 62
$V_{k,n}(z) = V_{k,n}^{(0)}(z)$	partial V polynomial, 214
$\mathbf{V}_n^{(m)}, \hat{\mathbf{V}}_n^{(m)}$	lower triangular Toeplitz matrices, 120,124
$\mathbf{W}_n^{(m)}, \hat{\mathbf{W}}_n^{(m)}$	lower triangular Toeplitz matrices, 120,125

$\mathbf{X}_n^{(m)}, \hat{\mathbf{X}}_n^{(m)}$	lower triangular Toeplitz matrices, 120,124
$\mathbf{Y}_n^{(m)}, \hat{\mathbf{Y}}_n^{(m)}$	lower triangular Toeplitz matrices, 120,125
Z^+, Z^-	index boundaries for zeros, 155
$Z^{(m)}(z), \hat{Z}^{(m)}(z)$	halves of a Laurent series, 38
$Z(z) = Z^{(0)}(z)$	Carathéodory function, 210
$\mathbb{Z}$	the set of integers, 39
$\alpha_n^{(m)}, \hat{\alpha}_n^{(m)}$	SS parameters, 30
$\alpha_n = \alpha_n^{(0)}$	reflection coefficient, 214
κ, κ_ρ	winding number, 156
$\lambda^{(m)}$	linear functional, 83
$\hat{\lambda}^{(m)}$	linear functional, 98
π_k	poles of meromorphic function, 156
$\rho_n^{(m)}$	ρ–parameter for a Laurent series, 77
$\hat{\rho}_n^{(m)}$	$\hat{\rho}$–parameter for a Laurent series, 79
$\sigma_n^{(m)}$	σ–parameter for a Laurent series, 77
$\hat{\sigma}_n^{(m)}$	$\hat{\sigma}$–parameter for a Laurent series, 79
$\tau_n^{(m)}(\cdot), \hat{\tau}_n^{(m)}(\cdot)$	Moebius transforms, 60
τ_n	transmission coefficient, 226
$\theta_n^{(m)}$	θ matrix of the recurrence, 55
ζ_k	zeros of meromorphic function, 156
$\Pi_{m:n}$	projection operator, 22
$\Pi_n^{(m)}(z)$	Π series for a fls, 57
$\hat{\Pi}_n(z) = \hat{\Pi}_n^{(0)}(z)$	$\hat{\Pi}$ series, 216
$\Pi_{k,n}^{(m)}(z), \hat{\Pi}_{k,n}^{(m)}(z)$	partial Π series for a fls, 62
$\Pi_{k,n}(z) = \Pi_{k,n}^{(0)}(z)$	Π series, 216
$\Gamma_n^{(m)}(z), \hat{\Gamma}_n^{(m)}(z)$	Γ and $\hat{\Gamma}$ series for a fls, 57
$\Gamma_n(z) = \Gamma_n^{(0)}(z)$	Γ series, 214

$\Gamma(z)$ — Schur function, 210

$\Lambda, \Lambda^{(-1)}$ — shift operator and its left inverse, 196

$\Omega_n^{(m)}(z), \hat{\Omega}_n^{(m)}(z)$ — Ω and $\hat{\Omega}$ series for a fls, 61

$\Omega_n(z) = \Omega_n^{(0)}(z)$ — Ω series, 217

$\Sigma_n^{(m)}(z), \hat{\Sigma}_n^{(m)}(z)$ — Σ and $\hat{\Sigma}$ series for a fls, 60

$\Sigma_n(z) = \Sigma_n^{(0)}(z)$ — Σ series, 217

$\Theta_n^{(m)}$ — Θ matrix of composite recurrence, 55

SUBJECT INDEX

Algorithms
  Algorithm 1, 31
  Algorithm 2, 34
  Algorithm 2a, 58
  Algorithm 3a, 69
  Algorithm 3b, 80
  Algorithm 4, 76
  Algorithm 5, 76
  Algorithm inverse 1a, 59
  Algorithm inverse 1b, 62
  Algorithm of Schur, 215
  Algorithm of Schur-Cohn, 216
  Algorithm of Trench-Zohar,
  Algorithm of Levinson, 221
  Algorithm of Pick-Nevanlinna, 229
  qd algorithm, 81
  $\pi\zeta$ algorithm, 81
  Gram-Schmidt algorithm, 118
  Cholesky algorithm, 118

Bilinear forms
  $<\cdot,\cdot>^{(m)}$, 84,218
  $[\cdot,\cdot]^{(m)}$, 98
  $\{\cdot,\cdot\}^{(m)}$, 101
Blaschke product, 208,215
Block structure
  of Padé table, 145
  of Laurent-Padé table, 149,219
  of two-point Padé table, 149
  of Chebyshev-Padé table, 219
  of Fourier-Padé table, 219
  of T-table, 163

Cauchy product, 23
Christoffel-Darboux formula
  for $<\cdot,\cdot>^{(m)}$, 95
  for $<\cdot,\cdot>^{(m)}$, 100
  for $\{\cdot,\cdot\}^{(m)}$, 102
Continued fraction, 18,47
  definition, 18
  convergent of, 18
  contraction of, 20
  expansions, 49,51
  forward evaluation scheme, 50
  determinant formula, 13,38,89
Contraction of a CF
  even contraction, 20
  odd contraction, 20
Coefficients
  parial correlation, 221
  reflection, 224
  transmission, 227
  Fourier, 195
  McLaurin, 197

Determinants
  Toeplitz determinants, 104,142,212
  Hankel determinants, 104
  asymptotics for Toeplitz det, 157,159
  Jacobi's identity for Toeplitz
    determinants, 105
  determinant formula, 13,38,89

Equations
  telegraphers equations, 224
  wave equations, 225
  Toeplitz operator equation, 195

Wiener–Hopf equation, 198
Yule–Walker equations, 220
Equivalence of pairs, 20
Extension
  pseudomeromorphic, 208,219

Factorization
  inner–outer factorization, 208
  Beurling factorization, 208
  of Toeplitz matrix, 115
  of Hankel matrix, 123
  of meromorphic fct, 156
  of chain scattering matrix, 229
  of Toeplitz operators, 197
Filter
  ARMA filtering, 230
  lattice filter, 223
  modeling filter, 222
  whitening filter, 222
  Wiener filter, 222
  backward error filter, 222
  forward error filter, 222
  minimal phase filter, 222
Flow graph
  see also Port
  definition, 14
  node of a flow graph, 14
  branch of a flow graph, 14
  transmittance of a flow graph, 14
  lattice flow graph, 15,21,223
  ladder flow graph, 15,22,223
Formal Laurent series
  Cauchy product of, 23
  definition, 22
  projection operator for, 22
  inverse of, 23
  quotient of, 23
  normal fls, 24
Functionals
  $\lambda^{(m)}$, 83
  $\hat{\lambda}^{(m)}$, 98
Functions
  inner function, 208

meromorphic function, 155,198
outer function, 208
positive real function, 210
Carathéodory function, 210
Schur function, 210,229
  contraction, 210
scattering function, 229
transmission function, 229
system function, 222
Function classes
  Carathéodory class, 210
  Schur class, 210
  IF class, 209

Gohberg–Semencul formula, 121
Gram–Schmidt, 118

Index of a function
  see winding number

Jacobi
  matrices, 110,128,179
  identity for Toeplitz det., 105

Laurent polynomial
  definition, 23
  B and $\hat{B}$ Laurent pols., 40

Matrices
  Toeplitz matrix, 104,112
  Hankel matrix, 104,122
  Jacobi matrix, 110,128,179
  inversion of Toeplitz matrix, 120,127
  inversion of Hankel matrix, 125
  factorization of Toeplitz matrix, 115
  factorization of Hankel matrix, 123
  anti–unit matrix, 104
  Gram matrix, 98,118,218
  θ matrix, 55,213
  scattering matrix, 228
  chain scattering matrix, 227,229
Moment problems, 207
Montessus de Ballore theorem, 167

Node
  node value, 14

sink node, 14
source node, 14

Operator
  delay operator, 222
  expectation operator, 219
  projection operator, 22
  Toeplitz operator, 195
  inverse of Toeplitz operator, 197
  shift operator, 196
Order
  of a fls, 23
Orthogonal
  orthogonality principle, 220
  biorthogonal polynomials for
    $<\cdot,\cdot>^{(m)}$, 85
  orthogonal polynomials for $[\cdot,\cdot]^{(m)}$,
    98
  orthogonal polynomials for $\{\cdot,\cdot\}^{(m)}$,
    101
  Szegö orthogonal polynomials, 218

Padé approximants, 24,37
  definition, 24
  Chebyshev-Padé approximant, 154
  Fourier-Padé approximant, 219
  Laurent-Padé approximant, 26,39,
    201,213,230
  two point Padé approximant, 27,43,
    82
Padé forms
  Padé form, 26,143
  Chebyshev-Padé form, 154,219
  Fourier-Padé form, 219
  Laurent-Padé form, 27,143,151
  two point Padé form, 28,143,150
Padé tables
  Padé table, 26,149
  Chebyshev-Padé table, 153,219
  Fourier-Padé table, 219
  Laurent-Padé table, 153
  two point Padé table, 150
Parahermitean conjugate, 83
Parameters

u and $\hat{u}$ parameters, 30,32,85,104,212
v and $\hat{v}$ parameters, 30,32,104,212
Schur-Szegö parameters, 30,85,104,
    184,219
a and b parameters, 65,104,
    184,193,212
$\hat{a}$ and $\hat{b}$ parameters, 78,184,193,212
F and G parameters, 73,213
$\hat{F}$ and $\hat{G}$ parameters, 79,184,193,213
ρ and σ parameters, 75,105,213
$\hat{\rho}$ and $\hat{\sigma}$ parameters, 79,101,105,213
  convergence of, 183,193
Paths
  sawtooth, 65
  row, 72,195
  staircase, 73
  diagonal, 75
  column, 173
Polynomials
  see also Laurent polynomials
  see also Orthogonal
  Q and $\hat{Q}$ polynomials, 30,213
  of the first kind, 33,213
  A and $\hat{A}$ polynomials, 38,87,213
  of the second kind, 38,87,213
  U and $\hat{U}$ polynomials, 44
  partial U and $\hat{U}$ polynomials, 62,214
  V and $\hat{V}$ polynomials, 44
  partial V and $\hat{V}$ polynomials, 62,214
  Hadamard polynomials, 167
  Rutishauser polynomials, 173,179,
    200
  dual Rutishauser polynomials,
    188,191
Port
  m-port, 14
  load of a port, 14
Prediction
  predictor, 220
  prediction error, 220
  forward prediction, 220

backward prediction, 220
Process
  autoregressive, 222
  regular, 222
  stochastic process, 219
  innovation process, 220
  white noise, 222
Projection
  projection operator, 22
  projection method, 196

Quadrature, 90

Reproducing kernel
  for $<\cdot,\cdot>^{(m)}$, 94,119
  for $<\cdot,\cdot>^{(m)}$, 100
  for $\{\cdot,\cdot\}^{(m)}$, 102
  recursion for, 97
  determinant expression for, 118,124
Residual, 25,29,32
Riesz–Herglotz representation, 210
Rhombus rules
  for ab parameters, 68
  for $\hat{ab}$ parameters, 78
  for FG parameters, 73
  for $\hat{FG}$ parameters, 81
  qd algorithm, 81
  $\pi\zeta$ algorithm, 82

Scattering
  lossless inverse scattering, 224
  scattering matrix, 229
  scattering function, 228
  chain scattering matrix, 227,229
Series
  see also Formal Laurent series
  Fourier series, 210,214
  Laurent series, 197
  McLaurin series, 167,197
  formal power series, 23
  P and $\hat{P}$ series, 32,213
  R and $\hat{R}$ series, 32,213
  Π and $\hat{\Pi}$ series, 57,213

partial Π and $\hat{\Pi}$ series, 62,214
  Γ and $\hat{\Gamma}$ series, 57,213
  Σ and $\hat{\Sigma}$ series, 60,213
  Ω and $\hat{\Omega}$ series, 61,213
Stochastic proces
  definition, 219
  wide sense stationary, 219
Symbol of Toeplitz operator, 197
System
  definition, 221
  impulse response of, 221
  input of, 221
  output of, 221
  system function, 222
  time invariant, 221

Transforms
  Moebius transforms definition, 11
  inverse of Moebius transform, 12
  Moebius transforms, 55,213
  dual Moebius transform, 13
  determinant formula, 13,38,89
  discrete Fourier transform, 219
Transmission line, 224

Wave
  equation, 225
  incoming, 225
  outgoing, 225
Wiener–Hopf equation, 198
Wiener–Kinchin theorem, 219
Winding number, 156,196,205
  definition, 156
Yule–Walker equations, 220

Integral Equations and Operator Theory

The journal is devoted to the publication of current research in integral equations, operator theory and related topics, with emphasis on the linear aspects of the theory. The very active and critical editorial board takes a broad view of the subject and puts a particularly strong emphasis on applications. The journal contains two sections, the main body consisting of refereed papers, and the second part containing short announcements of important results, open problems, information, etc. Manuscripts are reproduced directly by a photographic process, permitting rapid publication.

Please order from your bookseller
or write for a specimen copy to Birkhäuser Verlag
P.O. Box 133,
CH-4010 Basel/Switzerland

Prices are subject to change without notice 3/87

First published in 1978.
6 issues per year, approx. 900 pages per volume

Subscription Information
Annual subscription
sFr. 268.−/DM 336.−/
US$ 174.00
(plus postage)
Single copy
sFr. 49.−/DM 62.−/
US$ 32.00
(plus postage)

Birkhäuser Verlag
Basel · Boston · Stuttgart